Elder Olson
University of Chicago

MAJOR VOICES
20 BRITISH & AMERICAN POETS

McGraw-Hill Book Company

New York   St. Louis   San Francisco   Düsseldorf   Johannesburg
Kuala Lumpur   London   Mexico·   Montreal   New Delhi
Panama   Rio de Janeiro   Singapore   Sydney   Toronto

Library of Congress Cataloging in Publication Data

Olson, Elder, 1909-   comp.
  Major voices.

  1. English poetry (Collections) 2. American
poetry (Collections) I. Title.
PR1175.O55   821'.008   72-13260
ISBN 0-07-047654-3

MAJOR VOICES: 20 BRITISH & AMERICAN POETS

1234567890 DODO 79876543

This book was set in Palatino by Vail-Ballou Press, Inc.
The editors were David Edwards,
Robert Weber, and Susan Gamer;
the designer was J. E. O'Connor;
and the production supervisor was Joan M. Oppenheimer.
The printer and binder was R. R. Donnelley & Sons Company.

Cover photograph by Tad Nichols:
Concretions Weathering out of Eocene Limestone,
Kharga Oasis, Egypt.

ACKNOWLEDGMENTS

W. H. Auden, "Musée des Beaux Arts" and "The Unknown Citizen," copyright
   1940, renewed 1968 by W. H. Auden. From *Collected Shorter Poems 1927–1957*,
   by W. H. Auden. Reprinted by permission of Random House, Inc., and Faber
   and Faber, Ltd.
John Berryman, "Sonnet 23" from *Berryman's Sonnets*, copyright © 1952, 1967
   by John Berryman and "Dream Song 266" from *The Dream Songs* by John
   Berryman, copyright © 1959, 1962, 1963, 1964, 1965, 1966, 1967, 1968, 1969 by
   John Berryman. Reprinted with the permission of Farrar, Straus & Giroux, Inc.
Hart Crane, "To Brooklyn Bridge" from *The Collected Poems and Selected Let-
   ters and Prose of Hart Crane* by Hart Crane. Copyright © 1933, 1958, 1966 by
   Liveright Publishing Corporation. By permission of Liveright, Publishing, New
   York.

78067

E. E. Cummings, "Buffalo Bill's," copyright 1923, 1951 by E. E. Cummings from *Poems 1923–1954* by E. E. Cummings and "my sweet old etcetera," copyright 1926, by Horace Liveright; copyright, 1954, by E. E. Cummings. By permission of Harcourt Brace Jovanovich, Inc.

Emily Dickinson, "After Great Pain a Formal Feeling Comes" and "Forever Is Composed of Nows," (10 lines), copyright 1929, © 1957 by Mary L. Hampson. From *The Complete Poems of Emily Dickinson* edited by Thomas H. Johnson, by permission of Little, Brown and Co. "Because I could not stop for death," "I felt a funeral in my brain," "I heard a fly buzz when I died," "The last night that she lived," and "Forever is composed of nows," (2 lines), reprinted by permission of the publishers and the Trustees of Amherst College from Thomas H. Johnson, Editor, *The Poems of Emily Dickinson*, Cambridge, Mass.: The Belknap Press of Harvard University Press, copyright, 1951, 1955, by The President and Fellows of Harvard College. All other poems from *The Complete Poems of Emily Dickinson* edited by Thomas H. Johnson.

T. S. Eliot, "The Love Song of J. Alfred Prufrock," "Gerontion," "The Hollow Men," "Journey of the Magi," "Preludes," "Morning at the Window," and "Sweeney Among the Nightingales," from *Collected Poems 1909–1962* by T. S. Eliot, copyright, 1936, by Harcourt Brace Jovanovich, Inc.; copyright © 1963, 1964, by T. S. Eliot. Reprinted by permission of Harcourt Brace Jovanovich, Inc., and Faber and Faber, Ltd.

Robert Frost, "Directive," "Provide, Provide," "Mending Wall," "After Apple-Picking," "The Road Not Taken," "The Oven Bird," "Birches," "The Cow in Apple Time," "The Runaway," "Stopping by Woods on a Snowy Evening," "The Onset," "Once by the Pacific," "To Earthward," "Two Tramps in Mud Time," "Bereft," "The Gift Outright," "Design," and "Questioning Faces," from *The Poetry of Robert Frost* edited by Edward Connery Lathem. Copyright 1916, 1923, 1928, 1930, 1939, 1947, © 1969 by Holt, Rinehart and Winston, Inc. Copyright 1936, 1942, 1944, 1951, © 1956, 1958, 1962 by Robert Frost. Copyright © 1964, 1967, 1970 by Lesley Frost Ballantine. Reprinted by permission of Holt, Rinehart and Winston, Inc.

Thomas Hardy, "The Ruined Maid" and "Neutral Tones" from *Collected Poems* by Thomas Hardy. Copyright 1925 by The Macmillan Company. Reprinted with permission of The Macmillan Company, the Trustees of the Hardy Estate; Macmillan London & Basingstoke; and The Macmillan Company of Canada Limited.

Gerard Manley Hopkins, "The Wreck of the Deutschland," "The Habit of Perfection," "God's Grandeur," "The Starlight Night," "Spring," "The Windhover," "Pied Beauty," "Felix Randal," "Spring and Fall," "Inversnaid," "No Worst, There Is None," "I Wake and Feel the Fell of Dark," "Patience, Hard Thing!" "Thou Art Indeed Just Lord," from *Poems of Gerard Manley Hopkins*, edited by W. H. Gardiner and N. H. MacKenzie, copyright 1967 by Oxford University Press.

A. E. Housman, "To An Athlete Dying Young," from "A Shropshire Lad"—Authorised Edition—from *The Collected Poems of A. E. Housman*. Copyright 1939, 1940, © 1965 by Holt, Rinehart and Winston, Inc. Copyright © 1967, 1968 by Robert E. Symons. Reprinted by permission of Holt, Rinehart and Winston, Inc. and The Society of Authors as the literary representative of the Estate of A. E. Housman; and Jonathan Cape Ltd., publishers of A. E. Housman's *Collected Poems*.

Robert Lowell, "The Holy Innocents," from *Lord Weary's Castle*, copyright, 1946, by Robert Lowell. Reprinted by permission of Harcourt Brace Jovanovich, Inc.

Archibald MacLeish, "Ars Poetica," from *Collected Poems 1917–1952* by Archibald MacLeish. Copyright © 1962 by Archibald MacLeish. Reprinted by permission of the publisher Houghton Mifflin Company.

CONTENTS

JOHN DONNE (1572–1631)

JOHN MILTON (1608–1674)

ANDREW MARVELL (1621–1678)

PERCY BYSSHE SHELLEY (1792–1822)

JOHN KEATS (1795–1821)

ALFRED LORD TENNYSON (1809–1892)

ROBERT BROWNING (1812–1889)

WALT WHITMAN (1819–1892)

MATTHEW ARNOLD (1822–1888)

EMILY DICKINSON (1830–1886)

GERARD MANLEY HOPKINS (1844–1889)

WILLIAM BUTLER YEATS (1865–1939)

ROBERT FROST (1874–1963)

WALLACE STEVENS (1879–1955)

T. S. ELIOT (1888–1965)

ADDITIONAL POEMS

SIR THOMAS WYATT (1503?–1542)

EDMUND SPENSER (1552?–1599)

SIR PHILIP SIDNEY (1554–1586)

CHRISTOPHER MARLOWE (1564–1593)

THOMAS CAMPION (1567–1619)

JOHN BERRYMAN (1914–1972)

ROBERT LOWELL (1917–   )

INTRODUCTION

What is poetry?

People find the question "What is poetry?" either very easy or very difficult to answer. Those who find it easiest identify poetry with verse: for them, if something is in verse, it is poetry, and if not, not. Others—aware that not all verse is poetry and that not all poems are in verse—think of poetry as being distinguished from other literature by some special quality of thought, emotion, or language, although they are not in agreement as to what that quality might be. Still others think that poetry involves a certain kind of "structure," although they disagree as to what *this* might be. Such differences of view lead, of course, to many different definitions of poetry, but none has been universally accepted.

Because we are unlikely to succeed where many famous critics and philosophers have failed, there is little point in attempting to define poetry here. For our purposes the question does not matter. If no one seems to know what poetry is in general, almost everyone seems to know what it is in particular cases. That is, we can usually recognize a poem when we encounter one. No one mistakes a magazine article or a newspaper editorial for a poem, and no one supposes Shelley's "Ode to the West Wind" to be a weather report, or Shakespeare's "Hark! Hark! the Lark" to be a news item. We can see that such things are different, though we may not be able to agree exactly about what the differences are.

Indeed, precisely because we can tell what is a poem and what is not, there is general agreement that a large area of literature should be called poetry. We may dispute the exact boundaries of that area, but wherever the lines may be drawn, there is no doubt that certain works fall within them. No one denies, for example, that the works of Homer and Shakespeare are poems.

And so, if we cannot solve the question of how poetry differs from other literature—cannot solve it, at any rate, to everyone's satisfaction—we can at least see how poems differ from each other and what consequences these differences have. What the nature of poetry in general may be is a matter of hypothesis; how particular poems differ from each other, however, is a matter of fact that we can discover and verify by observation and comparison.

How poems differ

POEMS DIFFER IN WHAT THEY PRESENT

One important way that poems differ is in what they present to the reader. Some depict mental experiences, that is, the things happening in a person's mind. Some show one person acting upon someone else. Other poems show people *interacting*, acting upon and reacting to one another in turn. Others, while possibly doing all the things just mentioned, also tell a story. And still other poems present an argument and are intended to convince the reader of something. These are all differences of subject, but "subject" can mean many things, and so it is best for our purposes to state the differences in these terms.

Poems of mental experience

These poems, as we just said, exhibit what is happening in someone's mind; they show him perceiving, remembering, imagining, thinking, reasoning, feeling emotions—in short, they show him experiencing all that can occur in the privacy of the mind. He may speak to himself or to some listener or, perhaps, even to something that cannot understand or even hear him, like a bird or a cloud; but he does this only to express his inner and private experiences, for otherwise we could not know about them. In Browning's "Soliloquy of the Spanish Cloister," for example, a monk talks to himself; "Ulysses," in Tennyson's poem, speaks to his men; in "The Tyger," Blake addresses an animal that could not possibly understand him; and Keats, in "To Autumn," talks to a season which, of course, could not even hear him. In each of these cases the poet uses a different way to express to the reader what is going on in the speaker's mind.

Poems that show someone acting upon someone else

These poems are quite different from poems of mental experience, for here the speaker is not merely trying to express his feelings; he also is speaking in order to influence another person in the poem. Compare any of the poems just mentioned with Marvell's "To His Coy Mistress." The speaker in this poem is a lover attempting to persuade his mistress that she should no longer be coy. In poems of this kind a speaker wants not only to voice his inner thoughts and feelings but also to *affect* someone else. He may beseech, command, threaten, inform, or do any of the things that can be done with words.

Notice, however, that we cannot tell from Marvell's poem whether the lover persuades his mistress to consent or not, for we are given *his* action only. In this respect Marvell's poem is quite different from those that show people interacting.

Poems that show people interacting

In Browning's "The Bishop Orders His Tomb at Saint Praxed's Church," we also hear only the speaker's voice; but in this case the poet lets us know how the Bishop's sons react to each of his pleas. We can infer that they refuse one request after another, much as we can tell, in hearing one end of a telephone conversation, what has been said on the other. If we heard the sons' voices as well as the Bishop's, we then could follow the interaction very clearly.

Poems that tell a story

Many people think that a story is anything that is narrated, but a story can also be dramatized (as, it might be argued, is the case with the Browning poem just mentioned). And not everything that is narrated is a story; for example, "I picked a cherry" does not tell a story, even though it narrates something. A story involves more than a single simple event. It needs a succession of events, and even this, in itself, is not enough to make a story. "I picked a cherry and ate it" involves a succession but is not a story, for what it recounts is of no interest whatever. The events *might be made* to be of interest if they were related somehow to the fortunes or misfortunes of someone. What about the following?

A king planned to invade an enemy's country. He consulted an oracle and was told that if he invaded he would destroy a mighty empire.

Assured by this, he led his armies into battle after battle and at last was defeated utterly. He then realized what the oracle had really meant.

Even in this bare outline, it is clear that we have a story.

Poems that present arguments or explanations

Poems may also, as we said, present an argument or explanation to the reader. Often such poems seem to differ from essays and prose arguments only in that they use devices usually associated with poetry to make their point—devices such as alliteration, assonance, rhyme, and figurative and ornamental language. The premises or evidence offered in such poems may sometimes take the form of a story; however, in such cases, the story is not told for its own interest but, as in fables and parables, to prove a thesis or to point to a moral.

POEMS DIFFER IN LENGTH

That poems differ in length may seem to be so apparent that there is hardly any point in mentioning it, but more is here than meets the eye. If we leave aside the number and length of words used in a poem, length depends on two things: the extent of the subject treated and the scale on which it is treated. Thus, to illustrate the first point, a poem may range from a single perception, thought, emotion, or act (a single event of the simplest order) to whole sequences consisting of any number of events—from, for example, the events of the shortest lyric to those of the longest epic. To illustrate the scale whereby a subject may be treated, let us look back at our story of the king: a whole war is represented simply by the expression "battle after battle" (and even a single battle is, of course, very complicated). Obviously, the more detail a poet gives, the larger the scale; and the more he generalizes and avoids detail, the smaller the scale. Taken in this sense. Browning's poem about the Bishop shows a relatively short action on a large scale, while Coleridge's *Rime of the Ancient Mariner* presents a long action on a fairly small scale. The poet may, of course, and frequently does, vary the scale within a single poem. Coleridge does this in the *Ancient Mariner* by passing quickly over some events and dwelling on others.

POEMS DIFFER IN EMOTIONAL QUALITY

A third way that poems differ is in the emotional effect they produce in the reader, which is a matter of their being serious or comic and to what degree. Just as we can tell whether something is said earnestly or jokingly, so can we tell a serious play from a comedy, the ordinary serious play from the more extreme forms (such as the tragic and the heroic), and the ordinary comedy from its extreme (the farce). The serious forms of poetry seek to evoke the reader's grave concern for things which are presented as important. The comic forms, on the other hand, seek to eliminate any serious concerns; things are presented as unimportant.

POEMS DIFFER IN THEIR METHOD OF PRESENTATION

Poems also differ depending on whether the subject is presented through a dramatic or a narrative method, or through a mixture of the two. The importance of this difference to us as readers is that the dramatic method permits us to witness the events ourselves, whereas the narrative method allows us to know them only through someone else's account. The mixed method recounts certain parts and allows us to witness others for ourselves. These are, however, only *basic* methods of presentation, and they contain many subdivisions. Since there can be narrative portions in a drama or dramatic portions in a narrative, forms are classified according to their *overall* method, not according to the method used in a particular part. Although the above story of the defeated king was presented in purely narrative terms, it could also, of course, be made purely dramatic or treated in a mixture of the two.

POEMS DIFFER IN STYLE, OR DICTION

The language used in poetry either follows the norms of ordinary speech or words, syntax, and rhythms are used which depart from these norms to produce effects not possible otherwise—greater dignity or energy, for example. Indeed, when we say that a poet has a distinctive style, we are speaking precisely of his departures from ordinary language; it is impossible to have a distinctive style while using language as everyone else uses it.

There is, then, no such *single* thing as "poetic diction," although many critics have thought so and tried to discover and define its quality. We can find every sort of style in poetry, as you will see from the poems in this anthology. In general, however, it can be said that poetry tends to explore, in a way that nothing else does, the whole range of possibilities of expression in a given language. It tends, for example, to use figurative expressions much more frequently than do other forms of composition; but we readily accept, in poetry, language that would strike us as intolerably strained and affected in anything but a poem. We accept it because we understand that the poet is trying for effects which could not be achieved otherwise.

Let us examine some of the basic devices of language that poetry employs: similes, metaphors, and images.

Similes and metaphors

The simile, as its name implies, is an expressed *likening* of one thing to something else. The metaphor is closely related, for it also involves likeness; but the likeness—instead of being made grammatically explicit by the use of such words as "like" or "as"—is implied: the name of the thing to which something is likened is simply substituted for its own. Thus "He is brave as a lion" or "His bravery is like that of a lion" is a simile; "He is a lion for bravery" is a metaphor. Metaphors are clearly more compact and economical than similes, for they omit the words expressing the comparison. The simile, however, can be much more elaborately developed, can be drawn out to great length, can detail point after point of likeness, and can build an elaborate image of the thing to which something is likened.

The most famous kind of simile—the Homeric simile—does this last thing mentioned. Here is an example from Homer:

> As when the south wind has poured down a mist upon the peaks of a mountain, unfriendly to shepherds but friendly to the thief by night, and a man sees before him only so far as he can throw a stone, so was the dust raised beneath the feet of those who went forth.

An even more elaborate type of simile not merely likens things to each other as wholes, but also likens their corresponding parts. An example is the famous passage from Ecclesiastes which compares the body to a city: the eyes are watchers in the tower, the teeth are grinders in the mills, and so on, with each part being likened to part.

There are four kinds of metaphors, and as its etymology shows, "metaphor" involves the transference of words or names by substituting (1) a general name for a specific one, (2) a specific name for a general one, or (3) the name of one species within a given class for that of another species in the same class; finally, (4) the metaphor may be based upon a proportional likeness, that is, one in which $A:B::C:D$.

The following line from "Felix Randal," by Hopkins, illustrates the first three kinds of metaphors:

> Didst fettle for the great grey drayhorse his bright and battering sandal!

Here "fettle" (to prepare) is more general than "forge"; "battering" is more specific than "beating"; and "sandal" and "horseshoe" are two species of the general class of things with which feet are shod.

The proportional metaphor can be illustrated by Shakespeare's Sonnet 73:

> That time of year thou mayst in me behold
> When yellow leaves, or none, or few, do hang
> Upon those boughs which shake against the cold,
> Bare ruined choirs, where late the sweet birds sang;

Here the proportion is "Autumn is to the year as a man's past-prime is to his life." As a reading will show, the whole sonnet is built upon such proportions: the second quatrain says that the twilight is to day as the past-prime is to a man's life, and the last quatrain likens the life of a fire to the life of a man.

Similes and metaphors are not, of course, used only in poetry. Indeed, they abound even in common speech, slang, and criminal argot. The criminal, for instance, uses "snow" for "cocaine," "ice" for "diamonds," and "hit" for "kill." But whereas the poet always seeks new metaphors, those used in common speech have become *clichés*, stereotypes which automatically replace the literal terms and thus lose all significance as metaphors and, in fact, their very characteristics *as* metaphors; they have simply become other words for the objects they describe.

Comparisons may simply clarify, by likening something abstract or unfamiliar to something concrete or familiar, but they can do other things as well. For example, by likening the beauty or dignity of something to a thing of greater beauty or dignity, the poet can praise or elevate it; by likening it to an inferior thing, he can depreciate it.

While similes and metaphors point out a *likeness* between things, they may also be used *ironically*; and since irony reverses the meaning of what is being said, they can thus indicate a *difference* between things. Thus ironic praise is actually depreciation, and mock-seriousness is actually comic. A mock-epic poem like Pope's *Rape of the Lock* uses irony in this way as its chief structural device—a trivial action or event is likened, ironically, to the important action of an epic.

Some similes and metaphors are based upon a likeness that is obvious once the things have been compared; others compare things which are apparently so different that any resemblance between them seems impossible and the poet has to point out, sometimes even argue, the resemblance. The former class has no special name, but the latter are called *conceits*. We can see at once why the moon might be called a "silver lamp"; but what is the resemblance between lovers and a pair of compasses? Such comparisons are like riddles. (For the answer to this particular one, see the last three stanzas of "A Valediction: Forbidding Mourning" by John Donne.) Conceits of dazzling ingenuity are one of the principal features of the "metaphysical" poetry of the seventeenth century.

Images

An image is quite different from a simile or a metaphor. It is not a figure of speech in the sense of a particular form of grammatical expression; it may be a phrase or a clause or a sentence of any construction. *What it does* is what makes it an image; it stimulates the reader to an act of imagination whereby he can imagine what someone else is perceiving or feeling as though he were perceiving or feeling it himself. An image is always something concrete and particular, for all experience is of particular things. Imagery is not confined to presentations of the external senses, however, as many people think; *any* physical or mental experience can be imagined— for example, a stomach ache, a heart attack, or the thrill of a discovery.

In an image there are separate elements—two or more—which are immediately combined into a whole by the reader's or hearer's imagination.

There cannot be many elements, and the relationship between them must not be too intricate or precise, for then no image results. The imagination cannot grasp too many elements at a time or combine them very intricately. Moreover, while it can imagine things which are impossible, it cannot imagine things which are contradictory. It can imagine a creature that is half man and half serpent, though such a creature is an impossibility; but it cannot imagine a round square.

Basically there are two types of images, objective and subjective. Objective imagery renders something as anyone would perceive it; subjective imagery renders something as it would appear only to someone in a particular condition—for example, in a certain mental or physical state. "The dark-leaved, red-berried yew" is an objective image; but clouds seen as "Gloomy grammarians in golden gowns" is subjective. The objective primarily characterizes the object and does not characterize the perceiver; the subjective tells us primarily about the perceiver—what is significant is that he should see the object in that particular way. Similes and metaphors, too, may be classified as objective or subjective: they either tell us primarily about the thing which is likened to something else or tell us primarily about the person who sees the likeness.

Since images cause us to perceive something as someone else does, they are an important device for establishing our sympathy with that person. They may also, however, function to alienate him from us by setting forth a mind or character which we find repellent.

The forms of poetry

It is the usual practice of textbooks, in discussing the forms of poetry, to list and describe types such as epic, tragedy, comedy, ode, elegy, pastoral, lyric, epigram, mock-epic, satire, ballad, and so on. Every reader of poetry should no doubt know these types, but since a glossary is provided, there is no point in discussing them here. And a good encyclopedia will afford even more information.

A student should not suppose, however, that his knowledge of poetic forms is complete when he has looked up every item on the list. On the contrary, to make such a supposition is to impair very seriously his perception of poetic form. In the first place, not all the types in this and similar lists are, in a strict sense, *forms*. Pastoral and ballad, for example, are *conventions* which may be used in any number of different forms. Pastoral conventions appear in such diverse forms as pastoral romance, pastoral drama, pastoral elegy, and pastoral lyric; "pastoral" simply means that the subject matter will involve shepherds and their lives, usually treated in certain stylized ways. For example, Marlowe's "Passionate Shepherd to His Love" and Milton's "Lycidas" are both pastorals, but they have nothing in common as far as form goes. Moreover, even genuine forms such as epic and tragedy have certain conventions attached to them.

A convention is something that is sanctioned by custom or habit. But a good poet does not do something in his poem because it is sanctioned by custom or habit; he does whatever he does because it is sanctioned *by his poem*. He does it, that is, to make his poem more effective. He may very well employ conventions, but if he does so, he employs them not because they are sanctioned by the customary practice of other poets, but because they are useful to his poem. Conventions always involve a set of rules or prescriptions for those who wish to follow them; but *there are no rules or prescriptions for the writing of poetry*. Each poem makes its own requirements and demands, which are not rules or laws; the only sovereignty is that of the whole over its parts.

Such lists of types, moreover, tend to suggest that there are a finite number of fixed poetic forms. The history of poetry, however, clearly shows that poetic forms are not finite or fixed; on the contrary, new forms evolve from the old—as, for example, Greek tragedy evolved from epic and dithyramb—and any given form undergoes its own development. All the arts develop and, as they do, tend to influence fresh developments in each other. Theories of fixed and finite forms can neither account for such developments nor accommodate themselves to them, and so they are always ultimately discredited by them.

The best procedure for the student who wishes to gain a knowledge of poetic forms, therefore, is to address himself to individual poems. Using the ways in which poems differ, as outlined in this introduction, he ought to try to describe each poem as accurately as he can. He will then approach the problem of form, for these "ways of difference" relate to the form of any particular work. When he has studied a number of poems, he ought to compare them to see in what respects they are similar or different. In the course of such study he will discover that these ways of difference serving him as guidelines are, while basic, merely basic and no more, and that he will have to differentiate further and further on his own to achieve accurate description. For example, the distinction between narrative and dramatic method is perfectly sound, but too general. The student will find that there are many different kinds of narrative devices; he ought to try to distinguish these and discover how and why they are used. Confronting each poem, he should study the effect which each has upon him and try to find out how that effect is produced. Proceeding in this way, he will gain a sense, not merely of what poetry has been, but also of what it may be. Poetry is not a closed and dead art, but a living and growing one, and each new poet teaches us more about what poetry is.

WILLIAM SHAKESPEARE

1564–1616

The supreme dramatist William Shakespeare, we are told, was a gentle, witty man who liked to be jovial with friends. He was of middle-class stock and received little formal education. At eighteen he married Ann Hathaway and six months later was a father. Whether he left Stratford-on-Avon as a poacher, a runaway butcher's apprentice, or a restless country schoolteacher is not known, but he seems to have been drawn magnetically to the excitement and promise of the newly legitimized London theater. Certainly he also needed money, for his family had grown with the advent of twins, Hamnet and Judith. In any case, by 1592 he was well enough known as an actor and itinerant play doctor to be labelled an "upstart crow" by one Robert Greene. Shakespeare may have been Marlowe's apprentice for a time, and Marlowe's influence is clear in the early histories (especially *Richard III* and *King John*). While Shakespeare borrowed the plot skeletons of all but one of his dramas from histories, biographies, or even existing plays, it was his individual genius for construction and characterization that formed them into masterpieces. His characters were so true to life in their passions, frailties, tragic flaws, and moments of grandeur that they overreached the artificial world of the stage. Shakespeare knew how to juxtapose his characters so that they became foils to one another, thus further defining and developing them. His twenty years of active work in the theater also made him a superbly practical playwright, enabling him to balance action and words with unfailing craftsmanship.

Shakespeare began his writing career with variety. In the years up to 1594, when he acted before Queen Elizabeth as a member of Lord Chamberlain's Men, he wrote most of his poems, as well as three comedies, five histories and one tragedy. In December 1594 the *Comedy of Errors* was performed at Gray's Inn. The next seven years were mainly devoted to the comedies (*A Midsummer Night's Dream*, 1595, to *Twelfth Night*, 1600–1601), but this period also included four histories, two tragedies, *Romeo and Juliet* (1595) and *Julius Caesar* (1599). Shakespeare's son Hamnet died in 1596; 1599 saw the erection of the famous Globe Theatre. The following seven years produced the great tragedies: *Hamlet* (1601–1602); *Othello* (1604); *King Lear* (1605–1606); *Macbeth* (1606). The dramatic romances (especially *The Tempest*, 1611) show a rounding of Shakespeare's life and thought toward the end of his career. While men are still subject to universal laws of cause and effect, Shakespeare more often shows them choosing to ally themselves with those natural laws, thus avoiding the direst consequences. William Shakespeare died in his native Stratford on or around his fifty-second birthday, leaving most of his possessions to his daughter Susanna and "the second best bed, with the furniture" to his wife.

Winter

From LOVE'S LABOUR'S LOST

When icicles hang by the wall,
And Dick the shepherd blows his nail,
And Tom bears logs into the hall,
And milk comes frozen home in pail,
When blood is nipp'd, and ways be foul,   5
Then nightly sings the staring owl,
                              "Tu-who!
To-whit, tu-who!"—a merry note,
While greasy Joan doth keel the pot.

When all aloud the wind doth blow,   10
And coughing drowns the parson's saw,
And birds sit brooding in the snow,
And Marian's nose looks red and raw,
When roasted crabs hiss in the bowl,
Then nightly sings the staring owl,   15
                                        "Tu-who!
To-whit, tu-who!"—a merry note,
While greasy Joan doth keel the pot.

Under the greenwood tree

From AS YOU LIKE IT

Under the greenwood tree
Who loves to lie with me,
And turn his merry note
Unto the sweet bird's throat,
Come hither, come hither, come hither: 5
Here shall he see
No enemy
But winter and rough weather.

Who doth ambition shun,
And loves to lie i' the sun,   10
Seeking the food he eats,
And pleased with what he gets,
Come hither, come hither, come hither:
Here shall he see
No enemy   15
But winter and rough weather.

Blow, blow, thou winter wind

From AS YOU LIKE IT

Blow, blow, thou winter wind,
Thou art not so unkind
    As man's ingratitude;
Thy tooth is not so keen,
Because thou art not seen,   5
    Although thy breath be rude.

Heigh-ho! sing, heigh-ho! unto the green holly:
Most friendship is feigning, most loving mere folly:
    Then, heigh-ho, the holly!
    This life is most jolly.   *10*

    Freeze, freeze, thou bitter sky,
    That dost not bite so nigh
      As benefits forgot:
    Though thou the waters warp,
    Thy sting is not so sharp   *15*
      As friends remember'd not.
Heigh-ho! sing, heigh-ho! unto the green holly:
Most friendship is feigning, most loving mere folly:
    Then, heigh-ho, the holly!
    This life is most jolly.   *20*

It was a lover and his lass

From AS YOU LIKE IT

It was a lover and his lass,
    With a hey, and a ho, and hey nonino,
That o'er the green corn-field did pass
    In the spring time, the only pretty ring time,
When birds do sing, hey ding a ding, ding: *5*
Sweet lovers love the spring.

Between the acres of the rye,
    With a hey, and a ho, and a hey nonino,
These pretty country folk would lie,
    In the spring time, the only pretty ring time,   *10*
When birds do sing, hey ding a ding, ding:
Sweet lovers love the spring.

This carol they began that hour,
    With a hey, and a ho, and a hey nonino,
How that a life was but a flower   *15*
    In the spring time, the only pretty ring time,
When birds do sing, hey ding a ding, ding:
Sweet lovers love the spring.

And therefore take the present time,
    With a hey, and a ho, and a hey nonino,   *20*

For love is crowned with the prime
    In the spring time, the only pretty ring time,
When birds do sing, hey ding a ding, ding:
Sweet lovers love the spring.

Tell me, where is fancy bred

From THE MERCHANT OF VENICE

Tell me, where is fancy bred,
Or in the heart or in the head?
How begot, how nourished?
    Reply, reply.
It is engender'd in the eyes,   5
With gazing fed; and fancy dies
In the cradle where it lies.
    Let us all ring fancy's knell:
    I'll begin it,—Ding, dong bell.
Ding, dong, bell.   10

Come away, come away, death

From TWELFTH NIGHT

Come away, come away, death,
    And in sad cypress let me be laid;
Fly away, fly away, breath,
    I am slain by a fair cruel maid.
My shroud of white, stuck all with yew,   5
    Oh, prepare it!
My part of death, no one so true
    Did share it.

Not a flower, not a flower sweet,
    On my black coffin let there be strown;   10

Tell me: *1 fancy:* love. *2 Or . . . or:* Whether . . . or.
Come away: *2 sad cypress:* a cypress coffin. *7–8:* "Since I cannot play the
part of a lover, the only role left me is death; no lover who died was so true as I."

Not a friend, not a friend greet
    My poor corpse, where my bones shall be thrown.
A thousand, thousand sighs to save,
        Lay me, oh, where
Sad true lover never find my grave   15
        To weep there.

O Mistress mine, where are you roaming?

From TWELFTH NIGHT

O Mistress mine, where are you roaming?
O, stay and hear; your true love's coming,
    That can sing both high and low:
Trip no further, pretty sweeting;
Journeys end in lovers meeting,   5
    Every wise man's son doth know.

What is love? 'Tis not hereafter;
Present mirth hath present laughter;
    What's to come is still unsure:
In delay there lies no plenty;   10
Then, come kiss me, sweet and twenty,
    Youth's a stuff will not endure.

Hark, hark! the lark at heaven's gate sings

From CYMBELINE

Hark, hark! the lark at heaven's gate sings,
    And Phoebus 'gins arise,
His steeds to water at those springs
    On chalic'd flowers that lies;
And winking Mary-buds begin
    To ope their golden eyes.
With every thing that pretty is,
    My lady sweet, arise:
        Arise, arise!

Fear no more the heat o' the sun

From CYMBELINE

Fear no more the heat o' the sun,
   Nor the furious winter's rages;
Thou thy worldly task has done,
   Home art gone, and ta'en thy wages:
Golden lads and girls all must,   5
As chimney-sweepers, come to dust.

Fear no more the frown o' the great;
   Thou art past the tyrant's stroke;
Care no more to clothe and eat;
   To thee the reed is as the oak: 10
The sceptre, learning, physic, must
All follow this, and come to dust.

Fear no more the lightning-flash,
   Nor the all-dreaded thunder-stone;
Fear not slander, censure rash;   15
   Thou hast finished joy and moan:
All lovers young, all lovers must
Consign to thee, and come to dust.

No exorciser harm thee!
Nor no witchcraft charm thee!   20
Ghost unlaid forbear thee!
Nothing ill come near thee!
Quiet consummation have,
And renownéd be thy grave!

Full fathom five thy father lies

From THE TEMPEST

Full fathom five thy father lies,
   Of his bones are coral made;
Those are pearls that were his eyes;
   Nothing of him that doth fade,

Fear no more: *18 Consign:* to set one's seal or signature to, to subscribe or agree to; here, to do as you do, follow you. *19 exorciser:* a magician or conjurer who might have evil power over the dead. *21 Ghost unlaid:* an unappeased ghost who, therefore, might work evil. The general meaning of lines 19–21 is, "May neither conjurer nor witch nor ghost trouble you."

But doth suffer a sea change
Into something rich and strange.
Sea-nymphs hourly ring his knell:
                              Ding, dong.
Hark! Now I hear them—Ding, dong, bell.

Shall I compare thee to a summer's day?
SONNET 18

Shall I compare thee to a summer's day?
Thou are more lovely and more temperate;
Rough winds do shake the darling buds of May,
And summer's lease hath all too short a date;
Sometime too hot the eye of heaven shines,   5
And often is his gold complexion dimmed;
And every fair from fair sometime declines,
By chance, or nature's changing course untrimmed.
But thy eternal summer shall not fade,
Nor lose possession of that fair thou owest,   10
Nor shall death brag thou wander'st in his shade
When in eternal lines to time thou growest:
So long as men can breathe, or eyes can see,
So long lives this, and this gives life to thee.

Devouring Time, blunt thou the lion's paws
SONNET 19

Devouring Time, blunt thou the lion's paws,
And make the earth devour her own sweet brood;
Pluck the keen teeth from the fierce tiger's jaws
And burn the long-lived phoenix in her blood;
Make glad and sorry seasons as thou fleet'st,   5
And do whate'er thou wilt, swift-footed Time,
To the wide world and all her fading sweets,
But I forbid thee one most heinous crime:
O, carve not with thy hours my love's fair brow,
Nor draw no lines there with thine antique pen;   10
Him in thy course untainted do allow

For beauty's pattern to succeeding men.
Yet do thy worst, old Time: despite thy wrong,
My love shall in my verse ever live young.

When, in disgrace with Fortune and men's eyes
SONNET 29

When, in disgrace with Fortune and men's eyes,
I all alone beweep my outcast state,
And trouble deaf heaven with my bootless cries,
And look upon myself and curse my fate,
Wishing me like to one more rich in hope,   5
Featured like him, like him with friends possessed,
Desiring this man's art, and that man's scope,
With what I most enjoy contented least;
Yet in these thoughts myself almost despising,
Haply I think on thee, and then my state,   10
Like to the lark at break of day arising
From sullen earth, sings hymns at heaven's gate;
For thy sweet love rememb'red such wealth brings
That then I scorn to change my state with kings.

When I have seen by Time's fell hand defaced
SONNET 64

When I have seen by Time's fell hand defaced
The rich-proud cost of outworn buried age;
When sometime lofty towers I see down-razed,
And brass eternal slave to mortal rage;
When I have seen the hungry ocean gain   5
Advantage on the kingdom of the shore,
And the firm soil win of the watery main,
Increasing store with loss, and loss with store;
When I have seen such interchange of state,
Or state itself confounded to decay,   10
Ruin hath taught me thus to ruminate:
That Time will come and take my love away.
This thought is as a death, which cannot choose
But weep to have that which it fears to lose.

Since brass, nor stone, nor earth, nor boundless sea

SONNET 65

Since brass, nor stone, nor earth, nor boundless sea
But sad mortality o'ersways their power,
How with this rage shall beauty hold a plea,
Whose action is no stronger than a flower?
O, how shall summer's honey breath hold out   5
Against the wrackful siege of battering days,
When rocks impregnable are not so stout,
Nor gates of steel so strong, but Time decays?
O fearful meditation! where, alack,
Shall Time's best jewel from Time's chest lie hid?   10
Or what strong hand can hold his swift foot back?
Or who his spoil of beauty can forbid?
O, none, unless this miracle have might,
That in black ink my love may still shine bright.

That time of year thou mayst in me behold

SONNET 73

That time of year thou mayst in me behold
When yellow leaves, or none, or few, do hang
Upon those boughs which shake against the cold,
Bare ruined choirs, where late the sweet birds sang;
In me thou see'st the twilight of such day   5
As after sunset fadeth in the west,
Which by and by black night doth take away,
Death's second self, that seals up all in rest.
In me thou see'st the glowing of such fire
That on the ashes of his youth doth lie,   10
As the death-bed whereon it must expire,
Consumed with that which it was nourished by.
This thou perceiv'st, which makes thy love more strong,
To love that well which thou must leave ere long.

Sonnet 65: *1–2 Since . . . nor*, etc.: "Since neither brass nor stone . . ."; i.e.,
death has greater power than brass, stone, etc., despite the fact that they endure.

Farewell! thou art too dear for my possessing

SONNET 87

Farewell! thou art too dear for my possessing,
And like enough thou know'st thy estimate.
The charter of thy worth gives thee releasing;
My bonds in thee are all determinate.
For how do I hold thee but by thy granting,   5
And for that riches where is my deserving?
The cause of this fair gift in me is wanting,
And so my patent back again is swerving.
Thyself thou gav'st, thy own worth then not knowing,
Or me, to whom thou gav'st it, else mistaking;   10
So thy great gift, upon misprision growing,
Comes home again, on better judgment making.
Thus have I had thee as a dream doth flatter—
In sleep a king, but waking no such matter.

From you have I been absent in the spring

SONNET 98

From you I have been absent in the spring,
When proud-pied April, dressed in all his trim,
Hath put a spirit of youth in everything,
That heavy Saturn laughed and leaped with him.
Yet nor the lays of birds, nor the sweet smell   5
Of different flowers in odor and in hue,
Could make me any summer's story tell,
Or from their proud lap pluck them where they grew;
Nor did I wonder at the lily's white,
Nor praise the deep vermilion in the rose;   10
They were but sweet, but figures of delight,
Drawn after you, you pattern of all those.
Yet seemed it winter still, and, you away,
As with your shadow, I with these did play.

Sonnet 87:   *2 estimate:* worth, value.   *4 determinate:* ended, out of date.   *8 patent:* claim, privilege.   *11 misprision:* error, mistake.

Th' expense of spirit in a waste of shame

SONNET 129

Th' expense of spirit in a waste of shame
Is lust in action; and, till action, lust
Is perjured, murd'rous, bloody, full of blame,
Savage, extreme, rude, cruel, not to trust;
Enjoyed no sooner but despisèd straight;   5
Past reason hunted, and no sooner had,
Past reason hated as a swallowed bait
On purpose laid to make the taker mad:
Mad in pursuit, and in possession so;
Had, having, and in quest to have, extreme;   10
A bliss in proof, and proved, a very woe;
Before, a joy proposed; behind, a dream.
All this the world well knows; yet none knows well
To shun the heaven that leads men to this hell.

My mistress' eyes are nothing like the sun

SONNET 130

My mistress' eyes are nothing like the sun;
Coral is far more red than her lips' red;
If snow be white, why then her breasts are dun;
If hairs be wires, black wires grow on her head.
I have seen roses damasked, red and white,   5
But no such roses see I in her cheeks;
And in some perfumes is there more delight
Than in the breath that from my mistress reeks.
I love to hear her speak; yet well I know
That music hath a far more pleasing sound: 10
I grant I never saw a goddess go;
My mistress, when she walks, treads on the ground.
And yet, by heaven, I think my love as rare
As any she belied with false compare.

Sonnet 129: *5 despisèd straight:* despised immediately after being enjoyed. *11 proof:* experience; i.e., "A bliss in being experienced, but once experienced, a woe."

Poor soul, the center of my sinful earth

SONNET 146

Poor soul, the center of my sinful earth,
Thrall to these rebel powers that thee array,
Why dost thou pine within and suffer dearth,
Painting thy outward walls so costly gay?
Why so large cost, having so short a lease,   5
Dost thou upon thy fading mansion spend?
Shall worms, inheritors of this excess,
Eat up thy charge? Is this thy body's end?
Then, soul, live thou upon thy servant's loss,
And let that pine to aggravate thy store;   10
Buy terms divine in selling hours of dross;
Within be fed, without be rich no more:
So shalt thou feed on Death, that feeds on men,
And Death once dead, there's no more dying then.

My love is as a fever, longing still

SONNET 147

My love is as a fever, longing still
For that which longer nurseth the disease,
Feeding on that which doth preserve the ill,
The uncertain sickly appetite to please.
My reason, the physician to my love,   5
Angry that his prescriptions are not kept,
Hath left me, and I desperate now approve
Desire is death, which physic did except.
Past cure I am, now reason is past care,
And frantic-man with evermore unrest;   10
My thoughts and my discourse as madmen's are,
At random from the truth vainly expressed:
For I have sworn thee fair, and thought thee bright,
Who art as black as hell, as dark as night.

The Phoenix and the Turtle

Let the bird of loudest lay
   On the sole Arabian tree,
   Herald sad and trumpet be,
To whose sound chaste wings obey.

But thou shrieking harbinger,   5
   Foul precurrer of the fiend,
   Augur of the fever's end,
To this troop come thou not near.

From this session interdict
   Every fowl of tyrant wing   10
   Save the eagle, feathered king.
Keep the obsequy so strict.

Let the priest in surplice white
   That defunctive music can,
   Be the death-divining swan,   15
Lest the requiem lack his right.

And thou, treble-dated crow;
   That thy sable gender mak'st
   With the breath thou giv'st and tak'st,
'Mongst our mourners shalt thou go.   20

Here the anthem doth commence:—
   Love and constancy is dead;
   Phoenix and the turtle fled
In a mutual flame from hence.

So they loved, as love in twain   25
   Had the essence but in one;
   Two distincts, division none;
Number there in love was slain.

The Phoenix and the Turtle: *Title:* The Turtle is the turtledove. *1 lay:* song. The bird is perhaps the crane. *5 shrieking harbinger:* screech owl. *6 precurrer:* precursor, or harbinger. *11 Save:* except. *12 obsequy:* burial rite. *15 death-divining swan:* The swan supposedly could foretell its own death and, in its last moments, would sing. The swan here plays the part of a priest. *17 treble-date:* metaphorically speaking, living three times as long as others, i.e., "long-lived." *18–19 sable gender:* black offspring. The crow was thought in ancient times to conceive by the billing of male and female; hence, "the breath." *27 distincts:* separate beings. *28 Number:* Two are made one in love; since numbers are generated out of one, reduction to only one is seen as "slaying," or destroying, number.

Hearts remote, yet not asunder;
    Distance, and no space was seen   *30*
    'Twixt the turtle and his queen:
But in them it were a wonder.

So between them love did shine,
    That the turtle saw his right
    Flaming in the phoenix' sight;   *35*
Either was the other's mine.

Property was thus appalled,
    That the self was not the same;
    Single nature's double name
Neither two nor one was called.   *40*

Reason, in itself confounded,
    Saw division grow together;
    To themselves yet either neither;
Simple were so well compounded,

That it cried, "How true a twain   *45*
    Seemeth this concordant one!
    Love hath reason, reason none
If what parts can so remain."

Whereupon it made this threne
    To the phoenix and the dove,   *50*
    Co-supremes and stars of love,
As chorus to their tragic scene.

THRENOS

Beauty, truth, and rarity,
Grace in all simplicity,
Here enclosed in cinders lie.   *55*

Death is now the phoenix' nest;
And the turtle's loyal breast
To eternity doth rest,

Leaving no posterity:
'Twas not their infirmity,   *60*
It was married chastity.

32 But: except. *36 mine:* Whatever is one's property is also the other's; i.e.,
what is "mine" for one is "mine" for the other. *37–38:* Property is what belongs
to oneself; here, two distinct selves are one. *44:* That which is "simple" cannot
be divided into parts; that which is "compounded" is composed of parts. Shake-
speare is pursuing the paradox of two made one.

Truth may seem, but cannot be;
Beauty brag, but 'tis not she;
Truth and beauty buried be.

To this urn let those repair 65
That are either true or fair;
For these dead birds sigh a prayer.

JOHN DONNE
1572–1631

Donne was born of Catholic parents at a time when England was greatly influenced by Puritans (his brother died in prison for harboring a priest in 1591). By 1587 he had studied at Oxford and Cambridge for three years each, but he could not take a degree without recanting his faith. Through all these years he studied law and probably wrote many of the witty and seductive poems which appear in *Songs and Sonnets* (circulated only in manuscript during his life). In 1593 he did convert to Anglicanism, after much sincere turmoil. However, eight years of preparation for a brilliant political career at court were scotched when he eloped with his noble patron's sixteen-year-old niece in 1601. He was reconciled to his father-in-law by 1609, but a career at court was permanently out of the question. Finally, in 1615, he was ordained into the church, at the direct wish of King

James I. The inner debate leading up to this move can be found in Donne's *Essays in Divinity* (1614), and some of the *Holy Sonnets* can be traced as early as 1609.

After his wife died in childbirth in 1617, leaving him with seven children, Donne became more passionately committed than ever to the church and the world of spirit. By 1621, when he became Dean of St. Paul's, he was the outstanding cleric of his time. (His sermons, brilliant in reasoning and metaphysical imagination, are spectacular). While many of the divine poems were written in this period, as well as the exceedingly inward *Devotions Upon Emergent Occasions* (1623–1624), one cannot throw an easy wall between the sixteenth-century lover and the seventeenth-century mystic. Both key moods undoubtedly interpenetrated for many years, certainly up to 1617. Donne, at his most rakish, sought to express the touchstones unifying all transcendent experience, all ecstasies—emotional, divine, and intellectual. Donne, at his most orthodox, still felt the passions of creation keenly. Prescient of his impending death, John had a portrait painted of himself in a shroud for contemplation and, a few days before dying quite suddenly, preached his own funeral sermon.

Death be not proud, though some have called thee

HOLY SONNET 10

Death be not proud, though some have called thee
Mighty and dreadful, for, thou art not so;
For, those whom thou think'st thou dost overthrow,
Die not, poor death, nor yet canst thou kill me.
From rest and sleep, which but thy pictures be,   5
Much pleasure; then from thee, much more must flow,
And soonest our best men with thee do go,
Rest of their bones, and soul's delivery.
Thou art slave to Fate, Chance, kings, and desperate men,
And dost with poison, war, and sickness dwell,   10
And poppy, or charms can make us sleep as well,
And better than thy stroke; why swell'st thou then?
One short sleep past, we wake eternally,
And death shall be no more; death, thou shalt die.

The Good Morrow

I wonder, by my troth, what thou and I
Did till we loved? Were we not weaned till then,
But sucked on country pleasures, childishly?
Or snorted we in the Seven Sleepers' den?
'Twas so; but this, all pleasures fancies be.   5
If ever any beauty I did see,
Which I desired, and got, 'twas but a dream of thee.

And now good morrow to our waking souls,
Which watch not one another out of fear;
For love all love of other sights controls,   10
And makes one little room an everywhere.
Let sea-discoverers to new worlds have gone;
Let maps to other, worlds on worlds have shown;
Let us possess one world; each hath one, and is one.

My face in thine eye, thine in mine appears,   15
And true plain hearts do in the faces rest;
Where can we find two better hemispheres
Without sharp north, without declining west?
Whatever dies was not mixed equally;
If our two loves be one, or thou and I   20
Love so alike that none do slacken, none can die.

Song

Go and catch a falling star,
    Get with child a mandrake root,
Tell me where all past years are,
    Or who cleft the devil's foot,
Teach me to hear mermaids singing,   5
Or to keep off envy's stinging,
        And find
        What wind
Serves to advance an honest mind.

The Good Morrow: 4 *Seven Sleepers' den*: according to early Christian legend, a cave in which seven Christian youths of Ephesus took refuge from the persecution of the Emperor Decius (249–251) and fell into a sleep that lasted 230 years. 5 *but*: except for.

If thou beest born to strange sights,   *10*
   Things invisible to see,
Ride ten thousand days and nights,
   Till age snow white hairs on thee.
Thou, when thou return'st, wilt tell me
All strange wonders that befell thee,   *15*
      And swear
      No where
Lives a woman true and fair.

If thou find'st one, let me know:
   Such a pilgrimage were sweet;   *20*
Yet do not; I would not go,
   Though at next door we might meet.
Though she were true when you met her,
And last till you write your letter,
      Yet she   *25*
      Will be
False, ere I come, to two or three.

The Canonization

For Godsake hold your tongue, and let me love,
   Or chide my palsy, or my gout,
My five gray hairs, or ruin'd fortune flout,
    With wealth your state, your mind with arts improve,
      Take you a course, get you a place,   *5*
      Observe his honor, or his grace,
Or the King's reall, or his stamped face
   Contemplate, what you will, approve,
   So you will let me love.

Alas, alas, who's injur'd by my love?   *10*
   What merchants' ships have my sighs drown'd?
Who says my tears have overflow'd his ground?
    When did my colds a forward spring remove?
      When did the heats which my veins fill
      Add one more to the plaguy bill?   *15*

The Canonization: *7 the King's reall*, etc.: the king's real face or his face as stamped on a coin. *15 the plaguy bill:* the weekly list of those dead of the plague.

Soldiers find wars, and lawyers find out still
  Litigious men, which quarrels move,
  Though she and I do love.

Call us what you will, we are made such by love;
  Call her one, me another fly, 20
We'are tapers too, and at our own cost die,
  And we in us find the'eagle and the dove.
    The phoenix riddle hath more wit
    By us, we two being one, are it.
So, to one neutral thing both sexes fit, 25
  We die and rise the same, and prove
  Mysterious by this love.

We can die by it, if not live by love,
  And if unfit for tombs and hearse
Our legend be, it will be fit for verse; 30
  And if no piece of chronicle we prove,
    We'll build in sonnets pretty rooms;
    As well a well wrought urn becomes
The greatest ashes, as half-acre tombs,
  And by these hymns, all shall approve 35
  Us *Canoniz'd* for Love:

And thus invoke us; You whom reverend love
  Made one another's hermitage;
You, to whom love was peace, that now is rage;
  Who did the whole world's soul contract, and drove 40
    Into the glasses of your eyes
    (So made such mirrors, and such spies,
That they did all to you epitomize,)
  Countries, towns, Courts: Beg from above
  A pattern of your love! 45

Break of Day

'Tis true, 'tis day; what though it be?
Oh, wilt thou therefore rise from me?
  Why should we rise because 'tis light?
  Did we lie down because 'twas night?
Love which in spite of darkness brought us hither 5
Should, in despite of light, keep us together.

Light hath no tongue, but is all eye;
If it could speak as well as spy,
   This were the worst that it could say:
    That, being well, I fain would stay,   *10*
And that I loved my heart and honor so,
That I would not from him that had them go.

Must business thee from hence remove?
Oh, that's the worst disease of love;
   The poor, the foul, the false, love can   *15*
    Admit, but not the busied man.
He which hath business and makes love, doth do
Such wrong as when a married man doth woo.

A Nocturnal upon Saint Lucy's Day, Being the Shortest Day

'Tis the year's midnight, and it is the day's,
Lucy's, who scarce seven hours herself unmasks;
   The sun is spent, and now his flasks
    Send forth light squibs, no constant rays;
     The whole world's sap is sunk;   *5*
The general balm the hydroptic earth hath drunk,
Whither, as to the bed's feet, life is shrunk,
Dead and interred; yet all these seem to laugh,
Compared with me, who am their epitaph.

Study me then, you who shall lovers be   *10*
At the next world (that is, at the next spring),
   For I am every dead thing
    In whom love wrought new alchemy.
     For his art did express
A quintessence even from nothingness,   *15*
From dull privations, and lean emptiness;
He ruined me, and I am re-begot
Of absence, darkness, death: things which are not.

All others, from all things, draw all that's good,
Life, soul, form, spirit, whence they being have;   *20*

A Nocturnal upon Saint Lucy's Day: *1:* In the old reckoning, December 13,
Saint Lucy's Day, was the shortest day of the year; hence, in Donne's metaphor,
it is the "midnight" of the year. *3 flasks:* powder flasks. *4 squibs:* mere flashes,
like firework squibs, rather than "constant rays."

I, by Love's limbeck, am the grave
Of all, that's nothing. Oft a flood
   Have we two wept, and so
  Drown'd the whole world, us two; oft did we grow
To be two chaoses, when we did show   25
Care to ought else; and often absences
Withdrew our souls, and made us carcasses.

But I am by her death, (which word wrongs her)
Of the first nothing, the elixir grown;
   Were I a man, that I were one,   30
  I needs must know; I should prefer,
     If I were any beast,
Some ends, some means; Yea plants, yea stones detest,
And love; All, all some properties invest;
If I an ordinary nothing were,   35
As shadow, a light and body must be here.

But I am none; nor will my Sun renew.
Your lovers, for whose sake, the lesser Sun
   At this time to the Goat is run
    To fetch new lust, and give it you,   40
     Enjoy your summer all;
Since she enjoys her long night's festival,
Let me prepare towards her, and let me call
This hour her vigil, and her Eve, since this
Both the year's, and the day's deep midnight is.   45

A Valediction: Forbidding Mourning

As virtuous men pass mildly away,
  And whisper to their souls to go,
Whilst some of their sad friends do say,
  The breath goes now, and some say, No:

So let us melt, and make no noise,   5
  No tear-floods, nor sigh-tempests move;

21–22 *limbeck:* alembic, or still, used by alchemists. Donne uses an analogy be-
tween stages of alchemical transmutation and degrees of privation and negation. He
is not human, or he would know it; not a beast, for beasts select ends and
means; not a plant nor a stone, for they know attraction and repulsion (loving
and hating); nor is he even a shadow, for then light and body must be present.
He is, therefore, the very quintessence of nothing, its "elixir." *29 the first noth-
ing:* the nothingness that preceded the Creation. *39–40:* The sun is in the Goat,
the zodiacal sign of Capricorn. Goats are proverbially lustful.

'Twere profanation of our joys
   To tell the laity our love.

Moving of th' earth brings harms and fears,
   Men reckon what it did, and meant;   *10*
But trepidation of the spheres,
   Though greater far, is innocent.

Dull sublunary lovers' love
   —Whose soul is sense—cannot admit
Absence, because it doth remove   *15*
   Those things which elemented it.

But we by a love so much refined
   That ourselves know not what it is,
Inter-assurèd of the mind,
   Care less eyes, lips and hands to miss.   *20*

Our two souls therefore, which are one,
   Though I must go, endure not yet
A breach, but an expansion,
   Like gold to airy thinness beat.

If they be two, they are two so   *25*
   As stiff twin compasses are two;
Thy soul, the fix'd foot, makes no show
   To move, but doth, if th' other do.

And though it in the centre sit,
   Yet, when the other far doth roam,   *30*
It leans, and hearkens after it,
   And grows erect, as that comes home.

Such wilt thou be to me, who must,
   Like th' other foot, obliquely run;
Thy firmness makes my circle just,   *35*
   And makes me end where I begun.

The Ecstasy

Where, like a pillow on a bed,
   A pregnant bank swelled up to rest
The violet's reclining head,
   Sat we two, one another's best.

Our hands were firmly cèmented 5
　　With a fast balm, which thence did spring;
Our eye-beams twisted, and did thread
　　Our eyes upon one double string;
So to entergraft our hands, as yet
　　Was all the means to make us one, 10
And pictures in our eyes to get
　　Was all our propagation.
As, 'twixt two equal armies, fate
　　Suspends uncertain victory,
Our souls, which to advance their state 15
　　Were gone out, hung 'twixt her and me.
And whilst our souls negotiate there,
　　We like sepulchral statues lay;
All day, the same our postures were,
　　And we said nothing, all the day. 20
If any, so by love refined
　　That he soul's language understood,
And by good love were grown all mind,
　　Within convenient distance stood,
He, though he knew not which soul spake, 25
　　Because both meant, both spake the same,
Might thence a new concoction take
　　And part far purer than he came.
This ecstasy doth unperplex,
　　We said, and tell us what we love: 30
We see by this it was not sex,
　　We see we saw not what did move;
But as all several souls contain
　　Mixture of things, they know not what,
Love these mixed souls doth mix again 35
　　And makes both one, each this and that.
A single violet transplant,
　　The strength, the color, and the size,
All which before was poor and scant,
　　Redoubles still, and multiplies. 40
When love with one another so
　　Interinanimates two souls,
That abler soul, which thence doth flow,
　　Defects of loneliness controls.
We then, who are this new soul, know 45
　　Of what we are composed, and made,
For the atomies of which we grow
　　Are souls, whom no change can invade.
But O alas! so long, so far,
　　Our bodies why do we forbear? 50

They are ours, though they are not we; we are
    The intelligences, they the spheres.
We owe them thanks, because they thus
    Did us, to us, at first convey,
Yielded their forces, sense, to us,   55
    Nor are dross to us, but allay.
On man heaven's influence works not so,
    But that it first imprints the air;
So soul into the soul may flow,
    Though it to body first repair.   60
As our blood labors to beget
    Spirits, as like souls as it can,
Because such fingers need to knit
    That subtle knot, which makes us man,
So must pure lovers' souls descend   65
    To affections, and to faculties,
Which sense may reach and apprehend;
    Else a great prince in prison lies.
To our bodies turn we then, that so
    Weak men on love revealed may look;   70
Love's mysteries in souls do grow,
    But yet the body is his book.
And if some lover, such as we,
    Have heard this dialogue of one,
Let him still mark us, he shall see   75
    Small change when we're to bodies gone.

Love's Deity

I long to talk with some old lover's ghost
    Who died before the god of love was born.
I cannot think that he who then loved most,
    Sunk so low as to love one which did scorn.
But since this god produced a destiny   5
And that vice-nature, custom, lets it be,
    I must love her that loves not me.

Sure, they which made him god, meant not so much,
    Nor he in his young godhead practiced it.
But when an even flame two hearts did touch,   10
    His office was indulgently to fit

The Ecstasy: *56 allay:* alloy.

Actives to passives. Correspondency
Only his subject was; it cannot be
   Love, till I love her who loves me.

But every modern god will not extend   *15*
   His vast prerogative as far as Jove.
To rage, to lust, to write to, to commend,
   All is the purlieu of the god of love.
O! were we wakened by this tyranny
To ungod this child again, it could not be   *20*
   I should love her who loves not me.

Rebel and atheist too, why murmur I,
   As though I felt the worst that love could do?
Love may make me leave loving, or might try
   A deeper plague, to make her love me too;   *25*
Which, since she loves before, I'm loth to see.
Falsehood is worse than hate; and that must be,
   If she whom I love, should love me.

The Will

Before I sigh my last gasp, let me breathe,
Great Love, some legacies; here I bequeath
Mine eyes to Argus, if mine eyes can see;
If they be blind, then, Love, I give them thee;
My tongue to Fame; to ambassadors mine ears;   *5*
      To women or the sea, my tears;
    Thou, Love, hast taught me heretofore
  By making me serve her who had twenty more
That I should give to none, but such as had too much before.

My constancy I to the planets give;   *10*
My truth to them who at the court do live;
Mine ingenuity and openness,
To Jesuits; to buffoons my pensiveness;
My silence to any, who abroad have been;
      My money to a Capuchin: *15*
    Thou, Love, taught'st me, by appointing me
  To love there, where no love received can be,
Only to give to such as have an incapacity.

My faith I give to Roman Catholics;
All my good works unto the schismatics   20
Of Amsterdam; my best civility
And courtship to an University;
My modesty I give to shoulders bare;
  My patience let gamesters share:
   Thou, Love, taught'st me, by making me   25
  Love her that holds my love disparity,
Only to give to such as have an incapacity.

I give my reputation to those
Which were my friends; mine industry to foes;
To schoolmen I bequeath my doubtfulness;   30
My sickness to physicians, or excess;
To Nature all that I in rhyme have writ;
  And to my company my wit:
   Thou, Love, by making me adore
  Her, who begot this love in me before,   35
Taught'st me to make, as though I gave, when I do but restore.

To him, for whom the passing-bell next tolls,
I give my physic-books; my written rolls
Of moral counsels I to Bedlam give;
My brazen medals unto them which live   40
In want of bread; to them which pass among
  All foreigners, mine English tongue:
   Thou, Love, by making me love one
  Who thinks her friendship a fit portion
For younger lovers, dost my gifts thus disproportion.   45

Therefore I'll give no more, but I'll undo
The world by dying; because Love dies too.
Then all your beauties will be no more worth
Than gold in mines, where none doth draw it forth;
And all your graces no more use shall have,   50
  Than a sun-dial in a grave:
   Thou, Love, taught'st me, by making me
  Love her, who doth neglect both me and thee,
To invent & practice this one way to annihilate all three.

The Funeral

Whoever comes to shroud me, do not harm
    Nor question much
That subtle wreath of hair about mine arm;
The mystery, the sign you must not touch,
    For 'tis my outward soul,   5
Viceroy to that which, unto heav'n being gone,
    Will leave this to control
And keep these limbs, her provinces, from dissolution.

For if the sinewy thread my brain lets fall
    Through every part   10
Can tie those parts, and make me one of all;
These hairs, which upward grew, and strength and art
    Have from a better brain,
Can better do 't: except she meant that I
    By this should know my pain,   15
As prisoners then are manacled, when they're condemned to die.

Whate'er she meant by 't, bury it with me,
    For since I am
Love's martyr, it might breed idolatry
If into other hands these reliques came.   20
    As 't was humility
To afford to it all that a soul can do,
    So 't is some bravery
That, since you would have none of me, I bury some of you.

The Blossom

    Little think'st thou, poor flower,
    Whom I have watched six or seven days,
And seen thy birth, and seen what every hour
Gave to thy growth, thee to this height to raise,
And now dost laugh and triumph on this bough,   5
    Little think'st thou
That it will freeze anon, and that I shall
Tomorrow find thee fallen, or not at all.

    Little think'st thou, poor heart
    That labour'st yet to nestle thee,   10

And think'st by hovering here to get a part
In a forbidden or forbidding tree,
And hop'st her stiffness by long siege to bow;
  Little think'st thou,
That thou tomorrow, ere that sun doth wake,   *15*
Must with this sun and me a journey take.

 But thou which lov'st to be
  Subtle to plague thyself, wilt say,
Alas, if you must go, what's that to me?
Here lies my business, and here I will stay: *20*
You go to friends, whose love and means present
   Various content
To your eyes, ears, and tongue, and every part.
If then your body go, what need you a heart?

 Well then, stay here; but know,   *25*
  When thou hast stayed and done thy most;
A naked thinking heart, that makes no show,
Is to a woman but a kind of ghost;
How shall she know my heart; or having none,
  Know thee for one?   *30*
Practice may make her know some other part,
But take my word, she doth not know a heart.

 Meet me at London, then,
  Twenty days hence, and thou shalt see
Me fresher, and more fat, by being with men,   *35*
Than if I had stayed still with her and thee.
For God's sake, if you can, be you so too:
  I would give you
There to another friend, whom we shall find
As glad to have my body as my mind.   *40*

The Relic

  When my grave is broke up again
  Some second guest to entertain
(For graves have learned that womanhead
To be to more than one a bed),
  And he that digs it, spies   *5*
A bracelet of bright hair about the bone,
  Will he not let us alone,

And think that there a loving couple lies,
Who thought that this device might be some way
To make their souls, at the last busy day,   *10*
Meet at this grave, and make a little stay?

    If this fall in a time, or land,
    Where mis-devotion doth command,
      Then he that digs us up will bring
      Us to the Bishop and the King,   *15*
         To make us Relics; then
Thou shalt be a Mary Magdalen, and I
         A something else thereby;
All women shall adore us, and some men;
And since at such time, miracles are sought,   *20*
I would have that age by this paper taught
What miracles we harmless lovers wrought.

    First, we loved well and faithfully,
    Yet knew not what we loved, nor why;
      Difference of sex no more we knew   *25*
      Than our guardian angels do;
         Coming and going, we
Perchance might kiss, but not between those meals;
         Our hands ne'er touched the seals
Which nature, injured by late law, sets free: *30*
These miracles we did; but now, alas,
All measure, and all language, I should pass,
Should I tell what a miracle she was.

A Lecture upon the Shadow

    Stand still, and I will read to thee
    A lecture, love, in Love's philosophy.
      These three hours that we have spent,
      Walking here, two shadows went
Along with us, which we ourselves produced;   *5*
      But, now the sun is just above our head,
      We do those shadows tread,
And to brave clearness all things are reduced.
      So whilst our infant loves did grow,
      Disguises did, and shadows, flow   *10*
      From us and our cares; but, now 'tis not so.

That love hath not attained the highest degree,
Which is still diligent lest others see.

Except our loves at this noon stay,
We shall new shadows make the other way.   15
  As the first were made to blind
  Others, these which come behind
Will work upon ourselves, and blind our eyes.
  If our loves faint, and westwardly decline,
  To me thou, falsely, thine,   20
And I to thee, mine actions shall disguise.
  The morning shadows wear away,
  But these grow longer all the day;
  But oh, love's day is short, if love decay.

Love is a growing, or full constant light,   25
And his first minute after noon, is night.

I *am a little world made cunningly*

HOLY SONNET 5

I am a little world made cunningly
Of elements, and an angelic sprite,
But black sin hath betrayed to endless night
My world's both parts, and oh, both parts must die.
You which beyond that heaven which was most high   5
Have found new spheres, and of new lands can write,
Pour new seas in mine eyes, that so I might
Drown my world with my weeping earnestly,
Or wash it if it must be drowned no more;
But oh it must be burnt! Alas, the fire   10
Of lust and envy have burnt it heretofore,
And made it fouler; let their flames retire,
And burn me, O Lord, with a fiery zeal
Of Thee and Thy house, which doth in eating heal.

A Lecture: 14 *Except:* unless.

At the round earth's imagined corners, blow

HOLY SONNET 7

At the round earth's imagined corners, blow
Your trumpets, angels, and arise, arise
From death, you numberless infinities
Of souls, and to your scattered bodies go;
All whom the flood did, and fire shall o'erthrow,   5
All whom war, dearth, age, agues, tyrannies,
Despair, law, chance, hath slain, and you whose eyes
Shall behold God, and never taste death's woe.
But let them sleep, Lord, and me mourn a space,
For if, above all these, my sins abound,   10
'Tis late to ask abundance of Thy grace
When we are there; here on this lowly ground,
Teach me how to repent; for that's as good
As if Thou hadst sealed my pardon with Thy blood.

Batter my heart, three-personed God, for you

HOLY SONNET 14

Batter my heart, three-personed God, for you
As yet but knock, breathe, shine, and seek to mend;
That I may rise and stand, o'erthrow me, and bend
Your force to break, blow, burn and make me new.
I, like an usurped town, to another due,   5
Labour to admit you, but oh, to no end;
Reason your viceroy in me, me should defend,
But is captived, and proves weak or untrue.
Yet dearly I love you, and would be loved fain,
But am betrothed unto your enemy: 10
Divorce me, untie, or break that knot again,
Take me to you, imprison me, for I
Except you enthrall me, never shall be free,
Nor ever chaste, except you ravish me.

Holy Sonnet 14: *1 three-personed God:* the Trinity of Father, Son, and Holy Ghost. *5:* i.e., belonging to another, but usurped. *9 fain:* gladly. *13 Except:* unless.

Good Friday, 1613, Riding Westward

Let man's Soul be a sphere, and then, in this,
The intelligence that moves, devotion is.
And as the other spheres, by being grown
Subject to foreign motions, lose their own,
And being by others hurried every day,   5
Scarce in a year their natural form obey:
Pleasure or business, so, our souls admit
For their first mover, and are whirl'd by it.
Hence is't, that I am carried towards the West
This day, when my Soul's form bends toward the East.   10
There I should see a Sun, by rising set,
And by that setting endless day beget;
But that Christ on this Cross, did rise and fall,
Sin had eternally benighted all.
Yet dare I almost be glad, I do not see   15
That spectacle of too much weight for me.
Who sees God's face, that is self life, must die;
What a death were it then to see God die?
It made his own Lieutenant Nature shrink,
It made his footstool crack, and the Sun wink.   20
Could I behold those hands which span the poles,
And tune all spheres at once, pierc'd with those holes?
Could I behold that endless height which is
Zenith to us, and to our Antipodes,
Humbled below us? or that blood which is   25
The seat of all our Souls, if not of his,
Make dirt of dust, or that flesh which was worn
By God, for his apparel, ragg'd, and torn?
If on these things I durst not look, durst I
Upon his miserable mother cast mine eye,   30

Good Friday: *1 sphere:* Donne is using later modifications of the Ptolemaic conception of the universe. In this system the earth was the center around which all heavenly bodies revolved. These bodies were thought of as fastened in ten concentric spheres, all but the last of which were transparent. There were, thus, the spheres of the moon, of Mercury, of Venus, of the sun, of Mars, of Jupiter, of Saturn, and of the fixed stars, as well as the Crystalline sphere, and the *primum mobile*, or "first-moved," from which all other spheres derived their motions. God moved the *primum mobile*; an angel ("intelligence," line 2) presided over each of the other nine spheres to give it its proper motion. Donne is comparing the microcosm, or small universe of man, to the macrocosm, or great universe. The irregularities in the motions of the stars are like those in the lives of men who are turned from their natural course by the "foreign motions" of pleasure or business. *10 form:* nature. *20 footstool:* "Thus saith the Lord . . . the earth is my footstool" (Isa. 66:1). The whole line refers to the earthquake and eclipse which attended the Crucifixion (Matt. 27:45, 51).

Who was God's partner here, and furnish'd thus
Half of that sacrifice, which ransom'd us?
Though these things, as I ride, be from mine eye,
They'are present yet unto my memory,
For that looks towards them; and thou look'st towards me, 35
O Saviour, as thou hang'st upon the tree;
I turn my back to thee, but to receive
Corrections, till thy mercies bid thee leave.
O think me worth thine anger, punish me,
Burn off my rusts, and my deformity, 40
Restore thine image, so much, by thy grace,
That thou may'st know me, and I'll turn my face.

Hymn to God, My God, in My Sickness

Since I am coming to that holy room,
    Where, with thy choir of saints for evermore,
I shall be made thy music; as I come
    I tune the instrument here at the door,
    And what I must do then, think here before. 5

Whilst my physicians by their love are grown
    Cosmographers, and I their map, who lie
Flat on this bed, that by them may be shown
    That this is my south-west discovery
    Per fretum febris, by these straits to die, 10

I joy, that in these straits, I see my west;
    For, though their currents yield return to none,
What shall my west hurt me? As west and east
    In all flat maps (and I am one) are one,
    So death doth touch the Resurrection. 15

Is the Pacific sea my home? Or are
    The eastern riches? Is *Jerusalem*?
Anyan, and *Magellan*, and *Gibraltar*,

---

38 *leave:* stop, desist. The metaphor in lines 37–38 is of one who turns his back
in order to be lashed in corrective punishment.

Hymn to God: *10 Per fretum febris:* "through the raging of fever." Donne puns
on the Latin word *fretum*, which means both "raging" and "straits," as well as
on the English word *straits*, which can also mean "a distressed situation" (see
Matt. 7:13–14). *18 Anyan:* the Bering Strait.

All straits, and none but straits, are ways to them,
Whether where *Japhet* dwelt, or *Cham*, or *Sem*.   *20*

We think that *Paradise* and *Calvary*,
　Christ's cross, and *Adam's* tree, stood in one place;
Look, Lord, and find both *Adams* met in me;
　As the first *Adam's* sweat surrounds my face,
　May the last *Adam's* blood my soul embrace.   *25*

So, in his purple wrapped receive me Lord,
　By these his thorns give me his other crown;
And as to others' souls I preached thy word,
　Be this my text, my sermon to mine own,
　Therefore that he may raise the Lord throws down.   *30*

---

20 Japhet, Cham, Sem: the three sons of Noah. Japhet (or Japheth) was the ancestor of those who were to occupy the isles of the Gentiles (supposedly the Mediterranean lands of Europe and Asia Minor); Cham (or Ham) was the ancestor of those who were to occupy Egypt; Sem (or Shem) was the ancestor of the Semites. Hence, Europe, Africa, and Asia are implied.   *30:* See Ps. 145:14.

JOHN MILTON
1608–1674

M ilton was born a Puritan and, like John Donne, was superbly edu-
cated. Both began writing good poetry young (Milton when he
was fifteen), both wrote masterpieces of prose exposition, and both suffered
calamitous upsets to their busy careers. After receiving his M.A. from Cam-
bridge in 1632, Milton spent six years at Horton, his father's estate, study-
ing and, not incidentally, writing many of his better short poems. Lamen-
tably, when he married in 1643, his seventeen-year-old wife left him within
a month. Shortly after, he published a series of tracts urging that incom-
patibility should be considered legitimate grounds for divorce. *Of Education*
and *Areopagitica* (urging freedom of thought and of the press) followed the
next year. All his major earlier poems, including *L'Allegro, Il Penseroso,*
and *Lycidas* had been published by 1645. During the Commonwealth, he

defended Parliament, tyrannicide, and the execution of Charles I, becoming Latin Secretary in Cromwell's Office of Foreign Affairs. When the Restoration came in 1660, Milton found himself in jail for a time, and his public career ended.

For the past twenty years Milton had almost ignored poetry. Now he had plenty of time to write and, even though he had been blind since 1652, progressed apace with *Paradise Lost*, the greatest of all English epic poems, the goal of which was to "justify the ways of God to men." *Paradise Lost* was finished in 1665 and published in 1667. In 1671, *Paradise Regained* and *Samson Agonistes* were published. These poems, but especially *Paradise Lost*, show a unique landmark poet, usually considered second only to Shakespeare, who ignored the poetic schools of his time, including that of Donne, to create a grand language of his own. His main influences form a path from Spenser and the High Renaissance Italians Ariosto and Tasso back to the greatest epic Classical poets, Virgil and Homer. He truly brought the epic to English and his best work compares favorably with the best of any age and language.

Lycidas

In this Monody the Author bewails a learned Friend, unfortunately drowned in his passage from Chester on the Irish Seas, 1637, and, by occasion, foretells the ruin of our corrupted Clergy, then in their height.

Yet once more, O ye laurels, and once more,
Ye myrtles brown, with ivy never sere,
I come to pluck your berries harsh and crude,
And with forced fingers rude
Shatter your leaves before the mellowing year.   5
Bitter constraint and sad occasion dear
Compels me to disturb your season due;
For Lycidas is dead, dead ere his prime,
Young Lycidas, and hath not left his peer.
Who would not sing for Lycidas? he knew   10
Himself to sing, and build the lofty rhyme.
He must not float upon his watery bier
Unwept, and welter to the parching wind,
Without the meed of some melodious tear.
      Begin, then, Sisters of the sacred well   15

Lycidas: Milton contributed this poem to a collection of memorial poems to Edward King, a fellow student at Cambridge who drowned while on a journey to Ireland. *1–2:* Laurels, ivy, and myrtle are traditional symbols of poetry. *3 crude:* unripe. *15 Sisters:* the Muses. *sacred well:* the fountain of Aganippe on Mt. Helicon, sacred to the Muses.

That from beneath the seat of Jove doth spring;
Begin, and somewhat loudly sweep the string.
Hence with denial vain and coy excuse:
So may some gentle Muse
With lucky words favor *my* destined urn,   20
And as he passes turn,
And bid fair peace be to my sable shroud!
      For we were nursed upon the self-same hill,
Fed the same flock, by fountain, shade, and rill;
Together both, ere the high lawns appeared   25
Under the opening eyelids of the Morn,
We drove a-field, and both together heard
What time the gray-fly winds her sultry horn,
Battening our flocks with the fresh dews of night,
Oft till the star that rose at evening bright   30
Toward heaven's descent had sloped his westering wheel.
Meanwhile the rural ditties were not mute;
Tempered to the oaten flute
Rough Satyrs danced, and Fauns with cloven heel
From the glad sound would not be absent long;   35
And old Damoetas loved to hear our song.
      But, oh! the heavy change, now thou art gone,
Now thou art gone and never must return!
Thee, Shepherd, thee the woods and desert caves,
With wild thyme and the gadding vine o'ergrown,   40
And all their echoes, mourn.
The willows, and the hazel copses green,
Shall now no more be seen
Fanning their joyous leaves to thy soft lays.
As killing as the canker to the rose,   45
Or taint-worm to the weanling herds that graze,
Or frost to flowers that their gay wardrobe wear,
When first the white-thorn blows;
Such, Lycidas, thy loss to shepherd's ear.
      Where were ye, Nymphs, when the remorseless deep   50
Closed o'er the head of your loved Lycidas?
For neither were ye playing on the steep
Where your old bards, the famous Druids, lie,
Nor on the shaggy top of Mona high,
Nor yet where Deva spreads her wizard stream.   55

16 seat of Jove: an altar to Jove on Mt. Helicon. The spring, however, is not
in fact beneath the altar. *29 Battening:* feeding. *36 Damoetas:* usually taken
as a pastoral name for a Cambridge tutor. *50 Nymphs:* Milton is addressing
the Muses here. *54 Mona:* the island of Angelesy. *55 Deva:* the Dee River,
which empties into the Irish Sea. *wizard stream:* The river's shifting of its
channel was supposed to prophesy good fortune to England or to Wales, accord-
ing to the direction of shift.

Ay me! I fondly dream,
"Had ye been there," . . . for what could that have done?
What could the Muse herself that Orpheus bore,
The Muse herself, for her enchanting son,
Whom universal nature did lament,   60
When, by the rout that made the hideous roar,
His gory visage down the stream was sent,
Down the swift Hebrus to the Lesbian shore?
          Alas! what boots it with uncessant care
To tend the homely, slighted, shepherd's trade,   65
And strictly meditate the thankless Muse?
Were it not better done, as others use,
To sport with Amaryllis in the shade,
Or with the tangles of Neaera's hair?
Fame is the spur that the clear spirit doth raise.   70
(That last infirmity of noble mind)
To scorn delights and live laborious days;
But the fair guerdon when we hope to find,
And think to burst out into sudden blaze,
Comes the blind Fury with the abhorrèd shears   75
And slits the thin-spun life. "But not the praise,"
Phoebus replied, and touched my trembling ears:
"Fame is no plant that grows on mortal soil,
Nor in the glistering foil
Set off to the world, nor in broad rumor lies,   80
But lives and spreads aloft by those pure eyes
And perfect witness of all-judging Jove;
As he pronounces lastly on each deed,
Of so much fame in heaven expect thy meed."
          O fountain Arethuse, and thou honored flood,   85
Smooth-sliding Mincius, crowned with vocal reeds,
That strain I heard was of a higher mood.
But now my oat proceeds,
And listens to the Herald of the Sea
That came in Neptune's plea.   90
He asked the waves, and asked the felon winds,
What hard mishap hath doomed this gentle swain?
And questioned every gust of rugged wings,

---

56 fondly: foolishly. *58–63 Muse:* Calliope, mother of Orpheus and chief of the Muses. Orpheus was torn to pieces by Thracian maenads when he refused to take part in their bacchic ories; his head was cast into the Hebrus River and floated to the Isle of Lesbos. *64 boots:* profits, avails. *65 shepherd's trade:* the art of poetry. *68–69 Amaryllis . . . Neaera:* simply pastoral names for girls *73 guerdon:* reward. *75 the blind Fury:* Stropos, in fact not a Fury, but the one of the three Fates who cut the thread of life. *85 Arethuse:* Arethusa, a spring in Sicily associated with Sicilian pastoral poetry. *86 Mincius:* The Mincio River in Lombardy, associated with Latin pastoral poetry. Theocritus was born near Arethusa, Virgil near the Mincio.

That blows from off each beakèd promontory;
They knew not of his story, 95
And sage Hippotades their answer brings,
That not a blast was from his dungeon strayed:
The air was calm, and on the level brine
Sleek Panopé with all her sisters played.
It was that fatal and perfidious bark, 100
Built in the eclipse, and rigged with curses dark,
That sunk so low that sacred head of thine.
     Next, Camus, reverend sire, went footing slow,
His mantle hairy, and his bonnet sedge,
Inwrought with figures dim, and on the edge 105
Like to that sanguine flower inscribed with woe.
"Ah! who hath reft," quoth he, "my dearest pledge?"
Last came, and last did go,
The Pilot of the Galilean Lake;
Two massy keys he bore of metals twain 110
(The golden opes, the iron shuts amain).
He shook his mitred locks, and stern bespake:—
"How well could I have spared for thee, young swain,
Enow of such as, for their bellies' sake,
Creep, and intrude, and climb into the fold! 115
Of other care they little reckoning make
Than how to scramble at the shearers' feast
And shove away the worthy bidden guest.
Blind mouths! that scarce themselves know how to hold
A sheep-hook, or have learned ought else the least 120
That to the faithful herdman's art belongs!
What recks it them? What need they? They are sped;
And, when they list, their lean and flashy songs
Grate on their scrannel pipes of wretched straw;
The hungry sheep look up, and are not fed, 125
But, swoln with wind and the rank mist they draw,
Rot inwardly, and foul contagion spread;
Besides what the grim wolf with privy paw
Daily devours apace, and nothing said.
But that two-handed engine at the door 130

96 *Hippotades:* Aeolus, god of the winds. 99 *Panopé:* a sea nymph attending on the sea god. 103 *Camus:* a personification of the Cam River at Cambridge; here representative of the university. 106 *that sanguine flower,* etc.: the hyacinth, which sprang from the blood of Hyacinthus and was thought by the Greeks to be inscribed with the Greek word for "alas!" 109–111 *Pilot:* St. Peter, keeper of the keys of heaven and first bishop of the Roman Church. *amain:* violently. 120 *sheep-hook:* the pastoral staff of a bishop. 128 *grim wolf:* a reference to the Catholic conversions frequent at this time. 130 *two-handed engine:* This expression, no doubt purposely vague, has been interpreted in innumerable ways. One is as the two-handed sword wielded by the angel Michael (see *Paradise Lost* 6. 251).

Stands ready to smite once, and smite no more."
      Return, Alphëus; the dread voice is past
That shrunk thy streams; return, Sicilian Muse,
And call the vales, and bid them hither cast
Their bells and flowerets of a thousand hues.   *135*
Ye valleys low, where the mild whispers use
Of shades, and wanton winds, and gushing brooks,
On whose fresh lap the swart star sparely looks,
Throw hither all your quaint enameled eyes
That on the green turf suck the honeyed showers,   *140*
And purple all the ground with vernal flowers.
Bring the rathe primrose that forsaken dies,
The tufted crow-toe, and pale jessamine,
The white pink, and the pansy freaked with jet,
The glowing violet,   *145*
The musk-rose, and the well-attired woodbine,
With cowslips wan that hang the pensive head,
And every flower that sad embroidery wears;
Bid amaranthus all his beauty shed,
And daffadillies fill their cups with tears,   *150*
To strew the laureate hearse where Lycid lies.
For so, to interpose a little ease,
Let our frail thoughts dally with false surmise.
Ay me! whilst thee the shores and sounding seas
Wash far away, where'er thy bones are hurled;   *155*
Whether beyond the stormy Hebrides,
Where thou perhaps under the whelming tide
Visit'st the bottom of the monstrous world;
Or whether thou, to our moist vows denied,
Sleep'st by the fable of Bellerus old,   *160*
Where the great Vision of the guarded mount
Looks toward Namancos and Bayona's hold.
Look homeward, Angel, now, and melt with ruth:
And, O ye dolphins, waft the hapless youth.
      Weep no more, woeful shepherds, weep no more,   *165*
For Lycidas, your sorrow, is not dead,
Sunk though he be beneath the watery floor.

132 *Alphëus:* an Arcadian river. The meaning of this passage is that after the heroic outburst of St. Peter's speech, the poet resumes the simple pastoral strain. 138 *the swart star:* the Dog Star, which withers vegetation in the dog days. 142 *rathe:* early. 144 *freaked:* spotted. 151–153: The poet is *pretending* that Lycidas's body is on the bier, simply to gain some relief from his sorrow. 160 *Bellerus:* a name coined by Milton to stand for some mythical hero of Land's End in on Cornwall. He derives it from *Bellerium,* the Roman name for the region. 161 *Vision of the guarded mount:* The mountain is St. Michael's Mount, where the archangel was supposed to guard England from invaders and where he was also supposed to be seen from time to time; hence, "great Vision." 162 *Namancos and Bayona's hold:* two towns in Spain, England's old enemy.

So sinks the day-star in the ocean bed,
And yet anon repairs his drooping head,
And tricks his beams, and with new-spangled ore   *170*
Flames in the forehead of the morning sky:
So Lycidas sunk low, but mounted high,
Through the dear might of Him that walked the waves,
Where, other groves and other streams along,
With nectar pure his oozy locks he laves,   *175*
And hears the unexpressive nuptial song,
In the blest kingdoms meek of joy and love.
There entertain him all the Saints above,
In solemn troops, and sweet societies,
That sing, and singing in their glory move,   *180*
And wipe the tears for ever from his eyes.
Now, Lycidas, the shepherds weep no more;
Henceforth thou art the Genius of the shore,
In thy large recompense, and shalt be good
To all that wander in that perilous flood.   *185*
      Thus sang the uncouth swain to the oaks and rills,
While the still morn went out with sandals gray;
He touched the tender stops of various quills,
With eager thought warbling his Doric lay:
And now the sun had stretched out all the hills,   *190*
And now was dropped into the western bay.
At last he rose, and twitched his mantle blue:
To-morrow to fresh woods, and pastures new.

Ode on the Morning of Christ's Nativity

This is the month, and this the happy morn
Wherein the Son of Heaven's Eternal King
Of wedded maid and virgin mother born,
Our great redemption from above did bring;
For so the holy sages once did sing   *5*
That He our deadly forfeit should release,
And with His Father work us a perpetual peace.

That glorious Form, that Light unsufferable,
And that far-beaming blaze of Majesty

168 day-star: the sun. *173 Him that walked the waves:* Christ, who walked on
the water (Matt. 14:26). *176 unexpressible:* inexpressive. *nuptial song:* "the
marriage supper of the Lamb" (Rev. 19:9). *189 Doric:* here, simply "pastoral."

Wherewith He wont at Heaven's high council-table   10
To sit the midst of Trinal Unity,
He laid aside; and, here with us to be,
Forsook the courts of everlasting day,
And chose with us a darksome house of mortal clay.

Say, heavenly Muse, shall not thy sacred vein   15
Afford a present to the Infant God?
Hast thou no verse, no hymn, or solemn strain
To welcome Him to this His new abode,
Now while the heaven, by the sun's team untrod,
Hath took no print of the approaching light,   20
And all the spangled host keep watch in squadrons bright?

See how from far, upon the eastern road,
The star-led wizards haste with odours sweet:
O run, prevent them with thy humble ode
And lay it lowly at His blessed feet;   25
Have thou the honour first thy Lord to greet,
And join thy voice unto the Angel choir
From out His secret altar touch'd with hallow'd fire.

THE HYMN

It was the winter wild,
While the heaven-born Child,   30
All meanly wrapt in the rude manger lies;
Nature in awe to Him
Had doff'd her gaudy trim,
With her great Master so to sympathize:
It was no season then for her   35
To wanton with the sun, her lusty paramour.

Only with speeches fair
She woos the gentle air
To hide her guilty front with innocent snow;
And on her naked shame,   40
Pollute with sinful blame,
The saintly veil of maiden white to throw;
Confounded, that her Maker's eyes
Should look so near upon her foul deformities.

But He, her fears to cease,   45
Sent down the meek-eyed Peace;
She, crown'd with olive green, came softly sliding
Down through the turning sphere,

His ready harbinger,
With turtle wing the amorous clouds dividing,   50
And waving wide her myrtle wand,
She strikes a universal peace through sea and land.

No war, or battle's sound
Was heard the world around:
The idle spear and shield were high uphung;   55
The hookèd chariot stood
Unstain'd with hostile blood,
The trumpet spake not to the armèd throng
And kings sat still with awful eye,
As if they surely knew their sovran Lord was by.   60

But peaceful was the night
Wherein the Prince of Light
His reign of peace upon the earth began:
The winds, with wonder whist,
Smoothly the waters kist,   65
Whispering new joys to the mild ocean—
Who now hath quite forgot to rave,
While birds of calm sit brooding on the charmèd wave.

The stars, with deep amaze
Stand fix'd in steadfast gaze,   70
Bending one way their precious influence;
And will not take their flight,
For all the morning light,
Or Lucifer that often warn'd them thence;
But in their glimmering orbs did glow,   75
Until their Lord Himself bespake, and bid them go.

And though the shady gloom
Had given day her room,
The sun himself withheld his wonted speed,
And hid his head for shame,   80
As his inferior flame
The new-enlighten'd world no more should need;
He saw a greater Sun appear
Than his bright throne, or burning axletree could bear.

The shepherds on the lawn,   85
Or ere the point of dawn,
Sate simply chatting in a rustic row;
Full little thought they than
That the mighty Pan

Was kindly come to live with them below;   *90*
Perhaps their loves, or else their sheep,
Was all that did their silly thoughts so busy keep.

When such music sweet
Their hearts and ears did greet,
As never was by mortal finger strook—   *95*
Divinely-warbled voice
Answering the stringèd noise,
As all their souls in blissful rapture took;
The air, such pleasure loth to lose,
With thousand echoes still prolongs each heavenly close.   *100*

Nature, that heard such sound
Beneath the hollow round
Of Cynthia's seat the airy region thrilling,
Now was almost won
To think her part was done,   *105*
And that her reign had here its last fulfilling;
She knew such harmony alone
Could hold all Heaven and Earth in happier union.

At last surrounds their sight
A globe of circular light,   *110*
That with long beams the shamefaced night array'd;
The helmèd Cherubim
And sworded Seraphim,
Are seen in glittering ranks with wings display'd,
Harping in loud and solemn choir,   *115*
With unexpressive notes, to Heaven's new-born Heir.

Such music (as 'tis said)
Before was never made
But when of old the Sons of Morning sung,
While the Creator great   *120*
His constellations set,
And the well-balanced world on hinges hung,
And cast the dark foundations deep,
And bid the weltering waves their oozy channel keep.

Ring out, ye crystal spheres!   *125*
Once bless our human ears,
If ye have power to touch our senses so;
And let your silver chime
Move in melodious time;
And let the bass of heaven's deep organ blow;   *130*

And with your ninefold harmony
Make up full consort to the angelic symphony.

For if such holy song
Enwrap our fancy long,
Time will run back, and fetch the age of gold,   135
And speckled Vanity
Will sicken soon and die,
And leprous Sin will melt from earthly mould,
And Hell itself will pass away,
And leave her dolorous mansions to the peering day.   140

Yea, Truth, and Justice then
Will down return to men,
Orb'd in a rainbow; and, like glories wearing,
Mercy will sit between
Throned in celestial sheen,   145
With radiant feet the tissued clouds down steering;
And Heaven, as at some festival,
Will open wide the gates of her high palace hall.

But wisest Fate says No;
This must not yet be so;   150
The Babe yet lies in smiling infancy,
That on the bitter cross
Must redeem our loss;
So both Himself and us to glorify:
Yet first, to those ychaine'd in sleep,   155
The wakeful trump of doom must thunder through the deep.

With such a horrid clang
As on Mount Sinai rang
While the red fire and smouldering clouds outbrake:
The aged Earth aghast   160
With terror of that blast,
Shall from the surface to the centre shake;
When, at the world's last sessiòn,
The dreadful Judge in middle air shall spread His throne.

And then at last our bliss   165
Full and perfect is,
But now begins; for from this happy day
Th' old Dragon under ground
In straiter limits bound,

158: See Exod. 19:18–19. 168 Dragon: In Revelation, Satan is spoken of thus

Not half so far casts his usurpèd sway,
And wroth to see his kingdom fail,
Swings the scaly horror of his folded tail.

The Oracles are dumb;
No voice or hideous hum
Runs through the archèd roof in words deceiving.   175
Apollo from his shrine
Can no more divine,
With hollow shriek the steep of Delphos leaving.
No nightly trance or breathèd spell,
Inspires the pale-eyed priest from the prophetic cell.   180

The lonely mountains o'er,
And the resounding shore,
A voice of weeping heard, and loud lament:
From haunted spring and dale
Edged with poplar pale,   185
The parting Genius is with sighing sent;
With flower-inwoven tresses torn
The Nymphs in twilight shade of tangled thickets mourn.

In consecrated earth,
And on the holy hearth,   190
The Lars and Lemures moan with midnight plaint,
In urns, and altars round,
A drear and dying sound
Affrights the Flamens at their service quaint;
And the chill marble seems to sweat,   195
While each peculiar Power forgoes his wonted seat.

Peor and Baalim
Forsake their temples dim,
With that twice-batter'd god of Palestine,
And moonèd Ashtaroth   200
Heaven's queen and mother both,
Now sits not girt with tapers' holy shine;
The Lybic Hammon shrinks his horn,
In vain the Tyrian maids their wounded Thammuz mourn.

191 *Lars and Lemures:* The Lares were benign spirits of the sea, who were wor-
shipped by the Romans and given a special room ("holy hearth") in their houses;
the Lemures were hostile ghosts. 194 *Flamens:* priests of ancient Rome. 197
Peor and Baalim: different names of the Phoenician sun god (Baal-Peor). 199
god of Palestine: Dagon, worshipped by the Philistines (1 Sam. 5:1–4). 200 *Ash-
taroth:* the Phoenician moon goddess. 203 *Hammon:* an Egyptian god in the
form of a ram with curled horns. 204 *Tyrian maids:* girls of the city of Tyre.
Thammuz: Babylonian nature god, slain by a boar or by the fertility goddess
Ishtar, and restored to life by the goddess every spring.

And sullen Moloch, fled, 205
Hath left in shadows dread,
His burning idol all of blackest hue,
In vain with cymbals' ring,
They call the grisly king,
In dismal dance about the furnace blue; 210
The brutish gods of Nile as fast,
Isis, and Orus, and the dog Anubis haste.

Nor is Osiris seen
In Memphian grove, or green,
Trampling the unshower'd grass with lowings loud: 215
Nor can he be at rest
Within his sacred chest,
Nought but profoundest Hell can be his shroud,
In vain with timbrell'd anthems dark
The sable-stolèd sorcerers bear his worshipt ark. 220

He feels from Juda's land
The dreaded Infant's hand,
The rays of Bethlehem blind his dusky eyn;
Nor all the gods beside,
Longer dare abide, 225
Not Typhon huge ending in snaky twine:
Our Babe, to show His Godhead true,
Can in His swaddling bands control the damnèd crew.

So, when the sun in bed,
Curtain'd with cloudy red, 230
Pillows his chin upon an orient wave,
The flocking shadows pale,
Troop to the infernal jail,
Each fetter'd ghost slips to his several grave;
And the yellow-skirted fays, 235
Fly after the night-steeds leaving their moon-loved maze.

But see! the Virgin blest,
Hath laid her Babe to rest;
Time is, our tedious song should here have ending;
Heaven's youngest-teemèd star 240

205 *Moloch*: the Canaanitic and Assyrian god of fire; children were burned in his idol, which was filled with fire. 212 *Isis*: Egyptian earth goddess. *Orus*: Horus, the sun god. *Anubis*: the dog-headed son of Osiris. 213 *Osiris*: the nature god worshipped by the Egyptians in the form of the sacred bull Apis. 214 *Memphian*: near the Egyptian city of Memphis. 236 *Typhon*: in Greek mythology, the hundred-headed monster slain by Zeus; he was worshipped in Egypt in the form of a crocodile.

Hath fix'd her polish'd car,
Her sleeping Lord with hand-maid lamp attending:
And all about the courtly stable,
Bright-harness'd Angels sit in order serviceable.

O Nightingale, that on yon bloomy spray

O Nightingale, that on yon bloomy spray
Warbl'st at eve, when all the woods are still,
Thou with fresh hope the lover's heart dost fill,
While the jolly hours lead on propitious May.
Thy liquid notes that close the eye of day,   5
First heard before the shallow cuckoo's bill
Portend success in love; O if Jove's will
Have link'd that amorous power to thy soft lay,
Now timely sing, ere the rude bird of hate
Foretell my hopeless doom in some grove nigh: 10
As thou from year to year hast sung too late
For my relief; yet hadst no reason why,
Whether the Muse, or Love call thee his mate,
Both them I serve, and of their train am I.

L'Allegro

Hence, loathèd Melancholy,
    Of Cerberus and blackest Midnight born
In Stygian cave forlorn,
    'Mongst horrid shapes and shrieks, and sights unholy!
Find out some uncouth cell,   5
    Where brooding darkness spreads his jealous wings,
And the night-raven sings;
    There, under ebon shades and low-browed rocks,
As ragged as thy locks,
    In dark Cimmerian desert ever dwell.   10

L'Allegro: Title: "The Cheerful Man." 1–10: Milton personifies Melancholy and invents a parentage and birthplace for her: her father is Cerberus, the three-headed dog who guarded the entrance to Hades; her mother is Night; she was born in a cave near the River Styx. (In myth the husband of Nox, or Night, was Erebus, not Cerberus.) L'Allegro sends Melancholy into exile in a desert out of reach of the sun, where the fabled Cimmerians live in mist and darkness.

But come, thou goddess fair and free,
In heaven yclept Euphrosyne,
And by men heart-easing Mirth;
Whom lovely Venus, at a birth,
With two sister Graces more,   *15*
To ivy-crownèd Bacchus bore;
Or whether (as some sager sing)
The frolic wind that breathes the spring,
Zephyr, with Aurora playing,
As he met her once a-Maying,   *20*
There, on beds of violets blue,
And fresh-blown roses washed in dew,
Filled her with thee, a daughter fair,
So buxom, blithe, and debonair.
Haste thee, nymph, and bring with thee   *25*
Jest and youthful Jollity,
Quips and Cranks and wanton Wiles,
Nods and Becks and wreathèd Smiles,
Such as hang on Hebe's cheek,
And love to live in dimple sleek;   *30*
Sport, that wrinkled Care derides,
And Laughter holding both his sides.
Come, and trip it, as ye go,
On the light fantastic toe,
And in thy right hand lead with thee   *35*
The mountain-nymph, sweet Liberty.
And if I give thee honor due,
Mirth, admit me of thy crew,
To live with her, and live with thee,
In unreprovèd pleasures free: *40*
To hear the lark begin his flight,
And, singing, startle the dull night,
From his watch-tower in the skies,
Till the dappled dawn doth rise;
Then to come in spite of sorrow,   *45*
And at my window bid good morrow,
Through the sweetbriar or the vine
Or the twisted eglantine,

11–24: Euphrosyne (the Greek word means "Joy" or "Mirth") was one of the three Graces, born with her sisters Aglaia (Splendor) and Thalia (Pleasure) to Venus and Bacchus in one version of the myth or, as Milton prefers, to Aurora and Zephyr. Milton has in mind the innocent joy born of dawn and soft breezes, rather than of love and wine. *24 buxom:* lively. *27 Cranks:* odd turns of speech. *28 Becks:* beckonings. *29 Hebe:* goddess of youth, born to Jupiter and Juno. *40 unreprovèd:* innocent, blameless. *45 in spite of sorrow:* in contempt of sorrow.

While the cock, with lively din,
Scatters the rear of darkness thin.   50
And to the stack or the barn door
Stoutly struts his dames before;
Oft listening how the hounds and horn
Cheerly rouse the slumbering morn,
From the side of some hoar hill,   55
Through the high wood echoing shrill;
Sometime walking, not unseen.
By hedgerow elms, on hillocks green,
Right against the eastern gate,
Where the great sun begins his state,   60
Robed in flames and amber light,
The clouds in thousand liveries dight;
While the ploughman, near at hand,
Whistles o'er the furrowed land,
And the milkmaid singeth blithe,   65
And the mower whets his scythe,
And every shepherd tells his tale
Under the hawthorn in the dale.
Straight mine eye hath caught new pleasures,
Whilst the landskip round it measures: 70
Russet lawns and fallows gray,
Where the nibbling flocks do stray;
Mountains on whose barren breast
The laboring clouds do often rest;
Meadows trim, with daisies pied;   75
Shallow brooks and rivers wide.
Towers and battlements it sees
Bosomed high in tufted trees,
Where perhaps some beauty lies,
The cynosure of neighboring eyes.   80
Hard by, a cottage chimney smokes
From betwixt two agèd oaks,
Where Corydon and Thyrsis, met,
Are at their savory dinner set
Of herbs and other country messes.   85
Which the neat-handed Phillis dresses;
And then in haste her bower she leaves,
With Thestylis to bind the sheaves,
Or, if the earlier season lead,

---

62 *dight:* dressed, decked out. *67 tells his tale:* that is, he counts his sheep.
70: i.e., "While my eyes sweep over the whole landscape." *71 lawns:* open
fields. *fallows:* untilled land. *80 cynosure:* the constellation of Ursa Minor (the
Little Bear or Little Dipper), which contains the polestar (Polaris), by which
Tyrian sailors steered (literally, "dog's tail," in reference to its shape); hence,
something often looked at. *85–88:* The names in this passage are common ones
in pastoral poetry and denote only conventional pastoral characters.

To the tanned haycock in the mead.   90
Sometimes, with secure delight,
The upland hamlets will invite,
When the merry bells ring round,
And the jocund rebecks sound
To many a youth and many a maid   95
Dancing in the checkered shade;
And young and old come forth to play
On a sunshine holiday,
Till the livelong daylight fail.
Then to the spicy, nut-brown ale,   100
With stories told of many a feat:
How faery Mab the junkets eat;
She was pinched and pulled, she said;
And he, by friar's lanthorn led,
Tells how the drudging goblin sweat   105
To earn his cream-bowl duly set,
When in one night, ere glimpse of morn,
His shadowy flail hath threshed the corn
That ten day-laborers could not end;
Then lies him down the lubber fiend,   110
And, stretched out all the chimney's length,
Basks at the fire his hairy strength,
And, crop-full, out of doors he flings
Ere the first cock his matin rings.
Thus done the tales, to bed they creep,   115
By whispering winds soon lulled asleep.
Towered cities please us then,
And the busy hum of men,
Where throngs of knights and barons bold,
In weeds of peace, high triumphs hold,   120
With store of ladies, whose bright eyes
Rain influence, and judge the prize
Of wit or arms, while both contend
To win her grace whom all commend.
There let Hymen oft appear   125
In saffron robe, with taper clear,
And pomp and feast and revelry,

94 *rebecks:* fiddles, precursors of violins. *101–114:* This passage contains the
stories told: a serving maid tells how Queen Mab (*Romeo and Juliet* 1. 4. 53ff:),
who was traditionally the patroness and tormentor of serving maids, had eaten
the junkets (puddings) and pushed and pulled her about; a man tells how he
was led astray by Friar Rush's lantern (the will-o-the-wisp) and how Robin
Goodfellow, the plague and benefactor of farm laborers, had threshed all the
corn in one night, etc. Robin is "crop-full" because he has gorged on the bowl of
cream that was set out to ask his help and prevent his mischief. *114 matin:*
morning song. *120 weeds:* clothes or dress. *triumphs:* revels, processions. *125
Hymen:* god of marriage. Milton is thinking of wedding festivities.

With mask and antique pageantry;
Such sights as youthful poets dream
On summer eves by haunted stream. 130
Then to the well-trod stage anon,
If Jonson's learnèd sock be on,
Or sweetest Shakespeare, Fancy's child,
Warble his native wood-notes wild.
And ever, against eating cares, 135
Lap me in soft Lydian airs,
Married to immortal verse,
Such as the meeting soul may pierce,
In notes with many a winding bout
Of linkèd sweetness long drawn out 140
With wanton heed and giddy cunning,
The melting voice through mazes running,
Untwisting all the chains that tie
The hidden soul of harmony;
That Orpheus' self may heave his head 145
From golden slumber on a bed
Of heaped Elysian flowers, and hear
Such strains as would have won the ear
Of Pluto to have quite set free
His half-regained Eurydice. 150
These delights if thou canst give,
Mirth, with thee I mean to live.

Il Penseroso

Hence, vain, deluding joys,
   The brood of Folly without father bred!
How little you bestèd,
   Or fill the fixèd mind with all your toys!
Dwell in some idle brain, 5
   And fancies fond with gaudy shapes possess,

128 *mask:* an entertainment, usually dramatic. *132 sock:* a low slipper worn in comedies; the buskin, or high boot, was worn in tragedies. *136 Lydian airs:* soft and voluptuous music. *139 bout:* bend, turn. *145–150 Orpheus:* the legendary musician who drew his wife Eurydice from Hades and then lost her by glancing back to see if she was following. Milton's point is that this music is better even than Orpheus's and would have induced Pluto to free Eurydice.

Il Penseroso: Title: "The Pensive Man." *1–11:* Here, in a passage that parallels the opening lines of *L'Allegro*, the Pensive Man exiles trivial joys to "some idle brain"; such joys are the unfathered brood of Folly. *3 bestèd:* bestead, i.e., profit or benefit. *4 toys:* trifles.

As thick and numberless
   As the gay motes that people the sunbeams,
Or likest hovering dreams,
   The fickle pensioners of Morpheus' train.   *10*
But hail, thou goddess sage and holy!
Hail, divinest Melancholy!
Whose saintly visage is too bright
To hit the sense of human sight,
And therefore to our weaker view   *15*
O'erlaid with black, staid Wisdom's hue;
Black, but such as in esteem
Prince Memnon's sister might beseem,
Or that starred Ethiop queen that strove
To set her beauty's praise above   *20*
The sea-nymphs, and their powers offended.
Yet thou art higher far descended:
Thee bright-haired Vesta long of yore
To solitary Saturn bore;
His daughter she (in Saturn's reign   *25*
Such mixture was not held a stain).
Oft in glimmering bowers and glades
He met her, and in secret shades
Of woody Ida's inmost grove,
Whilst yet there was no fear of Jove.   *30*
Come, pensive nun, devout and pure,
Sober, steadfast, and demure,
All in a robe of darkest grain,
Flowing with majestic train,
And sable stole of cypress lawn   *35*
Over thy decent shoulders drawn.
Come, but keep thy wonted state,
With even step and musing gait
And looks commercing with the skies,
Thy rapt soul sitting in thine eyes;   *40*
There, held in holy passion still,
Forget thyself to marble, till
With a sad, leaden, downward cast

---

10 pensioners: attendants; i.e., a retinue. *Morpheus:* Morpheus was the god of sleep (dreams). *18 Prince Memnon's sister:* at the time of the Trojan War, Memnon was King of the Ethiopians; Odysseus reported him to be the handsomest man he had ever seen. The "sister" seems to be Milton's invention. *19 starred Ethiop queen:* Cassiopeia, who became a constellation. *23 Vesta:* This invented parentage of Melancholy makes her the daughter of the king of gods and the goddess of fire. *29 Ida:* Mount Ida, in Crete, the ancient kingdom of Saturn before the successful rebellion of his son Jupiter (Zeus). *35 cypress lawn:* black crepe. *42 Forget thyself to marble:* in deep thought, become still as stone. *43 sad:* serious.

Thou fix them on the earth as fast.
And join with thee calm Peace and Quiet,   45
Spare Fast, that oft with gods doth diet,
And hears the Muses in a ring
Aye round about Jove's altar sing;
And add to these retirèd Leisure,
That in trim gardens takes his pleasure;   50
But, first and chiefest, with thee bring
Him that yon soars on golden wing,
Guiding the fiery-wheelèd throne,
The cherub Contemplation;
And the mute Silence hist along,   55
'Less Philomel will deign a song,
In her sweetest, saddest plight,
Smoothing the rugged brow of night,
While Cynthia checks her dragon yoke
Gently o'er the accustomed oak.   60
Sweet bird, that shunn'st the noise of folly,
Most musical, most melancholy!
Thee, chauntress, oft the woods among
I woo, to hear thy even-song;
And, missing thee, I walk unseen   65
On the dry, smooth-shaven green,
To behold the wandering moon,
Riding near her highest noon,
Like one that had been led astray
Through the heaven's wide, pathless way,   70
And oft, as if her head she bowed,
Stooping through a fleecy cloud.
Oft, on a plat of rising ground,
I hear the far-off curfew sound,
Over some wide-watered shore,   75
Swinging slow with sullen roar;
Or, if the air will not permit,
Some still, removèd place will fit,
Where glowing embers through the room
Teach light to counterfeit a gloom,   80
Far from all resort of mirth,
Save the cricket on the hearth,
Or the bellman's drowsy charm
To bless the doors from nightly harm.
Or let my lamp at midnight hour   85
Be seen in some high, lonely tower,

52–54: See Ezek. 10.   55 *hist along:* lead while hushing.   56 *'Less Philomel:* unless the nightingale.   59 *Cynthia:* moon goddess.   60 *accustomed oak:* usually frequented by the nightingale.   74 *curfew:* curfew bell.   83 *bellman:* night watchman.

Where I may oft outwatch the Bear,
With thrice-great Hermes, or unsphere
The spirit of Plato to unfold
What worlds or what vast regions hold   90
The immortal mind that hath forsook
Her mansion in this fleshly nook;
And of those demons that are found
In fire, air, flood, or under ground,
Whose power hath a true consent   95
With planet or with element.
Sometime let gorgeous Tragedy
In sceptered pall come sweeping by,
Presenting Thebes, or Pelops' line,
Or the tale of Troy divine,   100
Or what (though rare) of later age
Ennobled hath the buskined stage.
But, O sad virgin, that thy power
Might raise Musaeus from his bower;
Or bid the soul of Orpheus sing   105
Such notes as, warbled to the string,
Drew iron tears down Pluto's cheek,
And made hell grant what love did seek;
Or call up him that left half told
The story of Cambuscan bold,   110
Of Camball, and of Algarsife,
And who had Canace to wife,
That owned the virtuous ring and glass,
And of the wondrous horse of brass
On which the Tartar king did ride;   115
And if aught else great bards beside
In sage and solemn tunes have sung,
Of tourneys, and of trophies hung,
Of forests, and enchantments drear,
Where more is meant than meets the ear.   120
Thus, Night, oft see me in thy pale career,
Till civil-suited Morn appear,
Not tricked and frounced, as she was wont

---

87 *outwatch the Bear:* "the Bear" refers to the constellation Ursa Major, which
never sets; hence, watching till dawn. 88 *thrice-great Hermes:* a mythical
learned Egyptian king to whom various books were attributed in the Middle
Ages. *unsphere:* call Plato's spirit from the heavenly sphere it inhabits. 98
pall: royal mantle. *99–100:* i.e., the tales which afford subjects for some of the
tragedies of Aeschylus, Sophocles, and Euripides. *102 buskined stage:* tragic
stage. The buskin (high boot) was worn in tragedy; the sock was worn in
comedy. *104 Musaeus:* Greek poet of the age of Orpheus. *110–115:* The lines
refer to Chaucer's *Squire's Tale.* *113 virtuous ring and glass:* magic ring and
mirror. The ring permitted one to converse with birds and know medical herbs;
the mirror disclosed dangers, etc.; the horse carried its rider immediately to
wherever he wished. *122 civil-suited:* soberly garbed. *123 frounced:* curled.

With the Attic boy to hunt,
But kerchiefed in a comely cloud,   125
While rocking winds are piping loud,
Or ushered with a shower still,
When the gust hath blown his fill,
Ending on the rustling leaves,
With minute-drops from off the eaves.   130
And when the sun begins to fling
His flaring beams, me, goddess, bring
To archèd walks of twilight groves,
And shadows brown, that Sylvan loves,
Of pine or monumental oak,   135
Where the rude axe with heavèd stroke
Was never heard the nymphs to daunt,
Or fright them from their hallowed haunt.
There in close covert by some brook,
Where no profaner eye may look,   140
Hide me from day's garish eye,
While the bee with honied thigh,
That at her flowery work doth sing,
And the waters murmuring,
With such consort as they keep,   145
Entice the dewy-feathered sleep:
And let some strange, mysterious dream
Wave at his wings, in airy stream
Of lively portraiture displayed,
Softly on my eyelids laid;   150
And, as I wake, sweet music breathe
Above, about, or underneath,
Sent by some spirit to mortals good,
Or the unseen genius of the wood.
But let my due feet never fail   155
To walk the studious cloister's pale,
And love the high embowèd roof,
With antique pillars massy proof,
And storied windows richly dight,
Casting a dim, religious light.   160
There let the pealing organ blow
To the full-voiced choir below,
In service high and anthems clear,
As may with sweetness, through mine ear,
Dissolve me into ecstasies,   165
And bring all heaven before mine eyes.
And may at last my weary age

---

124 *Attic boy:* refers to Cephalus, Aurora's lover. 134 *Sylvan:* god of forests
and fields. 156 *pale:* enclosure. 157 *embowèd:* vaulted. 159 *storied:* painted
with scenes from stories.

Find out the peaceful hermitage,
The hairy gown and mossy cell,
Where I may sit and rightly spell   170
Of every star that heaven doth shew,
And every herb that sips the dew,
Till old experience do attain
To something like prophetic strain.
These pleasures, Melancholy, give,   175
And I with thee will choose to live.

When I consider how my light is spent

When I consider how my light is spent,
Ere half my days, in this dark world and wide,
And that one talent which is death to hide,
Lodg'd with me useless, though my Soul more bent
To serve therewith my Maker, and present   5
My true account, lest he returning chide,
Doth God exact day-labor, light denied,
I fondly ask; But Patience to prevent
That murmur, soon replies, God doth not need
Either man's work or his own gifts, who best   10
Bear his mild yoke, they serve him best, his state
Is kingly. Thousands at his bidding speed
And post o'er land and ocean without rest:
They also serve who only stand and wait.

Hail, Holy Light

From PARADISE LOST, Book III

Hail, holy light, offspring of Heav'n first-born,
Or of th' Eternal Coeternal beam
May I express thee unblam'd? since God is light,
And never but in unapproached light
Dwelt from Eternity, dwelt then in thee,   5
Bright effluence of bright essence increate.
Or hearest thou rather pure Ethereal stream,
Whose Fountain who shall tell? before the Sun,
Before the Heavens thou wert, and at the voice

170 spell: study.

Of God, as with a Mantle didst invest   10
The rising world of water dark and deep,
Won from the void and formless infinite.
Thee I re-visit now with bolder wing,
Escaped the Stygian Pool, though long detained
In that obscure sojourn, while in my flight   15
Through utter and through middle darkness borne
With other notes then to th' Orphean Lyre
I sung of Chaos and Eternal Night,
Taught by the heavenly Muse to venture down
The dark descent, and up to reascend,   20
Though hard and rare: thee I revisit safe,
And feel thy sovereign vital Lamp; but thou
Revisit'st not these eyes, that roll in vain
To find thy piercing ray, and find no dawn;
So thick a drop serene hath quenched their Orbs,   25
Or dim suffusion veiled. Yet not the more
Cease I to wander where the Muses haunt
Clear Spring, or shady Grove, or Sunny Hill,
Smit with the love of sacred song; but chief
Thee Zion and the flowery Brooks beneath   30
That wash thy hallowed feet, and warbling flow,
Nightly I visit: nor sometimes forget
Those other two equalled with me in Fate,
So were I equalled with them in renown,
Blind Thamyris and blind Maeonides,   35
And Tiresias and Phineus Prophets old.
Then feed on thoughts, that voluntary move
Harmonious numbers; as the wakeful Bird
Sings darkling, and in shadiest Covert hid
Tunes her nocturnal Note. Thus with the Year   40
Seasons return, but not to me returns
Day, or the sweet approach of Even or Morn,
Or sight of vernal bloom, or Summer's Rose,
Or flocks, or herds, or human face divine;
But cloud instead, and ever-during dark   45
Surrounds me, from the cheerful ways of men
Cut off, and for the Book of knowledge fair
Presented with a Universal blank
Of Nature's works to me expung'd and raised,
And wisdom at one entrance quite shut out.   50
So much the rather thou Celestial light
Shine inward, and the mind through all her powers
Irradiate, there plant eyes, all mist from thence
Purge and disperse, that I may see and tell
Of things invisible to mortal sight.   55

ANDREW MARVELL
1622–1678

Finding yourself on one of opposing sides through birth or fortune, and sticking or changing, was the perilous portion of all who lived in the seventeenth century from Shakespeare to Pope. Marvell was the son of an Anglican clergyman who was said to have considered Catholicism as a recent graduate of Cambridge. Then, after extensive travels on the Continent during the Civil War (1642–1649) and serving as tutor to the retired Parliamentary General, he found himself in Puritan politics serving, at Milton's recommendation, within Cromwell's government. From 1659 he was Member of Parliament from Hull, bridging the gap into the Restoration world of Charles II (1660–1680) with exceptional ease. He became outspoken in urging toleration of others, and it is even said he was influential in saving Milton from stiff punishment or execution by Charles II. As in Donne's case and others', Marvell's poetry, though all written in the 1650s, was published posthumously (*Miscellaneous Poems*, 1681). Marvell hearkens ahead with a cavalier wit to match the best of Pope in concise clarity and reflects back upon the greatest of Donne's metaphysical "high seriousness." All these qualities of clarity, wit, and profundity make Marvell's small opus one of the fine touchstones of Baroque taste in English, or any, civilization.

To His Coy Mistress

Had we but world enough and time,
This coyness, lady, were no crime.
We would sit down and think which way
To walk, and pass our long love's day;
Thou by the Indian Ganges' side   5
Shouldst rubies find; I by the tide
Of Humber would complain. I would
Love you ten years before the Flood;
And you should, if you please, refuse
Till the conversion of the Jews.   10
My vegetable love should grow
Vaster than empires, and more slow.
An hundred years should go to praise
Thine eyes, and on thy forehead gaze;
Two hundred to adore each breast,   15
But thirty thousand to the rest;
An age at least to every part,
And the last age should show your heart.
For, lady, you deserve this state,
Nor would I love at lower rate.   20
      But at my back I always hear
Time's wingèd chariot hurrying near;
And yonder all before us lie
Deserts of vast eternity.
Thy beauty shall no more be found,   25
Nor in thy marble vault shall sound
My echoing song; then worms shall try
That long preserved virginity,
And your quaint honor turn to dust,
And into ashes all my lust.   30
The grave's a fine and private place,
But none, I think, do there embrace.
      Now therefore, while the youthful hue

Sits on thy skin like morning dew,
And while thy willing soul transpires   35
At every pore with instant fires,
Now let us sport us while we may;
And now, like amorous birds of prey,
Rather at once our time devour,
Than languish in his slow-chapped power.   40
Let us roll all our strength, and all
Our sweetness, up into one ball;
And tear our pleasures with rough strife
Through the iron gates of life.
Thus, though we cannot make our sun   45
Stand still, yet we will make him run.

The Garden

How vainly men themselves amaze
To win the palm, the oak, or bays;
And their incessant labours see
Crowned from some single herb, or tree,
Whose short and narrow-vergèd shade   5
Does prudently their toils upbraid;
While all flowers and all trees do close
To weave the garlands of repose!

Fair Quiet, have I found thee here,
And Innocence, thy sister dear?   10
Mistaken long, I sought you then
In busy companies of men.
Your sacred plants, if here below,
Only among the plants will grow;
Society is all but rude   15
To this delicious solitude.

No white nor red was ever seen
So amorous as this lovely green.
Fond lovers, cruel as their flame,
Cut in these trees their mistress' name: 20
Little, alas! they know or heed
How far these beauties hers exceed!
Fair trees! wheres'e'er your barks I wound
No name shall but your own be found.

When we have run our passion's heat, 25
Love hither makes his best retreat.
The gods, that mortal beauty chase,
Still in a tree did end their race;
Apollo hunted Daphne so,
Only that she might laurel grow; 30
And Pan did after Syrinx speed,
Not as a nymph, but for a reed.

What wondrous life is this I lead!
Ripe apples drop about my head;
The luscious clusters of the vine 35
Upon my mouth do crush their wine;
The nectarine, and curious peach,
Into my hands themselves do reach;
Stumbling on melons, as I pass.
Ensnared with flowers, I fall on grass. 40

Meanwhile, the mind, from pleasure less,
Withdraws into its happiness:
The mind, that ocean where each kind
Does straight its own resemblance find;
Yet it creates, transcending these, 45
Far other worlds, and other seas;
Annihilating all that's made
To a green thought in a green shade.

Here at the fountain's sliding foot,
Or at some fruit-tree's mossy root, 50
Casting the body's vest aside,
My soul into the boughs does glide:
There like a bird it sits, and sings,
Then whets and combs its silver wings;
And, till prepared for longer flight, 55
Waves in its plumes the various light.

Such was that happy garden-state,
While man there walked without a mate:
After a place so pure and sweet,
What other help could yet be meet? 60
But 'twas beyond a mortal's share
To wander solitary there:
Two paradises 'twere in one,
To live in paradise alone.

How well the skillful gardener drew 65
Of flowers, and herbs, this dial new;

Where, from above, the milder sun
Does through a fragrant zodiac run;
And, as it works, the industrious bee
Computes its time as well as we.   70
How could such sweet and wholesome hours
Be reckoned but with herbs and flowers!

The Mower to the Glow-worms

Ye living lamps, by whose dear light
The nightingale does sit so late,
And studying all the summer night,
Her matchless songs does meditate;

Ye county comets that portend   5
No war nor prince's funeral,
Shining unto no higher end
Than to presage the grass's fall;

Ye glow-worms, whose officious flame
To wand'ring mowers shows the way   10
That in the night have lost their aim
And after foolish fires do stray;

Your courteous lights in vain you waste,
Since Juliana here is come
For she my mind hath so displaced   15
That I shall never find my home.

A Dialogue Between the Resolved Soul and Created Pleasure

Courage, my soul! now learn to wield
The weight of thine immortal shield
Close on thy head thy helmet right.
Balance thy sword against the fight.
See where an army, strong as fair,   5
With silken banners spreads the air.
Now, if thou be'st that thing divine,
In this day's combat let it shine,

And show that nature wants an art
To conquer one resolved heart.   *10*

PLEASURE

Welcome the creation's guest,
Lord of earth and heaven's heir.
Lay aside that warlike crest,
And of nature's banquet share,
Where the souls of fruits and flowers   *15*
Stand prepared to heighten yours.

SOUL

I sup above and cannot stay
To bait so long upon the way.

PLEASURE

On these downy pillows lie,
Whose soft plumes will thither fly;   *20*
On these roses strowed so plain
Lest one leaf thy side should strain.

SOUL

My gentler rest is on a thought,
Conscious of doing what I ought.

PLEASURE

If thou be'st with perfumes pleased,   *25*
Such as oft the gods appeased,
Thou in fragrant clouds shalt show
Like another god below.

SOUL

A soul that knows not to presume
Is heaven's and its own perfume.   *30*

PLEASURE

Everything does seem to vie
Which should first attract thine eye;
But since none deserves that grace,
In this crystal view thy face.

SOUL

When the creator's skill is prized,   *35*
The rest is all but earth disguised.

PLEASURE

Hark, how music then prepares
For thy stay these charming airs;

Which the posting winds recall,
And suspend the river's fall.   *40*

SOUL

Had I but any time to lose,
On this I would it all dispose.
Cease, tempter, none can chain a mind
Whom this sweet cordage cannot bind.

CHORUS

Earth cannot show so brave a sight   *45*
As when a single soul does fence
The batteries of alluring sense,
And heaven views it with delight.
Then persevere, for still new charges sound;
And if thou overcom'st, thou shalt be crowned.   *50*

PLEASURE

All this fair, and cost, and sweet,
Which scatteringly doth shine,
Shall within one beauty meet,
And she be only thine.

SOUL

If things of sight such heavens be,   *55*
What heavens are those we cannot see?

PLEASURE

Wheresoe'er thy foot shall go
    The minted gold shall lie;
Till thou purchase all below,
    And want new worlds to buy.   *60*

SOUL

Were't not a price who'd value gold?
And that's worth nought that can be sold.

PLEASURE

Wilt thou all the glory have
    That war or peace commend?
Half the world shall be thy slave,   *65*
    The other half thy friend.

SOUL

What friends, if to myself untrue?
What slaves, unless I captive you?

Thou **shalt** know each hidden cause,
    And see the future time;   70
Try what depth the center draws,
    And then to heaven climb.

SOUL

None thither mounts by the degree
Of knowledge, but humility.

CHORUS

Triumph, triumph, victorious soul!   75
The world has not one pleasure more.
The rest does lie beyond the pole,
And is thine everlasting store.

A Dialogue Between the Soul and Body

SOUL

Oh, who shall from this dungeon raise
A soul enslaved so many ways?
With bolts of bones; that fettered stands
In feet, and manacled in hands;
Here blinded with an eye, and there   5
Deaf with the drumming of an ear;
A soul hung up, as 'twere, in chains
Of nerves and arteries and veins;
Tortured, besides each other part.
In a vain head and double heart.   10

BODY

Oh, who shall me deliver whole
From bonds of this tyrannic soul?
Which, stretched upright, impales me so
That mine own precipice I go;
And warms and moves this needless frame,   15
A fever could but do the same.
And, wanting where its spite to try,
Has made me live to let me die.
A body that could never rest,
Since this ill spirit it possessed.   20

What magic could me thus confine
Within another's grief to pine?
Where whatsoever it complain,
I feel, that cannot feel, the pain.
And all my care itself employs,   25
That to preserve which me destroys.
Constrained not only to endure
Diseases, but, what's worse, the cure;
And ready oft the port to gain,
Am shipwrecked into health again.   30

But physic yet could never reach
The maladies thou me dost teach:
Whom first the cramp of hope does tear,
And then the palsy shakes of fear;
The pestilence of love does heat,   35
Or hatred's hidden ulcer eat.
Joy's cheerful madness does perplex,
Or sorrow's other madness vex;
Which knowledge forces me to know,
And memory will not forgo.   40
What but a soul could have the wit
To build me up for sin so fit?
So architects do square and hew
Green trees that in the forest grew.

Bermudas

Where the remote Bermudas ride
In th' ocean's bosom unespied,
From a small boat that rowed along,
The list'ning winds received this song:

        What should we do but sing his praise   5
That led us through the wat'ry maze
Unto an isle so long unknown,
And yet far kinder than our own?
Where he the huge sea-monsters wracks,
That lift the deep upon their backs,   10
He lands us on a grassy stage,

Safe from the storms and prelates' rage.
He gave us this eternal spring
Which here enamels everything,
And sends the fowls to us in care,   15
On daily visits through the air.
He hangs in shades the orange bright,
Like golden lamps in a green night;
And does in the pomegranates close
Jewels more rich than Ormus shows.   20
He makes the figs our mouths to meet
And throws the melons at our feet,
But apples plants of such a price,
No tree could ever bear them twice.
With cedars, chosen by his hand,   25
From Lebanon, he stores the land,
And makes the hollow seas that roar
Proclaim the ambergris on shore.
He cast, of which we rather boast,
The Gospel's pearl upon our coast,   30
And in these rocks for us did frame
A temple, where to sound his name.
Oh, let our voice his praise exalt,
Till it arrive at heaven's vault;
Which thence, perhaps, rebounding, may   35
Echo beyond the Mexic Bay.

        Thus sung they in the English boat
An holy and a cheerful note,
And all the way, to guide their chime,
With falling oars they kept the time.   40

The Definition of Love

My love is of a birth as rare
As 'tis for object strange and high:
It was begotten by Despair
Upon Impossibility.

Magnanimous Despair alone   5
Could show me so divine a thing,
Where feeble Hope could ne'er have flown
But vainly flapped its tinsel wing.

And yet I quickly might arrive
Where my extended soul is fixed,   10
But Fate does iron wedges drive,
And always crowds itself betwixt.

For Fate with jealous eye does see
Two perfect loves, nor lets them close:
Their union would her ruin be,   15
And her tyrannic power depose.

And therefore her decrees of steel
Us the distant poles have placed,
(Though love's whole world on us doth wheel)
Not by themselves to be embraced,   20

Unless the giddy heaven fall,
And earth some new convulsion tear,
And, us to join, the world should all
Be cramped into a planisphere.

As lines, so loves oblique may well   25
Themselves in every angle greet;
But ours, so truly parallel,
Though infinite, can never meet.

Therefore the love which us doth bind,
But fate so enviously debars,   30
Is the conjunction of the mind,
And opposition of the stars.

ALEXANDER POPE
1688–1744

Pope was born a Catholic of elderly parents. He was ill much, contracting tuberculosis of the spine as a child of twelve, and was fragile the whole of his fifty-six years. Compensating, perhaps, he studied intensively on his own—discrimination against his religion made normal channels and opportunities unavailable. However, the literary profession was comparatively open, and Pope applied his great intelligence and bursting energies to conquering the society of wits. Pope lived in a time which prided itself upon improvement of established forms. In poetry these included such types as the elegy, epic, pindaric, pastoral, heroic and familiar epistle, imitation, translation, and occasional verse, and Pope mastered them all, polishing and honing until his essentially conservative process of perfecting tradition and the mechanics of form exceeded that of all his contemporaries. Such attention to craft brought forth a need for great criticism of parts and technical definition. Pope here was also the master, construing concepts of *judgment, wit, genius,* and *taste* to their highest and most integral level for the purposes of neo-Classical composition, indeed for the whole period between Milton and Wordsworth. His *Essay on Criticism* (1771) is his chief document here and did much to establish his reputation. The kind of work Pope did, and the neo-Classical quality of mind, became alien to most gifted minds after 1789. The crisply righteous attitudes that man was the undoubted pinnacle of creation, that reason was a well-lit highway to truth, and that nature was less interesting than the social or intellectual concoctions of cultivated consensus became a minority view with the Romantics and has remained so. Pope's most accessible work for the present generation is undoubtedly *The Rape of the Lock* (1712–1714) which rewards even the most reluctant first reading with indelible recollections that become pleasurable and treasured sooner or later.

The Rape of the Lock

CANTO I

What dire offense from am'rous causes springs,
What mighty contests rise from trivial things,
I sing—This verse to Caryl, Muse! is due:
This, even Belinda may vouchsafe to view:
Slight is the subject, but not so the praise,   5
If She inspire, and He approve my lays.
       Say what strange motive, Goddess! could compel
A well-bred Lord t' assault a gentle Belle?
O say what stranger cause, yet unexplored,
Could make a gentle Belle reject a Lord?   10
In tasks so bold, can little men engage,
And in soft bosoms dwells such mighty Rage?
       Sol through white curtains shot a tim-rous ray,
And oped those eyes that must eclipse the day:
Now lap-dogs give themselves the rousing shake,   15
And sleepless lovers, just at twelve, awake:
Thrice rung the bell, the slipper knocked the ground,
And the pressed watch returned a silver sound.
Belinda still her downy pillow prest,
Her guardian Sylph prolonged the balmy rest: 20
'Twas He had summoned to her silent bed
The morning-dream that hovered o'er her head;

17 *bell . . . slipper:* two ways to summon servants.   18 *pressed watch:* a repeater which chimed the hours and quarters when the pin was pressed.

A Youth more glitt'ring than a Birth-night Beau,
(That even in slumber caused her cheek to glow)
Seemed to her ear his winning lips to lay,   25
And thus in whispers said, or seemed to say.
        Fairest of mortals, thou distinguished care
Of thousand bright Inhabitants of Air!
If e'er one vision touched thy infant thought,
Of all the Nurse and all the Priest have taught;   30
Of airy Elves by moonlight shadows seen,
The silver token, and the circled green,
Or virgins visited by Angel-powers,
With golden crowns and wreaths of heav'nly flowers;
Hear and believe! thy own importance know,   35
Nor bound thy narrow views to things below.
Some secret truths, from learnèd pride concealed,
To Maids alone and Children are revealed:
What though no credit doubting Wits may give?
The Fair and Innocent shall still believe.   40
Know, then, unnumbered Spirits round thee fly,
The light Militia of the lower sky:
These, though unseen, are ever on the wing,
Hang o'er the Box, and hover round the Ring.
Think what an equipage thou hast in Air,   45
And view with scorn two Pages and a Chair.
As now your own, our beings were of old,
And once inclosed in Woman's beauteous mould;
Thence, by a soft transition, we repair
From earthly Vehicles to these of air.   50
Think not, when Woman's transient breath is fled,
That all her vanities at once are dead;
Succeeding vanities she still regards,
And though she plays no more, o'erlooks the cards.
Her joy in gilded Chariots, when alive,   55
And love of Ombre, after death survive.
For when the Fair in all their pride expire,
To their first Elements their Souls retire:
The Sprites of fiery Termagants in Flame
Mount up, and take a Salamander's name.   60
Soft yielding minds to Water glide away,
And sip, with Nymphs, their elemental Tea.
The graver Prude sinks downward to a Gnome,

23 *Birth-night Beau:* Splendid clothing was worn for royal birthdays. 44 *Box:* a
box in the theater. *Ring:* circular drive in Hyde Park, a fashionable place to
drive. 50 *Vehicles:* Here a pun is intended to link the notion of the body as
vehicle of the soul with "vehicle" in the ordinary sense. 55 *Chariots:* coaches.
56 *Ombre:* a card game that will be explained in Canto III; it is pronounced
om'ber.

In search of mischief still on Earth to roam.
The light Coquettes in Sylphs aloft repair,   65
And sport and flutter in the fields of Air.
   Know further yet; whoever fair and chaste
Rejects mankind, is by some Sylph embraced:
For Spirits, freed from mortal laws, with ease
Assume what sexes and what shapes they please.   70
What guards the purity of melting Maids,
In courtly balls, and midnight masquerades,
Safe from the treach'rous friend, the daring spark,
The glance by day, the whisper in the dark,
When kind occasion prompts their warm desires,   75
When music softens, and when dancing fires?
'Tis but their Sylph, the wise Celestials know,
Though Honor is the word with Men below.
   Some nymphs there are, too conscious of their face,
For life predestined to the Gnomes' embrace.   80
These swell their prospects and exalt their pride,
When offers are disdained, and love denied:
Then gay Ideas crowd the vacant brain,
While Peers, and Dukes, and all their sweeping train,
And Garters, Stars, and Coronets appear,   85
And in soft sounds, Your Grace salutes their ear.
'Tis these that early taint the female soul,
Instruct the eyes of young Coquettes to roll,
Teach Infant-cheeks a bidden blush to know,
And little hearts to flutter at a Beau.   90
   Oft, when the world imagine women stray,
The Sylphs through mystic mazes guide their way,
Through all the giddy circle they pursue,
And old impertinence expel by new.
What tender maid but must a victim fall   95
To one man's treat, but for another's ball?
When Florio speaks what Virgin could withstand,
If gentle Damon did not squeeze her hand?
With varying vanities, from every part,
They shift the moving Toyshop of their heart;   100
Where wigs with wigs, with sword-knots sword-knots strive,
Beaux banish beaux, and coaches coaches drive.
This erring mortals Levity may call;
Oh blind to truth! the Sylphs contrive it all.
   Of these am I, who they protection claim,   105
A watchful sprite, and Ariel is my name.
Late, as I ranged the crystal wilds of air,
In the clear Mirror of thy ruling Star
I saw, alas! some dread event impend,

Ere to the main this morning sun descend,   *110*
But heaven reveals not what, or how, or where:
Warned by the Sylph, oh pious maid, beware!
This to disclose in all thy guardian can:
Beware of all, but most beware of Man!
      He said; when Shock, who thought she slept too long,   *115*
Leaped up, and waked his mistress with his tongue.
'Twas then, Belinda, if report say true,
Thy eyes first opened on a Billet-doux;
Wounds, Charms, and Ardors were no sooner read,
But all the Vision vanished from thy head.   *120*
      And now, unveiled, the Toilet stands displayed,
Each silver Vase in mystic order laid.
First, robed in white, the Nymph intent adores,
With head uncovered, the Cosmetic powers.
A heav'nly image in the glass appears,   *125*
To that she bends, to that her eyes she rears;
Th' inferior Priestess, at her altar's side,
Trembling begins the sacred rites of Pride.
Unnumbered treasures ope at once, and here
The various off'rings of the world appear;   *130*
From each she nicely culls with curious toil,
And decks the Goddess with the glitt'ring spoil.
This casket India's glowing gems unlocks,
And all Arabia breathes from yonder box.
The Tortoise here and Elephant unite,   *135*
Transformed to combs, the speckled, and the white.
Here files of pins extend their shining rows,
Puffs, Powders, Patches, Bibles, Billet-doux.
Now awful Beauty puts on all its arms;
The fair each moment rises in her charms,   *140*
Repairs her smiles, awakens every grace,
And calls forth all the wonders of her face;
Sees by degrees a purer blush arise,
And keener lightnings quicken in her eyes.
The busy Sylphs surround their darling care,   *145*
These set the head, and those divide the hair,
Some fold the sleeve, whilst others plait the gown;
And Betty's praised for labors not her own.

CANTO II

Not with more glories, in th' etherial plain,
The Sun first rises o'er the purpled main,   *150*

115 *Shock:* Belinda's lapdog; the name comes from "shock" or "shough," a kind
of dog. *118 Billet-doux:* love letter. *148 Betty:* Belinda's maid.

Than, issuing forth, the rival of his beams
Launched on the bosom of the silver Thames.
Fair Nymphs, and well-drest Youths around her shone,
But every eye was fixed on her alone.
On her white breast a sparkling Cross she wore,   155
Which Jews might kiss, and Infidels adore.
Her lively looks a sprightly mind disclose,
Quick as her eyes, and as unfixed as those:
Favors to none, to all she smiles extends;
Oft she rejects, but never once offends.   160
Bright as the sun, her eyes the gazers strike,
And, like the sun, they shine on all alike.
Yet graceful ease, and sweetness void of pride,
Might hide her faults, if Belles had faults to hide:
If to her share some female errors fall,   165
Look on her face, and you'll forget 'em all.
      This Nymph, to the destruction of mankind,
Nourished two Locks, which graceful hung behind
In equal curls, and well conspired to deck
With shining ringlets the smooth iv'ry neck.   170
Love in these labyrinths his slaves detains,
And mighty hearts are held in slender chains.
With hairy springes we the birds betray,
Slight lines of hair surprise the finny prey,
Fair tresses man's imperial race ensnare,   175
And beauty draws us with a single hair.
      Th' advent'rous Baron the bright locks admired;
He saw, he wished, and to the prize aspired.
Resolved to win, he meditates the way,
By force to ravish, or by fraud betray;   180
For when success a Lover's toil attends,
Few ask, if fraud or force attained his ends.
      For this, ere Phoebus rose, he had implored
Propitious heaven, and every power adored,
But chiefly Love—to Love an Altar built,   185
Of twelve vast French Romances, neatly gilt.
There lay three garters, half a pair of gloves;
And all the trophies of his former loves;
With tender Billet-doux he lights the pyre,
And breathes three am'rous sighs to raise the fire.   190
Then prostrate falls, and begs with ardent eyes
Soon to obtain, and long possess the prize:
The powers gave ear, and granted half his prayer,
The rest, the winds dispersed in empty air.
      But now secure the painted vessel glides,   195
The sun-beams trembling on the floating tides:

While melting music steals upon the sky,
And softened sounds along the waters die;
Smooth flow the waves, the Zephyrs gently play,
Belinda smiled, and all the world was gay.   200
All but the Sylph—with careful thoughts opprest,
Th' impending woe sat heavy at his breast.
He summons strait his Denizens of air;
The lucid squadrons round the sails repair:
Soft o'er the shrouds aërial whispers breathe,   205
That seemed but Zephyrs to the train beneath.
Some to the sun their insect-wings unfold,
Waft on the breeze, or sink in clouds of gold;
Transparent forms, too fine for mortal sight,
Their fluid bodies half dissolved in light,   210
Loose to the wind their airy garments flew,
Thin glitt'ring textures of the filmy dew,
Dipt in the richest tincture of the skies,
Where light disports in ever-mingling dyes,
While every beam new transient colors flings,   215
Colors that change whene'er they wave their wings.
Amid the circle, on the gilded mast,
Superior by the head, was Ariel placed;
His purple pinions opening to the sun,
He raised his azure wand, and thus begun.   220
        Ye Sylphs and Sylphids, to your chief give ear!
Fays, fairies, Genii, Elves, and Daemons, hear!
Ye know the spheres and various tasks assigned
By laws eternal to th' aërial kind.
Some in the fields of purest Aether play,   225
And bask and whiten in the blaze of day.
Some guide the course of wand'ring orbs on high,
Or roll the planets through the boundless sky.
Some less refined, beneath the moon's pale light
Pursue the stars that shoot athwart the night,   230
Or suck the mists in grosser air below,
Or dip their pinions in the painted bow,
Or brew fierce tempests on the wintry main,
Or o'er the glebe distil the kindly rain.
Others on earth o'er human race preside,   235
Watch all their ways, and all their actions guide:
Of these the chief the care of Nations own,
And guard with Arms divine the British Throne.
        Our humbler province is to tend the Fair,
Not a less pleasing, though less glorious care;   240

218 *Superior by the head:* In epic poetry the hero is commonly a head taller than
any other character.

To save the powder from too rude a gale,
Nor let th' imprisoned essences exhale;
To draw fresh colors from the vernal flowers;
To steal from rainbows ere they drop in showers
A brighter wash; to curl their waving hairs,   245
Assist their blushes, and inspire their airs;
Nay oft, in dreams, invention we bestow,
To change a Flounce, or add a Furbelow.
    This day, black Omens threat the brightest Fair,
That e'er deserved a watchful spirit's care;   250
Some dire disaster, or by force, or slight;
But what, or where, the fates have wrapt in night.
Whether the nymph shall break Diana's law,
Or some frail China jar receive a flaw;
Or stain her honor or her new brocade;   ῀55
Forget her prayers, or miss a masquerade;
Or lose her heart, or necklace, at a ball;
Or whether Heaven has doomed that Shock must fall.
Haste, then, ye spirits! to your charge repair:
The flutt'ring fan be Zephyretta's care;   260
The drops to thee, Brillante, we consign;
And, Momentilla, let the watch be thine;
Do thou, Crispissa, tend her fav'rite Lock;
Ariel himself shall be the guard of Shock.
    To fifty chosen Sylphs, of special note,   265
We trust th' important charge, the Petticoat:
Oft have we known that seven-fold fence to fail,
Though stiff with hoops, and armed with ribs of whale;
Form a strong line about the silver bound,
And guard the wide circumference around.   270
    Whatever spirit, careless of his charge,
His post neglects, or leaves the fair at large,
Shall feel sharp vengeance soon o'ertake his sins,
Be stopped in vials, or transfixed with pins;
Or plunged in lakes of bitter washes lie,   75
Or wedged whole ages in a bodkin's eye:
Gums and Pomatums shall his flight restrain,
While clogged he beats his silken wings in vain;
Or Alum styptics with contracting power
Shrink his thin essence like a riveled flower: 280
Or, as Ixion fixed, the wretch shall feel
The giddy motion of the whirling Mill,

---

248 *Furbelow:* a gathered flounce on a dress, or any showy trimming.   253 *Diana's law:* i.e., the law of chastity.   260–263 *Zephyretta, Brillante,* etc.: names of sylphs. 276 *bodkin:* needle.   277 *Pomatums:* pomades.   281 *Ixion:* In punishment, Jove had him fastened to a revolving fiery wheel.

In fumes of burning Chocolate shall glow,
And tremble at the sea that froths below!
    He spoke; the spirits from the sails descend;   285
Some, orb in orb, around the nymph extend;
Some thrid the mazy ringlets of her hair;
Some hang upon the pendants of her ear:
With beating hearts the dire event they wait,
Anxious, and trembling for the birth of Fate.   290

CANTO III

Close by those meads, forever crowned with flowers,
Where Thames with pride surveys his rising towers,
There stands a structure of majestic frame,
Which from the neighb'ring Hampton takes its name ·
Here Britain's statesmen oft the fall foredoom   295
Of foreign Tyrants and of Nymphs at home;
Here thou, great Anna! whom three realms obey,
Dost sometimes counsel take—and sometimes Tea.
    Hither the heroes and the nymphs resort,
To taste awhile the pleasures of a Court;   300
In various talk th' instructive hours they past,
Who gave the ball, or paid the visit last;
One speaks the glory of the British Queen,
And one describes a charming Indian screen;
A third interprets motions, looks, and eyes;   305
At every word a reputation dies.
Snuff, or the fan, supply each pause of chat,
With singing, laughing, ogling, *and all that.*
    Meanwhile, declining from the noon of day,
The sun obliquely shoots his burning ray;   310
The hungry Judges soon the sentence sign,
And wretches hang that jury-men may dine;
The merchant from th' Exchange returns in peace,
And the long labors of the Toilet cease.
Belinda now, whom thirst of fame invites,   315
Burns to encounter two advent'rous Knights,
At Ombre singly to decide their doom;
And swells her breast with conquests yet to come.
Straight the three bands prepare in arms to join,
Each band the number of the sacred nine.   320

---

297 Anna: Queen Anne. *315:* The game of Ombre (see line 56, page 74) now begins. It requires three players and a pack of forty cards—the full pack minus all the 8s, 9s, and 10s. The principal player, the Ombre (from Spanish *hombre,* "man"), endeavors to win more tricks than either of the others. Each player is dealt nine cards, the remaining thirteen cards being the stock. The Ombre declares the trump; if he wins, he is said to have got *sacada;* if he loses, *codille.*

Soon as she spreads her hand, th' aërial guard
Descend, and sit on each important card:
First Ariel perched upon a Matadore,
Then each, according to the rank they bore;
For Sylphs, yet mindful of their ancient race,   325
Are, as when women, wondrous fond of place.
　　　Behold, four Kings in majesty revered,
With hoary whiskers and a forky beard;
And four fair Queens whose hands sustain a flower,
Th' expressive emblem of their softer power;   330
Four Knaves in garbs succinct, a trusty band,
Caps on their heads, and halberts in their hand;
And particolored troops, a shining train,
Draw forth to combat on the velvet plain.
　　　The skilful Nymph reviews her force with care: 335
Let Spades be trumps! she said, and trumps they were.
　　　Now move to war her sable Matadores,
In show like leaders of the swarthy Moors.
Spadillio first, unconquerable Lord!
Led off two captive trumps, and swept the board.   340
As many more Manillio forced to yield,
And marched a victor from the verdant field.
Him Basto followed, but his fate more hard
Gained but one trump and one Plebeian card.
With his broad sabre next, a chief in years,   345
The hoary Majesty of Spades appears,
Puts forth one manly leg, to sight revealed,
The rest, his many-colored robe concealed.
The rebel Knave, who dares his prince engage,
Proves the just victim of his royal rage.   350
Even mighty Pam, that Kings and Queens o'erthrew
And mowed down armies in the fights of Lu,
Sad chance of war! now destitute of aid,
Falls undistinguished by the victor spade!
　　　Thus far both armies to Belinda yield;   355
Now to the Baron fate inclines the field.
His warlike Amazon her host invades,
Th' imperial consort of the crown of Spades.
The Club's black Tyrant first her victim dyed,
Spite of his haughty mien, and barb'rous pride: 360
What boots the regal circle on his head,

337 The principal trumps are called *Matadores.* 339 *Spadillio:* the ace of spades,
the first trump in this game. 341 *Manillio:* the deuce of trumps when trumps
are black; the seven when they are red. It is the second trump of the game. 343
Basto: the ace of clubs. 351 *Pam:* the knave (jack) of clubs, the highest card in
the card game of Loo.

His giant limbs, in state unwieldy spread;
That long behind he trails his pompous robe,
And, of all monarchs, only grasps the globe?
    The Baron now his Diamonds pours apace; 365
Th' embroidered King who shows but half his face,
And his refulgent Queen, with powers combined
Of broken troops an easy conquest find.
Clubs, Diamonds, Hearts, in wild disorder seen,
With throngs promiscuous strow the level green. 370
Thus when dispersed a routed army runs,
Of Asia's troops, and Afric's sable sons,
With like confusion different nations fly,
Of various habit, and of various dye,
The pierced battalions dis-united fall, 375
In heaps on heaps; one fate o'erwhelms them all.
    The Knave of Diamonds tries his wily arts,
And wins (oh shameful chance!) the Queen of Hearts.
At this, the blood the virgin's cheek forsook,
A livid paleness spreads o'er all her look; 380
She sees, and trembles at th' approaching ill,
Just in the jaws of ruin, and Codille.
And now (as oft in some distempered State)
On one nice Trick depends the general fate.
An Ace of Hearts steps forth: The King unseen 385
Lurked in her hand, and mourned his captive Queen:
He springs to Vengeance with an eager pace,
And falls like thunder on the prostrate Ace.
The nymph exulting fills with shouts the sky;
The walls, the woods, and long canals reply. 390
    Oh thoughtless mortals! ever blind to fate,
Too soon dejected, and too soon elate.
Sudden, these honors shall be snatched away,
And cursed for ever this victorious day.
    For lo! the board with cups and spoons is crowned, 395
The berries crackle, and the mill turns round;
On shining Altars of Japan they raise
The silver lamp; the fiery spirits blaze:
From silver spouts the grateful liquors glide,
While China's earth receives the smoking tide: 400
At once they gratify their scent and taste,
And frequent cups prolong the rich repast.
Straight hover round the Fair her airy band;
Some, as she sipped, the fuming liquor fanned,

---

382 *Codille:* i.e., loss of the game. *385–390:* Belinda takes the decisive trick and wins the game. *396 berries:* coffee berries. *mill:* coffee mill. *397 Altars of Japan:* jappaned, or lacquered, tables.

Some o'er her lap their careful plumes displayed, 405
Trembling, and conscious of the rich brocade.
Coffee, (which makes the politician wise,
And see through all things with his half-shut eyes)
Sent up in vapors to the Baron's brain
New Strategems, the radiant Lock to gain. 410
Ah cease, rash youth! desist ere 'tis too late,
Fear the just Gods, and think of Scylla's Fate!
Changed to a bird, and sent to flit in air,
She dearly pays for Nisus' injured hair!
      But when to mischief mortals bend their will, 415
How soon they find fit instruments of ill!
Just then, Clarissa drew with tempting grace
A two-edged weapon from her shining case:
So Ladies in Romance assist their Knight,
Present the spear, and arm him for the fight. 420
He takes the gift with rev'rence, and extends
The little engine on his fingers' ends;
This just behind Belinda's neck he spread,
As o'er the fragrant steams she bends her head.
Swift to the Lock a thousand Sprites repair, 425
A thousand wings, by turns, blow back the hair;
And thrice they twitched the diamond in her ear;
Thrice she looked back, and thrice the foe drew near.
Just in that instant, anxious Ariel sought
The close recesses of the Virgin's thought; 430
As on the nosegay in her breast reclined,
He watched th' Ideas rising in her mind,
Sudden he viewed, in spite of all her art,
An earthly Lover lurking at her heart.
Amazed, confused, he found his power expired, 435
Resigned to fate, and with a sigh retired.
      The Peer now spreads the glitt'ring Forfex wide,
T' inclose the Lock; now joins it, to divide.
Even then, before the fatal engine closed,
A wretched Sylph too fondly interposed; 440
Fate urged the shears, and cut the Sylph in twain,
(But airy substance soon unites again)
The meeting points the sacred hair dissever
From the fair head, forever, and forever!
      Then flashed the living lightning from her eyes, 445
And screams of horror rend th' affrighted skies.
Not louder shrieks to pitying heaven are cast,

---

412 *Scylla:* the daughter of King Nisus; she plucked from his head the purple hair on which the safety of his kingdom depended and gave it to her lover Minos. For this action she was changed into a bird. 437 *Forfex:* a pair of scissors or shears.

When husbands, or when lap-dogs breathe their last;
Or when rich China vessels fall'n from high,
In glitt'ring dust and painted fragments lie!   450
        Let wreaths of triumph now my temples twine,
(The victor cried) the glorious Prize is mine!
While fish in streams, or birds delight in air,
Or in a coach and six the British Fair,
As long as Atalantis shall be read,   455
Or the small pillow grace a Lady's bed,
While visits shall be paid on solemn days,
When num'rous wax-lights in bright order blaze,
While nymphs take treats, or assignations give,
So long my honor, name, and praise shall live!   460
What Time would spare, from Steel receives its date,
And monuments, like men, submit to fate!
Steel could the labor of the Gods destroy,
And strike to dust th' imperial towers of Troy;
Steel could the works of mortal pride confound,   465
And hew triumphal arches to the ground.
What wonder then, fair nymph! thy hairs should feel,
The conq'ring force of unresisted steel?

CANTO IV

But anxious cares the pensive nymph oppressed,
And secret passions labored in her breast.   470
Not youthful kings in battle seized alive,
Not scornful virgins who their charms survive,
Not ardent lovers robbed of all their bliss,
Not ancient ladies when refused a kiss,
Not tyrants fierce that unrepenting die,   175
Not Cynthia when her manteau's pinned awry,
E'er felt such rage, resentment, and despair,
As thou, sad Virgin! for thy ravished Hair.
        For, that sad moment when the Sylphs withdrew
And Ariel weeping from Belinda flew,   480
Umbriel, a dusky, melancholy sprite,
As ever sullied the fair face of light,
Down to the central earth, his proper scene,
Repaired to search the gloomy Cave of Spleen.
        Swift on his sooty pinions flits the Gnome,   485
And in a vapor reached the dismal dome.
No cheerful breeze this sullen region knows,
The dreaded East is all the wind that blows.
Here in a grotto, sheltered close from air,

455 *Atalantis:* a scandalous book of the time by Mrs. Manley.

And screened in shades from day's detested glare, 490
She sighs forever on her pensive bed,
Pain at her side, and Megrim at her head.
     Two handmaids wait the throne: alike in place,
But diff'ring far in figure and in face.
Here stood Ill-nature like an ancient maid, 195
Her wrinkled form in black and white arrayed;
With store of prayers, for mornings, nights, and noons,
Her hand is filled; her bosom with lampoons.
     There Affectation, with a sickly mien,
Shows in her cheek the roses of eighteen, 500
Practised to lisp, and hang the head aside,
Faints into airs, and languishes with pride,
On the rich quilt sinks with becoming woe,
Wrapt in a gown, for sickness, and for show.
The fair one feels such maladies as these, 505
When each new night-dress gives a new disease.
     A constant Vapor o'er the palace flies;
Strange phantoms rising as the mists arise;
Dreadful, as hermit's dreams in haunted shades,
Or bright, as visions of expiring maids. 510
Now glaring fields, and snakes on rolling spires,
Pale specters, gaping tombs, and purple fires:
Now lakes of liquid gold, Elysian scenes,
And crystal domes, and angels in machines.
     Unnumbered throngs on every side are seen, 515
Of bodies changed to various forms by Spleen.
Here living Tea-pots stand, one arm held out,
One bent; the handle this, and that the spout:
A Pipkin there, like Homer's Tripod walks;
Here sighs a Jar, and there a Goose-pie talks; 520
Men prove with child, as powerful fancy works,
And maids turned bottles, call aloud for corks.
     Safe past the Gnome through this fantastic band,
A branch of healing Spleenwort in his hand.
Then thus addressed the power: "Hail, wayward Queen! 525
Who rule the sex to fifty from fifteen:
Parent of vapors and of female wit,
Who give th' hysteric or poetic fit,
On various tempers act by various ways,
Make some take physic, others scribble plays; 530
Who cause the proud their visits to delay,
And send the godly in a pet to pray.
A nymph there is, that all thy power disdains,

492 Megrim: migraine.

And thousands more in equal mirth maintains.
But oh! if e'er thy Gnome could spoil a grace,   535
Or raise a pimple on a beauteous face,
Like Citron-waters matrons' cheeks inflame,
Or change complexions at a losing game;
If e'er with airy horns I planted heads,
Or rumpled petticoats, or tumbled beds,   540
Or caus'd suspicion when no soul was rude,
Or discomposed the head-dress of a Prude,
Or e'er to costive lap-dog gave disease,
Which not the tears of brightest eyes could ease:
Hear me, and touch Belinda with chagrin,   545
That single act gives half the world the spleen."
    The Goddess with a discontented air
Seems to reject him, though she grants his prayer.
A wondrous Bag with both her hands she binds,
Like that where once Ulysses held the winds;   550
There she collects the force of female lungs,
Sighs, sobs, and passions, and the war of tongues.
A Vial next she fills with fainting fears,
Soft sorrows, melting griefs, and flowing tears.
The Gnome rejoicing bears her gifts away,   555
Spreads his black wings, and slowly mounts to day.
    Sunk in Thalestris' arms the nymph he found,
Her eyes dejected and her hair unbound.
Full o'er their heads the swelling bag he rent,
And all the Furies issued at the vent.   560
Belinda burns with more than mortal ire,
And fierce Thalestris fans the rising fire.
"Oh wretched maid!" she spread her hands, and cried,
(While Hampton's echoes, "Wretched maid!" replied)
"Was it for this you took such constant care   565
The bodkin, comb, and essence to prepare?
For this your locks in paper durance bound,
For this with torturing irons wreathed around?
For this with fillets strained your tender head,
And bravely bore the double loads of lead?   570
Gods! shall the ravisher display your hair,
While the Fops envy, and the Ladies stare!
Honor forbid! at whose unrivaled shrine
Ease, pleasure, virtue, all our sex resign.
Methinks already I your tears survey,   575
Already hear the horrid things they say,
Already see you a degraded toast,
And all your honor in a whisper lost!

567 *durance:* imprisonment.   569 *fillets:* bands.

How shall I, then, your helpless fame defend?
'Twill then be infamy to seem your friend!   580
And shall this prize, th' inestimable prize,
Exposed through crystal to the gazing eyes,
And heightened by the diamond's circling rays,
On that rapacious hand forever blaze?
Sooner shall grass in Hyde-park Circus grow,   585
And wits take lodgings in the sound of Bow;
Sooner let earth, air, sea, to Chaos fall,
Men, monkeys, lap-dogs, parrots, perish all!"
    She said; then raging to Sir Plume repairs,
And bids her Beau demand the precious hairs: 590
(Sir Plume of amber snuff-box justly vain,
And the nice conduct of a clouded cane)
With earnest eyes, and round unthinking face,
He first the snuff-box opened, then the case,
And thus broke out—"My Lord, why, what the devil?   595
Z—ds! damn the lock! 'fore Gad, you must be civil!
Plague on't! 'tis past a jest—nay prithee, pox!
Give her the hair"—he spoke, and rapped his box.
    "It grieves me much" (replied the Peer again)
"Who speaks so well should ever speak in vain.   600
But by this Lock, this sacred Lock I swear,
(Which never more shall join its parted hair;
Which never more its honors shall renew,
Clipped from the lovely head where late it grew)
That while my nostrils draw the vital air,   605
This hand, which won it, shall for ever wear."
He spoke, and speaking, in proud triumph spread
The long-contended honors of her head.
    But Umbriel, hateful Gnome! forbears not so;
He breaks the Vial whence the sorrows flow.   610
Then see! the nymph in beauteous grief appears,
Her eyes half-languishing, half-drowned in tears;
On her heaved bosom hung her drooping head,
Which, with a sigh, she raised; and thus she said.
    "Forever cursed be this detested day,   615
Which snatched my best, my fav'rite curl away!
Happy! ah ten times happy had I been,
If Hampton-Court these eyes had never seen!
Yet am not I the first mistaken maid,
By love of Courts to numerous ills betrayed.   620
Oh had I rather un-admired remained
In some lone isle, or distant Northern land;

585 *Hyde-park Circus:* the Ring mentioned in Canto I (line 44), where constant traffic kept the grass from growing. 586 *Bow:* Bow Bells, the bells of St. Mary-le-Bow in the unfashionable quarter of town. 596 *Z — ds:* Zounds!

Where the gilt Chariot never marks the way,
Where none learn Ombre, none e'er taste Bohea!
There kept my charms concealed from mortal eye,   625
Like roses, that in deserts bloom and die.
What moved my mind with youthful Lords to roam?
Oh had I stayed, and said my prayers at home!
'Twas this, the morning omens seemed to tell,
Thrice from my trembling hand the patch-box fell;   630
The tott'ring China shook without a wind,
Nay, Poll sat mute, and Shock was most unkind!
A Sylph too warned me of the threats of fate,
In mystic visions, now believed too late!
See the poor remnants of these slighted hairs!   635
My hands shall rend what even thy rapine spares:
These in two sable ringlets taught to break,
Once gave new beauties to the snowy neck;
The sister-lock now sits uncouth, alone,
And in its fellow's fate foresees its own;   640
Uncurled it hangs, the fatal shears demands,
And tempts once more, thy sacrilegious hands.
Oh hadst thou, cruel! been content to seize
Hairs less in sight, or any hairs but these!"

CANTO V

She said: the pitying audience melt in tears.   645
But Fate and Jove had stopped the Baron's ears.
In vain Thalestris with reproach assails,
For who can move when fair Belinda fails?
Not half so fixed the Trojan could remain,
While Anna begged and Dido raged in vain,   650
Then grave Clarissa graceful waved her fan;
Silence ensued, and thus the nymph began.
　　　"Say why are Beauties praised and honored most,
The wise man's passion, and the vain man's toast?
Why decked with all that land and sea afford,   655
Why Angels called, and Angel-like adored?
Why round our coaches crowd the white gloved Beaux,
Why bows the side-box from its inmost rows;
How vain are all these glories, all our pains,
Unless good sense preserve what beauty gains: 660
That men may say, when we the front-box grace:
"Behold the first in virtue as in face!"
Oh! if to dance all night, and dress all day,

624 *Bohea:* a kind of black tea. 632 *Poll:* the parrot. 649–650 *Trojan:* Aeneas,
who resolved to leave Carthage despite the rage of Dido and the entreaties of
her sister Anna (see *Aeneid* 4. 440).

Charmed the small-pox, or chased old-age away;
Who would not scorn what housewife's cares produce,   665
Or who would learn one earthly thing of use?
To patch, nay ogle, might become a Saint,
Nor could it sure be such a sin to paint.
But since, alas! frail beauty must decay,
Curled or uncurled, since Locks will turn to grey;   670
Since painted, or not painted, all shall fade,
And she who scorns a man, must die a maid;
What then remains but well our power to use,
And keep good-humor still whate'er we lose?
And trust me, dear! good-humor can prevail,   675
When airs, and flights, and screams, and scolding fail.
Beauties in vain their pretty eyes may roll;
Charms strike the sight, but merit wins the soul."
        So spoke the Dame, but no applause ensued;
Belinda frowned, Thalestris called her Prude.   680
"To arms, to arms!" the fierce Virago cries,
And swift as lightning to the combat flies.
All side in parties, and begin th' attack;
Fans clap, silks rustle, and tough whalebones crack;
Heroes' and Heroines' shouts confus'dly rise,   685
And bass and treble voices strike the skies.
No common weapons in their hands are found,
Like Gods they fight, nor dread a mortal wound.
        So when bold Homer makes the Gods engage,
And heavenly breasts with human passions rage;   690
'Gainst Pallas, Mars; Latona, Hermes arms;
And all Olympus rings with loud alarms:
Jove's thunder roars, heaven trembles all around,
Blue Neptune storms, the bellowing deeps resound:
Earth shakes her nodding towers, the ground gives way,   695
And the pale ghosts start at the flash of day!
        Triumphant Umbriel on a sconce's height
Clapped his glad wings, and sat to view the fight:
Propped on their bodkin spears, the Sprites survey
The growing combat, or assist the fray.   700
        While through the press enraged Thalestris flies,
And scatters death around from both her eyes,
A Beau and Witling perished in the throng,
One died in metaphor, and one in song.
"O cruel nymph! a living death I bear,"   705
Cried Dapperwit, and sunk beside his chair.
A mournful glance Sir Fopling upwards cast,
'Those eyes are made so killing'—was his last.
Thus on Maeander's flowery margin lies

Th' expiring Swan, and as he sings he dies. 710
      When bold Sir Plume had drawn Clarissa down,
Chloe stepped in, and killed him with a frown;
She smiled to see the doughty hero slain,
But, at her smile, the Beau revived again.
      Now Jove suspends his golden scales in air, 715
Weighs the Men's wits against the Lady's hair;
The doubtful beam long nods from side to side;
At length the wits mount up, the hairs subside.
      See, fierce Belinda on the Baron flies,
With more than usual lightning in her eyes: 720
Nor feared the Chief th' unequal fight to try,
Who sought no more than on his foe to die.
But this bold Lord with manly strength endued,
She with one finger and a thumb subdued:
Just where the breath of life his nostrils drew, 725
A charge of Snuff the wily virgin threw;
The Gnomes direct, to every atom just,
The pungent grains of titillating dust.
Sudden, with starting tears each eye o'erflows,
And the high dome re-echoes to his nose. 730
      Now meet thy fate, incensed Belinda cried,
And drew a deadly bodkin from her side.
(The same, his ancient personage to deck,
Her great great grandsire wore about his neck,
In three seal-rings; which after, melted down, 735
Formed a vast buckle for his widow's gown:
Her infant grandame's whistle next it grew,
The bells she jingled, and the whistle blew;
Then in a bodkin graced her mother's hairs,
Which long she wore, and now Belinda wears.) 740
      "Boast not my fall" (he cried) "insulting foe!
Thou by some other shalt be laid as low;
Nor think, to die dejects my lofty mind:
All that I dread is leaving you behind!
Rather than so, ah let me still survive, 745
And burn in Cupid's flames—but burn alive."
      "Restore the Lock!" she cries; and all around
"Restore the Lock!" the vaulted roofs rebound.
Not fierce Othello in so loud a strain
Roared for the handkerchief that caused his pain. 750
But see how oft ambitious aims are crossed,
And chiefs contend till all the prize is lost!
The Lock, obtained with guilt, and kept with pain,
In every place is sought, but sought in vain:

749–750: See Othello 4. 1.

With such a prize no mortal must be blest,
So heaven decrees! with heaven who can contest?
    Some thought it mounted to the Lunar sphere,
Since all things lost on earth are treasured there.
There Heroes' wits are kept in pond'rous vases,
And beaux' in snuff-boxes and tweezer-cases.   760
There broken vows and death-bed alms are found,
And lovers' hearts with ends of riband bound,
The courtier's promises, and sick man's prayers,
The smiles of harlots, and the tears of heirs,
Cages for gnats, and chains to yoke a flea,   765
Dried butterflies, and tomes of casuistry.
    But trust the Muse—she saw it upward rise,
Though marked by none but quick, poetic eyes:
(So Rome's great founder to the heavens withdrew,
To Proculus alone confessed in view)   770
A sudden Star, it shot through liquid air,
And drew behind a radiant trail of hair.
Not Berenice's Locks first rose so bright,
The heavens bespangling with disheveled light.
The Sylphs behold it kindling as it flies,   775
And pleased pursue its progress through the skies.
    This the Beau monde shall from the Mall survey,
And hail with music its propitious ray.
This the blest Lover shall for Venus take,
And send up vows from Rosamonda's lake.   780
This Partridge soon shall view in cloudless skies,
When next he looks through Galileo's eyes;
And hence th' egregious wizard shall foredoom
The fate of Louis, and the fall of Rome.
    Then cease, bright Nymph! to mourn thy ravished hair,   785
Which adds new glory to the shining sphere!
Not all the tresses that fair head can boast,
Shall draw such envy as the Lock you lost.
For, after all the murders of your eye,
When, after millions slain, yourself shall die: 790
When those fair suns shall set, as set they must,
And all those tresses shall be laid in dust,
This Lock, the Muse shall consecrate to fame,
And 'midst the stars inscribe Belinda's name.

770 *Proculus:* a Roman senator; it was Proculus alone to whom Romulus, the founder of Rome, taken to heaven by Mars, later appeared. 773 *Berenice's Locks:* "Berenice's Hair," a group of stars in the constellation Leo. 777 *the Mall:* It was fashionable to take an evening walk in the mall in St. James's Park. 780 *Rosamonda's lake:* a pond associated with unlucky love in the southwest corner of St. James's Park. 781 *Partridge:* John Partridge (1644–1715), an astrologist who was the frequent butt of jokes because of his absurd predictions. 782 *Galileo's eyes:* the telescope. 784 *Louis:* King Louis XIV of France.

Epistle to Miss Blount

ON HER LEAVING THE TOWN, AFTER THE CORONATION

As some fond virgin, whom her mother's care
Drags from the town to wholesome country air,
Just when she learns to roll a melting eye,
And hear a spark, yet think no danger nigh;
From the dear man unwilling she must sever,   5
Yet takes one kiss before she parts forever:
Thus from the world fair Zephalinda flew,
Saw others happy, and with sighs withdrew;
Not that their pleasures caused her discontent;
She sighed not that they stayed, but that she went.   10
    She went to plain-work, and to purling brooks,
Old-fashioned halls, dull aunts, and croaking rooks:
She went from opera, park, assembly, play,
To morning walks, and prayers three hours a day;
To part her time 'twixt reading and bohea,   15
To muse, and spill her solitary tea,
Or o'er cold coffee trifle with the spoon,
Count the slow clock, and dine exact at noon;
Divert her eyes with pictures in the fire,
Hum half a tune, tell stories to the squire;   20
Up to her godly garret after seven,
There starve and pray, for that's the way to heaven.
    Some squire, perhaps, you take delight to rack,
Whose game is whist, whose treat a toast in sack;
Who visits with a gun, presents you birds,   25
Then gives a smacking buss, and cries—"No words!"
Or with his hounds comes hollowing from the stable,
Makes love with nods and knees beneath a table;
Whose laughs are hearty, though his jests are coarse,
And loves you best of all things—but his horse.   30
    In some fair evening, on your elbow laid,
You dream of triumphs in the rural shade;
In pensive thought recall the fancied scene,
See coronations rise on every green:
Before you pass the imaginary sights   35
Of lords and earls and dukes and gartered knights,
While the spread fan o'ershades your closing eyes;

Epistle to Miss Blount: *Title*: Teresa Blount, the sister of Pope's friend, Martha. The coronation was that of George I in 1714. *4 hear a spark*: listen to the addresses of a wooer. *7 Zephalinda*: a name which Teresa assumed in her correspondence. *11 plain-work*: plain needlework, as opposed to embroidery. *15 bohea*: a black tea.

Then gives one flirt, and all the vision flies.
Thus vanish scepters, coronets, and balls,
And leave you in lone woods, or empty walls!   40
        So when your slave, at some dear idle time
(Not plagued with headaches or the want of rhyme)
Stands in the streets, abstracted from the crew,
And while he seems to study, thinks of you;
Just when his fancy points your sprightly eyes,   45
Or sees the blush of soft Parthenia rise,
Gay pats my shoulder, and you vanish quite;
Streets, chairs, and coxcombs rush upon my sight;
Vexed to be still in town, I knit my brow,
Look sour, and hum a tune—as you may now.   50

Elegy to the Memory of an Unfortunate Lady

        What beckoning ghost, along the moonlight shade
Invites my steps, and points to yonder glade?
'Tis she!—but why that bleeding bosom gored,
Why dimly gleams the visionary sword?
O ever beauteous, every friendly! tell,   5
Is it, in Heaven, a crime to love too well?
To bear too tender, or too firm a heart,
To act a lover's or a Roman's part?
Is there no bright reversion in the sky,
For those who greatly think, or bravely die?   10
        Why bade ye else, ye Powers! her soul aspire
Above the vulgar flight of low desire?
Ambition first sprung from your blest abodes;
The glorious fault of angels and of gods:
Thence to their images on earth it flows,   15
And in the breasts of kings and heroes glows.
Most souls, 'tis true, but peep out once an age,
Dull sullen prisoners in the body's cage:
Dim lights of life, that burn a length of years
Useless, unseen, as lamps in sepulchers;   20

38 flirt: a flirt of the fan; here, since the fan is open, a brisk closing of it.   41
slave: Pope calls himself her "slave" in compliment.   45 points: gives or directs
attention to.   46 Parthenia: Martha Blount.   47 Gay: John Gay (1685–1732),
English poet and playwright.

Elegy to the Memory: Title: The subject is imaginary.   1 beckoning ghost:
Ghosts were thought to beckon when they had something to disclose.   8 Ro-
man's part: to commit suicide when troubles were beyond remedy.

Like Eastern kings a lazy state they keep,
And close confined to their own palace, sleep.
    From these perhaps (ere Nature bade her die)
Fate snatched her early to the pitying sky.
As into air the purer spirits flow,   25
And separate from their kindred dregs below;
So flew the soul to its congenial place.
Nor left one virtue to redeem her race.
    But thou, false guardian of a charge too good,
Thou, mean deserter of thy brother's blood!   30
See on these ruby lips the trembling breath,
These cheeks, now fading at the blast of death;
Cold is that breast which warmed the world before,
And those love-darting eyes must roll no more.
Thus, if Eternal Justice rules the ball,   35
Thus shall your wives, and thus your children fall:
On all the line a sudden vengeance waits,
And frequent hearses shall besiege your gates.
There passengers shall stand, and pointing say
(While the long funerals blacken all the way),   40
Lo these were they, whose souls the Furies steeled,
And cursed with hearts unknowing how to yield.
Thus unlamented pass the proud away,
The gaze of fools, and pageant of a day!
So perish all, whose breast ne'er learned to glow   45
For others' good, or melt at others' woe.
    What can atone (oh, ever-injured shade!)
Thy fate unpitied, and thy rites unpaid?
No friend's complaint, no kind domestic tear
Pleased thy pale ghost, or graced thy mournful bier.   50
By foreign hands thy dying eyes were closed,
By foreign hands thy decent limbs composed,
By foreign hands thy humble grave adorned,
By strangers honored, and by strangers mourned!
What though no friends in sable weeds appear,   55
Grieve for an hour, perhaps, then mourn a year,
And bear about the mockery of woe
To midnight dances, and the public show?
What though no weeping Loves thy ashes grace,
Nor polished marble emulate thy face?   60
What though no sacred earth allow thee room,
Nor hallowed dirge be muttered o'er thy tomb?
Yet shall thy grave with rising flowers be dressed,
And the green turf lie lightly on thy breast:

35 *ball:* the orb representing the world, often held by statues depicting Justice.

There shall the morn her earliest tears bestow,   65
There the first roses of the year shall blow;
While angels with their silver wings o'ershade
The ground, now sacred by thy reliques made.
        So peaceful rests, without a stone, a name,
What once had beauty, titles, wealth, and fame.   70
How loved, how honored once, avails thee not,
To whom related, or by whom begot;
A heap of dust alone remains of thee,
'Tis all thou art, and all the proud shall be!
        Poets themselves must fall, like those they sung,   75
Deaf the praised ear, and mute the tuneful tongue.
Even he, whose soul now melts in mournful lays,
Shall shortly want the generous tear he pays;
Then from his closing eyes thy form shall part,
And the last pang shall tear thee from his heart,   80
Life's idle business at one gasp be o'er,
The Muse forgot, and thou beloved no more!

Engraved on the Collar of a Dog, Which I Gave to His Royal Highness

I am his Highness' dog at Kew;
Pray tell me, sir, whose dog are you?

Engraved on the Collar: *1 Kew:* Kew Palace, in Kew Gardens, west of London
on the Thames.

WILLIAM BLAKE

1757–1827

Ignored and at odds with the repressions of his time, Blake, a visionary individualist, has become comprehensible to many readers only amid the moral and artistic revisions of the twentieth century. Still in many ways far ahead of our own time, Blake was apprenticed and trained as an artist, but he read widely on his own and developed, in *Songs of Innocence* (1789), a unique vehicle for combining his lyric prophecies with striking hand-colored engravings. *Songs of Experience* (1794) attacks those diseases of perception and society which destroy the clarity of childlike innocence and block the soul's evolution. The "contrary" states of the human soul and "double vision" to see truth beyond confusion and deception were of prime interest to William Blake. In 1803 a three-year attempt to accept society in the form of a patron's kindness failed. His one bid for recognition, an ambitious one-man show, failed in 1809. Continuing to live in low-income London, Blake worked his way alone, developing the unique visionary system for expressing cosmic themes in his "prophetic books," notably *Milton* and *Jerusalem* (1804–1820).

To Spring

O thou with dewy locks, who lookest down
Thro' the clear windows of the morning, turn
Thine angel eyes upon our western isle,
Which in full choir hails thy approach, O Spring!

The hills tell each other, and the list'ning   5
Valleys hear; all our longing eyes are turned
Up to thy bright pavilions: issue forth,
And let thy holy feet visit our clime.

Come o'er the eastern hills, and let our winds
Kiss thy perfumed garments; let us taste   10
Thy morn and evening breath; scatter thy pearls
Upon our love-sick land that mourns for thee.

O deck her forth with thy fair fingers; pour
Thy soft kisses on her bosom; and put
Thy golden crown upon her languish'd head,   15
Whose modest tresses were bound up for thee!

To the Evening Star

Thou fair-hair'd angel of the evening,
Now, whilst the sun rests on the mountains, light
Thy bright torch of love; thy radiant crown
Put on, and smile upon our evening bed!
Smile on our loves, and, while thou drawest the   5
Blue curtains of the sky, scatter thy silver dew
On every flower that shuts its sweet eyes
In timely sleep. Let thy west wind sleep on
The lake; speak silence with thy glimmering eyes,
And wash the dusk with silver. Soon, full soon,   10

Dost thou withdraw; then the wolf rages wide,
And the lion glares thro' the dun forest:
The fleeces of our flocks are cover'd with
Thy sacred dew: protect them with thine influence.

Song

How sweet I roam'd from field to field,
   And tasted all the summer's pride,
'Til I the prince of love beheld,
   Who in the sunny beams did glide!

He shew'd me lilies for my hair,   5
   And blushing roses for my brow;
He led me through his gardens fair,
   Where all his golden pleasures grow.

With sweet May dews my wings were wet,
   And Phoebus fir'd my vocal rage;   10
He caught me in his silken net,
   And shut me in his golden cage.

He loves to sit and hear me sing,
   Then, laughing, sports and plays with me;
Then stretches out my golden wing,   15
   And mocks my loss of liberty.

Song

My silks and fine array,
   My smiles and languish'd air,
By love are driv'n away;
   And mournful lean Despair
Brings me yew to deck my grave: 5
Such end true lovers have.

His face is fair as heav'n,
   When springing buds unfold;
O why to him was't giv'n,
   Whose heart is wintry cold?   10

His breast is love's all worship'd tomb,
Where all love's pilgrims come.

Bring me an axe and spade,
   Bring me a winding sheet;
When I my grave have made,   *15*
   Let winds and tempests beat:
Then down I'll lie, as cold as clay.
True love doth pass away!

To the Muses

Whether on Ida's shady brow
   Or in the chambers of the East,
The chambers of the Sun, that now
   From ancient melody have ceased;

Whether in heaven ye wander fair,   *5*
   Or the green corners of the earth,
Or the blue regions of the air
   Where the melodious winds have birth;

Whether on crystal rocks ye rove,
   Beneath the bosom of the sea,   *10*
Wandering in many a coral grove;
   Fair Nine, forsaking Poetry;

How have you left the ancient love
   That bards of old enjoy'd in you!
The languid strings do scarcely move,   *15*
   The sound is forced, the notes are few.

Introduction

From SONGS OF INNOCENCE

Piping down the valleys wild,
   Piping songs of pleasant glee,
On a cloud I saw a child,
   And he laughing said to me:

To the Muses: *12 Fair Nine:* The Muses.

"Pipe a song about a Lamb!"   5
    So I piped with merry cheer.
"Piper, pipe that song again;"
    So I piped: he wept to hear.

"Drop thy pipe, thy happy pipe;
    Sing thy songs of happy cheer!"   10
So I sung the same again,
    While he wept with joy to hear.

"Piper, sit thee down and write
    In a book that all may read."
So he vanish'd from my sight;   15
    And I pluck'd a hollow reed,

And I made a rural pen,
    And I stain'd the water clear,
And I wrote my happy songs
    Every child may joy to hear.   20

The Lamb

    Little Lamb, who made thee?
    Dost thou know who made thee?
Gave thee life, and bid thee feed,
By the stream and o'er the mead;
Gave thee clothing of delight,   5
Softest clothing, woolly, bright;
Gave thee such a tender voice,
Making all the vales rejoice?
    Little Lamb, who made thee?
    Dost thou know who made thee?   10

    Little Lamb, I'll tell thee,
    Little Lamb, I'll tell thee:
He is callèd by thy name,
For He calls Himself a Lamb.
He is meek, and He is mild;   15
He became a little child.
I a child, and thou a lamb,
We are callèd by His name.
    Little Lamb, God bless thee!
    Little Lamb, God bless thee!   20

The Sick Rose

O rose, thou art sick!
The invisible worm
That flies in the night,
In the howling storm,

Has found out thy bed
Of crimson joy,
And his dark secret love
Does thy life destroy.

The Tyger

Tyger! Tyger! burning bright
In the forests of the night,
What immortal hand or eye
Could frame thy fearful symmetry?

In what distant deeps or skies   5
Burnt the fire of thine eyes?
On what wings dare he aspire?
What the hand dare seize the fire?

And what shoulder, and what art,
Could twist the sinews of thy heart?   10
And when thy heart began to beat,
What dread hand? and what dread feet?

What the hammer? what the chain?
In what furnace was thy brain?
What the anvil? what dread grasp   15
Dare its deadly terrors clasp?

When the stars threw down their spears,
And water'd heaven with their tears,
Did he smile his work to see?
Did he who made the Lamb make thee?   20

Tyger! Tyger! burning bright
In the forests of the night,
What immortal hand or eye,
Dare frame thy fearful symmetry?

The Garden of Love

I went to the Garden of Love,
And saw what I never had seen:
A Chapel was built in the midst,
Where I used to play on the green.

And the gates of this Chapel were shut,   *5*
And "Thou shalt not" writ over the door;
So I turn'd to the Garden of Love
That so many sweet flowers bore;

And I saw it was filled with graves,
And tomb-stones where flowers should be;   *10*
And Priests in black gowns were walking their rounds,
And binding with briars my joys and desires.

A Poison Tree

I was angry with my friend:
I told my wrath, my wrath did end.
I was angry with my foe:
I told it not, my wrath did grow.

And I water'd it in fears,   *5*
Night and morning with my tears;
And I sunned it with smiles,
And with soft deceitful wiles.

And it grew both day and night,
Till it bore an apple bright;   *10*
And my foe beheld it shine,
And he knew that it was mine,

And into my garden stole
When the night had veil'd the pole:
In the morning glad I see   *15*
My foe outstretch'd beneath the tree.

I Saw a Chapel All of Gold

I saw a Chapel all of gold
That none did dare to enter in,
And many weeping stood without,
Weeping, mourning, worshipping.

I saw a Serpent rise between   5
The white pillars of the door,
And he forc'd and forc'd and forc'd;
Down the golden hinges tore,

And along the pavement sweet,
Set with pearls and rubies bright,   10
All his shining length he drew,
Till upon the altar white

Vomiting his poison out
On the Bread and on the Wine.
So I turned into a sty,   15
And laid me down among the swine.

To See a World

From AUGURIES OF INNOCENCE

To see a World in a grain of sand,
And a Heaven in a wild flower,
Hold Infinity in the palm of your hand,
And Eternity in an hour.

Mock On, Mock On

Mock on, mock on, Voltaire, Rousseau,
  Mock on, mock on; 'tis all in vain;
You throw the sand against the wind
  And the wind blows it back again.

And every sand becomes a gem   5
  Reflected in the beams divine;

Blown back, they blind the mocking eye,
　　But still in Israel's paths they shine.

The atoms of Democritus
　　And Newton's particles of light　　　　10
Are sands upon the Red Sea shore,
　　Where Israel's tents do shine so bright.

And Did Those Feet

From MILTON

And did those feet in ancient time
　　Walk upon England's mountains green?
And was the holy Lamb of God
　　On England's pleasant pastures seen?

And did the Countenance Divine　　　　5
　　Shine forth upon our clouded hills?
And was Jerusalem builded here
　　Among these dark Satanic Mills?

Bring me my bow of burning gold!
　　Bring me my arrows of desire!　　　　10
Bring me my spear! O clouds, unfold!
　　Bring me my chariot of fire!

I will not cease from mental fight,
　　Nor shall my sword sleep in my hand
Till we have built Jerusalem　　　　15
　　In England's green and pleasant land.

WILLIAM WORDSWORTH
1770–1850

Born in the sparsely settled Lake District he would make famous, Wordsworth found formal education at Cambridge less fulfilling than vacation explorations in the Alps or his moody, but natural, rustic childhood. A vivid democrat and enthusiast of the French Revolution, Wordsworth was forced by war between England and France to abandon his lover, Annette Vallon, and a daughter. Divided loyalties and the effects of time made reunion impossible. In 1798, he and Coleridge—friends since college—set forth a revolutionary change of style and spirit in poetry through the publication of *Lyrical Ballads*, whose preface by Wordsworth defended and underlined his position. In spite of his longevity, most of Wordsworth's great poetry came within ten fertile years and was finished by 1807, the publication date of his *Poems in Two Volumes. The Prelude,* his great long poem on youth's nurture to mystical and practical enlightenment through nature, was begun in 1798 and completed in first full draft by 1805. A poet who specialized in recapturing his past in order to unlock the moral and esthetic lessons of creation, Wordsworth may have exhausted his primary lode of inspiration by 1815, when his career as a public poet was firmly launched and his first collected edition as well as *The Excursion*, a less successful long poem, appeared. Wordsworth revised *The Prelude* until his death in 1850, when it was finally published.

Ode

INTIMATIONS OF IMMORTALITY
FROM RECOLLECTIONS OF EARLY CHILDHOOD

The Child is father of the Man;
And I could wish my days to be
Bound each to each by natural piety.

I
There was a time when meadow, grove, and stream,
The earth, and every common sight,
    To me did seem
    Apparelled in celestial light,
The glory and the freshness of a dream.   *5*
It is not now as it hath been of yore;—
    Turn wheresoe'er I may,
      By night or day,
The things which I have seen I now can see no more.

II
    The Rainbow comes and goes,   *10*
    And lovely is the Rose,
    The Moon doth with delight
Look round her when the heavens are bare,
    Waters on a starry night
    Are beautiful and fair;   *15*
  The sunshine is a glorious birth;
  But yet I know, where'er I go,
That there hath past away a glory from the earth.

III
Now, while the birds thus sing a joyous song,
    And while the young lambs bound   *20*
      As to the tabor's sound,

Ode: *Epigraph:* See "My Heart Leaps Up," page 115.

To me alone there came a thought of grief:
A timely utterance gave that thought relief,
     And I again am strong:
The cataracts blow their trumpets from the steep;   *25*
No more shall grief of mine the season wrong;
I hear the Echoes through the mountains throng,
The Winds come to me from the fields of sleep,
     And all the earth is gay;
        Land and sea   *30*
   Give themselves up to jollity,
     And with the heart of May
Doth every beast keep holiday;—
     Thou Child of Joy,
Shout round me, let me hear thy shouts, thou happy Shepherd-
  boy!   *35*

      IV

Ye blessèd Creatures, I have heard the call
     Ye to each other make; I see
The heavens laugh with you in your jubilee;
     My heart is at your festival,
     My head hath its coronal,   *40*
The fullness of your bliss, I feel—I feel it all.
     Oh evil day! if I were sullen
     While Earth herself is adorning,
        This sweet May-morning,
     And the children are culling   *45*
        On every side,
In a thousand valleys far and wide,
     Fresh flowers; while the sun shines warm,
And the Babe leaps up on his mother's arm:—
     I hear, I hear, with joy I hear!   *50*
     —But there's a Tree, of many, one,
A single Field which I have looked upon,
Both of them speak of something that is gone:
     The Pansy at my feet
     Doth the same tale repeat: *55*
Whither is fled the visionary gleam?
Where is it now, the glory and the dream?

      V

Our birth is but a sleep and a forgetting:
The Soul that rises with us, our life's Star,
     Hath had elsewhere its setting,   *60*
        And cometh from afar:
     Not in entire forgetfulness,
     And not in utter nakedness,

But trailing clouds of glory do we come
      From God, who is our home: 65
Heaven lies about us in our infancy!
Shades of the prison-house begin to close
      Upon the growing Boy,
But he beholds the light, and whence it flows,
      He sees it in his joy;   70
The Youth, who daily farther from the east
      Must travel, still is Nature's priest,
      And by the vision splendid
      Is on his way attended;
At length the Man perceives it die away,   75
And fade into the light of common day.

VI

Earth fills her lap with pleasures of her own;
Yearnings she hath in her own natural kind,
And, even with something of a mother's mind,
      And no unworthy aim,   80
      The homely nurse doth all she can
To make her Foster-child, her inmate Man,
      Forget the glories he hath known,
And that imperial palace whence he came.

VII

Behold the Child among his new-born blisses,   85
A six years' darling of a pigmy size!
See, where 'mid work of his own hand he lies,
Fretted by sallies of his mother's kisses,
With light upon him from his father's eyes!
See, at his feet, some little plan or chart,   90
Some fragment from his dream of human life,
Shaped by himself with newly-learnèd art;
      A wedding or a festival,
      A mourning or a funeral;
        And this hath now his heart,   95
      And unto this he frames his song:
        Then will he fit his tongue
To dialogues of business, love, or strife;
      But it will not be long
      Ere this be thrown aside,   100
      And with new joy and pride
The little Actor cons another part;
Filling from time to time his 'humorous stage'
With all the Persons, down to palsied Age,
That Life brings with her in her equipage;   105

As if his whole vocation
Were endless imitation.

VIII

Thou, whose exterior semblance doth belie
    Thy soul's immensity;
Thou best philosopher, who yet dost keep   110
Thy heritage, thou eye among the blind,
That, deaf and silent, read'st the Eternal Deep,
Haunted forever by the Eternal Mind,—
    Mighty prophet! seer blest!
    On whom those truths do rest,   115
Which we are toiling all our lives to find,
In darkness lost, the darkness of the grave;
Thou, over whom thy Immortality
Broods like the Day, a master o'er a slave,
A Presence which is not to be put by;   120
Thou little Child, yet glorious in the might
Of heaven-born freedom on thy being's height,
Why with such earnest pains dost thou provoke
The years to bring the inevitable yoke,
Thus blindly with thy blessedness at strife?   125
Full soon thy Soul shall have her earthly freight,
And custom lie upon thee with a weight,
Heavy as frost, and deep almost as life!

IX

    O joy! that in our embers
    Is something that doth live,   130
    That nature yet remembers
    What was so fugitive!
The thought of our past years in me doth breed
Perpetual benediction; not indeed
For that which is most worthy to be blest;   135
Delight and liberty, the simple creed
Of childhood, whether busy or at rest,
With new-fledged hope still fluttering in his breast:—
    Not for these I raise
    The song of thanks and praise;   140
    But for those obstinate questionings
    Of sense and outward things,
    Fallings from us, vanishings;
    Blank misgivings of a Creature
Moving about in worlds not realized,   145
High instincts before which our mortal nature
Did tremble like a guilty thing surprised:

But for those first affections,
　　Those shadowy recollections,
　　　Which, be they what they may,　　　　　　　　*150*
Are yet the fountain-light of all our day,
Are yet a master-light of all our seeing;
Uphold us, cherish, and have power to make
Our noisy years seem moments in the being
Of the Eternal Silence: truths that wake,　　　　　*155*
　　　To perish never:
Which neither listlessness, nor mad endeavor,
　　　Nor man nor boy,
Nor all that is at enmity with joy,
Can utterly abolish or destroy!　　　　　　　　　　*160*
　　　Hence in a season of calm weather
　　　Though inland far we be,
Our souls have sight of that immortal sea
　　　Which brought us hither,
　　　Can in a moment travel thither,　　　　　　　*165*
And see the children sport upon the shore,
And hear the mighty waters rolling evermore.

X

Then sing, ye Birds, sing, sing a joyous song!
　　And let the young Lambs bound
　　As to the tabor's sound!　　　　　　　　　　*170*
We in thought will join your throng,
　　Ye that pipe and yet that play,
　　Ye that through your hearts to-day
　　Feel the gladness of the May!
What though the radiance which was once so bright　*175*
Be now forever taken from my sight,
　　Though nothing can bring back the hour
Of splendor in the grass, of glory in the flower;
　　We will grieve not, rather find
　　Strength in what remains behind;　　　　　　*180*
　　In the primal sympathy
　　Which having been must ever be;
　　In the soothing thoughts that spring
　　Out of human suffering;
　　In the faith that looks through death,　　　　*185*
In years that bring the philosophic mind.

XI

And O, ye Fountains, Meadows, Hills, and Groves,
Forebode not any severing of our loves!
Yet in my heart of hearts I feel your might;

I only have relinquished one delight   190
To live beneath your more habitual sway.
I love the Brooks which down their channels fret,
Even more than when I tripped lightly as they;
The innocent brightness of a new-born Day
                    Is lovely yet;   195
The Clouds that gather round the setting sun
Do take a sober coloring from an eye
That hath kept watch o'er man's mortality;
Another race hath been, and other palms are won.
Thanks to the human heart by which we live,   200
Thanks to its tenderness, its joys, and fears,
To me the meanest flower that blows can give
Thoughts that do often lie too deep for tears.

Lines Composed a Few Miles Above Tintern Abbey

Five years have past; five summers, with the length
Of five long winters! and again I hear
These waters, rolling from their mountain-springs
With a soft inland murmur.—Once again
Do I behold these steep and lofty cliffs,   5
That on a wild secluded scene impress
Thoughts of more deep seclusion; and connect
The landscape with the quiet of the sky.
The day is come when I again repose
Here, under this dark sycamore, and view   10
These plots of cottage-ground, these orchard-tufts,
Which at this season, with their unripe fruits,
Are clad in one green hue, and lose themselves
'Mid groves and copses. Once again I see
These hedge-rows, hardly hedge-rows, little lines   15
Of sportive wood run wild: these pastoral farms,
Green to the very door; and wreaths of smoke
Sent up, in silence, from among the trees!
With some uncertain notice, as might seem
Of vagrant dwellers in the houseless woods,   20
Or of some hermit's cave, where by his fire
The hermit sits alone.

                    These beauteous forms,
Through a long absence, have not been to me
As is a landscape to a blind man's eye:

But oft, in lonely rooms, and 'mid the din   25
Of towns and cities, I have owed to them,
In hours of weariness, sensations sweet,
Felt in the blood, and felt along the heart;
And passing even into my purer mind,
With tranquil restoration:—feelings too   30
Of unremembered pleasure: such, perhaps,
As have no slight or trivial influence
On that best portion of a good man's life,
His little, nameless, unremembered, acts
Of kindness and of love. Nor less, I trust,   35
To them I may have owed another gift,
Of aspect more sublime; that blessed mood,
In which the burthen of the mystery,
In which the heavy and the weary weight
Of all this unintelligible world,   40
Is lightened:—that serene and blessed mood,
In which the affections gently lead us on,—
Until, the breath of this corporeal frame
And even the motion of our human blood
Almost suspended, we are laid asleep   45
In body, and become a living soul:
While with an eye made quiet by the power
Of harmony, and the deep power of joy,
We see into the life of things.

                        If this
Be but a vain belief, yet, oh! how oft—   50
In darkness and amid the many shapes
Of joyless daylight; when the fretful stir
Unprofitable, and the fever of the world,
Have hung upon the beatings of my heart—
How oft, in spirit, have I turned to thee,   55
O sylvan Wye! thou wanderer thro' the woods,
How often has my spirit turned to thee!
    And now, with gleams of half-extinguished thought,
With many recognitions dim and faint,
And somewhat of a sad perplexity,   60
The picture of the mind revives again:
While here I stand, not only with the sense
Of present pleasure, but with pleasing thoughts
That in this moment there is life and food
For future years. And so I dare to hope,   65
Though changed, no doubt, from what I was when first
I came among these hills; when like a roe

56 Wye: the Wye River.

I bounded o'er the mountains, by the sides
Of the deep rivers, and the lonely streams,
Wherever nature led: more like a man   70
Flying from something that he dreads than one
Who sought the thing he loved. For nature then
(The coarser pleasures of my boyish days,
And their glad animal movements all gone by)
To me was all in all.—I cannot paint   75
What then I was. The sounding cataract
Haunted me like a passion: the tall rock,
The mountain, and the deep and gloomy wood,
Their colors and their forms, were then to me
An appetite; a feeling and a love,   80
That had no need of a remoter charm,
By thought supplied, nor any interest
Unborrowed from the eye.—That time is past,
And all its aching joys are now no more,
And all its dizzy raptures. Not for this   85
Faint I, nor mourn nor murmur; other gifts
Have followed; for such loss, I would believe,
Abundant recompense. For I have learned
To look on nature, not as in the hour
Of thoughtless youth; but hearing oftentimes   90
The still, sad music of humanity,
Nor harsh nor grating, though of ample power
To chasten and subdue. And I have felt
A presence that disturbs me with the joy
Of elevated thoughts; a sense sublime   95
Of something far more deeply interfused,
Whose dwelling is the light of setting suns,
And the round ocean and the living air,
And the blue sky, and in the mind of man;
A motion and a spirit, that impels   100
All thinking things, all objects of all thought,
And rolls through all things. Therefore am I still
A lover of the meadows and the woods,
And mountains; and of all that we behold
From this green earth; of all the mighty world   105
Of eye, and ear,—both what they half create,
And what perceive; well pleased to recognise
In nature and the language of the sense,
The anchor of my purest thoughts, the nurse,
The guide, the guardian of my heart, and soul   110
Of all my moral being.

                Nor perchance,
If I were not thus taught, should I the more

Suffer my genial spirits to decay:
For thou art with me here upon the banks
Of this fair river; thou my dearest Friend,　　　　115
My dear, dear Friend; and in thy voice I catch
The language of my former heart, and read
My former pleasures in the shooting lights
Of thy wild eyes. Oh! yet a little while
May I behold in thee what I was once,　　　　120
My dear, dear Sister! and this prayer I make,
Knowing that Nature never did betray
The heart that loved her; 'tis her privilege,
Through all the years of this our life, to lead
From joy to joy: for she can so inform　　　　125
The mind that is within us, so impress
With quietness and beauty, and so feed
With lofty thoughts, that neither evil tongues,
Rash judgments, nor the sneers of selfish men,
Nor greetings where no kindness is, nor all　　　　130
The dreary intercourse of daily life,
Shall e'er prevail against us, or disturb
Our cheerful faith, that all which we behold
Is full of blessings. Therefore let the moon
Shine on thee in thy solitary walk;　　　　135
And let the misty mountain-winds be free
To blow against thee: and, in after years,
When these wild ecstasies shall be matured
Into a sober pleasure; when thy mind
Shall be a mansion for all lovely forms,　　　　140
Thy memory be as a dwelling-place
For all sweet sounds and harmonies; oh! then,
If solitude, or fear, or pain, or grief,
Should be thy portion, with what healing thoughts
Of tender joy wilt thou remember me,　　　　145
And these my exhortations! Nor, perchance—
If I should be where I no more can hear
Thy voice, nor catch from thy wild eyes these gleams
Of past existence—wilt thou then forget
That on the banks of this delightful stream　　　　150
We stood together; and that I, so long
A worshipper of Nature, hither came
Unwearied in that service: rather say
With warmer love—oh! with far deeper zeal
Of holier love. Nor wilt thou then forget　　　　155
That after many wanderings, many years
Of absence, these steep woods and lofty cliffs,
And this green pastoral landscape, were to me
More dear, both for themselves and for thy sake!

She Dwelt Among the Untrodden Ways

She dwelt among the untrodden ways
    Beside the springs of Dove,
A maid whom there were none to praise
    And very few to love:

A violet by a mossy stone   5
    Half hidden from the eye!
—Fair as a star, when only one
    Is shining in the sky.

She lived unknown, and few could know
    When Lucy ceased to be;   10
But she is in her grave, and, oh,
    The difference to me!

A Slumber Did My Spirit Seal

A slumber did my spirit seal;
    I had no human fears:
She seemed a thing that could not feel
    The touch of earthly years.

No motion has she now, no force;
    She neither hears nor sees;
Rolled round in earth's diurnal course,
    With rocks, and stones, and trees.

My Heart Leaps Up

My heart leaps up when I behold
    A rainbow in the sky;
So was it when my life began;
So is it now I am a man;

She Dwelt: *2 Dove:* This is probably the stream in Yorkshire, although there are several streams in England so named.

So be it when I shall grow old.
  Or let me die!
The Child is father of the Man;
And I could wish my days to be
Bound each to each by natural piety.

Composed upon Westminister Bridge

SEPTEMBER 3, 1802

Earth has not anything to show more fair:
Dull would he be of soul who could pass by
A sight so touching in its majesty:
This City now doth, like a garment, wear
The beauty of the morning; silent, bare,   5
Ships, towers, domes, theaters, and temples lie
Open unto the fields, and to the sky;
All bright and glittering in the smokeless air.
Never did sun more beautifully steep
In his first splendor, valley, rock, or hill;   10
Ne'er saw I, never felt, a calm so deep!
The river glideth at his own sweet will:
Dear God! the very houses seem asleep;
And all that mighty heart is lying still!

It Is a Beauteous Evening

It is a beauteous evening, calm and free;
The holy time is quiet as a Nun
Breathless with adoration; the broad sun
Is sinking down in its tranquility;
The gentleness of heaven broods o'er the Sea: 5
Listen! the mighty Being is awake,
And doth with his eternal motion make
A sound like thunder—everlastingly.
Dear Child! dear Girl! that walkest with me here,
If thou appear untouched by solemn thought,   10
Thy nature is not therefore less divine:
Thou liest in Abraham's bosom all the year,
And worship'st at the Temple's inner shrine,
God being with thee when we know it not.

She Was a Phantom of Delight

She was a Phantom of delight
When first she gleamed upon my sight;
A lovely Apparition, sent
To be a moment's ornament;
Her eyes as stars of Twilight fair;   5
Like Twilight's, too, her dusky hair;
But all things else about her drawn
From May-time and the cheerful Dawn;
A dancing Shape, an Image gay,
To haunt, to startle, and way-lay.   10

I saw her upon nearer view,
A Spirit, yet a Woman too!
Her household motions light and free,
And steps of virgin-liberty;
A countenance in which did meet   15
Sweet records, promises as sweet;
A Creature not too bright or good
For human nature's daily food;
For transient sorrows, simple wiles,
Praise, blame, love, kisses, tears, and smiles.   20

And now I see with eyes serene
The very pulse of the machine;
A Being breathing thoughtful breath,
A Traveller between life and death;
The reason firm, the temperate will,   25
Endurance, foresight, strength, and skill;
A perfect Woman, nobly planned,
To warn, to comfort, and command;
And yet a Spirit still, and bright
With something of angelic light.   30

The Solitary Reaper

Behold her, single in the field,
    Yon solitary Highland lass!
Reaping and singing by herself;
    Stop here, or gently pass!

Alone she cuts and binds the grain,   *5*
And sings a melancholy strain;
O listen! for the Vale profound
Is overflowing with the sound.

No Nightingale did ever chaunt
   More welcome notes to weary bands   *10*
Of travelers in some shady haunt,
   Among Arabian sands:
A voice so thrilling ne'er was heard
In spring-time from the Cuckoo-bird,
Breaking the silence of the seas   *15*
Among the farthest Hebrides.

Will no one tell me what she sings?—
   Perhaps the plaintive numbers flow
For old, unhappy, far-off things,
   And battles long ago: *20*
Or is it some more humble lay,
Familiar matter of to-day?
Some natural sorrow, loss, or pain,
That has been, and may be again?

Whate'er the theme, the Maiden sang   *25*
   As if her song could have no ending;
I saw her singing at her work,
   And o'er the sickle bending;—
I listened, motionless and still;
And, as I mounted up the hill,   *30*
The music in my heart I bore,
Long after it was heard no more.

I Wandered Lonely as a Cloud

I wandered lonely as a cloud
That floats on high o'er vales and hills,
When all at once I saw a crowd,
A host, of golden daffodils;
Beside the lake, beneath the trees,   *5*
Fluttering and dancing in the breeze.

Continuous as the stars that shine
And twinkle on the milky way,

They streached in never-ending line
Along the margin of a bay: 10
Ten thousand saw I at a glance,
Tossing their heads in sprightly dance.

The waves beside them danced; but they
Out-did the sparkling waves in glee:
A poet could not but be gay,   15
In such a jocund company:
I gazed—and gazed—but little thought
What wealth the show to me had brought:

For oft, when on my couch I lie
In vacant or in pensive mood,   20
They flash upon that inward eye
Which is the bliss of solitude;
And then my heart with pleasure fills,
And dances with the daffodils.

London, 1802

Milton! thou shouldst be living at this hour:
England hath need of thee; she is a fen
Of stagnant waters: altar, sword, and pen,
Fireside, the heroic wealth of hall and bower,
Have forfeited their ancient English dower   5
Of inward happiness. We are selfish men;
Oh! raise us up, return to us again;
And give us manners, virtue, freedom, power.
Thy soul was like a Star, and dwelt apart:
Thou hadst a voice whose sound was like the sea: 10
Pure as the naked heavens, majestic, free,
So didst thou travel on life's common way,
In cheerful godliness; and yet thy heart
The lowliest duties on herself did lay.

The World Is Too Much with Us

The world is too much with us; late and soon,
Getting and spending, we lay waste our powers:
Little we see in Nature that is ours;
We have given our hearts away, a sordid boon!
The Sea that bares her bosom to the moon;   5
The winds that will be howling at all hours,
And are up-gathered now like sleeping flowers;
For this, for everything, we are out of tune;
It moves us not.—Great God! I'd rather be
A Pagan suckled in a creed outworn;   10
So might I, standing on this pleasant lea,
Have glimpses that would make me less forlorn;
Have sight of Proteus rising from the sea;
Or hear old Triton blow his wreathèd horn.

SAMUEL TAYLOR COLERIDGE
1772–1834

Coleridge was said to be an almost hypnotically attractive man, immense in potentialities against which he, and many of his friends, measured his achievements as small. A college drop-out and an inept cavalryman for a short while in 1794, he launched a long failure of a marriage as part of a communal scheme which he abandoned in the planning stage. He met Wordsworth in 1795, and their mutual stimulation led to the *Lyrical Ballads* three years later. For instance, the technique of combined description and meditation in *Frost at Midnight* influenced Wordsworth directly in *Tintern Abbey*. By 1801 Coleridge had become dependent upon opium while trying to treat a variety of painful diseases. *Kubla Khan* speaks of a visionary state which may link the inspiration of the poem to a dose of laudanum (opium in an alcohol solution). Coping with addiction became a lifelong effort, made possible by living with a doctor friend. Philosophy and criticism occupied much more of Coleridge's sporadic creative life than poetry. Like Wordsworth, life moved him to the right, but generally in a gentle, profoundly theorizing way. Coleridge was a versatile and brilliant man, as one may judge from the variety in his small body of poetry and the adventurous range of thought in his critical landmark, *Biographia Literaria* (1817).

The Rime of the Ancient Mariner

PART I

An ancient Mariner meeteth three gallants bidden to a wedding feast, and detaineth one.

It is an ancient Mariner,
And he stoppeth one of three.
"By thy long grey beard and glittering eye,
Now wherefore stopp'st thou me?

The Bridegroom's doors are open'd wide,   5
And I am next of kin;
The guests are met, the feast is set:
May'st hear the merry din."

He holds him with his skinny hand,
"There was a ship," quoth he.   10
"Hold off! Unhand me, grey-beard loon!"
Eftsoons his hand dropt he.

The Wedding-Guest is spellbound by the eye of the old seafaring man, and constrained to hear his tale.

He holds him with his glittering eye—
The Wedding-Guest stood still,
And listens like a three years' child: 15
The Mariner hath his will.

The Wedding-Guest sat on a stone:
He cannot choose but hear;
And thus spake on that ancient man,
The bright-eyed Mariner.   20

"The ship was cheer'd, the harbour clear'd,
Merrily did we drop
Below the kirk, below the hill,
Below the lighthouse top.

The Mariner tells how the ship sailed southward with a good wind and fair weather, till it reach'd the Line.

The Sun came up upon the left,   25
Out of the sea came he!

And he shone bright, and on the right
Went down into the sea.

Higher and higher every day,
Till over the mast at noon——"   30
The Wedding-Guest here beat his breast,
For he heard the loud bassoon.

*The Wedding-
Guest heareth
the bridal music;
but the Mariner
continueth his tale.*
The bride hath paced into the hall,
Red as a rose is she;
Nodding their heads before her goes   35
The merry minstrelsy.

The Wedding-Guest he beat his breast,
Yet he cannot choose but hear;
And thus spake on that ancient man,
The bright-eyed Mariner.   40

*The ship driven
by a storm to-
ward the South
Pole.*
"And now the Storm-blast came, and he
Was tyrannous and strong:
He struck with his o'ertaking wings,
And chased us south along.

With sloping masts and dipping prow,   45
As who pursued with yell and blow
Still treads the shadow of his foe,
And forward bends his head,
The ship drove fast, loud roar'd the blast,
And southward aye we fled.   50

And now there came both mist and snow,
And it grew wondrous cold:
And ice, mast-high, came floating by,
As green as emerald.

*The land of ice,
and of fearful
sounds, where
no living thing
was to be seen.*
And through the drifts the snowy clifts   55
Did send a dismal sheen:
Nor shapes of men nor beasts we ken—
The ice was all between.

The ice was here, the ice was there,
The ice was all around: 60
It crack'd and growl'd, and roar'd and howled,
Like noises in a swound!

50 *aye:* ever.   57: i.e., neither men nor beasts were to be seen.   62 *swound:*
dream, swoon.

Till a great sea-
bird, called the
Albatross, came
through the snow-
fog, and was
received with
great joy and
hospitality.

At length did cross an Albatross,
Through the fog it came;
As if it had been a Christian soul,   65
We hail'd it in God's name.

It ate the food it ne'er had eat,
And round and round it flew.
The ice did split with a thunder-fit;
The helmsman steer'd us through!   70

And lo! the
Albatross proveth
a bird of good
omen, and follow-
eth the ship as it
returned north-
ward through fog
and floating ice.

And a good south wind sprung up behind;
The Albatross did follow,
And every day, for food or play,
Came to the mariners' hollo!

In mist or cloud, on mast or shroud,   75
It perch'd for vespers nine;
Whiles all the night, through fog-smoke white,
Glimmer'd the white moonshine."

"God save thee, ancient Mariner,
From the fiends, that plague thee thus!—   80
Why look'st thou so?"—"With my crossbow
I shot the Albatross.

PART II

"The Sun now rose upon the right:
Out of the sea came he,
Still hid in mist, and on the left   85
Went down into the sea.

And the good south wind still blew behind,
But no sweet bird did follow,
Nor any day for food or play
Came to the mariners' hollo!   90

His shipmates cry
out against the
ancient Mariner
for killing the bird
of good luck.

And I had done an hellish thing,
And it would work 'em woe:
For all averr'd I had kill'd the bird
That made the breeze to blow.
Ah wretch! said they, the bird to slay,   95
That made the breeze to blow!

But when the fog
cleared off, they
justify the same,
and thus make
themselves accom-
plices in the crime.

Nor dim nor red, like God's own head,
The glorious Sun uprist:

74 hollo: greeting or call.   76 vespers nine: nine evenings.

Then all averr'd I had kill'd the bird
That brought the fog and mist.   *100*
'Twas right, said they, such birds to slay,
That bring the fog and mist.

The fair breeze blew, the white foam flew,
The furrow follow'd free;
We were the first that ever burst   *105*
Into that silent sea.

Down dropt the breeze, the sails dropt down,
'Twas sad as sad could be;
And we did speak only to break
The silence of the sea!   *110*

All in a hot and copper sky,
The bloody Sun, at noon,
Right up above the mast did stand,
No bigger than the Moon.

Day after day, day after day,   *115*
We stuck, nor breath nor motion;
As idle as a painted ship
Upon a painted ocean.

Water, water, everywhere,
And all the boards did shrink;   *120*
Water, water, everywhere,
Nor any drop to drink.

The very deep did rot: O Christ!
That ever this should be!
Yea, slimy things did crawl with legs   *125*
Upon the slimy sea.

About, about, in reel and rout
The death-fires danced at night;
The water, like a witch's oils,
Burnt green, and blue, and white.   *130*

And some in dreams assurèd were
Of the Spirit that plagued us so;
Nine fathom deep he had follow'd us
From the land of mist and snow.

And every tongue, through utter drought,   135
Was wither'd at the root;
We could not speak, no more than if
We had been choked with soot.

*The shipmates, in
their sore distress,
would fain throw
the whole guilt on
the ancient
Mariner: in sign
whereof they hang
the dead sea-bird
round his neck.*
Ah! well a-day! what evil looks
Had I from old and young!   140
Instead of the cross, the Albatross
About my neck was hung.

PART III

"There passed a weary time. Each throat
Was parch'd, and glazed each eye.
A weary time! a weary time!   145
How glazed each weary eye!
*The ancient
Mariner beholdeth
a sign in the
element afar off.*
When, looking westward, I beheld
A something in the sky.

At first it seem'd a little speck,
And then it seem'd a mist;   150
It moved and moved, and took at last
A certain shape, I wist.

A speck, a mist, a shape, I wist!
And still it near'd and near'd:
As if it dodged a water-sprite,   155
It plunged, and tack'd and veer'd.

*At its nearer
approach, it
seemeth him to be
a ship; and at a
dear ransom he
freeth his speech
from the bonds of
thirst.*
With throats unslaked, with black lips baked,
We could nor laugh nor wail;
Through utter drought all dumb we stood!
I bit my arm, I suck'd the blood,   160
And cried, A sail! a sail!

With throats unslaked, with black lips baked,
Agape they heard me call:
A flash of joy;
Gramercy! they for joy did grin,
And all at once their breath drew in,   165
As they were drinking all.

*And horror
follows. For can
it be a ship that
comes onward
without wind or
tide?*
See! see! (I cried) she tacks no more!
Hither to work us weal—

152 *wist:* knew.   164 *Gramercy:* Great thanks!   167 *tacks:* sailing by manag-
ing sails and helm so as to come up into the wind.   168 *weal:* to work weal is to
do good.

Without a breeze, without a tide,
She steadies with upright keel!   170

The western wave was all aflame,
The day was wellnigh done!
Almost upon the western wave
Rested the broad, bright Sun;
When that strange shape drove suddenly   175
Betwixt us and the Sun.

*It seemeth him
but the skeleton
of a ship.*
And straight the Sun was fleck'd with bars
(Heaven's Mother send us grace!),
As if through a dungeon-grate he peer'd
With broad and burning face.   180

Alas! (thought I, and my heart beat loud)
How fast she nears and nears!
Are those her sails that glance in the Sun,
Like restless gossameres?

*And its ribs are
seen as bars on
the face of the
setting sun.
The Spectre-
Woman and her
Deathmate, and no
other, on board
the skeleton ship.
Like vessel,
like crew!*
Are those her ribs through which the Sun   185
Did peer, as through a grate?
And is that Woman all her crew
Is that a Death? and are there two?
Is Death that Woman's mate?

Her lips were red, her looks were free,   190
Her locks were yellow as gold:
Her skin was as white as leprosy,
The Nightmare Life-in-Death was she,
Who thicks man's blood with cold.

*Death and Life-
in-Death have
diced for the
ship's crew and
she (the latter)
winneth the
ancient Mariner.*
The naked hulk alongside came,   195
And the twain were casting dice;
"The game is done! I've won! I've won!"
Quoth she, and whistles thrice.

*No twilight
within the courts
of the Sun.*
The Sun's rim dips; the stars rush out:
At one stride comes the dark;   200
With far-heard whisper, o'er the sea,
Off shot the spectre-bark.

We listen'd and look'd sideways up!
Fear at my heart, as at a cup,
My life-blood seem'd to sip!   205
The stars were dim, and thick the night,
The steersman's face by his lamp gleam'd white;

From the sails the dew did drip—
At the rising
of the Moon.
Till clomb above the eastern bar
The hornèd Moon, with one bright star   210
Within the nether tip.

One after
another,
One after one, by the star-dogg'd Moon,
Too quick for groan or sigh,
Each turn'd his face with a ghastly pang,
And cursed me with his eye.   215

His shipmates
drop down dead.
Four times fifty living men
(And I heard nor sigh nor groan),
With heavy thump, a lifeless lump,
They dropp'd down one by one.

But Life-in-Death
begins her work
on the ancient
Mariner.
The souls did from their bodies fly—   220
They fled to bliss or woe!
And every soul, it pass'd me by
Like the whizz of my crossbow!"

PART IV

The Wedding-
Guest feareth that
a spirit is talking
to him.
"I fear thee, ancient Mariner!
I fear thy skinny hand!   225
And thou art long, and lank, and brown,
As is the ribb'd sea-sand.

I fear thee and thy glittering eye,
And thy skinny hand so brown."—
But the ancient
Mariner assureth
him of his bodily
life, and pro-
ceedeth to relate
his horrible
penance.
"Fear not, fear not, thou Wedding-Guest!   230
This body dropt not down.

Alone, alone, all all alone,
Alone on a wide, wide sea!
And never a saint took pity on
My soul in agony.   235

He despiseth the
creatures of the
calm.
The many men, so beautiful!
And they all dead did lie:
And a thousand thousand slimy things
Lived on; and so did I.

And envieth that
they should live,
and so many
lie dead.
I look'd upon the rotting sea,   240
And drew my eyes away;
I look'd upon the rotting deck,
And there the dead men lay.

I look'd to heaven, and tried to pray;
But or ever a prayer had gusht,   245
A wicked whisper came, and made
My heart as dry as dust.

I closed my lids, and kept them close,
And the balls like pulses beat;
But the sky and the sea and the sea and the sky,   250
Lay like a load on my weary eye,
And the dead were at my feet.

*But the curse
liveth for him
in the eye of
the dead men.*
The cold sweat melted from their limbs,
Nor rot nor reek did they:
The look with which they look'd on me   255
Had never pass'd away.

An orphan's curse would drag to hell
A spirit from on high;
*In his loneliness
and fixedness
he yearneth
towards the
journeying Moon,
and the stars that
still sojourn, yet
still move onward;
and everywhere
the blue sky
belongs to them,
and is their
appointed rest and
their native
country and their
own natural
homes, which they
enter unan-
nounced, as lords
that are certainly
expected, and yet
there is a silent
joy at their arrival.*
But oh! more horrible than that
Is the curse in a dead man's eye!   260
Seven days, seven nights, I saw that curse,
And yet I could not die.

The moving Moon went up the sky,
And nowhere did abide;
Softly she was going up,   265
And a star or two beside—

Her beams bemock'd the sultry main,
Like April hoar-frost spread;
But where the ship's huge shadow lay,
The charmèd water burnt alway   270
A still and awful red.

*By the light of
the Moon he
beholdeth God's
creatures of the
great calm.*
Beyond the shadow of the ship,
I watch'd the water-snakes:
They moved in tracks of shining white
And when they rear'd, the elfish light   275
Fell off in hoary flakes.

Within the shadow of the ship
I watch'd their rich attire:
Blue, glossy green, and velvet black,

The Rime of the Ancient Mariner   **129**

They coil'd and swam; and every track   *280*
Was a flash of golden fire.

O happy living things! no tongue
Their beauty might declare:
A spring of love gush'd from my heart,
And I bless'd them unaware: *285*
Sure my kind saint took pity on me,
And I bless'd them unaware.

The selfsame moment I could pray;
And from my neck so free
The Albatross fell off, and sank   *290*
Like lead into the sea.

PART V

"O sleep! it is a gentle thing,
Beloved from pole to pole!
To Mary Queen the praise be given!
She sent the gentle sleep from Heaven,   *295*
That slid into my soul.

The silly buckets on the deck,
That had so long remain'd,
I dreamt that they were fill'd with dew;
And when I awoke, it rain'd.   *300*

My lips were wet, my throat was cold,
My garments all were dank;
Sure I had drunken in my dreams,
And still my body drank.

I moved, and could not feel my limbs: *305*
I was so light—almost
I thought that I had died in sleep,
And was a blessèd ghost.

And soon I heard a roaring wind:
It did not come anear;   *310*
But with its sound it shook the sails,
That were so thin and sere.

The upper air burst into life;
And a hundred fire-flags sheen;
To and fro they were hurried about!   *315*

And to and fro, and in and out,
The wan stars danced between.

And the coming wind did roar more loud,
And the sails did sigh like sedge;
And the rain pour'd down from one black cloud;   *320*
The Moon was at its edge.

The thick black cloud was cleft, and still
The Moon was at its side;
Like waters shot from some high crag,
The lightning fell with never a jag,   *325*
A river steep and wide.

The bodies of the ship's crew are inspired and the ship moves on;
The loud wind never reach'd the ship,
Yet now the ship moved on!
Beneath the lightning and the Moon
The dead men gave a groan.   *330*

They groan'd, they stirr'd, they all uprose,
Nor spake, nor moved their eyes;
It had been strange, even in a dream,
To have seen those dead men rise.

The helmsman steer'd, the ship moved on;   *335*
Yet never a breeze up-blew;
The mariners all 'gan work the ropes,
Where they were wont to do;
They raised their limbs like lifeless tools—
We were a ghastly crew.   *340*

But not by the souls of the men, nor by demons of earth or middle air, but by a blessed troop of angelic spirits, sent down by the invocation of the guardian saint.
The body of my brother's son
Stood by me, knee to knee:
The body and I pull'd at one rope,
But he said naught to me."

"I fear thee, ancient Mariner!"   *345*
"Be calm, thou Wedding-Guest:
'Twas not those souls that fled in pain,
Which to their corses came again,
But a troop of spirits blest:

For when it dawn'd—they dropp'd their arms,   *350*
And cluster'd round the mast;
Sweet sounds rose slowly through their mouths,
And from their bodies pass'd.

Around, around, flew each sweet sound,
Then darted to the Sun;   355
Slowly the sounds came back again,
Now mix'd, now one by one.

Sometimes a-dropping from the sky
I heard the skylark sing;
Sometimes all little birds that are,   360
How they seem'd to fill the sea and air
With their sweet jargoning!

And now 'twas like all instruments,
Now like a lonely flute;
And now it is an angel's song,   365
That makes the Heavens be mute.

It ceased; yet still the sails made on
A pleasant noise till noon,
A noise like of a hidden brook
In the leafy month of June,   370
That to the sleeping woods all night
Singeth a quiet tune.

Till noon we quietly sail'd on,
Yet never a breeze did breathe:
Slowly and smoothly went the ship,   375
Moved onward from beneath.

*The lonesome
Spirit from the
South Pole carries
on the ship as far
as the Line, in
obedience to the
angelic troop, but
still requireth
vengeance.*

Under the keel nine fathom deep,
From the land of mist and snow,
The Spirit slid: and it was he
That made the ship to go.   380
The sails at noon left off their tune,
And the ship stood still also.

The Sun, right up above the mast,
Had fix'd her to the ocean:
But in a minute she 'gan stir,   385
With a short uneasy motion—
Backwards and forwards half her length
With a short uneasy motion.

Then like a pawing horse let go,
She made a sudden mound: 390
It flung the blood into my head,
And I fell down in a swound.

The Polar Spirit's
fellow demons, the
invisible inhabi-
tants of the ele-
ment, take part
in his wrong; and
two of them
relate, one to the
other, that penance
long and heavy
for the ancient
Mariner hath been
accorded to the
Polar Spirit, who
returneth
southward.

How long in that same fit I lay,
I have not to declare;
But ere my living life return'd,   395
I heard, and in my soul discern'd
Two voices in the air.

"Is it he?" quoth one, "is this the man?
By Him who died on cross,
With his cruel bow he laid full low   400
The harmless Albatross.

The Spirit who bideth by himself
In the land of mist and snow,
He loved the bird that loved the man
Who shot him with his bow."   405

The other was a softer voice,
As soft as honey-dew:
Quoth he, "The man hath penance done,
And penance more will do."

PART VI

First Voice:
"But tell me, tell me! speak again,   410
Thy soft response renewing—
What makes that ship drive on so fast?
What is the Ocean doing?"

Second Voice:
"Still as a slave before his lord,
The Ocean hath no blast;   415
His great bright eye most silently
Up to the Moon is cast—

If he may know which way to go;
For she guides him smooth or grim.
See, brother, see! how graciously   420
She looketh down on him."

First Voice:
The Mariner hath
been cast into a   "But why drives on that ship so fast,
trance; for the   Without or wave or wind?"
angelic power
causeth the vessel
to drive northward   *Second Voice:*
faster than human
life could endure.   "The air is cut away before,
And closes from behind.   425

The Rime of the Ancient Mariner **133**

Fly, brother, fly! more high, more high!
Or we shall be belated:
For slow and slow that ship will go,
When the Mariner's trance is abated."

*The supernatural
motion is retarded;
the Mariner
awakes, and his
penance begins
anew.*
I woke, and we were sailing on   430
As in a gentle weather:
'Twas night, calm night, the Moon was high;
The dead men stood together.

All stood together on the deck,
For a charnel-dungeon fitter: 435
All fix'd on me their stony eyes,
That in the Moon did glitter.

The pang, the curse, with which they died,
Had never pass'd away:
I could not draw my eyes from theirs,   440
Nor turn them up to pray.

*The curse is
finally expiated.*
And now this spell was snapt: once more
I viewed the ocean green,
And look'd far forth, yet little saw
Of what had else been seen—   445

Like one that on a lonesome road
Doth walk in fear and dread,
And having once turn'd round, walks on,
And turns no more his head;
Because he knows a frightful fiend   450
Doth close behind him tread.

But soon there breathed a wind on me,
Nor sound nor motion made:
Its path was not upon the sea,
In ripple or in shade.   455

It raised my hair, it fann'd my cheek
Like a meadow-gale of spring—
It mingled strangely with my fears,
Yet it felt like a welcoming.

Swiftly, swiftly flew the ship,   460
Yet she sail'd softly too:
Sweetly, sweetly blew the breeze—
On me alone it blew.

O dream of joy! is this indeed
The lighthouse top I see?   465
Is this the hill? is this the kirk?
Is this mine own countree?

We drifted o'er the harbour-bar,
And I with sobs did pray—
O let me be awake, my God!   470
Or let me sleep away.

The harbour-bay was clear as glass,
So smoothly it was strewn!
And on the bay the moonlight lay,
And the shadow of the Moon.   475

The rock shone bright, the kirk no less
That stands above the rock;
The moonlight steep'd in silentness
The steady weathercock.

And the bay was white with silent light   480

The angelic spirits leave the dead bodies,

Till rising from the same,
Full many shapes, that shadows were,
In crimson colours came.

A little distance from the prow
Those crimson shadows were: 485
I turn'd my eyes upon the deck—
O Christ! what saw I there!

And appear in their own forms of light.

Each corse lay flat, lifeless and flat,
And, by the holy rood!
A man all light, a seraph-man,   490
On every corse there stood.

This seraph-band, each waved his hand:
It was a heavenly sight!
They stood as signals to the land,
Each one a lovely light;   495

This seraph-band, each waved his hand,
No voice did they impart—
No voice; but O, the silence sank
Like music on my heart.

But soon I heard the dash of oars,   500
I heard the Pilot's cheer;

My head was turn'd perforce away,
And I saw a boat appear.

The Pilot and the Pilot's boy,
I heard them coming fast: 505
Dear Lord in Heaven! it was a joy
The dead men could not blast.

I saw a third—I heard his voice:
It is the Hermit good!
He singeth loud his godly hymns   510
That he makes in the wood.
He'll shieve my soul, he'll wash away
The Albatross's blood."

PART VII

The Hermit
of the Wood "This Hermit good lives in that wood
Which slopes down to the sea.   515
How loudly his sweet voice he rears!
He loves to talk with marineres
That come from a far countree.

He kneels at morn, and noon, and eve—
He hath a cushion plump.   520
It is the moss that wholly hides
The rotted old oak-stump.

The skiff-boat near'd: I heard them talk,
"Why, this is strange, I trow!
Where are those lights so many and fair,   525
That signal made but now?"

Approacheth the
ship with wonder. "Strange, by my faith!" the Hermit said—
"And they answer'd not our cheer!
The planks look warp'd! and see those sails,
How thin they are and sere!   530
I never saw aught like to them,
Unless perchance it were

Brown skeletons of leaves that lag
My forest-brook along;
When the ivy-tod is heavy with snow,   535
And the owlet whoops to the wolf below,
That eats the she-wolf's young."

"Dear Lord! it hath a fiendish look—
(The Pilot made reply)

I am a-fear'd."—"Push on, push on!"   540
Said the Hermit cheerily.

The boat came closer to the ship,
But I nor spake nor stirr'd;
The boat came close beneath the ship,
And straight a sound was heard.   545

The ship suddenly sinketh.

Under the water it rumbled on
Still louder and more dread:
It reach'd the ship, it split the bay;
The ship went down like lead.

The ancient Mariner is saved in the Pilot's boat.

Stunn'd by that loud and dreadful sound,   550
Which sky and ocean smote,
Like one that hath been seven days drown'd
My body lay afloat;
But swift as dreams, myself I found
Within the Pilot's boat.   555

Upon the whirl, where sank the ship,
The boat spun round and round;
And all was still, save that the hill
Was telling of the sound.

I moved my lips—the Pilot shriek'd   560
And fell down in a fit;
The holy Hermit raised his eyes,
And pray'd where he did sit.

I took the oars; the Pilot's boy,
Who now doth crazy go,   565
Laugh'd loud and long, and all the while
His eyes went to and fro.
"Ha! ha!" quoth he, "full plain I see
The Devil knows how to row."

And now, all in my own countree,   570
I stood on the firm land!
The Hermit stepp'd forth from the boat,
And scarcely he could stand.

The ancient Mariner earnestly entreateth the Hermit to shrieve him; and the penance of life falls on him.

"O shrieve me, shrieve me, holy man!"
The Hermit cross'd his brow.   575
"Say quick," quoth he, "I bid thee say—
What manner of man art thou?"

574 *shrieve:* archaic form of "shrive."

Forthwith this frame of mine was wrench'd
With a wofeul agony,
Which forced me to begin my tale;   *580*
And then it left me free.

And ever and anon throughout his future life an agony constraineth him to travel from land to land;

Since then, at an uncertain hour,
That agony returns:
And till my ghastly tale is told,
This heart within me burns.   *585*

I pass, like night, from land to land;
I have strange power of speech;
That moment that his face I see,
I know the man that must hear me:
To him my tale I teach.   *590*

What loud uproar bursts from that door!
The wedding-guests are there:
But in the garden-bower the bride
And bride-maids singing are:
And hark, the little vesper bell,   *595*
Which biddeth me to prayer!

O Wedding-Guest! this soul hath been
Alone on a wide, wide sea:
So lonely 'twas, that God Himself
Scarce seemèd there to be.   *600*

O sweeter than the marriage-feast,
'Tis sweeter far to me,
To walk together to the kirk
With a goodly company!—

To walk together to the kirk,   *605*
And all together pray,
While each to his great Father bends,
Old men, and babes, and loving friends,
And youths and maidens gay!

And to teach, by his own example, love and reverence to all things that God made and loveth.

Farewell, farewell! but this I tell   *610*
To thee, thou Wedding-Guest!
He prayeth well, who loveth well
Both man and bird and beast.

He prayeth best, who loveth best
All things both great and small;   *615*

For the dear God who loveth us,
He made and loveth all."

The Mariner, whose eye is bright,
Whose beard with age is hoar,
Is gone: and now the Wedding-Guest   620
Turn'd from the bridegroom's door.

He went like one that hath been stunn'd,
And is of sense forlorn:
A sadder and a wiser man
He rose the morrow morn.   625

Kubla Khan

In Xanadu did Kubla Khan
A stately pleasure-dome decree:
Where Alph, the sacred river, ran
Through caverns measureless to man
   Down to a sunless sea.   5
So twice five miles of fertile ground
With walls and towers were girdled round:
And there were gardens bright with sinuous rills,
Where blossomed many an incense-bearing tree;
And here were forests ancient as the hills,   10
Enfolding sunny spots of greenery.

But oh! that deep romantic chasm which slanted
Down the green hill athwart a cedarn cover!
A savage place! as holy and enchanted
As e'er beneath a waning moon was haunted   15
By woman wailing for her demon-lover!
And from this chasm, with ceaseless turmoil seething,
As if this earth in fast thick pants were breathing,
A mighty fountain momently was forced:
Amid whose swift half-intermitted burst   20
Huge fragments vaulted like rebounding hail,
Or chaffy grain beneath the thresher's flail:
And 'mid these dancing rocks at once and ever
It flung up momently the sacred river.

Kubla Khan: *Title:* Kublai the Cham (1215?–1294), Mongol emperor and founder
of the Yuan dynasty of China. *1 Xanadu:* in Tartary. *13 cedarn cover:* a wood
of ceders.

Five miles meandering with a mazy motion   *25*
Through wood and dale the sacred river ran,
Then reached the caverns measureless to man,
And sank in tumult to a lifeless ocean:
And 'mid this tumult Kubla heard from far
Ancestral voices prophesying war!   *30*

   The shadow of the dome of pleasure
   Floated midway on the waves;
   Where was heard the mingled measure
   From the fountain and the caves.
It was a miracle of rare device,   *35*
A sunny pleasure-dome with caves of ice!

   A damsel with a dulcimer
   In a vision once I saw:
   It was an Abyssinian maid,
   And on her dulcimer she played,   *40*
   Singing of Mount Abora.
   Could I revive within me
   Her symphony and song,
   To such a deep delight 'twould win me,
That with music loud and long,   *45*
I would build that dome in air,
That sunny dome! those caves of ice!
And all who heard should see them there,
And all should cry, Beware! Beware!
His flashing eyes, his floating hair!   *50*
Weave a circle round him thrice,
And close your eyes with holy dread,
For he on honey-dew hath fed,
And drunk the milk of Paradise.

Frost at Midnight

   The Frost performs its secret ministry,
   Unhelped by any wind. The owlet's cry
   Came loud—and hark, again! loud as before.
   The inmates of my cottage, all at rest,
   Have left me to that solitude, which suits   *5*

41 *Mount Abora:* Prof. Lane Cooper has suggested that this is really Milton's
Mount Amara, an earthly paradise in Abyssinia.

Abstruser musings: save that at my side
My cradled infant slumbers peacefully.
'Tis calm indeed! so calm, that it disturbs
And vexes meditation with its strange
And extreme silentness. Sea, hill, and wood,   10
This populous village! Sea, and hill, and wood,
With all the numberless goings-on of life,
Inaudible as dreams! the thin blue flame
Lies on my low-burnt fire, and quivers not;
Only that film, which fluttered on the grate,   15
Still flutters there, the sole unquiet thing.
Methinks, its motion in this hush of nature
Gives it dim sympathies with me who live,
Making it a companionable form,
Whose puny flaps and freaks the idling Spirit   20
By its own moods interprets, every where
Echo or mirror seeking of itself,
And makes a toy of Thought.

                    But O! how oft,
How oft, at school, with most believing mind,
Presageful, have I gazed upon the bars,   25
To watch that fluttering stranger! and as oft
With unclosed lids, already had I dreamt
Of my sweet birth-place, and the old church-tower,
Whose bells, the poor man's only music, rang
From morn to evening, all the hot Fair-day   30
So sweetly, that they stirred and haunted me
With a wild pleasure, falling on mine ear
Most like articulate sound of things to come!
So gazed I, till the soothing things, I dreamt,
Lulled me to sleep, and sleep prolonged my dreams!   35
And so I brooded all the following morn,
Awed by the stern preceptor's face, mine eye
Fixed with mock study on my swimming book:
Save if the door half opened, and I snatched
A hasty glance, and still my heart leaped up,   40
For still I hoped to see the *stranger's* face,
Townsman, or aunt, or sister more beloved,
My play-mate when we both were clothed alike!

Dear Babe, that sleepest cradled by my side,
Whose gentle breathings, heard in this deep calm,   45
Fill up the interspersèd vacancies
And momentary pauses of the thought!
My babe so beautiful! it thrills my heart

With tender gladness, thus to look at thee,
And think that thou shalt learn far other lore,   *50*
And in far other scenes! For I was reared
In the great city, pent 'mid cloisters dim,
And saw nought lovely but the sky and stars.
But thou, my babe! shalt wander like a breeze
By lakes and sandy shores, beneath the crags   *55*
Of ancient mountain, and beneath the clouds,
Which image in their bulk lakes and shores
And mountain crags: so shalt thou see and hear
The lovely shapes and sounds intelligible
Of that eternal language, which thy God   *60*
Utters, who from eternity doth teach
Himself in all, and all things in himself.
Great universal Teacher! he shall mould
Thy spirit, and by giving make it ask.

Therefore all seasons shall be sweet to thee,   *65*
Whether the summer clothe the general earth
With greeness, or the redbreast sit and sing
Betwixt the tufts of snow on the bare branch
Of mossy apple-tree, while the nigh thatch
Smokes in the sun-thaw; whether the eave-drops fall   *70*
Heard only in the trances of the blast,
Or if the secret ministry of frost
Shall hang them up in silent icicles,
Quietly shining to the quiet Moon.

Youth and Age

Verse, a breeze mid blossoms straying,
Where Hope clung feeding, like a bee—
Both were mine! Life went a-maying
      With Nature, Hope, and Poesy,
          When I was young!

When I was young?—Ar, woful When!   *5*
Ah! for the change 'twixt Now and Then!
This breathing house not built with hands,
This body that does me grievous wrong,
O'er aery cliffs and glittering sands,
How lightly then it flashed along:—   *10*

Like those trim skiffs, unknown of yore,
On winding lakes and rivers wide,
That ask no aid of sail or oar,
That fear no spite of wind or tide!
Nought cared this body for wind or weather   *15*
When Youth and I lived in't together.

Flowers are lovely; Love is flower-like;
Friendship is a sheltering tree;
O! the joys, that came down shower-like,
Of Friendship, Love, and Liberty,
                    Ere I was old!   *20*

Ere I was old? Ah woful Ere,
Which tells me, Youth's no longer here!
O Youth! for years so many and sweet,
'Tis known, that Thou and I were one,
I'll think it but a fond conceit—   *25*
It cannot be that Thou art gone!
Thy vesper-bell hath not yet toll'd:—
And thou wert aye a masker bold!
What strange disguise hast now put on,
To make believe, that thou art gone?   *30*
I see these locks in silvery slips,
This drooping gait, this altered size:
But Spring-tide blossoms on thy lips,
And tears take sunshine from thine eyes!
Life is but thought: so think I will   *35*
That Youth and I are house-mates still.

Dew-drops are the gems of morning,
But the tears of mournful eve!
Where no hope is, life's a warning
That only serves to make us grieve,
                When we are old: *40*

That only serves to make us grieve
With oft and tedious taking-leave,
Like some poor nigh-related guest,
That may not rudely be dismist;
Yet hath outstay'd his welcome while,   *45*
And tells the jest without the smile.

Time, Real and Imaginary

AN ALLEGORY

On the wide level of a mountain's head,
(I knew not where, but 'twas some faery place)
Their pinions, ostrich-like, for sails out-spread,
Two lovely children run an endless race,
  A sister and a brother!   5
  This far outstripp'd the other;
 Yet ever runs she with reverted face,
 And looks and listens for the boy behind:
  For he, alas! is blind!
O'er rough and smooth with even step he passed, 10
And knows not whether he be first or last.

PERCY BYSSHE SHELLEY

1792–1822

Shelley is one of the younger Romantics, over twenty years junior to Wordsworth, who outlived him by twenty-eight years. Shelley was at odds with society from as early as his expulsion from Oxford for writing *The Necessity of Atheism* (1810) right up to his death by drowning in Italy, foreseen in the last passage of *Adonais*. *Prometheus Unbound* and *The Cenci* (both from 1819, his outstanding year) reflect his hatred of all tyrannies, political or domestic. Noble resolves and theories of free love harried his conjugal life, with its shifting passions, while exposing him to censure from friends and bigots alike. Though disapproving of marriage, he eloped at eighteen, then later fell in love with someone else. Rejecting his proposal that they all live together, his wife Harriet drowned herself. Shelley lost custody of their children, and in 1818 and 1819 his children by his new wife, Mary, also died. Mary, the author of *Frankenstein*, was the daughter of William Godwin, a "radical" but respectable intellectual Shelley helped feed. Shelley's work was accomplished despite depression and uproar. His great master is Plato, who instructed that behind the material world is a dimension of ideas, "pure forms" which correspond to the grosser aspects of life and are the repository of Beauty, Truth, and Ultimate Reality. Thus, beyond the present and tangible, Shelley found refuge for his ideals and freedom from tyranny or misunderstanding, and his poetry is abstract as well as sensuous. These qualities, and his platonism, can be measured in the *Hymn to Intellectual Beauty* (1816).

Ode to the West Wind

O wild West Wind, thou breath of Autumn's being,
Thou, from whose unseen presence the leaves dead
Are driven, like ghosts from an enchanter fleeing,
Yellow, and black, and pale, and hectic red,
Pestilence-stricken multitudes: O thou 5
Who chariotest to their dark wintry bed
The wingéd seeds, where they lie cold and low,
Each like a corpse within its grave, until
Thine azure sister of the Spring shall blow
Her clarion o'er the dreaming earth, and fill 10
(Driving sweet buds like flocks to feed in air)
With living hues and odours plain and hill:
Wild Spirit, which art moving everywhere;
Destroyer and Preserver; Hear, oh hear!

Thou on whose stream, 'mid the steep sky's commotion, 15
Loose clouds like earth's decaying leaves are shed,
Shook from the tangled boughs of Heaven and Ocean,
Angels of rain and lightning; there are spread
On the blue surface of thine airy surge,
Like the bright hair uplifted from the head 20
Of some fierce Maenad, ev'n from the dim verge
Of the horizon to the zenith's height—
The locks of the approaching storm. Thou dirge
Of the dying year, to which this closing night
Will be the dome of a vast sepulchre, 25
Vaulted with all thy congregated might
Of vapours, from whose solid atmosphere
Black rain, and fire, and hail, will burst; oh, hear!

21 *Maenad:* a priestess of Bacchus.

Thou who didst waken from his summer-dreams
The blue Mediterranean, where he lay, 30
Lull'd by the coil of his crystalline streams,

Beside a pumice isle in Baiae's bay,
And saw in sleep old palaces and towers
Quivering within the wave's intenser day,

All overgrown with azure moss and flowers 35
So sweet, the sense faints picturing them! Thou
For whose path the Atlantic's level powers

Cleave themselves into chasms, while far below
The sea-blooms and the oozy woods which wear
The sapless foliage of the ocean, know 40

Thy voice, and suddenly grow grey with fear
And tremble and despoil themselves: oh, hear!

If I were a dead leaf thou mightest bear;
If I were a swift cloud to fly with thee;
A wave to pant beneath thy power, and share 45

The impulse of thy strength, only less free
Than thou, O uncontrollable! If even
I were as in my boyhood, and could be

The comrade of thy wanderings over heaven,
As then, when to outstrip thy skiey speed 50
Scarce seem'd a vision, I would ne'er have striven

As thus with thee in prayer in my sore need.
Oh, lift me as a wave, a leaf, a cloud!
I fall upon the thorns of life! I bleed!

A heavy weight of hours has chain'd and bow'd 55
One too like thee: tameless, and swift, and proud.

Make me thy lyre, ev'n as the forest is:
What if my leaves are felling like its own?
The tumult of thy mighty harmonies

Will take from both a deep autumnal tone, 60
Sweet though in sadness. Be thou, Spirit fierce,
My spirit! be thou me, impetuous one!

Drive my dead thoughts over the universe
Like wither'd leaves to quicken a new birth;
And, by the incantation of this verse, 65

Scatter, as from an unextinguish'd hearth
Ashes and sparks, my words among mankind!
Be through my lips to unawaken'd earth

The trumpet of a prophecy! O Wind,
If Winter comes, can Spring be far behind? 70

32 *Baiae's bay*: near Naples.

Hymn to Intellectual Beauty

The awful shadow of some unseen Power
  Floats through unseen among us,—visiting
  This various world with as inconstant wing
As summer winds that creep from flower to flower;
Like moonbeams that behind some piny mountain shower,   5
    It visits with inconstant glance
    Each human heart and countenance:
Like hues and harmonies of evening,—
    Like clouds in starlight widely spread,—
    Like memory of music fled,—   10
    Like aught that for its grace may be
Dear, and yet dearer for its mystery.

Spirit of Beauty, that dost consecrate
  With thine own hues all thou dost shine upon
  Of human thought or form,—where art thou gone?   15
Why dost thou pass away and leave our state,
This dim vast vale of tears, vacant and desolate?
    Ask why the sunlight not forever
    Weaves rainbows o'er yon mountain river,
Why aught should fail and fade that once is shown,   20
    Why fear and dream and death and birth
    Cast on the daylight of this earth
    Such gloom,—why man has such a scope
For love and hate, despondency and hope?

No voice from some sublimer world hath ever   25
  To sage or poet these responses given—
  Therefore the names of Daemon, Ghost, and Heaven,
Remain the records of their vain endeavor,
Frail spells—whose uttered charm might not avail to sever,
    From all we hear and all we see,   30
    Doubt, chance, and mutability.
Thy light alone—like mist o'er mountains driven,
    Or music by the night wind sent
    Through strings of some still instrument,
    Or moonlight on a midnight stream,   35
Gives grace and truth to life's unquiet dream.

Love, Hope, and Self-esteem, like clouds depart
  And come, for some uncertain moments lent.
  Man were immortal, and omnipotent,
Didst thou, unknown and awful as thou art,   40

Keep with thy glorious train firm state within his heart.
    Thou messenger of sympathies,
    That wax and wane in lovers' eyes—
Thou—that to human thought art nourishment,
    Like darkness to a dying flame!   45
    Depart not as thy shadow came,
    Depart not—lest the grave should be,
Like life and fear, a dark reality.

While yet a boy I sought for ghosts, and sped
    Through many a listening chamber, cave and ruin,   50
    And starlight wood, with fearless steps pursuing
Hopes of high talk with the departed dead.
I called on poisonous names with which our youth is fed;
    I was not heard—I saw them not—
    When musing deeply on the lot   55
Of life, at that sweet time when winds are wooing
    All vital things that wake to bring
    News of birds and blossoming,—
    Sudden, thy shadow fell on me;
I shrieked, and clasped my hands in ecstasy!   60

I vowed that I would dedicate my powers
    To thee and thine—have I not kept the vow?
    With beating heart and streaming eyes, even now
I call the phantoms of a thousand hours
Each from his voiceless grave: they have in visioned bowers   65
    Of studious zeal or love's delight
    Outwatched with me the envious night—
They know that never joy illumed my brow
    Unlinked with hope that thou wouldst free
    This world from its dark slavery,   70
    That thou—O awful Loveliness,
Wouldst give whate'er these words cannot express.

The day becomes more solemn and serene
    When noon is past—there is a harmony
    In autumn, and a lustre in its sky,   75
Which through the summer is not heard or seen,
As if it could not be, as if it had not been!
    Thus let thy power, which like the truth
    Of nature on thy passive youth
Descended, to my onward life supply   80
    Its calm—to one who worships thee,
    And every form containing thee,
    Whom, Spirit fair, thy spells did bind
To fear himself, and love all human kind.

Ozymandias

I met a traveler from an antique land
Who said: Two vast and trunkless legs of stone
Stand in the desert. Near them, on the sand,
Half sunk, a shattered visage lies, whose frown,
And wrinkled lip, and sneer of cold command,   5
Tell that its sculptor well those passions read
Which yet survive, stamped on these lifeless things,
The hand that mocked them and the heart that fed;
And on the pedestal these words appear:
"My name is Ozymandias, king of kings: 10
Look on my works, ye Mighty, and despair!"
Nothing beside remains. Round the decay
Of that colossal wreck, boundless and bare
The lone and level sands stretch far away.

The Indian Serenade

I arise from dreams of thee
In the first sweet sleep of night,
When the winds are breathing low,
And the stars are shining bright:
I arise from dreams of thee,   5
And a spirit in my feet
Hath led me—who knows how?
To thy chamber window, Sweet!

The wandering airs they faint
On the dark, the silent stream—   10
The Champak odors fail
Like sweet thoughts in a dream;
The nightingale's complaint,
It dies upon her heart;—
As I must on thine,   15
Oh, belovèd as thou art!

Oh lift me from the grass!
I die! I faint! I fail!
Let thy love in kisses rain

The Indian Serenade: *11 Champak:* a tree of the magnolia family.

On my lips and eyelids pale.   20
My cheek is cold and white, alas!
My heart beats loud and fast;—
Oh! press it to thine own again,
Where it will break at last.

Music, When Soft Voices Die

Music, when soft voices die,
Vibrates in the memory—
Odours, when sweet violets sicken,
Live within the sense they quicken.

Rose leaves, when the rose is dead,
Are heap'd for the beloved's bed;
And so thy thoughts, when thou art gone,
Love itself shall slumber on.

One Word Is Too Often Profaned

One word is too often profaned
    For me to profane it;
One feeling too falsely disdain'd
    For thee to disdain it;
One hope is too like despair   5
    For prudence to smother;
And pity from thee more dear
    Than that from another.

I can give not what men call love:
    But wilt thou accept not   10
The worship the heart lifts above
    And the heavens reject not,
The desire of the moth for the star,
    Of the night for the morrow,
The devotion to something afar   15
    From the sphere of our sorrow?

Adonais

I weep for Adonais—he is dead!
Oh weep for Adonais! though our tears
Thaw not the frost which binds so dear a head!
And thou, sad Hour, selected from all years
To mourn our loss, rouse thy obscure compeers,   5
And teach them thine own sorrow! Say: 'With me
Died Adonais; till the Future dares
Forget the Past, his fate and fame shall be
An echo and a light unto Eternity!'

Where wert thou, mighty Mother, when he lay,   10
When thy son lay, pierced by the shaft which flies
In darkness? where was lorn Urania
When Adonais died? With veilèd eyes,
'Mid listening Echoes, in her paradise
She sate, while one, with soft enamored breath,   15
Rekindled all the fading melodies,
With which, like flowers that mock the corse beneath,
He had adorned and hid the coming bulk of death.

Oh, weep for Adonais—he is dead!
Wake, melancholy Mother, wake and weep!   20
Yet wherefore? Quench within their burning bed
Thy fiery tears, and let thy loud heart keep
Like his, a mute and uncomplaining sleep;
For he is gone, where all things wise and fair
Descend. Oh, dream not that the amorous Deep   25
Will yet restore him to the vital air;
Death feeds on his mute voice, and laughs at our despair.

Most musical of mourners, weep again!
Lament anew, Urania!—He died,
Who was the sire of an immortal strain,   30
Blind, old, and lonely, when his country's pride,
The priest, the slave, and the liberticide,
Trampled and mocked with many a loathèd rite
Of lust and blood; he went, unterrified,
Into the gulf of death; but his clear Sprite   35
Yet reigns o'er earth, the third among the sons of light.

Adonais: *Title:* the poet John Keats, for whom this poem is an elegy.   *12 Urania:* the heavenly Muse.   *29 He:* John Milton.   *36:* The other two "sons of light" are probably Homer and Dante.

Most musical of mourners, weep anew!
Not all to that bright station dared to climb;
And happier they their happiness who knew,
Whose tapers yet burn through that night of time   40
In which suns perished; others more sublime,
Struck by the envious wrath of man or God,
Have sunk, extinct in their refulgent prime;
And some yet live, treading the thorny road,
Which leads, through toil and hate, to Fame's serene abode.   45

But now, thy youngest, dearest one has perished,
The nursling of thy widowhood, who grew,
Like a pale flower by some sad maiden cherished,
And fed with true-love tears instead of dew;
Most musical of mourners, weep anew!   50
Thy extreme hope, the loveliest and the last,
The bloom, whose petals nipped before they blew,
Died on the promise of the fruit, is waste;
The broken lily lies—the storm is overpast.

To that high Capital, where kingly Death   55
Keeps his pale court in beauty and decay,
He came; and bought, with price of purest breath,
A grave among the eternal.—Come away!
Haste, while the vault of blue Italian day
Is yet his fitting charnel-roof! while still   60
He lies, as if in dewy sleep he lay;
Awake him not! surely he takes his fill
Of deep and liquid rest, forgetful of all ill.

He will awake no more, oh, never more!
Within the twilight chamber spreads apace   65
The shadow of white Death, and at the door
Invisible Corruption waits to trace
His extreme way to her dim dwelling-place;
The eternal Hunger sits, but pity and awe
Soothe her pale rage, nor dares she to deface   70
So fair a prey, till darkness, and the law
Of change, shall o'er his sleep the mortal curtain draw.

Oh, weep for Adonais!—The quick Dreams,
The passion-wingèd ministers of thought,
Who were his flocks, whom near the living streams   75
Of his young spirit he fed, and whom he taught
The love which was its music, wander not,—
Wander no more, from kindling brain to brain,

But droop there, whence they sprung; and mourn their lot
Round the cold heart, where, after their sweet pain,   80
They ne'er will gather strength, or find a home again.

And one with trembling hands clasps his cold head,
And fans him with her moonlight wings, and cries;
"Our love, our hope, our sorrow, is not dead;
See, on the silken fringe of his faint eyes   85
Like dew upon a sleeping flower, there lies
A tear some Dream has loosened from his brain."
Lost Angel of a ruined paradise!
She knew not 'twas her own; as with no stain
She faded, like a cloud which had outwept its rain.   90

One from a lucid urn of starry dew
Washed his light limbs as if embalming them;
Another clipped her profuse locks, and threw
The wreath upon him, like an anadem,
Which frozen tears instead of pearls begem;   95
Another in her wilful grief would break
Her bow and winged reeds, as if to stem
A greater loss with one which was more weak;
And dull the barbèd fire against his frozen cheek.

Another Splendor on his mouth alit,   100
That mouth, whence it was wont to draw the breath
Which gave it strength to pierce the guarded wit,
And pass into the panting heart beneath
With lightning and with music: the damp death
Quenched its caress upon his icy lips;   105
And, as a dying meteor stains a wreath
Of moonlight vapor, which the cold night clips,
It flushed through his pale limbs, and passed to its eclipse.

And others came—Desires and Adorations,
Wingèd Persuasions and veiled Destinies,   110
Splendors, and Glooms, and glimmering Incarnations
Of hopes and fears, and twilight Fantasies;
And Sorrow, with her family of Sighs,
And Pleasure, blind with tears, led by the gleam
Of her own dying smile instead of eyes,   115
Came in slow pomp;—the moving pomp might seem
Like pageantry of mist on an autumnal stream.

All he had loved, and molded into thought,
From shape, and hue, and odor, and sweet sound,

Lamented Adonais. Morning sought
Her eastern watch-tower, and her hair unbound,
Wet with tears which should adorn the ground,
Dimmed the aërial eyes that kindle day;
Afar the melancholy thunder moaned,
Pale Ocean in unquiet slumber lay,
And the wild winds flew round, sobbing in their dismay.

Lost Echo sits amid the voiceless mountains,
And feeds her grief with his remembered lay,
And will no more reply to winds or fountains,
Or amorous birds perched on the young green spray,
Or herdsmen's horn, or bell at closing day;
Since she can mimic not his lips, more dear
Than those for whose disdain she pined away
Into a shadow of all sounds:—a drear
Murmur, between their songs, is all the woodmen hear.

Grief made the young Spring wild, and she threw down
Her kindling buds, as if she Autumn were,
Or they dead leaves; since her delight is flown,
For whom should she have waked the sullen year?
To Phoebus was not Hyacinth so dear
Nor to himself Narcissus, as to both
Thou, Adonais: wan they stand and sere
Amid the faint companions of their youth,
With dew all turned to tears; odor, to sighing ruth.

Thy spirit's sister, the lorn nightingale
Mourns not her mate with such melodious pain;
Not so the eagle, who like thee could scale
Heaven, and could nourish in the sun's domain
Her mighty youth with morning, doth complain,
Soaring and screaming round her empty nest,
As Albion wails for thee: the curse of Cain
Light on his head who pierced thy innocent breast,
And scared the angel soul that was its earthly guest!

Ah, woe is me! Winter is come and gone,
But grief returns with the revolving year;
The airs and streams renew their joyous tone;
The ants, the bees, the swallows reappear;
Fresh leaves and flowers deck the dead Seasons' bier;
The amorous birds now pair in every brake,
And build their mossy homes in fields and brere;
And the green lizard, and the golden snake,
Like unimprisoned flames, out of their trance awake.

120

125

130

135

140

145

150

155

160

Through wood and stream and field and hill and ocean
A quickening life from the Earth's heart has burst
As it has ever done, with change and motion,   *165*
From the great morning of the world when first
God dawned on Chaos; in its stream immersed,
The lamps of Heaven flash with a softer light;
All baser things pant with life's sacred thirst;
Diffuse themselves; and spend in love's delight,   *170*
The beauty and the joy of their renewèd might.

The leprous corpse, touched by this spirit tender,
Exhales itself in flowers of gentle breath;
Like incarnations of the stars, when splendor
Is changed to fragrance, they illumine death   *175*
And mock the merry worm that wakes beneath;
Nought we know dies. Shall that alone which knows
Be as a sword consumed before the sheath
By sightless lightning?—the intense atom glows
A moment, then is quenched in a most cold repose.   *180*

Alas! that all we loved of him should be,
But for our grief, as if it had not been,
And grief itself be mortal! Woe is me!
Whence are we, and why are we? of what scene
The actors or spectators? Great and mean   *185*
Meet massed in death, who lends what life must borrow.
As long as skies are blue, and fields are green,
Evening must usher night, night urge the morrow,
Month follow month with woe, and year wake year to sorrow.

He will awake no more, oh, never more!   *190*
"Wake thou," cried misery, "childless Mother, rise
Out of thy sleep, and slake, in thy heart's core,
A wound more fierce than his, with tears and sighs."
And all the Dreams that watched Urania's eyes,
And all the Echoes whom their sister's song   *195*
Had held in holy silence, cried: "Arise!"
Swift as a Thought by the snake Memory stung,
From her ambrosial rest the fading Splendor sprung.

She rose like an autumnal Night, that springs
Out of the East, and follows wild and drear   *200*
The golden Day, which, on eternal wings,
Even as a ghost abandoning a bier,
Had left the Earth a corpse:—sorrow and fear
So struck, so roused, so rapt Urania;

So saddened round her like an atmosphere
Of stormy mist; so swept her on her way
Even to the mournful place where Adonais lay.

Out of her secret paradise she sped.
Through camps and cities rough with stone, and steel,
And human hearts, which to her airy tread
Yielding not, wounded the invisible
Palms of her tender feet where'er they fell:
And barbèd tongues, and thoughts more sharp than they,
Rent the soft Form they never could repel,
Whose sacred blood, like the young tears of may,
Paved with eternal flowers that undeserving way.

In the death-chamber for a moment Death,
Shamed by the presence of that living Might,
Blushed to annihilation, and the breath
Revisited those lips, and Life's pale light
Flashed through those limbs, so late her dear delight.
"Leave me not wild and drear and comfortless,
As silent lightning leaves the starless night!
Leave me not!" cried Urania: her distress
Roused Death: Death rose and smiled, and met her vain caress.

"Stay yet awhile! speak to me once again;
Kiss me, so long but as a kiss may live;
And in my heartless breast and burning brain
That word, that kiss, shall all thoughts else survive,
With food of saddest memory kept alive,
Now thou art dead, as if it were a part
Of thee, my Adonais! I would give
All that I am to be as thou now art!
But I am chained to Time, and cannot thence depart!

"O gentle child, beautiful as thou wert,
Why didst thou leave the trodden paths of men
Too soon, and with weak hands though mighty heart
Dare the unpastured dragon in his den?
Defenseless as thou wert, oh, where was then
Wisdom the mirrored shield, or scorn the spear?
Or hadst thou waited the full cycle when
Thy spirit should have filled its crescent sphere,
The monsters of life's waste had fled from thee like deer.

"The herded wolves, bold only to pursue;
The obscene ravens, clamorous o'er the dead;

The vultures to the conqueror's banner true
Who feed where Desolation first has fed,
And whose wings rain contagion;—how they fled,
When, like Apollo, from his golden bow
The Pythian of the age one arrow sped   250
And smiled!—The spoilers tempt no second blow,
They fawn on the proud feet that spurn them lying low.

"The sun comes forth, and many reptiles spawn;
He sets, and each ephemeral insect then
Is gathered into death without a dawn,   255
And the immortal stars awake again;
So is it in the world of living men:
A godlike mind soars forth, in its delight
Making earth bare and veiling heaven, and when
It sinks, the swarms that dimmed or shared its light   260
Leave to its kindred lamps the spirit's awful night."

Thus ceased she: and the mountain shepherds came,
Their garlands sere, their magic mantles rent;
The Pilgrim of Eternity, whose fame
Over his living head like Heaven is bent,   265
An early but enduring monument,
Came, veiling all the lightnings of his song
In sorrow; from her wilds Ierne sent
The sweetest lyrist of her saddest wrong,
And love taught grief to fall like music from his tongue. 270

Midst others of less note, came one frail Form,
A phantom among men; companionless
As the last cloud of an expiring storm
Whose thunder is its knell; he, as I guess,
Had gazed on Nature's naked loveliness,   275
Actaeon-like, and now he fled astray
With feeble steps o'er the world's wilderness,
And his own thoughts, along that rugged way,
Pursued, like raging hounds, their father and their prey.

A pardlike Spirit beautiful and swift—   280
A Love in desolation masked;—a Power
Girt round with weakness;—it can scarce uplift
The weight of the superincumbent hour;

249–250: Apollo killed the monster Python with an arrow. Lord Byron, the poet,
is here likened to him. Byron "slew" the critics with his poem *English Bards and
Scotch Reviewers.* 264 *Pilgrim:* Byron again, because of *Childe Harold's Pil-
grimage.* 268 *Ierne:* Ireland. 269 *sweetest lyrist:* Thomas Moore (1779–1852).

It is a dying lamp, a falling shower,
A breaking billow;—even whilst we speak   285
Is it not broken? On the withering flower
The killing sun smiles brightly: on a cheek
The life can burn in blood, even while the heart may break.

His head was bound with pansies overblown,
And faded violets, white, and pied, and blue;   290
And a light spear topped with a cypress cone,
Round whose rude shaft dark ivy-tresses grew
Yet dripping with the forest's noonday dew,
Vibrated, as the ever-beating heart
Shook the weak hand that grasped it; of that crew   295
He came the last, neglected and apart;
A herd-abandoned deer struck by the hunter's dart.

All stood aloof, and at his partial moan
Smiled through their tears; well knew that gentle band
Who in another's fate now wept his own,   300
As in the accents of an unknown land
He sung new sorrow; sad Urania scanned
The stranger's mien, and murmured: "Who art thou?"
He answered not, but with a sudden hand
Made bare his branded and ensanguined brow,   305
Which was like Cain's or Christ's—oh! that it should be so!

What softer voice is hushed over the dead?
Athwart what brow is that dark mantle thrown?
What form leans sadly o'er the white death-bed,
In mockery of monumental stone,   310
The heavy heart heaving without a moan?
If it be he, who, gentlest of the wise,
Taught, soothed, loved, honored the departed one,
Let me not vex, with inharmonious sighs,
The silence of that heart's accepted sacrifice.   315

Our Adonais has drunk poison—oh,
What deaf and viperous murderer could crown
Life's early cup with such a draught of woe?
The nameless worm would now itself disown:
It felt, yet could escape, the magic tone   320
Whose prelude held all envy, hate, and wrong,
But what was howling in one breast alone,
Silent with expectation of the song,
Whose master's hand is cold, whose silver lyre unstrung.

Live thou, whose infamy is not thy fame!   325
Live! fear no heavier chastisement from me,
Thou noteless blot on a remembered name!
But be thyself, and know thyself to be!
And ever at thy season be thou free
To spill the venom when thy fangs o'erflow: 330
Remorse and Self-Contempt shall cling to thee;
Hot Shame shall burn upon thy secret brow,
And like a beaten hound tremble thou shalt—as now.

Nor let us weep that our delight is fled
Far from these carrion kites that scream below;   335
He wakes or sleeps with the enduring dead;
Thou canst not soar where he is sitting now.—
Dust to the dust! but the pure spirit shall flow
Back to the burning fountain whence it came,
A portion of the Eternal, which must glow   340
Through time and change, unquenchably the same,
Whilst thy cold embers choke the sordid hearth of shame.

Peace, peace! he is not dead, he doth not sleep—
He hath awakened from the dream of life—
'Tis we, who, lost in stormy visions, keep   345
With phantoms an unprofitable strife,
And in mad trance, strike with our spirit's knife
Invulnerable nothings. *We* decay
Like corpses in a charnel; fear and grief
Convulse us and consume us day by day,   350
And cold hopes swarm like worms within our living clay.

He has outsoared the shadow of our night;
Envy and calumny and hate and pain,
And that unrest which men miscall delight,
Can touch him not and torture not again;   355
From the contagion of the world's slow stain
He is secure, and now can never mourn
A heart grown cold, a head grown gray in vain;
Nor, when the spirit's self has ceased to burn,
With sparkless ashes load an unlamented urn.   360

He lives, he wakes—'tis Death is dead, not he;
Mourn not for Adonais.—Thou young Dawn,
Turn all thy dew to splendor, for from thee
The spirit thou lamentest is not gone;
Ye caverns and ye forests, cease to moan!   365
Cease, ye faint flowers and fountains, and thou air,

Which like a mourning veil thy scarf hadst thrown
O'er the abandoned Earth, now leave it bare
Even to the joyous stars which smile on its despair!

He is made one with Nature: there is heard   370
His voice in all her music, from the moan
Of thunder, to the song of night's sweet bird;
He is a presence to be felt and known
In darkness and in light, from herb and stone,
Spreading itself where'er that Power may move   375
Which has withdrawn his being to its own;
Which wields the world with never-wearied love,
Sustains it from beneath, and kindles it above.

He is a portion of the loveliness
Which once he made more lovely: he doth bear   380
His part, while the one Spirit's plastic stress
Sweeps through the dull dense world, compelling there
All new successions to the forms they wear,
Torturing the unwilling dross that checks its flight
To its own likeness, as each mass may bear;   385
And bursting in its beauty and its might
From trees and beasts and men into the Heaven's light.

The splendors of the firmament of time
May be eclipsed, but are extinguished not;
Like stars to their appointed height they climb,   390
And death is a low mist which cannot blot
The brightness it may veil. When lofty thought
Lifts a young heart above its mortal lair,
And love and life contend in it for what
Shall be its earthly doom, the dead live there   395
And move like winds of light on dark and stormy air.

The inheritors of unfulfilled renown
Rose from their thrones, built beyond mortal thought,
Far in the Unapparent. Chatterton
Rose pale,—his solemn agony had not   400
Yet faded from him; Sidney, as he fought
And as he fell and as he lived and loved
Sublimely mild, a Spirit without spot,
Arose; and Lucan, by his death approved:
Oblivion as they rose shrank like a thing reproved. 405

399 *Chatterton:* Thomas Chatterton (1752–1770), a poet who poisoned himself.
401 *Sidney:* Sir Philip Sidney (1554–1586), who was killed in battle. 404 *Lucan:*
(39–65), Roman poet who killed himself to escape execution.

And many more, whose names on earth are dark,
But whose transmitted effluence cannot die
So long as fire outlives the parent spark,
Rose, robed in dazzling immortality.
"Thou art become as one of us," they cry,   410
"It was for thee yon kingless sphere has long
Swung blind in unascended majesty,
Silent alone amid an heaven of song.
Assume thy wingèd throne, thou Vesper of our throng!"

Who mourns for Adonais? Oh, come forth,   415
Fond wretch! and know thyself and him aright.
Clasp with thy panting soul the pendulous earth;
As from a center, dart by thy spirit's light
Beyond all worlds, until its spacious might
Satiate the void circumference: then shrink   420
Even to a point within our day and night;
And keep thy heart light lest it make thee sink
When hope has kindled hope, and lured thee to the brink.

Or go to Rome, which is the sepulcher,
Oh, not of him, but of our joy: 'tis nought   425
That ages, empires, and religions there
Lie buried in the ravage they have wrought;
For such as he can lend,—they borrow not
Glory from those who made the world their prey;
And he is gathered to the kings of thought   430
Who waged contention with their time's decay,
And of the past are all that cannot pass away.

Go thou to Rome,—at once the Paradise,
The grave, the city, and the wilderness;
And where its wrecks like shattered mountains rise,   435
And flowering weeds and fragrant copses dress
The bones of Desolation's nakedness,
Pass, till the Spirit of the spot shall lead
Thy footsteps to a slope of green access
Where, like an infant's smile, over the dead   440
A light of laughing flowers along the grass is spread;

And gray walls molder round, on which dull Time
Feeds, like slow fire, upon a hoary brand;
And one keen puramid with wedge sublime,
Pavilioning the dust of him who planned   445
This refuge for his memory, doth stand
Like flame transformed to marble; and beneath,

A field is spread, on which a newer band
Have pitched in Heaven's smile their camp of death,
Welcoming him we lose with scarce extinguished breath.   450

Here pause: these graves are all too young as yet
To have outgrown the sorrow which consigned
Its charge to each; and if the seal is set,
Here, on one fountain of a mourning mind,
Break it not thou! too surely shalt thou find   455
Thine own well full, if thou returnest home,
Of tears and gall. From the world's bitter wind
Seek shelter in the shadow of the tomb.
What Adonais is, why fear we to become?

The One remains, the many change and pass;   460
Heaven's light forever shines, Earth's shadows fly;
Life, like a dome of many-colored glass,
Stains the white radiance of Eternity,
Until Death tramples it to fragments.—Die,
If thou wouldst be with that which thou dost seek!   465
Follow where all is fled!—Rome's azure sky,
Flowers, ruins, statues, music, words, are weak
The glory they transfuse with fitting truth to speak.

Why linger, why turn back, why shrink, my heart?
Thy hopes are gone before: from all things here   470
They have departed; thou shouldst now depart!
A light is passed from the revolving year,
And man, and woman; and what still is dear
Attracts to crush, repels to make thee wither.
The soft sky smiles,—the low wind whispers near: 475
'Tis Adonais calls! oh, hasten thither,
No more let Life divide what Death can join together.

That Light whose smile kindles the Universe,
That Beauty in which all things work and move,
That Benediction which the eclipsing Curse   480
Of birth can quench not, that sustaining Love
Which through the web of being blindly wove
By man and beast and earth and air and sea,
Burns bright or dim, as each are mirrors of
The fire for which all thirst; now beams on me,   485
Consuming the last clouds of cold mortality.

The breath whose might I have invoked in song
Descends on me; my spirit's bark is driven,

Far from the shore, far from the trembling throng
Whose sails were never to the tempest given;   *490*
The massy earth and spherèd skies are riven!
I am borne darkly, fearfully, afar:
Whilst, burning through the inmost veil of Heaven,
The soul of Adonais, like a star,
Beacons from the abode where the Eternal are.   *495*

The World's Great Age

From HELLAS

The world's great age begins anew,
   The golden years return,
The earth doth like a snake renew
   Her winter weeds outworn:
Heaven smiles, and faiths and empires gleam,   *5*
Like wrecks of a dissolving dream.

A brighter Hellas rears its mountains
   From waves serener far;
A new Peneus rolls his fountains
   Against the morning star.   *10*
Where fairer Tempes bloom, there sleep
Young Cyclads on a sunnier deep.

A loftier Argo cleaves the main,
   Fraught with a later prize;
Another Orpheus sings again,   *15*
   And loves, and weeps, and dies.
A new Ulysses leaves once more
Calypso for his native shore.

The World's Great Age: The Greek war for independence seemed to Shelley
to herald a new Golden Age (a legendary era of innocence and happiness) and
inspired him to compose the lyrical drama *Hellas*, from which these lines are a
chorus. *4 weeds*: garb, robes; i.e., "The earth renews its verdure as a snake
renews its skin." *5 faiths and empires*: creeds and monarchies, both of which
Shelley detested. *7 Hellas*: originally a district in Thessaly, but here standing
for all Greece. *9 Peneus*: a river that flows through the Vale of Tempe in Thes-
saly. *11 Tempes*: valleys like the Vale of Tempe, which was famous for its
beauty. *12 Cyclads*: the Cyclades, islands that surround the Greek island of
Delos. *13 Argo*: the ship in which Jason sailed in quest of the Golden Fleece.
15 Orpheus: the legendary poet. *17 Ulysses*: the hero of *The Odyssey*. *18
Calypso*: the goddess who fell in love with Ulysses and kept him on Ogygia, her
island. Her name means "the concealer.'

Oh, write no more the tale of Troy,
   If earth Death's scroll must be!   *20*
Nor mix with Laian rage the joy
   Which dawns upon the free:
Although a subtler Sphinx renew
Riddles of death Thebes never knew.

Another Athens shall arise,   *25*
   And to remoter time
Bequeath, like sunset to the skies,
   The splendor of its prime;
And leave, if naught so bright may live,
All earth can take or Heaven can give.   *30*

Saturn and Love their long repose
   Shall burst, more bright and good
Than all who fell, than One who rose,
   Than many unsubdued:
Not gold, not blood, their altar dowers,   *35*
But votive tears and symbol flowers.

Oh, cease! must hate and death return?
   Cease! must men kill and die?
Cease! drain not to its dregs the urn
   Of bitter prophecy.   *40*
The world is weary of the past,
Oh, might it die or rest at last!

*W*hen the Lamp Is Shatter'd

When the lamp is shatter'd
The light in the dust lies dead—
   When the cloud is scatter'd,
The rainbow's glory is shed.

19 *Troy:* i.e., of the Trojan War.   *21 Laian:* a reference to the tragic destinies that befell members of King Laius's house in Thebes. His son Oedipus, who solved the riddle of the Sphinx, unknowingly killed his father and married his mother, Jocasta. These events occurred after the Golden Age, and thus Shelley is voicing a hope that the New Golden Age will continue forever and not be succeeded by disasters. *31 Saturn and Love:* deities of the Golden Age.   *33 all who fell:* the pagan gods who fell at the birth of Christ (see Milton's "On the Morning of Christ's Nativity," page 43). *One who rose:* Jesus, whom Shelley viewed not as the son of God, but as "a sublime human character." *34 many unsubdued:* Shelley remarks that he means "the monstrous objects of the idolatry of China, India, the Antarctic islands, and the native tribes of America."

When the lute is broken,   5
Sweet tones are remember'd not;
When the lips have spoken,
Loved accents are soon forgot.

As music and splendour
Survive not the lamp and the lute,   10
The heart's echoes render
No song when the spirit is mute—
No song but sad dirges,
Like the wind through a ruin'd cell,
Or the mournful surges   15
That ring the dead seaman's knell.

When hearts have once mingled,
Love first leaves the well-built nest;
The weak one is singled
To endure what it once possess'd.   20
O Love! who bewailest
The frailty of all things here,
Why choose you the frailest
For your cradle, your home, and your bier?

Its passions will rock thee   25
As the storms rock the ravens on high;
Bright reason will mock thee
Like the sun from a wintry sky.
From thy nest every rafter
Will rot, and thine eagle home   30
Leave thee naked to laughter,
When leaves fall and cold winds come.

JOHN KEATS
1795-1821

K eats's father kept a stable and died in falling from a horse when
Keats was eight. His mother died of tuberculosis when he was
fourteen. Keats studied medicine in London and qualified as an apothecary
in 1816. The same year he achieved his first major poem, the sonnet "On
First Looking into Chapman's Homer," and soon after came *Sleep and
Poetry*, in which he declared his ambition to match the highest poetic
achievements. From his letters we know Keats worked laboriously for four
years prior to his twentieth birthday, and then he found his key and evolved
astoundingly. In 1817 he wrote *Endymion*, which he judged slipshod and
merely an experiment. He gave up *Hyperion* because he felt himself falling
too much under Milton's magnetism.

In 1818 Keats watched his brother die of pneumonia; from a walking tour he himself contracted a chronically ulcerated throat. Another brother went broke in Kentucky, and Keats found himself trying to support the whole family. He fell in love, but that was doomed too. Mid all this, during nine months of 1819, he wrote all his major work: the six *Odes*, a number of sonnets, "The Eve of St. Agnes," "La Belle Dame sans Merci," and *Lamia*. Then, one night in February, 1820, he coughed up blood and knew, from experience with his brother and his mother, what was fated. He tried to improve his health by moving to Italy but died a year later. His odes and sonnets show how fully his senses apprehended life and how totally he could value and capture experience in the act of living up to his highest technical ideals as a poet.

To Autumn

Season of mists and mellow fruitfulness,
    Close bosom-friends of the maturing sun:
Conspiring with him how to load and bless
    With fruit the vines that round the thatch-eves run;
To bend with apples the mossed cottage-trees,   5
    And fill all fruit with ripeness to the core;
        To swell the gourd, and plump the hazel shells
With a sweet kernel; to set budding more,
    And still more, later flowers for the bees,
    Until they think warm days will never cease,   10
        For Summer has o'er-brimmed their clammy cells.

Who hath not seen thee oft amid thy store?
    Sometimes whoever seeks abroad may find
Thee sitting careless on a granary floor,
    Thy hair soft-lifted by the winnowing wind;   15
Or on a half-reaped furrow sound asleep,
    Drowsed with the fume of poppies, while thy hook
       Spares the next swath and all its twinèd flowers:
And sometimes like a gleaner thou dost keep
    Steady thy laden head across a brook;   20
    Or by a cider-press, with patient look,
        Thou watchest the last oozings hours by hours.

Where are the songs of Spring? Ay, where are they?
    Think not of them, thou hast thy music too,—
While barrèd clouds bloom the soft-dying day,   25
And touch the stubble-plains with rosy hue;

Then in a wailful choir the small gnats mourn
   Among the river sallows, borne aloft
      Or sinking as the light wind lives or dies;
And full-grown lambs loud bleat from hilly bourn;   *30*
   Hedge-crickets sing; and now with treble soft
   The red-breast whistles from a garden-croft;
   And gathering swallows twitter in the skies.

On First Looking into Chapman's Homer

Much have I travelled in the realms of gold,
And many goodly states and kingdoms seen;
Round many western islands have I been
Which bards in fealty to Apollo hold.
Oft of one wide expanse had I been told   *5*
That deep-browed Homer ruled as his demesne;
Yet did I never breathe its pure serene
Till I heard Chapman speak out loud and bold:

Then felt I like some watcher of the skies
When a new planet swims into his ken;   *10*
Or like stout Cortez when with eagle eyes
He stared at the Pacific—and all his men
Looked at each other with a wild surmise—
Silent, upon a peak in Darien.

When I Have Fears

When I have fears that I may cease to be
Before my pen has gleaned my teeming brain,
Before high-pilèd books, in charact'ry,
Hold like rich garners the full-ripened grain;
When I behold, upon the night's starred face,   *5*

On First Looking: *Title:* George Chapman (1559?–1634) was an English poet, dramatist, and translator who translated *The Iliad* (1612) and *The Odyssey* 1614–1615). Keats, who knew no Greek, came to know the grandeur of Homer through Chapman's translations. *11 Cortez:* the Spanish conquistador who conquered Mexico. It was not Cortez but Balboa who discovered the Pacific. *14 Darien:* in the eastern part of Panama.

Huge cloudy symbols of a high romance,
And think that I may never live to trace
Their shadows, with the magic hand of chance;

And when I feel, fair creature of an hour!
That I shall never look upon thee more,   10
Never have relish in the faery power
Of unreflecting love;—then on the shore
Of the wide world I stand alone, and think,
Till Love and Fame to nothingness do sink.

The Eve of St. Agnes

St. Agnes' Eve—Ah, bitter chill it was!
The owl, for all his feathers, was a-cold;
The hare limp'd trembling through the frozen grass,
And silent was the flock in woolly fold:
Numb were the beadsman's fingers, while he told   5
His rosary, and while his frosted breath,
Like pious incense from a censer old,
Seem'd taking flight for heaven, without a death,
Past the sweet Virgin's picture, while his prayer he saith.

His prayer he saith, this patient, holy man;   10
Then takes his lamp, and riseth from his knees,
And back returneth, meager, barefoot, wan,
Along the chapel aisle by slow degrees:
The sculptur'd dead, on each side, seem to freeze,
Emprison'd in black, purgatorial rails: 15
Knights, ladies, praying in dumb orat'ries,
He passeth by; and his weak spirit fails
To think how they may ache in icy hoods and mails.

Northward he turneth through a little door,
And scarce three steps, ere Music's golden tongue   20
Flatter'd to tears this aged man and poor;
But no—already had his deathbed rung:
The joys of all his life were said and sung:
His was harsh penance on St. Agnes' Eve:

The Eve of St. Agnes: 1 St. Agnes' Eve: the night preceding January 21. St.
Agnes was the patron saint of young girls, who could see visions of their future
husbands by performing certain rites.   5–9 told: i.e., he fingered the beads of his
rosary, saying a prayer for each.   16 orat'ries: chapels.

Another way he went, and soon among   25
    Rough ashes sat he for his soul's reprieve,
And all night kept awake, for sinners' sake to grieve.

    That ancient beadsman heard the prelude soft;
    And so it chanc'd, for many a door was wide,
    From hurry to and fro. Soon, up aloft,   30
    The silver, snarling trumpets 'gan to chide:
    The level chambers, ready with their pride,
    Were glowing to receive a thousand guests:
    The carved angels, ever eager-eyed,
    Star'd, where upon their heads the cornice rests,   35
With hair blown back, and wings put cross-wise on their breasts.

    At length burst in the argent revelry,
    With plume, tiara, and all rich array,
    Numerous as shadows haunting fairily
    The brain, new stuff'd, in youth, with triumphs gay   40
    Of old romance. These let us wish away,
    And turn, sole-thoughted, to one lady there,
    Whose heart had brooded, all that wintry day,
    On love, and wing'd St. Agnes' saintly care,
As she had heard old dames full many times declare.   45

    They told her how, upon St. Agnes' Eve,
    Young virgins might have visions of delight,
    And soft adorings from their loves receive
    Upon the honey'd middle of the night,
    If ceremonies due they did aright;   50
    As, supperless to bed they must retire,
    And couch supine their beauties, lily white;
    Nor look behind, nor sideways, but require
Of Heaven with upward eyes for all that they desire.

    Full of this whim was thoughtful Madeline: 55
    The music, yearning like a god in pain,
    She scarcely heard: her maiden eyes divine,
    Fix'd on the floor, saw many a sweeping train
    Pass by—she heeded not at all: in vain
    Came many a tiptoe, amorous cavalier,   60
    And back retir'd; not cool'd by high disdain,
    But she saw not: her heart was otherwhere:
She sigh'd for Agnes' dreams, the sweetest of the year.

    She danc'd along with vague regardless eyes,
    Anxious her lips, her breathing quick and short: 65

The hallow'd hour was near at hand: she sighs
Amid the timbrels, and the throng'd resort
Of whisperers in anger, or in sport;
'Mid looks of love, defiance, hate, and scorn,
Hoodwink'd with faery fancy; all amort,   *70*
Save to St. Agnes and her lambs unshorn,
And all the bliss to be before tomorrow morn.

So, purposing each moment to retire,
She linger'd still. Meantime, across the moors,
Had come young Porphyro, with heart on fire   *75*
For Madeline. Beside the portal doors,
Buttress'd from moonlight, stands he, and implores
All saints to give him sight of Madeline,
But for one moment in the tedious hours,
That he might gaze and worship all unseen;   *80*
Perchance speak, kneel, touch, kiss—in sooth such things
      have been.

He ventures in: let no buzz'd whisper tell:
All eyes be muffled, or a hundred swords
Will storm his heart, Love's fev'rous citadel:
For him, those chambers held barbarian hordes,   *85*
Hyena foemen, and hot-blooded lords,
Whose very dogs would execrations howl
Against his lineage: not one breast affords
Him any mercy, in that mansion foul,
Save one old beldame, weak in body and in soul.   *90*

Ah, happy chance! the aged creature came,
Shuffling along with ivory-headed wand,
To where he stood, hid from the torch's flame,
Behind a broad hall-pillar, far beyond
The sound of merriment and chorus bland: *95*
He startled her; but soon she knew his face,
And grasp'd his fingers in her palsied hand,
Saying, "Mercy, Porphyro! hie thee from this place:
They are all here tonight, the whole blood-thirsty race!

"Get hence! get hence! there's dwarfish Hildebrand;   *100*
He had a fever late, and in the fit
He cursed thee and thine, both house and land:
Then there's that old Lord Maurice, not a whit

---

70 amort: dead.   *71 unshorn:* On the anniversary of the martyrdom of St. Agnes, two lambs were blessed, then shorn, and the wool was woven into cloth by nuns. *86 foemen:* enemies.   *90 beldame:* old woman.

More tame for his gray hairs—Alas me! flit!
Flit like a ghost away."—"Ah, gossip dear,
We're safe enough; here in this armchair sit,
And tell me how"—"Good Saints! not here, not here;
Follow me, child, or else these stones will be thy bier."

He follow'd through a lowly arched way,
Brushing the cobwebs with his lofty plume,
And as she mutter'd "Well-a—well-a-day!"
He found him in a little moonlight room,
Pale, lattic'd, chill, and silent as a tomb.
"Now tell me where is Madeline," said he,
"O tell me, Angela, by the holy loom
Which none but secret sisterhood may see,
When they St. Agnes' wool are weaving piously."

"St. Agnes! Ah! it is St. Agnes' Eve—
Yet men will murder upon holy days:
Thou must hold water in a witch's sieve,
And be liege-lord of all the elves and fays,
To venture so: it fills me with amaze
To see thee, Porphyro!—St. Agnes' Eve!
God's help! my lady fair the conjuror plays
This very night: good angels her deceive!
But let me laugh awhile, I've mickle time to grieve."

Feebly she laugheth in the languid moon,
While Porphyro upon her face doth look,
Like puzzled urchin on an aged crone
Who keepeth clos'd a wond'rous riddle-book,
As spectacled she sits in chimney nook.
But soon his eyes grew brilliant, when she told
His lady's purpose; and he scarce could brook
Tears, at the thought of those enchantments cold,
And Madeline asleep in lap of legends old.

Sudden a thought came like a full-blown rose,
Flushing his brow, and in his pained heart
Made purple riot: then doth he propose
A stratagem, that makes the beldame start:
"A cruel man and impious thou art:
Sweet lady, let her pray, and sleep, and dream
Alone with her good angels, far apart
From wicked men like thee. Go, go!—I deem
Thou canst not surely be the same that thou didst seem."

105

110

115

120

125

130

135

140

126 *mickle:* much.

"I will not harm her, by all saints I swear," 145
Quoth Porphyro: "O may I ne'er find grace
When my weak voice shall whisper its last prayer,
If one of her soft ringlets I displace,
Or look with ruffian passion in her face:
Good Angela, believe me by these tears; 150
Or I will, even in a moment's space,
Awake, with horrid shout, my foemen's ears,
And beard them, though they may be more fang'd than wolves
    and bears."

"Ah! why wilt thou affright a feeble soul?
A poor, weak palsy-stricken, churchyard thing, 155
Whose passing-bell may ere the midnight toll;
Whose prayers for thee, each morn and evening,
Were never miss'd."—Thus plaining, doth she bring
A gentler speech from burning Porphyro;
So woful, and of such deep sorrowing, 160
That Angela gives promise she will do
Whatever he shall wish, betide her weal or woe.

Which was, to lead him, in close secrecy.
Even to Madeline's chamber, and there hide
Him in a closet, of such privacy 165
That he might see her beauty unespied,
And win perhaps that night a peerless bride,
While legion'd fairies pac'd the coverlet,
And pale enchantment held her sleepy-eyed.
Never on such a night have lovers met, 170
Since Merlin paid his demon all the monstrous debt.

"It shall be as thou wishest," said the dame:
"All cates and dainties shall be stored there
Quickly on this feast-night: by the tambour frame
Her own lute thou wilt see: no time to spare, 175
For I am slow and feeble, and scarce dare
On such a catering trust my dizzy head.
Wait here, my child, with patience; kneel in prayer
The while. Ah! thou must needs the lady wed,
Or may I never leave my grave among the dead." 180

So saying, she hobbled off with busy fear.
The lover's endless minutes slowly pass'd;

---

153 *beard*: confront. 162 *betide* . . .: if good or evil befall her. 171: Merlin,
magician of King Arthur's court, was the son of a demon; he was destroyed by
Vivien, who used the spells that he had taught to her because he was infatuated.
173 *cates*: delicacies. 174 *tambour frame*: an embroidery frame.

The dame return'd, and whisper'd in his ear
To follow her; with aged eyes aghast
From fright of dim espial. Safe at last,   185
Through many a dusky gallery, they gain
The maiden's chamber, silken, hush'd, and chaste;
Where Porphyro took covert, pleas'd amain.
His poor guide hurried back with agues in her brain.

Her falt'ring hand upon the balustrade,   190
Old Angela was feeling for the stair,
When Madeline, St. Agnes' charmed maid,
Rose, like a mission'd spirit, unaware:
With silver taper's light, and pious care,
She turn'd, and down the aged gossip led   195
To a safe level matting. Now prepare,
Young Porphyro, for gazing on that bed;
She comes, she comes again, like ringdove fray'd and fled.

Out went the taper as she hurried in;
Its little smoke, in pallid moonshine, died: 200
She clos'd the door, she panted, all akin
To spirits of the air, and visions wide:
No uttered syllable, or, woe betide!
But to her heart, her heart was voluble,
Paining with eloquence her balmy side;   205
As though a tongueless nightingale should swell
Her throat in vain, and die, heart-stifled, in her dell.

A casement high and triple-arch'd there was,
All garlanded with carven imag'ries
Of fruits, and flowers, and bunches of knot-grass,   210
And diamonded with panes of quaint device,
Innumerable of stains and splendid dyes,
As are the tiger-moth's deep-damask'd wings;
And in the midst, 'mid thousand heraldries,
And twilight saints, and dim emblazonings,   215
A shielded scutcheon blush'd with blood of queens and kings.

Full on this casement shone the wintry moon,
And threw warm gules on Madeline's fair breast,
As down she knelt for heaven's grace and boon;
Rose-bloom fell on her hands, together prest,   220
And on her silver cross soft amethyst,
And on her hair a glory, like a saint:

188 *amain:* exceedingly. 198 *fray'd:* frightened. Doves proverbially are timid.
218 *gules:* rays of blood-red color (a heraldic term).

She seem'd a splendid angel, newly drest,
Save wings, for heaven:—Porphyro grew faint:
She knelt, so pure a thing, so free from mortal taint.   225

Anon his heart revives: her vespers done,
Of all its wreathed pearls her hair she frees;
Unclasps her warmed jewels one by one;
Loosens her fragrant bodice; by degrees
Her rich attire creeps rustling to her knees: 230
Half-hidden, like a mermaid in sea-weed,
Pensive awhile she dreams awake, and sees
In fancy, fair St. Agnes in her bed,
But dares not look behind, or all the charm is fled.

Soon, trembling in her soft and chilly nest,   235
In sort of wakeful swoon, perplex'd she lay,
Until the poppied warmth of sleep oppress'd
Her soothed limbs, and soul fatigued away;
Flown, like a thought, until the morrow-day;
Blissfully haven'd both from joy and pain;   240
Clasp'd like a missal where swart Paynims pray;
Blinded alike from sunshine and from rain,
As though a rose should shut, and be a bud again.

Stol'n to this paradise, and so entranced,
Porphyro gazed upon her empty dress,   245
And listen'd to her breathing, if it chanced
To wake into a slumbrous tenderness;
Which when he heard, that minute did he bless,
And breath'd himself: then from the closet crept,
Noiseless as fear in a wide wilderness,   250
And over the hush'd carpet, silent, stept,
And 'tween the curtain peep'd, where, lo!—how fast she slept.

Then by the bed-side, where the faded moon
Made a dim, silver twilight, soft he set
A table, and, half anguish'd, threw thereon   255
A cloth of woven crimson, gold, and jet:—
O for some drowsy Morphean amulet!
The boisterous, midnight, festive clarion,
The kettle-drum, and far-heard clarinet,
Affray his ears, though but in dying tone:—   260
The hall door shuts again, and all the noise is gone.

241 *missal:* Christian prayer book, which would remain closed among pagans.

And still she slept an azure-lidded sleep,
In blanched linen, smooth, and lavender'd,
While he from forth the closet brought a heap
Of candied apple, quince, and plum, and gourd;   265
With jellies soother than the creamy curd,
And lucent syrups, tinct with cinnamon;
Manna and dates, in argosy transferr'd
From Fez; and spiced dainties, every one,
From silken Samarcand to cedar'd Lebanon.   270

These delicacies he heap'd with glowing hand
On golden dishes and in baskets bright
Of wreathed silver: sumptuous they stand
In the retired quiet of the night,
Filling the chilly room with perfume light.—   275
"And now, my love, my seraph fair, awake!
Thou art my heaven, and I thine eremite:
Open thine eyes, for meek St. Agnes' sake,
Or I shall drowse beside thee, so my soul doth ache."

Thus whispering, his warm, unnerved arm   280
Sank in her pillow. Shaded was her dream
By the dusk curtains:—'twas a midnight charm
Impossible to melt as iced stream:
The lustrous salvers in the moonlight gleam;
Broad golden fringe upon the carpet lies: 285
It seem'd he never, never could redeem
From such a steadfast spell his lady's eyes;
So mus'd awhile, entoil'd in woofed phantasies.

Awakening up, he took her hollow lute,—
Tumultuous,—and, in chords that tenderest be,   290
He play'd an ancient ditty, long since mute,
In Provence call'd, "La belle dame sans mercy:"
Close to her ear touching the melody;—
Wherewith disturb'd, she utter'd a soft moan:
He ceased—she panted quick—and suddenly   295
Her blue affrayed eyes wide open shone:
Upon his knees he sank, pale as smooth-sculptured stone.

Her eyes were open, but she still beheld,
Now wide awake, the vision of her sleep:
There was a painful change, that nigh expell'd   300

266 *soother:* softer, smoother.   277 *eremite:* hermite; here, simply one dedicated
to worship.   288 *woofed:* woven.   292 *"La belle . . .":* See page 180.

The blisses of her dream so pure and deep
At which fair Madeline began to weep,
And moan forth witless words with many a sigh;
While still her gaze on Porphyro would keep;
Who knelt, with joined hands and piteous eye,   305
Fearing to move or speak, she look'd so dreamingly.

"Ah, Porphyro!" said she, "but even now
Thy voice was at sweet tremble in mine ear,
Made tuneable with every sweetest vow;
And those sad eyes were spiritual and clear: 310
How chang'd thou art! how pallid, chill, and drear!
Give me that voice again, my Porphyro,
Those looks immortal, those complainings dear!
Oh leave me not in this eternal woe,
For if thou diest, my love, I know not where to go."   315

Beyond a mortal man impassion'd far
At these voluptuous accents, he arose,
Ethereal, flush'd, and like a throbbing star
Seen mid the sapphire heaven's deep repose;
Into her dream he melted, as the rose   320
Blendeth its odor with the violet,—
Solution sweet: meantime the frostwind blows
Like Love's alarum pattering the sharp sleet
Against the window-panes; St. Agnes' moon hath set.

'Tis dark: quick pattereth the flaw-blown sleet: 325
"This is no dream, my bride, my Madeline!"
'Tis dark: the iced gusts still rave and beat:
"No dream, alas! alas! and woe is mine!
Porphyro will leave me here to fade and pine.—
Cruel! what traitor could thee hither bring?   330
I curse not, for my heart is lost in thine,
Though thou forsakest a deceived thing;—
A dove forlorn and lost with sick unpruned wing."

"My Madeline! sweet dreamer! lovely bride!
Say, may I be for aye thy vassal blest?   335
Thy beauty's shield, heart-shap'd and vermeil-dyed?
Ah, silver shrine, here will I take my rest
After so many hours of toil and quest,
A famish'd pilgrim,—sav'd by miracle.
Though I have found, I will not rob thy nest   340
Saving of thy sweet self; if thou think'st well
To trust, fair Madeline, to no rude infidel.

"Hark! 'tis an elfin-storm from faery land,
Of haggard seeming, but a boon indeed:
Arise—arise! the morning is at hand;—   345
The bloated wassaillers will never heed:—
Let us away, my love, with happy speed;
There are no ears to hear, or eyes to see,—
Drown'd all in Rhenish and the sleepy mead:
Awake! arise! my love, and fearless be,   350
For o'er the southern moors I have a home for thee."

She hurried at his words, beset with fears,
For there were sleeping dragons all around,
At glaring watch, perhaps, with ready spears—
Down the wide stairs a darkling way they found.—   355
In all the house was heard no human sound.
A chain-droop'd lamp was flickering by each door;
The arras, rich with horseman, hawk, and hound,
Flutter'd in the besieging wind's uproar;
And the long carpets rose along the gusty floor.   360

They glide, like phantoms, into the wide hall;
Like phantoms, to the iron porch, they glide;
Where lay the porter in uneasy sprawl,
With a huge empty flagon by his side:
The wakeful bloodhound rose, and shook his hide,   365
But his sagacious eye an inmate owns:
By one and one, the bolts full easy slide:—
The chains lie silent on the footworn stones;—
The key turns, and the door upon its hinges groans.

And they are gone: aye, ages long ago   370
These lovers fled away into the storm.
That night the Baron dreamt of many a woe,
And all his warrior-guests, with shade and form
Of witch, and demon, and large coffin-worm,
Were long be-nightmar'd. Angela the old   375
Died palsy-twitch'd, with meager face deform;
The beadsman after thousand aves told,
For aye unsought-for slept among his ashes cold.

349 *Rhenish:* Rhine Wine. *mead:* a highly intoxicating brew made of honey.
366: The bloodhound recognizes Madeline as one of the household and does not
bark.

La Belle Dame sans Merci

O what can ail thee, knight-at-arms,
    Alone and palely loitering?
The sedge has withered from the lake,
    And no birds sing.

O what can ail thee, knight-at-arms,   5
    So haggard and so woe-begone?
The squirrel's granary is full,
    And the harvest's done.

I see a lily on thy brow
    With anguish moist and fever dew,   10
And on thy cheek a fading rose
    Fast withereth too.

I met a lady in the meads,
    Full beautiful—a faery's child:
Her hair was long, her foot was light,   15
    And her eyes were wild.

I made a garland for her head,
    And bracelets too, and fragrant zone;
She looked at me as she did love,
    And made sweet moan.   20

I set her on my pacing steed,
    And nothing else saw all day long,
For sidelong would she bend, and sing
    A faery's song.

She found me roots of relish sweet,   25
    And honey wild, and manna dew,
And sure in language strange she said—
    "I love thee true!"

She took me to her elfin grot,
    And there she wept and sighed full sore,   30
And there I shut her wild wild eyes
    With kisses four.

La Belle Dame: Title: "The Beautiful Lady without Pity," a poem by Alain Chartier (1385?–1433?), court poet of Charles II of France. *29 grot:* grotto.

And there she lullèd me asleep,
   And there I dreamed—ah! woe betide!
The latest dream I ever dreamed   35
   On the cold hill's side.

I saw pale kings and princes too,
   Pale warriors, death-pale were they all;
They cried—"La Belle Dame sans Merci
   Hath thee in thrall!"   40

I saw their starved lips in the gloam,
   With horrid warning gapèd wide,
And I awoke and found me here,
   On the cold hill's side.

And this is why I sojourn here,   45
   Alone and palely loitering,
Though the sedge is withered from the lake
   And no birds sing.

Ode on Melancholy

No, no, go not to Lethe, neither twist
   Wolfs-bane, tight-rooted, for its poisonous wine;
Nor suffer thy pale forehead to be kiss'd
   By nightshade, ruby grape of Proserpine;
Make not your rosary of yew-berries,   5
   Nor let the beetle, nor the death-moth be
     Your mournful Psyche, nor the downy owl
A partner in your sorrow's mysteries;
   For shade to shade will come too drowsily,
     And drown the wakeful anguish of the soul.   10

But when the melancholy fit shall fall
   Sudden from heaven like a weeping cloud,
That fosters the droop-headed flowers all,
   And hides the green hill in an April shroud;
Then glut thy sorrow on a morning rose,   15

Ode on Melancholy: *1 Lethe:* a river in the underworld; its waters brought oblivion. *4 Proserpine:* Queen of Hades; here used to symbolize the world of death. Wolf's-bane (monkshood), nightshade, and yew-berries are all poisonous. *7 Psyche:* the soul, conventionally symbolized as a butterfly.

Or on the rainbow of the salt sand-wave,
 Or on the wealth of the globèd peonies;
Or if thy mistress some rich anger shows,
 Emprison her soft hand, and let her rave,
  And feed deep, deep upon her peerless eyes.   *20*

She dwells with Beauty—Beauty that must die;
 And Joy, whose hand is ever at his lips
Bidding adieu; and aching Pleasure nigh,
 Turning to poison while the bee-mouth sips:
Ay, in the very temple of Delight   *25*
 Veil'd Melancholy has her sovereign shrine,
  Though seen of none save him whose strenuous tongue
Can burst Joy's grape against his palate fine;
His soul shall taste the sadness of her might,
 And be among her cloudy trophies hung.   *30*

*O*de to a Nightingale

My heart aches, and a drowsy numbness pains
 My sense, as though of hemlock I had drunk,
Or emptied some dull opiate to the drains
 One minute past, and Lethe-wards had sunk:
'Tis not through envy of thy happy lot,   *5*
 But being too happy in thine happiness—
  That thou, light wingèd Dryad of the trees,
   In some melodious plot
 Of beechen green, and shadows numberless,
  Singest of summer in full-throated ease.   *10*

O for a draught of vintage! that hath been
 Cooled a long age in the deep delvèd earth,
Tasting of Flora and the country green,
 Dance, and Provençal song, and sunburnt mirth!
O for a beaker full of the warm South,   *15*
 Full of the true, the blushful Hippocrene,
  With beaded bubbles winking at the brim,
   And purple-stainèd mouth;
 That I might drink, and leave the world unseen,
  And with thee fade away into the forest dim: *20*

Ode to a Nightingale: 4 *Lethe-wards:* to the forgetfulness of death. 7 *Dryad:*
a wood-nymph. *16 Hippocrene:* a fountain of the Muses on Mt. Helicon.

Fade away, dissolve, and quite forget
　　What thou among the leaves hast never known,
The weariness, the fever, and the fret
　　Here, where men sit and hear each other groan;
Where palsy shakes a few, sad, last gray hairs, 　　　　　25
　　Where youth grows pale, and specter-thin, and dies;
　　　　Where but to think is to be full of sorrow
　　　　　　And leaden-eyed despairs,
　　Where Beauty cannot keep her lustrous eyes,
　　Or new Love pine at them beyond to-morrow. 　　　　30

Away! away! for I will fly to thee,
　　Not charioted by Bacchus and his pards,
But on the viewless wings of Poesy,
　　Though the dull brain perplexes and retards:
Already with thee! tender is the night, 　　　　　　　35
　　And haply the Queen-Moon is on her throne,
　　　　Clustered around by all her starry Fays;
　　　　　　But here there is no light,
　　Save what from heaven is with the breezes blown
　　　　Through verdurous glooms and winding mossy ways. 　40

I cannot see what flowers are at my feet,
　　Nor what soft incense hangs upon the boughs,
But, in embalmèd darkness, guess each sweet
　　Wherewith the seasonable month endows
The grass, the thicket, and the fruit-tree wild; 　　　　45
　　White hawthorn, and the pastoral eglantine;
　　　　Fast-fading violets covered up in leaves;
　　　　　　And mid-May's eldest child,
　　The coming musk-rose, full of dewy wine,
　　　　The murmurous haunt of flies on summer eves. 　　50

Darkling I listen; and for many a time
　　I have been half in love with easeful Death,
Called him soft names in many a musèd rhyme,
　　To take into the air my quiet breath;
Now more than ever seems it rich to die, 　　　　　　55
　　To cease upon the midnight with no pain,
　　　　While thou art pouring forth thy soul abroad
　　　　　　In such an ecstasy!
　　Still wouldst thou sing, and I have ears in vain—
　　　　To thy high requiem become a sod. 　　　　　60

32 *Bacchus:* the god of wine. *pards:* leopards; they attended Bacchus. 37 *Fays:*
fairies.

Thou wast not born for death, immortal Bird!
  No hungry generations tread thee down;
The voice I hear this passing night was heard
  In ancient days by emperor and clown:
Perhaps the self-same song that found a path 65
    Through the sad heart of Ruth, when, sick for home,
      She stood in tears amid the alien corn;
        The same that oft-times hath
    Charmed magic casements, opening on the foam
      Of perilous seas, in faery lands forlorn. 70

Forlorn! the very word is like a bell
  To toll me back from thee to my sole self!
Adieu! the fancy cannot cheat so well
  As she is famed to do, deceiving elf.
Adieu! adieu! thy plaintive anthem fades 75
    Past the near meadows, over the still stream,
      Up the hill-side; and now 'tis buried deep
        In the next valley-glades:
    Was it a vision, or a waking dream?
      Fled is that music:—Do I wake or sleep? 80

Ode on a Grecian Urn

Thou still unravished bride of quietness,
  Thou foster-child of silence and slow time,
Sylvan historian, who canst thus express
  A flowery tale more sweetly than our rhyme:
What leaf-fringed legend haunts about thy shape 5
    Of deities or mortals, or of both,
      In Tempe or the dales of Arcady?
What men or gods are these? What maidens loth?
    What mad pursuit? What struggle to escape?
      What pipes and timbrels? What wild ecstasy? 10

Heard melodies are sweet, but those unheard
  Are sweeter; therefore, ye soft pipes, play on;
Not to the sensual ear, but, more endeared,
  Pipe to the spirit ditties of no tone:

Ode on a Grecian Urn: *3 Sylvan historian:* recorder of sylvan events or scenes.
7 Tempe: the Vale of Tempe in Thessaly. *Arcady:* a mountainous region in
Greece, associated with the notion of simple people leading a happy rural life.

Fair youth, beneath the trees, thou canst not leave   *15*
 Thy song, nor ever can those trees be bare;
  Bold Lover, never never canst thou kiss,
Though winning near the goal—yet, do not grieve;
 She cannot fade, though thou hast not thy bliss,
  For ever wilt thou love, and she be fair!   *20*

Ah, happy, happy boughs! that cannot shed
 Your leaves, nor ever bid the Spring adieu;
And, happy melodist unwearièd,
 For ever piping songs for ever new;
More happy love! more happy, happy love!   *25*
 For ever warm and still to be enjoyed,
  For ever panting, and for ever young;
All breathing human passion far above,
 That leaves a heart high-sorrowful and cloyed,
  A burning forehead, and a parching tongue.   *30*

Who are these coming to the sacrifice?
 To what green altar, O mysterious priest,
Lead'st thou that heifer lowing at the skies,
 And all her silken flanks with garlands dressed?
What little town by river or sea shore,   *35*
 Or mountain-built with peaceful citadel,
  Is emptied of its folk, this pious morn?
And, little town, thy streets for evermore
 Will silent be; and not a soul, to tell
  Why thou art desolate, can e'er return.   *40*

O Attic shape! Fair attitude! with brede
 Of marble men and maidens overwrought,
With forest branches and the trodden weed;
 Thou, silent form, dost tease us out of thought
As doth eternity: Cold Pastoral!   *45*
 When old age shall this generation waste,
  Thou shalt remain, in midst of other woe
Than ours, a friend to man, to whom thou say'st,
 "Beauty is truth, truth beauty,"—that is all
  Ye know on earth, and all ye need to know.   *50*

41 Attic: native of Athens or Attica.   *brede:* braid or embroidery.

Bright Star!

Bright star! would I were steadfast as thou art—
Not in lone splendour hung aloft the night,
And watching, with eternal lids apart,
Like Nature's patient sleepless Eremite,
The moving waters at their priestlike task   5
Of pure ablution round earth's human shores,
Or gazing on the new soft-fallen mask
Of snow upon the mountains and the moors—

No—yet still steadfast, still unchangeable,
Pillowed upon my fair love's ripening breast,   10
To feel for ever its soft fall and swell,
Awake for ever in a sweet unrest,
Still, still to hear her tender-taken breath,
And so live ever—or else swoon to death.

Bright Star: 4 *Eremite:* hermit.

ALFRED
LORD TENNYSON
1809–1892

Tennyson was a gentle, unhappy man from a disordered home when a group of gifted Cambridge undergraduates—"The Apostles" urged him to devote his life to poetry. He was not born with "the finest ear . . . of any English poet." He had to learn metrics, and he worked hard. His first volumes (1830 and 1832) were scoffed, but by 1842 he was writing fine poetry highly acceptable to his time. Living in poverty too unremitting even to marry, he slowly forged *In Memoriam*, an elegy to his closest "Apostle" friend, Arthur Hallam, who died in 1833. When *In Memoriam* was published in 1850, Tennyson became poet laureate (following Wordsworth), and he was able to marry.

In Memoriam is more than a statement of grief. It examines the entire process of reconciliation to death and life and all the leading pertinent ideas of the time in religion, philosophy, and the evolutionary sciences of geology and biology. Tennyson wrote many occasional poems as laureate, even propagandizing about issues, as in *The Charge of the Light Brigade*. His fascination with legend and tradition produced the ambitious *Idylls of the King* (1859–1888). Primarily a poet of the countryside, he nevertheless joined that company of great "modern" poets from Wordsworth to Pound who seriously attempted to match the ancient crafts of poetry to the human needs of the industrial urban age.

Some have argued that success was fatal for Tennyson. Certainly his reputation—as well as the scope of his work—became so huge that reaction blotted out his stature for over half a century after his death.

Morte d'Arthur

So all day long the noise of battle roll'd
Among the mountains by the winter sea;
Until King Arthur's table, man by man,
Had fall'n in Lyonnesse about their Lord,
King Arthur: then, because his wound was deep,   5
The bold Sir Bedivere uplifted him,
Sir Bedivere, the last of all his knights,
And bore him to a chapel nigh the field,
A broken chancel with a broken cross,
That stood on a dark strait of barren land.   10
On one side lay the Ocean, and on one
Lay a great water, and the moon was full.
        Then spake King Arthur to Sir Bedivere:
'The sequel of to-day unsolders all
The goodliest fellowship of famous knights   15
Whereof this world holds record. Such a sleep
They sleep—the men I loved. I think that we
Shall never more, at any future time,
Delight our souls with talk of knightly deeds,
Walking about the gardens and the halls   20
Of Camelot, as in the days that were.
I perish by this people which I made—
Tho' Merlin sware that I should come again
To rule once more—but let what will be, be,
I am so deeply smitten thro' the helm   25

Morte d'Arthur: *Title:* "The Death of Arthur." In King Arthur's absence his son Mordred usurped his kingdom; they fought when he returned. In the battle Arthur killed Mordred and was himself fatally wounded. *4 Lyonnesse:* supposedly in Cornwall. *21 Camelot:* capital of Arthur's kingdom. *23 Merlin:* the magician of Arthur's court.

That without help I cannot last till morn.
Thou therefore take my brand Excalibur,
Which was my pride: for thou rememberest how
In those old days, one summer noon, an arm
Rose up from out the bosom of the lake, 30
Clothed in white samite, mystic, wonderful,
Holding the sword—and how I row'd across
And took it, and have worn it, like a king:
And, wheresoever I am sung or told
In aftertime, this also shall be known: 35
But now delay not: take Excalibur,
And fling him far into the middle mere:
Watch what thou seest, and lightly bring me word!
    To him replied the bold Sir Bedivere:
'It is not meet, Sir King, to leave thee thus, 40
Aidless, alone, and smitten thro' the helm.
A little thing may harm a wounded man.
Yet I thy hest will all perform at full,
Watch what I see, and lightly bring thee word.'
    So saying, from the ruin'd shrine he stept 45
And in the moon athwart the place of tombs,
Where lay the mighty bones of ancient men,
Old knights, and over them the sea-wind sang
Shrill, chill, with flakes of foam. He, stepping down
By zig-zag paths, and juts of pointed rock, 50
Came on the shining levels of the lake.
    There drew he forth the brand Excalibur,
And o'er him, drawing it, the winter moon,
Brightening the skirts of a long cloud, ran forth
And sparkled keen with frost against the hilt: 55
For all the haft twinkled with diamond sparks,
Myriads of topaz-lights, and jacinth-work
Of subtlest jewellery. He gazed so long
That both his eyes were dazzled, as he stood,
This way and that dividing the swift mind, 60
In act to throw: but at the last it seem'd
Better to leave Excalibur conceal'd
There in the many-knotted waterflags,
That whistled stiff and dry about the marge.
So strode he back slow to the wounded King. 65
    Then spake King Arthur to Sir Bedivere:
'Hast thou perform'd my mission which I gave?
What is it thou hast seen? or what host heard?'

27 *brand Excalibur:* King Arthur's sword, which was called "Excalibur." 31
samite: a heavy silk fabric. 37 *middle mere:* in the middle of the lake. 43 *hest:*
command. 63 *waterflags:* water iris. 64 *marge:* edge of the lake.

And answer made the bold Sir Bedivere:
'I heard the ripple washing in the reeds,   70
And the wild water lapping on the crag.'
    To whom replied King Arthur, faint and pale:
'Thou hast betray'd thy nature and thy name,
Not rendering true answer, as beseem'd
Thy fealty, nor like a noble knight: 75
For surer sign had follow'd, either hand,
Or voice, or else a motion of the mere.
This is a shameful thing for men to lie.
Yet now, I charge thee, quickly do again
As thou art lief and dear, and do the thing   80
I bade thee, watch, and lightly bring me word.'
    Then went Sir Bedivere the second time
Across the ridge, and paced beside the mere,
Counting the dewy pebbles, fix'd in thought;
But when he saw the wonder of the hilt,   85
How curiously and strangely chased, he smote
His palms together, and he cried aloud,
        'And if indeed I cast the brand away,
Surely a precious thing, one worthy note,
Should thus be lost for ever from the earth,   90
Which might have pleased the eyes of many men.
What good should follow this, if this were done?
What harm, undone? deep harm to disobey,
Seeing obedience is the bond of rule.
Were it well to obey, then, if a king demand   95
An act unprofitable, against himself?
The King is sick, and knows not what he does.
What record, or what relic of my lord
Should be to aftertime, but empty breath
And rumours of a doubt? but were this kept,   100
Stored in some treasure-house of mighty kings,
Some one might show it at a joust of arms,
Saying, "King Arthur's sword, Excalibur,
Wrought by the lonely maiden of the Lake.
Nine years she wrought it, sitting in the deeps   105
Upon the hidden bases of the hills."
So might some old man speak in the aftertime
To all the people, winning reverence.
But now much honour and much fame were lost.'
        So spake he, clouded with his own conceit,   110
And hid Excalibur the second time,
And so strode back slow to the wounded King.

---

80 *lief:* beloved. 86 *smote:* struck. 104 *lonely maiden:* the Lady of the Lake,
who made Excalibur and gave it to Arthur.

Then spoke King Arthur, breathing heavily:
'What is it thou has seen? or what hast heard?'
    And answer made the bold Sir Bedivere: *115*
'I heard the water lapping on the crag,
And the long ripple washing in the reeds.'
    To whom replied King Arthur, much in wrath:
'Ah, miserable and unkind, untrue,
Unknightly, traitor-hearted! Woe is me!   *120*
Authority forgets a dying king,
Laid widow'd of the power in his eye
That bow'd the will. I see thee what thou art,
For thou, the latest-left of all my knights,
In whom should meet the offices of all,   *125*
Thou wouldst betray me for the precious hilt;
Either from lust of gold, or like a girl
Valuing the giddy pleasure of the eyes.
Yet, for a man may fail in duty twice,
And the third time may prosper, get thee hence: *130*
But, if thou spare to fling Excalibur,
I will arise and slay thee with my hands.'
    Then quickly rose Sir Bedivere, and ran,
And, leaping down the ridges lightly, plunged
Among the bulrush-beds, and clutch'd the sword,   *135*
And strongly wheel'd and threw it. The great brand
Made lightnings in the splendour of the moon,
And flashing round and round, and whirl'd in an arch,
Shot like a streamer of the northern morn,
Seen where the moving isles of winter shock   *140*
By night, with noises of the northern sea.
So flash'd and fell the brand Excalibur:
But ere he dipt the surface, rose an arm
Clothed in white samite, mystic, wonderful,
And caught him by the hilt, and brandish'd him   *145*
Three times, and drew him under in the mere.
And lightly went the other to the King.
    Then spoke King Arthur, drawing thicker breath:
'Now see I by thine eyes that this is done.
Speak out: what is it thou hast heard, or seen?'   *150*
    And answer made the bold Sir Bedivere:
'Sir King, I closed mine eyelids, lest the gems
Should blind my purpose, for I never saw,
Nor shall see, here or elsewhere, till I die,
Not tho' I live three lives of mortal men,   *155*
So great a miracle as yonder hilt.

---

124 *latest-left:* only survivor.   143 *he:* In imitation of an archaic style, Tennyson here uses "he" and "him" for "it"; the pronouns refer to the sword.

Then with both hands I flung him, wheeling him;
But when I look'd again, behold an arm,
Clothed in white samite, mystic, wonderful,
That caught him by the hilt, and brandish'd him   160
Three times, and drew him under in the mere.'
      And answer made King Arthur, breathing hard:
'My end draws nigh; 'tis time that I were gone.
Make broad thy shoulders to receive my weight,
And bear me to the margin; yet I fear   165
My wound hath taken cold, and I shall die.'
      So saying, from the pavement he half rose,
Slowly, with pain, reclining on his arm,
And looking wistfully with wide blue eyes
As in a picture. Him Sir Bedivere   170
Remorsefully regarded thro' his tears,
And would have spoken, but he found not words,
Then took with care, and kneeling on one knee,
Oe'r both his shoulders drew the languid hands,
And rising bore him thro' the place of tombs.   175
      But as he walk'd, King Arthur panted hard
Like one that feels a nightmare on his bed
When all the house is mute. So sigh'd the King,
Muttering and murmuring at his ear, 'Quick, quick!
I fear it is too late, and I shall die.'   180
But the other swiftly strode from ridge to ridge,
Clothed with his breath, and looking, as he walk'd
Larger than human on the frozen hills.
He heard the deep behind him, and a cry
Before. His own thought drove him, like a goad.   185
Dry clash'd his harness in the icy caves
And barren chasms, and all to left and right
The bare black cliff clang'd round him, as he based
His feet on juts of slippery crag that rang
Sharp-smitten with the dint of armed heels—   190
And on a sudden, lo! the level lake,
And the long glories of the winter moon.
      Then saw they how there hove a dusky barge,
Dark as a funeral scarf from stem to stern,
Beneath them; and descending they were ware   195
That all the decks were dense with stately forms
Black-stoled, black-hooded, like a dream—by these
Three Queens with crowns of gold—and from them rose
A cry that shiver'd to the tingling stars,
And, as it were one voice, an agony   200

165 *margin:* the edge of the lake.   193 *hove:* floated.

Of lamentation, like a wind, that shrills
All night in a waste, where no one comes,
Or hath come, since the making of the world.

    Then murmur'd Arthur, 'Place me in the barge,'
And to the barge they came. There those three Queens   *205*
Put forth their hands, and took the King, and wept.
But she, that rose the tallest of them all
And fairest, laid his head upon her lap,
And loosed the shatter'd casque, and chafed his hands,
And call'd him by his name, complaining loud,   *210*
And dropping bitter tears against his brow
Striped with dark blood: for all his face was white
And colourless, and like the wither'd moon
Smote by the fresh beam of the springing east;
And all his greaves and cuisses dash'd with drops   *215*
Of onset; and the light and lustrous curls—
That made his forehead like a rising sun
High from the dais-throne—were parch'd with dust;
Or, clotted into points and hanging loose,
Mix'd with the knightly growth that fringed his lips.   *220*
So like a shatter'd column lay the King;
Not like that Arthur who, with lance in rest,
From spur to plume a star of tournament,
Shot thro' the lists at Camelot, and charged
Before the eyes of ladies and of kings.   *225*

    Then loudly cried the bold Sir Bedivere,
'Ah! my Lord Arthur, whither shall I go?
Where shall I hide my forehead and my eyes?
For now I see the true old times are dead,
When every morning brought a noble chance,   *230*
And every chance brought out a noble knight.
Such times have been not since the light that led
The holy Elders with the gift of myrrh.
But now the whole ROUND TABLE is dissolved
Which was an image of the mighty world;   *235*
And I, the last, go forth companionless,
And the days darken round me, and the years,
Among new men, strange faces, other minds.'

    And slowly answered Arthur from the barge:
'The old order changeth, yielding place to new,   *240*
And God fulfils Himself in many ways,
Lest one good custom should corrupt the world.

---

209 casque: helmet.   *215–216 greaves:* armor worn below the knee. *cuisses:*
thigh armor. *drops of onset:* sweat or blood of battle.   *224 lists:* tilting field.
232–233: The Star of Bethlehem led the Three Wise Men to the crib of Jesus.

Comfort thyself: what comfort is in me?
I have lived my life, and that which I have done
May He within Himself make pure! but thou,   *245*
If thou shouldst never see my face again,
Pray for my soul. More things are wrought by prayer
Than this world dreams of. Wherefore let thy voice
Rise like a fountain for me night and day.
For what are men better than sheep or goats   *250*
That nourish a blind life within the brain,
If, knowing God, they lift not hands of prayer
Both for themselves and those who call them friend?
For so the whole round earth is every way
Bound by gold chains about the feet of God.   *255*
But now farewell. I am going a long way
With these thou seest—if indeed I go—
(For all my mind is clouded with doubt)
To the island-valley of Avilion;
Where falls not hail, or rain, or any snow,   *260*
Nor ever wind blows loudly; but it lies
Deep-meadow'd, happy, fair with orchard-lawns
And bowery hollows crown'd with summer sea,
Where I will heal me of my grievous wound.'
      So said he, and the barge with oar and sail   *265*
Move from the brink, like some full-breasted swan
That, fluting a wild carol ere her death,
Ruffles her pure cold plume, and takes the flood
With swarthy webs. Long stood Sir Bedivere
Revolving many memories, till the hull   *270*
Look'd one black dot against the verge of dawn,
And on the mere the wailings died away.

Choric Song

From THE LOTUS-EATERS *

There is sweet music here that softer falls
Than petals from blown roses on the grass,
Or night-dews on still waters between walls

---

249 *Avilion:* Avalon, the Celtic paradise.

* The Lotus-Eaters lived on the coast of Africa near Syrtes; Ulysses came upon their country on his return from Troy. (See *Odyssey* 10. 83–97, where Homer remarks that those who ate the lotus lost all desire to return home.) The speakers here are companions of Ulysses who partook of the "flowery food." The exact nature of this plant remains unknown.

Of shadowy granite, in a gleaming pass;
Music that gentlier on the spirit lies,
Than tired eyelids upon tired eyes;
Music that brings sweet sleep down from the blissful skies.
Here are cool mosses deep
And through the moss the ivies creep,
And in the stream the long-leaved flowers weep,
And from the craggy ledge the poppy hangs in sleep.

Why are we weighed upon with heaviness,
And utterly consumed with sharp distress,
While all things else have rest from weariness?
All things have rest; why should we toil alone,
We only toil, who are the first of things,
And make perpetual moan,
Still from one sorrow to another thrown;
Nor ever fold our wings,
And cease from wanderings,
Nor steep our brows in slumber's holy balm;
Nor harken what the inner spirit sings,
"There is no joy but calm!"—
Why should we only toil, the roof and crown of things?

Lo! in the middle of the wood,
The folded leaf is wooed from out the bud
With winds upon the branch, and there
Grows green and broad, and takes no care,
Sun-steeped at noon, and in the moon
Nightly dew-fed; and turning yellow
Falls, and floats adown the air.
Lo! sweetened with the summer light,
The full-juiced apple, waxing over-mellow,
Drops in a silent autumn night.
All its allotted length of days
The flower ripens in its place,
Ripens and fades, and falls, and hath no toil,
Fast-rooted in the fruitful soil.

Hateful is the dark-blue sky,
Vaulted o'er the dark-blue sea.
Death is the end of life; ah, why
Should life all labour be?
Let us alone. Time driveth onward fast,
And in a little while our lips are dumb.
Let us alone. What is it that will last?

5

10

15

20

25

30

35

40

45

All things are taken from us, and become
Portions and parcels of the dreadful past.
Let us alone. What pleasure can we have
To war with evil? Is there any peace
In ever climbing up the climbing wave?   50
All things have rest, and ripen toward the grave
In silence—ripen, fall, and cease;
Give us long rest or death, dark death, or dreamful ease.

How sweet it were, hearing the downward stream
With half-shut eyes ever to seem   55
Falling asleep in a half-dream!
To dream and dream, like yonder amber light,
Which will not leave the myrrh-bush on the height;
To hear each other's whispered speech;
Eating the Lotos day by day,   60
To watch the crisping ripples on the beach,
And tender curving lines of creamy spray;
To lend our hearts and spirits wholly
To the influence of mild-minded melancholy;
To muse and brood and live again in memory,   65
With those old faces of our infancy
Heaped over with a mound of grass,
Two handfuls of white dust, shut in an urn of brass!

Dear is the memory of our wedded lives,
And dear the last embraces of our wives   70
And their warm tears; but all hath suffered change;
For surely now our household hearths are cold,
Our sons inherit us, our looks are strange,
And we should come like ghosts to trouble joy.
Or else the island princes over-bold   75
Have eat our substance, and the minstrel sings
Before them of the ten years' war in Troy,
And our great deeds, as half-forgotten things.
Is there confusion in the little isle?
Let what is broken so remain.   80
The gods are hard to reconcile;
'Tis hard to settle order once again.
There *is* confusion worse than death,
Trouble on trouble, pain on pain,
Long labour unto aged breath,   85

50 *ever*: always. 77 *ten years' war in Troy*: When the Trojan Paris abducted
Helen from the house of her husband King Menelaus and took her to Troy,
ten years of war ensued between the Greeks and the Trojans; it ended with the
destruction of Troy.

Sore tasks to hearts worn out by many wars
And eyes grown dim with gazing on the pilot-stars.

But, propped on beds of amaranth and moly,
How sweet—while warm airs lull us, blowing lowly—
With half-dropped eyelid still,   90
Beneath a heaven dark and holy;
To watch the long bright river drawing slowly
His waters from the purple hill—
To hear the dewy echoes calling
From cave to cave through the thick-twined vine—   95
To watch the emerald-coloured water falling
Through many a woven acanthus-wreath divine!
Only to hear and see the far-off sparkling brine,
Only to hear were sweet, stretched out beneath the pine.

The Lotos blooms below the barren peak,   100
The Lotos blows by every winding creek;
All day the wind breathes low with mellower tone;
Through every hollow cave and alley lone
Round and round the spicy downs the yellow Lotos-dust is
    blown.
We have had enough of action, and of motion we,   105
Rolled to starboard, rolled to larboard, when the surge was
    seething free,
Where the wallowing monster spouted his foam-fountains in
    the sea.
Let us swear an oath, and keep it with an equal mind,
In the hollow Lotos-land to live and lie reclined
On the hills like gods together, careless of mankind.   110
For they lie beside their nectar, and the bolts are hurled
Far below them in the valleys, and the clouds are lightly curled
Round their golden houses, girdled with the gleaming world;
Where they smile in secret, looking over wasted lands,
Blight and famine, plague and earthquake, roaring deeps and
    fiery sands,   115
Clanging fights, and flaming towns, and sinking ships, and
    praying hands.
But they smile, they find a music centered in a doleful song
Steaming up, a lamentation and an ancient tale of wrong,
Like a tale of little meaning though the words are strong;
Chanted from an ill-used race of men that cleave the soil,   120

87 *pilot-stars:* stars by which sailors navigated. 8 *amaranth:* fabulous flower
supposed never to fade. *moly:* the magic herb Hermes gave to Ulysses to pro-
tect him from Circe's magic. 97 *acanthus-wreath:* a genus of prickly herbs of
the Mediterranean region. 107 *wallowing monster:* the whale.

Sow the seed, and reap the harvest with enduring toil,
Storing yearly little dues of wheat, and wine and oil;
Till they perish and they suffer—some, 'tis whispered—down
   in hell
Suffer endless anguish, others in Elysian valleys dwell,
Resting weary limbs at last on beds of asphodel.   *125*
Surely, surely, slumber is more sweet than toil, the shore
Than labour in the deep mid-ocean, wind and wave and oar;
O rest ye, brother mariners, we will not wander more.

Ulysses*

It little profits that an idle king,
By this still hearth, among these barren crags,
Matched with an aged wife, I mete and dole
Unequal laws unto a savage race,
That hoard, and sleep, and feed, and know not me.   *5*
I cannot rest from travel; I will drink
Life to the lees. All times I have enjoyed
Greatly, have suffered greatly, both with those
That loved me, and alone; on shore, and when
Through scudding drifts the rainy Hyades   *10*
Vexed the dim sea. I am become a name;
For always roaming with a hungry heart
Much have I seen and known—cities of men
And manners, climates, councils, governments,
Myself not least, but honoured of them all—   *15*
And drunk delight of battle with my peers,
Far on the ringing plains of windy Troy.
I am a part of all that I have met;
Yet all experience is an arch wherethrough
Gleams that untraveled world whose margin fades   *20*
Forever and forever when I move.
How dull it is to pause, to make an end,
To rust unburnished, not to shine in use!
As though to breathe were life! Life piled on life
Were all too little, and of one to me   *25*

---

124 *Elysian valleys:* such as might be found in Elysium, the dwelling place of the happy dead.   125 *asphodel:* a species of narcissus.

* After Ulysses had returned from Troy, he embarked on another and final expedition. Tennyson here has him explain why he intends to set forth on it.   10 *Hyades:* seven stars in the constellation Taurus, supposed to signify rain.

Little remains; but every hour is saved
From that eternal silence, something more,
A bringer of new things; and vile it were
For some three suns to store and hoard myself,
And this grey spirit yearning in desire   30
To follow knowledge like a sinking star,
Beyond the utmost bound of human thought.
      This is my son, mine own Telemachus,
To whom I leave the scepter and the isle—
Well-loved of me, discerning to fulfill   35
This labour, by slow prudence to make mild
A rugged people, and through soft degrees
Subdue them to the useful and the good.
Most blameless is he, centered in the sphere
Of common duties, decent not to fail   40
In offices of tenderness, and pay
Meet adoration to my household gods,
When I am gone. He works his work, I mine.
      There lies the port; the vessel puffs her sail;
There gloom the dark, broad seas. My mariners,   45
Souls that have toiled, and wrought, and thought with me—
That ever with a frolic welcome took
The thunder and the sunshine, and opposed
Free hearts, free foreheads—you and I are old;
Old age hath yet his honour and his toil.   50
Death closes all; but something ere the end,
Some work of noble note, may yet be done,
Not unbecoming men that strove with gods.
The lights begin to twinkle from the rocks;
The long day wanes; the slow moon climbs; the deep   55
Moans round with many voices. Come, my friends,
'Tis not too late to seek a newer world.
Push off, and sitting well in order smite
The sounding furrows; for my purpose holds
To sail beyond the sunset, and the baths   60
Of all the western stars, until I die.
It may be that the gulfs will wash us down;
It may be we shall touch the Happy Isles,
And see the great Achilles, whom we knew.
Though much is taken, much abides; and though   65
We are not now that strength which in old days
Moved earth and heaven, that which we are, we are—
One equal temper of heroic hearts,
Made weak by time and fate, but strong in will
To strive, to seek, to find, and not to yield.   70

63 *Happy Isles:* the Isles of the Blest, earthly paradise of the Greeks.

The Splendor Falls

From THE PRINCESS

The splendor falls on castle walls
   And snowy summits old in story;
The long light shakes across the lakes,
   And the wild cataract leaps in glory.
Blow, bugle, blow, set the wild echoes flying,   5
Blow, bugle; answer, echoes, dying, dying, dying.

O, hark, O, hear! how thin and clear,
   And thinner, clearer, farther going!
O, sweet and far from cliff and scar
   The horns of Elfland faintly blowing!   10
Blow, let us hear the purple glens replying,
Blow, bugle; answer, echoes, dying, dying, dying.

O love, they die in yon rich sky,
   They faint on hill or field or river;
Our echoes roll from soul to soul,   15
   And grow for ever and for ever.
Blow, bugle, blow, set the wild echoes flying,
And answer, echoes, answer, dying, dying, dying.

Tears, Idle Tears

From THE PRINCESS

Tears, idle tears, I know not what they mean,
Tears from the depth of some divine despair
Rise in the heart, and gather to the eyes,
In looking on the happy autumn-fields,
And thinking of the days that are no more.   5

Fresh as the first beam glittering on a sail,
That brings our friends up from the underworld,
Sad as the last which reddens over one
That sinks with all we love below the verge;
So sad, so fresh, the days that are no more.   10

The Splendor Falls: *9 scar*: a steep, rocky eminence.

Ah, sad and strange as in dark summer dawns
The earliest pipe of half-awaken'd birds
To dying ears, when unto dying eyes
The casement slowly grows a glimmering square;
So sad, so strange, the days that are no more.   15

Dear as remember'd kisses after death,
And sweet as those by hopeless fancy feign'd
On lips that are for others; deep as love,
Deep as first love, and wild with all regret;
O Death in Life, the days that are no more!   20

Ask Me No More

From THE PRINCESS

Ask me no more: the moon may draw the sea;
    The cloud may stoop from heaven and take shape,
    With fold to fold, of mountain or of cape;
But O too fond, when have I answer'd thee?
        Ask me no more.   5

Ask me no more: what answer should I give?
    I love not hollow cheek or faded eye:
    Yet O my friend, I will not have thee die!
Ask me no more, lest I should bid thee live;
        Ask me no more.   10

Ask me no more: thy fate and mine are seal'd:
    I strove against the stream and all in vain:
    Let the great river take me to the main:
No more, dear love, for at a touch I yield;
        Ask me no more.   15

Now Sleeps the Crimson Petal

From THE PRINCESS

Now sleeps the crimson petal, now the white;
Nor waves the cypress in the palace walk;
Nor winks the gold fin in the porphyry font:
The fire-fly wakens: waken thou with me.

Now droops the milkwhite peacock like a ghost,　　5
And like a ghost she glimmers on to me.

Now lies the Earth all Danaë to the stars,
And all thy heart lies open unto me.

Now slides the silent meteor on, and leaves
A shining furrow, as thy thoughts in me.　　　10

Now folds the lily all her sweetness up,
And slips into the bosom of the lake:
So fold thyself, my dearest, thou, and slip
Into my bosom and be lost in me.

Come Down, O Maid

From THE PRINCESS

Come down, O maid, from yonder mountain height.
What pleasure lives in height (the shepherd sang),
In height and cold, the splendor of the hills?
But cease to move so near the heavens, and cease
To glide a sunbeam by the blasted pine,　　　　　5
To sit a star upon the sparkling spire;
And come, for Love is of the valley, come,
For Love is of the valley, come thou down
And find him; by the happy threshold, he,
Or hand in hand with Plenty in the maize,　　　　10
Or red with spirited purple of the vats,
Or foxlike in the vine; nor cares to walk
With Death and Morning on the Silver Horns,
Nor wilt thou snare him in the white ravine,
Nor find him dropt upon the firths of ice,　　　　15
That huddling slant in furrow-cloven falls
To roll the torrent out of dusky doors.
But follow; let the torrent dance thee down
To find him in the valley; let the wild
Lean-headed eagles yelp alone, and leave　　　　　20
The monstrous ledges there to slope, and spill
Their thousand wreaths of dangling water-smoke,
That like a broken purpose waste in air.

Now Sleeps:　7 *Danaë*: Zeus visited Danae in the form of a golden shower; the
earth lies open to the stars as did Danae to the shower.

So waste not thou, but come; for all the vales
Await thee; azure pillars of the hearth   25
Arise to thee; the children call, and I
Thy shepherd pipe, and sweet is every sound,
Sweeter thy voice, but every sound is sweet;
Myriads of rivulets hurrying thro' the lawn,
The moan of doves in immemorial elms,   30
And murmuring of innumerable bees.

Old Yew, Which Graspest at the Stones

From IN MEMORIAM A. H. H.*

Old yew, which graspest at the stones
  That name the underlying dead,
  Thy fibres net the dreamless head,
Thy roots are wrapt about the bones.

The seasons bring the flower again,   5
  And bring the firstling to the flock;
  And in the dusk of thee the clock
Beats out the little lives of men.

O, not for thee the glow, the bloom,
  Who changest not in any gale,   10
  Nor branding summer suns avail
To touch thy thousand years of gloom;

And gazing on thee, sullen tree,
  Sick for thy stubborn hardihood,
  I seem to fail from out my blood   15
And grow incorporate into thee.

* The poems that make up *In Memoriam A. H. H.* were written in memory of
Arthur Henry Hallam, Tennyson's close friend who died in Vienna in 1833.
Containing over 130 poems, this long sequence was written over a period extend-
ing from Hallam's death to the year of their publication (1850). While the poems
were composed with no general plan in mind and with no thought of publication,
Tennyson later arranged them to exhibit the soul working its way from bereave-
ment to final consolation through faith. The poems appearing here are numbers
2, 7, 15, 50, and 106 in the sequence.

Dark House, by Which Once More I Stand

From IN MEMORIAM A. H. H.

Dark house, by which once more I stand
  Here in the long unlovely street,
  Doors, where my heart was used to beat
So quickly, waiting for a hand,

A hand that can be clasp'd no more—   5
  Behold me, for I cannot sleep,
  And like a guilty thing I creep
At earliest morning to the door.

He is not here; but far away
  The noise of life begins again,   10
  And ghastly thro' the drizzling rain
On the bald street breaks the blank day.

To-night the Winds Begin

From IN MEMORIAM A. H. H.

To-night the winds begin to rise
  And roar from yonder dropping day:
  The last red leaf is whirl'd away,
The rooks are blown about the skies;

The forest crack'd, the waters curl'd,   5
  The cattle huddled on the lea;
  And wildly dash'd on tower and tree
The sunbeam strikes along the world:

And but for fancies, which aver
  That all thy motions gently pass   10
  Athwart a plane of molten glass,
I scarce could brook the strain and stir

That make the barren branches loud;
  And but for fear it is not so,

To-night the Winds Begin: *4 rook:* a bird of the crow family. *9–11:* "And except for my fancy telling me that you are borne along a smooth sea like a plane of molten glass. . . ."

The wild unrest that lives in woe   15
Would dote and pore on yonder cloud

That rises upward always higher,
    And onward drags a labouring breast,
    And topples round the dreary west,
A looming bastion fringed with fire.   20

Be Near Me When My Light Is Low

From IN MEMORIAM A. H. H.

Be near me when my light is low,
    When the blood creeps, and the nerves prick
    And tingle; and the heart is sick,
And all the wheels of being slow.

Be near me when the sensuous frame   5
    Is rack'd with pangs that conquer trust;
    And Time, a maniac scattering dust,
And Life, a Fury slinging flame.

Be near me when my faith is dry,
    And men the flies of latter spring,   10
    That lay their eggs, and sting and sing
And weave their petty cells and die.

Be near me when I fade away,
    To point the term of human strife,
    And on the low dark verge of life   15
The twilight of eternal day.

Ring Out, Wild Bells, to the Wild Sky

From IN MEMORIAM A. H. H.

Ring out, wild bells, to the wild sky,
    The flying cloud, the frosty light:
    The year is dying in the night;
Ring out, wild bells, and let him die.

Ring out the old, ring in the new,
   Ring, happy bells, across the snow:
   The year is going, let him go;
Ring out the false, ring in the true.

Ring out the grief that saps the mind,
   For those that here we see no more;   10
   Ring out the feud of rich and poor,
Ring in redress to all mankind.

Ring out a slowly dying cause,
   And ancient forms of party strife;
   Ring in the nobler modes of life,   15
With sweeter manners, purer laws.

Ring out the want, the care, the sin,
   The faithless coldness of the times;
   Ring out, ring out my mournful rhymes,
But ring the fuller minstrel in.   20

Ring out false pride in place and blood,
   The civic slander and the spite;
   Ring in the love of truth and right,
Ring in the common love of good.

Ring out old shapes of foul disease;   25
   Ring out the narrowing lust of gold;
   Ring out the thousand wars of old,
Ring in the thousand years of peace.

Ring in the valiant man and free,
   The larger heart, the kindlier hand;   30
   Ring out the darkness of the land,
Ring in the Christ that is to be.

In Love, If Love Be Love

From MERLIN AND VIVIEN

In Love, if Love be Love, if Love be ours,
Faith and unfaith can ne'er be equal powers:
Unfaith in aught is want of faith in all.

It is the little rift within the lute,
That by and by will make the music mute,   5
And ever widening slowly silence all.

The little rift within the lover's lute,
Or little pitted speck in garner'd fruit,
That rotting inward slowly moulders all.

It is not worth the keeping: let it go: 10
But shall it? answer, darling, answer, no.
And trust me not at all or all in all.

ROBERT BROWNING
1812–1889

Educated from the books in his father's library, Browning followed trails in history and philosophy that were obscure to normally schooled contemporaries. When early poems such as "Pauline" (1833), were attacked as grandiose and immodest, Browning retreated from the personal voice in poetry and applied his fascination with theater to his poems, developing the dramatic monologue to unique new levels. The publication of *Men and Women* (1855) brought his best developments forth.

Following Shelley into atheism as a youth, Browning reacted later and became highly mystical, affecting millions of readers with his optimistic affirmations. He had faith in the perfection of ultimate things and envisioned a sublime setting where the imperfections of the universe are reconciled.

During the final twenty years of his life, Browning's reputation came to rival Tennyson's. Yet his privacy remained sealed behind the shifting masks in his rich and elaborate dramatic poems.

The Bishop Orders His Tomb at Saint Praxed's Church

[ROME, 15—.]

Vanity, saith the preacher, vanity!
Draw round my bed: is Anselm keeping back?
Nephews—sons mine . . . ah God, I know not! Well—
She, men would have to be your mother once,
Old Gandolf envied me, so fair she was!   5
What's done is done, and she is dead beside,
Dead long ago, and I am Bishop since,
And as she died so must we die ourselves,
And thence ye may perceive the world's a dream.
Life, how and what is it? As here I lie   10
In this state-chamber, dying by degrees,
Hours and long hours in the dead night, I ask
"Do I live, am I dead?" Peace, peace seems all.
Saint Praxed's ever was the church for peace;
And so, about this tomb of mine. I fought   15
With tooth and nail to save my niche, ye know:
—Old Gandolf cozened me, despite my care;
Shrewd was that snatch from out the corner South
He graced his carrion with, God curse the same!
Yet still my niche is not so cramped but thence   20
One sees the pulpit o' the epistle-side,
And somewhat of the choir, those silent seats,
And up into the aery dome where live
The angels, and a sunbeam's sure to lurk:
And I shall fill my slab of basalt there,   25
And 'neath my tabernacle take my rest,
With those nine columns round me, two and two,
The odd one at my feet where Anselm stands:
Peach-blossom marble all, the rare, the ripe
As fresh-poured red wine of a mighty pulse.   30
—Old Gandolf with his paltry onion-stone,
Put me where I may look at him! True peach,
Rosy and flawless: how I earned the prize!

31 *onion-stone:* a poor marble.

Draw close: that conflagration of my church
—What then? So much was saved if aught were missed!   *35*
My sons, ye would not be my death? Go dig
The white-grape vineyard where the oil-press stood,
Drop water gently till the surface sinks,
And if ye find . . . Ah, God I know not, I! . . .
Bedded in store of rotten figleaves soft,   *40*
And corded up in a tight olive-frail,
Some lump, ah God, of *lapis lazuli*,
Big as a Jew's head cut off at the nape,
Blue as a vein o'er the Madonna's breast . . .
Sons, all have I bequeathed you, villas, all,   *45*
That brave Frascati villa with its bath,
So, let the blue lump poise between my knees,
Like God the Father's globe on both His hands
Ye worship in the Jesu Church so gay,
For Gandolf shall not choose but see and burst!   *50*
Swift as a weaver's shuttle fleet our years:
Man goeth to the grave, and where is he?
Did I say basalt for my slab, sons? Black—
'Twas ever antique-black I meant! How else
Shall ye contrast my frieze to come beneath?   *55*
The bas-relief in bronze ye promised me,
Those Pans and Nymphs ye wot of, and perchance
Some tripod, thyrsus, with a vase or so,
The Saviour at his sermon on the mount,
Saint Praxed in a glory, and one Pan   *60*
Ready to twitch the Nymph's last garment off,
And Moses with the tables . . . but I know
Ye mark me not! What do they whisper thee,
Child of my bowels, Anselm? Ah, ye hope
To revel down my villas while I gasp   *65*
Bricked o'er with beggar's mouldy travertine
Which Gandolf from his tomb-top chuckles at!
Nay, boys, ye love me—all of jasper, then!
'Tis jasper ye stand pledged to, lest I grieve.
My bath must needs be left behind, alas!   *70*
One block, pure green as a pistachio-nut,
There's plenty jasper somewhere in the world—
And have I not Saint Praxed's ear to pray
Horses for ye, and brown Greek manuscripts,
And mistresses with great smooth marbly limbs?   *75*
—That's if ye carve my epitaph aright,

41 olive-frail: olive basket. *42 lapis lazuli:* an expensive blue stone. *49 Jesu Church:* the Jesuit church in Rome. *58 thyrsus:* a staff used in the rites of Bacchus. *66 travertine:* an inexpensive limestone.

Choice Latin, picked phrase, Tully's every word,
No gaudy ware like Gandolf's second line—
Tully, my masters? Ulpian serves his need!
And then how I shall lie through centuries,   80
And hear the blessed mutter of the mass,
And see God made and eaten all day long,
And feel the steady candle-flame, and taste
Good strong thick stupefying incense-smoke!
For as I lie here, hours of the dead night,   85
Dying in state and by such slow degrees,
I fold my arms as if they clasped a crook,
And stretch my feet forth straight as stone can point,
And let the bedclothes for a mortcloth drop
Into great laps and folds of sculptor's-work: 90
And as yon tapers dwindle, and strange thoughts
Grow, with a certain humming in my ears,
About the life before I lived this life,
And this life too, Popes, Cardinals and Priests,
Saint Praxed at his sermon on the mount,   95
Your tall pale mother with her talking eyes,
And new-found agate urns as fresh as day,
And marble's language, Latin pure, discreet,
—Aha, ELUCESCEBAT quoth our friend?
No Tully, said I, Ulpian at the best!   100
Evil and brief hath been my pilgrimage.
All *lapis*, all, sons! Else I gave the Pope
My villas: will ye ever eat my heart?
Ever your eyes were as a lizard's quick,
They glitter like your mother's for my soul,   105
Or ye would heighten my impoverished frieze,
Piece out its starved design, and fill my vase
With grapes, and add a vizor and a Term,
And to the tripod ye would tie a lynx
That in his struggle throws the thyrsus down,   110
To comfort me on my entablature
Whereon I am to lie till I must ask
"Do I live, am I dead?" There, leave me, there!
For ye have stabbed me with ingratitude
To death—ye wish it—God, ye wish it! Stone—   115
Gritstone, a-crumble! Clammy squares which sweat
As if the corpse they keep were oozing through—

77 *Tully:* Cicero (106–43 B.C.); therefore, the phrase would be "pure" Latin. 79
Ulpian: Ulpianus (170–228), who wrote late Latin which was inferior.   89 *mort-
cloth:* the drapery of the dead.   99 *Elucescebat:* "to shine forth"; the classical
form in the best Latin (Ciceronian) is *Elucebat*.   108 *Term:* a figure of the
Roman god Terminus, who presided over limits.

And no more *lapis* to delight the world!
Well, go! I bless ye. Fewer tapers there,
But in a row: and, going, turn your backs   120
—Ay, like departing altar-ministrants,
And leave me in my church, the church for peace,
That I may watch at leisure if he leers—
Old Gandolf, at me, from his onion-stone,
As still he envied me, so fair she was!   125

Sibrandus Schafnaburgensis

From GARDEN FANCIES

I

Plague take all your pedants, say I!
    He who wrote what I hold in my hand,
Centuries back was so good as to die,
    Leaving this rubbish to cumber the land;
This, that was a book in its time,   5
    Printed on paper and bound in leather,
Last month in the white of a matin-prime
    Just when the birds sang all together.

II

Into the garden I brought it to read,
    And under the arbute and laurustine   10
Read it, so help me grace in my need,
    From title page to closing line.
Chapter on chapter did I count,
    As a curious traveller counts Stonehenge;
Added up the mortal amount;   15
    And then proceeded to my revenge.

III

Yonder's a plum-tree with a crevice
    An owl would build in, were he but sage;
For a lap of moss, like a fine pont-levis
    In a castle of the Middle Age,   20
Joins to a lip of gum, pure amber;
    When he'd be private, there might he spend

Sibrandus Schafnaburgensis: *7 matin-prime:* prime of the morning. *10 arbute and laurustine:* arbutus and laurustine, evergreen shrubs or trees. *19 pont-levis:* drawbridge.

Hours alone in his lady's chamber:
    Into this crevice I dropped our friend.

IV

Splash, went he, as under he ducked,   25
    —I knew at the bottom rain-drippings stagnate;
Next a handful of blossoms I plucked
    To bury him with, my bookshelf's magnate;
Then I went indoors, brought out a loaf,
    Half a cheese, and a bottle of Chablis;   30
Lay on the grass and forgot the oaf
    Over a jolly chapter of Rabelais.

V

Now, this morning, betwixt the moss
    And gum that locked our friend in limbo,
A spider had spun his web across,   35
    And sat in the midst with arms akimbo:
So, I took pity, for learning's sake,
    And, *de profundis, accentibus laetis,*
Cantate! quoth I, as I got a rake,
    And up I fished his delectable treatise.   40

VI

Here you have it, dry in the sun,
    With all the binding all of a blister,
And great blue spots where the ink has run,
    And reddish streaks that wink and glister
O'er the page so beautifully yellow: 45
    Oh, well have the droppings played their tricks!
Did he guess how toadstools grow, this fellow?
    Here's one stuck in his chapter six!

VII

How did he like it when the live creatures
    Tickled and toused and browsed him all over,   50
And worm, slug, eft, with serious features,
    Came in, each one, for his right of trover?
—When the water-beetle with great blind deaf face
    Made of her eggs the stately deposit,
And the newt borrowed just so much of the preface   55
    As tiled in the top of his black wife's closet?

---

28 *magnate:* a prominent or great person; here, the biggest book on the shelf.
38–39 *de profundis*, etc.: "From the depths, sin with joyful accents!"   52 *trover:*
found property.

VIII

All that life and fun and romping,
    All that frisking and twisting and coupling,
While slowly our poor friend's leaves were swamping
    And clasps were cracking and covers suppling!   60
As if you had carried sour John Knox
    To the play-house at Paris, Vienna or Munich,
Fastened him into a front-row box,
    And danced off the ballet with trousers and tunic.

IX

Come, old martyr! What, torment enough is it?   65
    Back to my room shall you take your sweet self!
Good-bye, mother-beetle; husband-eft, *sufficit!*
    See the snug niche I have made on my shelf.
A.'s book shall prop you up, B.'s shall cover you,
    Here's C. to be grave with, or D. to be gay,   70
And with E. on each side, and F. right over you,
    Dry-rot at ease till the Judgment-day!

Porphyria's Lover

The rain set early in to-night,
    The sullen wind was soon awake,
It tore the elm-tops down for spite,
    And did its worst to vex the lake.
    I listened with heart fit to break.   5
When glided in Porphyria; straight
    She shut the cold out and the storm,
And kneeled and made the cheerless grate
    Blaze up, and all the cottage warm;
    Which done, she rose, and from her form   10
Withdrew the dripping cloak and shawl,
    And laid her soiled gloves by, untied
Her hat and let the damp hair fall,
    And, last, she sat down by my side
    And called me. When no voice replied,   15
She put my arm about her waist,
    And made her smooth white shoulder bare,

---

61 *John Knox:* (1513?–1572), the founder of Scottish Presbyterianism.   67 *sufficit:*
"That's enough."

And all her yellow hair displaced,
 And, stooping, made my cheek lie there,
 And spread o'er all her yellow hair,   *20*
Murmuring how she loved me—she
 Too weak, for all her heart's endeavour
To set its struggling passion free
 From pride, and vainer ties dissever,
 And give herself to me for ever.   *25*
But passion sometimes would prevail,
 Nor could to-night's gay feast restrain
A sudden thought of one so pale
 For love of her, and all in vain:
 So, she was come through wind and rain.   *30*
Be sure I looked up at her eyes
 Happy and proud; at last I knew
Porphyria worshipped me; surprise
 Made my heart swell, and still it grew
 While I debated what to do.   *35*
That moment she was mine, mine, fair,
 Perfectly pure and good: I found
A thing to do, and all her hair
 In one long yellow string I wound
 Three times her little throat around,   *40*
And strangled her. No pain felt she;
 I am quite sure she felt no pain.
As a shut bud that holds a bee,
 I warily oped her lids; again
 Laughed the blue eyes without a stain.   *45*
And I untightened next the tress
 About her neck; her cheek once more
Blushed bright beneath my burning kiss:
 I propped her head up as before,
 Only, this time *my* shoulder bore   *50*
Her head, which droops upon it still:
 The smiling rosy little head,
So glad it has its utmost will,
 That all it scorned at once is fled,
 And I, its love, am gained instead!   *55*
Porphyria's love: she guessed not how
 Her darling one wish would be heard.
And thus we sit together now,
 And all night long we have not stirred,
 And yet God has not said a word!   *60*

My Last Duchess

FERRARA

That's my last Duchess painted on the wall,
Looking as if she were alive. I call
That piece a wonder, now: Frà Pandolf's hands
Worked busily a day, and there she stands.
Will't please you sit and look at her? I said   5
"Frà Pandolf" by design, for never read
Strangers like you that pictured countenance,
The depth and passion of its earnest glance,
But to myself they turned (since none puts by
The curtain I have drawn for you, but I)   10
And seemed as they would ask me, if they durst,
How such a glance came there; so, not the first
Are you to turn and ask thus. Sir, 'twas not
Her husband's presence only, called that spot
Of joy into the Duchess' cheek: perhaps   15
Frà Pandolf chanced to say "Her mantle laps
Over my Lady's wrist too much," or "Paint
Must never hope to reproduce the faint
Half-flush that dies along her throat;" such stuff
Was courtesy, she thought, and cause enough   20
For calling up that spot of joy. She had
A heart—how shall I say?—too soon made glad,
Too easily impressed; she liked whate'er
She looked on, and her looks went everywhere.
Sir, 'twas all one! My favour at her breast,   25
The dropping of the daylight in the West,
The bough of cherries some officious fool
Broke in the orchard for her, the white mule
She rode with round the terrace—all and each
Would draw from her alike the approving speech,   30
Or blush, at least. She thanked men,—good! but thanked
Somehow—I know not how—as if she ranked
My gift of a nine-hundred-years-old name
With anybody's gift. Who'd stoop to blame
This sort of trifling? Even had you skill   35
In speech—(which I have not)—to make your will
Quite clear to such an one, and say "Just this
Or that in you disgusts me; here you miss,

My Last Duchess: *Ferrara:* either the city, which is the capital of the province of Ferrara in northcentral Italy, or the province itself. The artists mentioned are imaginary. Note that Frà Pandolf is a monk.

Or there exceed the mark"—and if she let
Herself be lessoned so, nor plainly set 40
Her wits to yours, forsooth, and made excuse,
—E'en then would be some stooping, and I choose
Never to stoop. Oh, sir, she smiled, no doubt,
Whene'er I passed her; but who passed without
Much the same smile? This grew; I gave commands; 45
Then all smiles stopped together. There she stands
As if alive. Will't please you rise? We'll meet
The company below, then. I repeat,
The Count your Master's known munificence
Is ample warrant that no just pretence 50
Of mine for dowry will be disallowed;
Though his fair daughter's self, as I avowed
At starting, is my object. Nay, we'll go
Together down, sir. Notice Neptune, though,
Taming a sea-horse, thought a rarity, 55
Which Claus of Innsbruck cast in bronze for me.

Soliloquy of the Spanish Cloister

I

Gr-r-r—there go, my heart's abhorrence!
   Water your damned flower-pots, do!
If hate killed men, Brother Lawrence,
   God's blood, would not mine kill you!
What? your myrtle-bush wants trimming? 5
   Oh, that rose has prior claims—
Needs its leaden vase filled brimming?
   Hell dry you up with its flames!

II

At the meal we sit together:
   Salve tibi! I must hear 10
Wise talk of the kind of weather,
   Sort of season, time of year:
Not a plenteous cork-crop: scarcely
   Dare we hope oak-galls, I doubt:
What's the Latin name for "parsley"? 15
   What's the Greek name for Swine's Snout?

Soliloquy: *10 Salve tibi:* "God save you!" or "Greetings!"

III

Whew! We'll have our platter burnished,
　Laid with care on our own shelf!
With a fire-new spoon we're furnished,
　And a goblet for ourself,　　　　　　20
Rinsed like something sacrificial
　Ere 'tis fit to touch our chaps—
Marked with L. for our initial!
　(He-he! There his lily snaps!)

IV

Saint, forsooth! While brown Dolores　25
　Squats outside the Convent bank,
With Sanchicha, telling stories,
　Steeping tresses in the tank,
Blue-black, lustrous, thick like horse-hairs,
　—Can't I see his dead eye glow,　　　30
Bright as 'twere a Barbary corsair's?
　(That is, if he'd let it show!)

V

When he finishes refection,
　Knife and fork he never lays
Cross-wise, to my recollection,　　　　35
　As do I, in Jesu's praise.
I, the Trinity illustrate,
　Drinking watered orange-pulp—
In three sips the Arian frustrate;
　While he drains his at one gulp!　　　40

VI

Oh, those melons! If he's able
　We're to have a feast; so nice!
One goes to the Abbot's table,
　All of us get each a slice.
How go on your flowers? None double?　45
　Not one fruit-sort can you spy?
Strange!—And I, too, at such trouble,
　Keep them close-nipped on the sly!

VII

There's a great text in Galatians,
　Once you trip on it, entails　　　　　50
Twenty-nine distinct damnations,

---

31 *corsair:* pirate or free-booter.　*39 Arian:* a follower of Arius (280?–336), who
denied the Trinity and the divinity of Christ as the Son of God.

One sure, if another fails:
If I trip him just a-dying,
   Sure of Heaven as sure as can be,
Spin him round and send him flying   55
   Off to Hell, a Manichee?

VIII

Or, my scrofulous French novel
   On grey paper with blunt type!
Simply glance at it, you grovel
   Hand and foot in Belial's gripe: 60
If I double down its pages
   At the woeful sixteenth print,
When he gathers his greengages,
   Ope a sieve and slip it in't?

IX

Or, there's Satan!—one might venture   65
   Pledge one's soul to him, yet leave
Such a flaw in the indenture
   As he'd miss till, past retrieve,
Blasted lay that rose-acacia
   We're so proud of! *Hy, Zy, Hine* . . .   70
'St, there's Vespers! *Plena gratiâ*
   Ave, Virgo! Gr-r-r—you swine!

"Childe Roland to the Dark Tower Came"

See EDGAR'S SONG in "LEAR"

My first thought was, he lied in every word,
   That hoary cripple, with malicious eye
   Askance to watch the working of his lie
On mine, and mouth scarce able to afford
Suppression of the glee that pursed and scored   5
   Its edge at one more victim gained thereby.

What else should he be set for, with his staff?
   What, save to waylay with his lies, ensnare
   All travellers that might find him posted there,

56 *Manichee:* a follower of Mani (216?–276?), who held there were two principles, good (light) and evil (dark).   60 *Belial:* a name for Satan.   63 *greengages:* plums. 70 *Hy, Zy, Hine* . . .: Scholars have not been able to determine the meaning of these words.   71–72 *Plena gratiâ,* etc.: "Hail, Virgin, full of grace!"

And ask the road? I guessed what skull-like laugh   10
Would break, what crutch 'gin write my epitaph
   For pastime in the dusty thoroughfare,

If at his counsel I should turn aside
   Into that ominous trace which, all agree,
   Hides the Dark Tower. Yet acquiescingly   15
I did turn as he pointed; neither pride
Nor hope rekindling at the end descried,
   So much as gladness that some end might be.

For, what with my whole world-wide wandering,
   What with my search drawn out thro' years, my hope   20
   Dwindled into a ghost not fit to cope
With that obstreperous joy success would bring,—
I hardly tried now to rebuke the spring
   My heart made, finding failure in its scope.

As when a sick man very near to death   25
   Seems dead indeed, and feels begin and end
   The tears and takes the farewell of each friend,
And hears one bid the other go, draw breath
Freelier outside, ("since all is o'er," he saith,
   "And the blow fallen no grieving can amend;")   30

While some discuss if near the other graves
   Be room enough for this, and when a day
   Suits best for carrying the corpse away,
With care about the banners, scarves and staves,—
And still the man hears all, and only craves   35
   He may not shame such tender love and stay.

Thus, I had so long suffered in this quest,
   Heard failure prophesied so oft, been writ
   So many times among "The Band"—to wit,
The knights who to the Dark Tower's search addressed   40
Their steps—that just to fail as they, seemed best,
   And all the doubt was now—should I be fit.

So, quiet as despair, I turned from him,
   That hateful cripple, out of his highway
   Into the path he pointed. All the day   45
Had been a dreary one at best, and dim
Was settling to its close, yet shot one grim
   Red leer to see the plain catch its estray.

Childe Roland: *48 estray:* one who had strayed into it; here, the knight.

For mark! no sooner was I fairly found
  Pledged to the plain, after a pace or two,   50
  Than, pausing to throw backward a last view
To the safe road, 'twas gone; grey plain all round:
Nothing but plain to the horizon's bound.
  I might go on; nought else remained to do.

So, on I went. I think I never saw   55
  Such starved ignoble nature; nothing throve:
  For flowers—as well expect a cedar grove!
But cockle, spurge, according to their law
Might propagate their kind, with none to awe,
  You'd think; a burr had been a treasure-trove.   60

No! penury, inertness and grimace,
  In some strange sort, were the land's portion. "See
  Or shut your eyes," said Nature peevishly,
"It nothing skills: I cannot help my case:
'Tis the Last Judgment's fire must cure this place,   65
  Calcine its clods and set my prisoners free."

If there pushed any ragged thistle-stalk
  Above its mates, the head was chopped—the bents
  Were jealous else. What made those holes and rents
In the dock's harsh swarth leaves—bruised as to baulk   70
All hope of greenness? 'tis a brute must walk
  Pashing their life out, with a brute's intents.

As for the grass, it grew as scant as hair
  In leprosy; thin dry blades pricked the mud
  Which underneath looked kneaded up with blood.   75
One stiff blind horse, his every bone a-stare,
Stood stupefied, however he came there:
  Thrust out past service from the devil's stud!

Alive? he might be dead for aught I know,
  With that red, gaunt and colloped neck a-strain,   80
  And shut eyes underneath the rusty mane;
Seldom went such grotesqueness with such woe;
I never saw a brute I hated so;
  He must be wicked to deserve such pain.

I shut my eyes and turned them on my heart.   85
  As a man calls for wine before he fights,
  I asked one draught of earlier, happier sights,

64 *skills:* avails. 68 *bents:* grass stalks. 70 *dock:* weed. 80 *colloped:* with
ridges of flesh.

Ere fitly I could hope to play my part.
Think first, fight afterwards—the soldier's art:
   One taste of the old time sets all to rights!   *90*

Not it! I fancied Cuthbert's reddening face
   Beneath its garniture of curly gold,
   Dear fellow, till I almost felt him fold
An arm in mine to fix me to the place,
That way he used. Alas, one night's disgrace!   *95*
   Out went my heart's new fire and left it cold.

Giles, then, the soul of honour—there he stands
   Frank as ten years ago when knighted first.
   What honest men should dare (he said) he durst.
Good—but the scene shifts—faugh! what hangman's hands   *100*
Pin to his breast a parchment? his own bands
   Read it. Poor traitor, spit upon and curst!

Better this Present than a Past like that;
   Back therefore to my darkening path again.
   No sound, no sight as far as eye could strain.   *105*
Will the night send a howlet or a bat?
I asked: when something on the dismal flat
   Came to arrest my thoughts and change their train.

A sudden little river crossed my path
   As unexpected as a serpent comes.   *110*
   No sluggish tide congenial to the glooms—
This, as it frothed by, might have been a bath
For the fiend's glowing hoof—to see the wrath
   Of its black eddy bespate with flakes and spumes.

So petty yet so spiteful! all along,   *115*
   Low scrubby alders kneeled down over it;
   Drenched willows flung them headlong in a fit
Of mute despair, a suicidal throng:
The river which had done them all the wrong,
   Whate'er that was, rolled by, deterred no whit.   *120*

Which, while I forded,—good saints, how I feared
   To set my foot upon a dead man's cheek,
   Each step, or feel the spear I thrust to seek
For hollows, tangled in his hair or beard!
—It may have been a water-rat I speared,   *125*
   But, ugh! it sounded like a baby's shriek.

106 howlet: owlet.   *114 bespate:* bespattered.   *120 no whit:* not at all.

Glad was I when I reached the other bank.
   Now for a better country. Vain presage!
   Who were the strugglers, what war did they wage
Whose savage trample thus could pad the dank   130
Soil to a plash? toads in a poisoned tank,
   Or wild cats in a red-hot iron cage—

The fight must so have seemed in that fell cirque.
   What penned them there, with all the plain to choose?
   No foot-print leading to that horrid mews,   135
None out of it. Mad brewage set to work
Their brains, no doubt, like galley-slaves the Turk
   Pits for his pastime, Christians against Jews.

And more than that—a furlong on—why, there!
   What bad use was that engine for, that wheel,   140
   Or brake, not wheel–that harrow fit to reel
Men's bodies out like silk? with all the air
Of Tophet's tool, on earth left unaware,
   Or brought to sharpen its rusty teeth of steel.

Then came a bit of stubbed ground, once a wood,   145
   Next a marsh, it would seem, and now mere earth
   Desperate and done with; (so a fool finds mirth,
Makes a thing and then mars it, till his mood
Changes and off he goes!) within a rood—
   Bog, clay and rubble, sand and stark black dearth.   150

Now blotches rankling, coloured gay and grim,
   Now patches where some leanness of the soil's
   Broke into moss or substances like boils;
Then came some palsied oak, a cleft in him
Like a distorted mouth that splits its rim   155
   Gaping at death, and dies while it recoils.

And just as far as ever from the end!
   Nought in the distance but the evening, nought
   To point my footstep further! At the thought,
A great black bird, Apollyon's bosom-friend,   160
Sailed past, nor beat his wide wing dragon-penned
   That brushed my cap—perchance the guide I sought.

131 *plash:* a puddle. 133 *cirque:* a circle. 135 *mews:* a cage, coop, or enclo-
sure. 143 *Tophet:* hell. 149 *rood:* seven or eight yards. 160 *Appolyon:* the
Angel of the Bottomless Pit (see Rev. 9:2). 161 *dragon-penned:* his wing is pin-
ioned like a dragon's.

For, looking up, aware I somehow grew,
   'Spite of the dusk, the plain had given place
   All round to mountains—with such name to grace   *165*
Mere ugly heights and heaps now stolen in view.
How thus they had surprised me,—solve it, you!
   How to get from them was no clearer case.

Yet half I seemed to recognise some trick
   Of mischief happened to me, God knows when—   *170*
   In a bad dream perhaps. Here ended, then,
Progress this way. When, in the very nick
Of giving up, one time more, came a click
   As when a trap shuts—you're inside the den!

Burningly it came on me all at once,   *175*
   This was the place! those two hills on the right,
   Crouched like two bulls locked horn in horn in fight;
While to the left, a tall scalped mountain . . . Dunce,
Fool, to be dozing at the very nonce,
   After a life spent training for the sight!   *180*

What in the midst lay but the Tower itself?
   The round squat turret, blind as the fool's heart,
   Built of brown stone, without a counterpart
In the whole world. The tempest's mocking elf
Points to the shipman thus the unseen shelf   *185*
   He strikes on, only when the timbers start.

Not see? because of night perhaps?—Why, day
   Came back again for that! before it left,
   The dying sunset kindled through a cleft:
The hills, like giants at a hunting, lay,   *190*
Chin upon hand, to see the game at bay,—
   "Now stab and end the creature—to the heft!"

Not hear? when noise was everywhere! it tolled
   Increasing like a bell. Names in my ears,
   Of all the lost adventurers my peers,—   *195*
How such a one was strong, and such was bold,
And such was fortunate, yet each of old
   Lost, lost! one moment knelled the woe of years.

There they stood, ranged along the hillsides, met
   To view the last of me, a living frame   *200*
   For one more picture! in a sheet of flame
I saw them and I knew them all. And yet

Dauntless the slug-horn to my lips I set,
  And blew, *"Childe Roland to the Dark Tower came."*

Andrea Del Sarto

(CALLED "THE FAULTLESS PAINTER")

But do not let us quarrel any more,
No, my Lucrezia; bear with me for once:
Sit down and all shall happen as you wish.
You turn your face, but does it bring your heart?
I'll work then for your friend's friend, never fear,   *5*
Treat his own subject after his own way,
Fix his own time, accept too his own price,
And shut the money into this small hand
When next it takes mine. Will it? tenderly?
Oh, I'll content him,—but to-morrow, Love!   *10*
I often am much wearier than you think,
This evening more than usual, and it seems
As if—forgive now—should you let me sit
Here by the window with your hand in mine
And look a half hour forth on Fiesole,   *15*
Both of one mind, as married people use,
Quietly, quietly, the evening through,
I might get up to-morrow to my work
Cheerful and fresh as ever. Let us try.
To-morrow how you shall be glad for this!   *20*
Your soft hand is a woman of itself,
And mine the man's bared breast she curls inside.
Don't count the time lost, either; you must serve
For each of the five pictures we require—
It saves a model. So! keep looking so—   *25*
My serpentining beauty, rounds on rounds!
—How could you ever prick those perfect ears,
Even to put the pearl there! oh, so sweet—
My face, my moon, my everybody's moon,
Which everybody looks on and calls his,   *30*
And, I suppose, is looked on by in turn,
While she looks—no one's: very dear, no less!
You smile? why, there's my picture ready made,
There's what we painters call our harmony!
A common greyness silvers everything,—   *35*

Andrea Del Sarto: *15 Fiesole:* Italian town near Florence.

All in a twilight, you and I alike
—You, at the point of your first pride in me
(That's gone you know),—but I, at every point;
My youth, my hope, my art, being all toned down
To yonder sober pleasant Fiesole.   40
There's the bell clinking from the chapel-top;
That length of convent-wall across the way
Holds the trees safer, huddled more inside;
The last monk leaves the garden; days decrease
And autumn grows, autumn in everything.   45
Eh? the whole seems to fall into a shape
As if I saw alike my work and self
And all that I was born to be and do,
A twilight-piece. Love, we are in God's hand.
How strange now, looks the life He makes us lead!   50
So free we seem, so fettered fast we are!
I feel He laid the fetter: let it lie!
This chamber for example—turn your head—
All that's behind us! you don't understand
Nor care to understand about my art,   55
But you can hear at least when people speak;
And that cartoon, the second from the door
—It is the thing, Love! so such things should be—
Behold Madonna! I am bold to say.
I can do with my pencil what I know,   60
What I see, what at bottom of my heart
I wish for, if I ever wish so deep–
Do easily, too—when I say perfectly
I do not boast, perhaps: yourself are judge
Who listened to the Legate's talk last week,   65
And just as much they used to say in France.
At any rate 'tis easy, all of it,
No sketches first, no studies, that's long past—
I do what many dream of all their lives
—Dream? strive to do, and agonise to do,   70
And fail in doing. I could count twenty such
On twice your fingers, and not leave this town,
Who strive—you don't know how the others strive
To paint a little thing like that you smeared
Carelessly passing with your robes afloat,—   75
Yet do much less, so much less, Someone says,
(I know his name, no matter)—so much less!
Well, less is more, Lucrezia! I am judged.
There burns a truer light of God in them,

65 *Legate:* a papal ambassador.

In their vexed, beating, stuffed and stopped-up brain,   *80*
Heart, or whate'er else, than goes on to prompt
This low-pulsed forthright craftsman's hand of mine.
Their works drop groundward, but themselves, I know,
Reach many a time a heaven that's shut to me,
Enter and take their place there sure enough,   *85*
Though they come back and cannot tell the world.
My works are nearer heaven, but I sit here.
The sudden blood of these men! at a word—
Praise them, it boils, or blame them, it boils too.
I, painting from myself and to myself,   *90*
Know what I do, am unmoved by men's blame
Or their praise either. Somebody remarks
Morello's outline there is wrongly traced,
His hue mistaken—what of that? or else,
Rightly traced and well ordered—what of that?   *95*
Speak as they please, what does the mountain care?
Ah, but a man's reach should exceed his grasp,
Or what's a Heaven for? all is silver-grey
Placid and perfect with my art—the worse!
I know both what I want and what might gain—   *100*
And yet how profitless to know, to sigh
"Had I been two, another and myself,
Our head would have o'erlooked the world!" No doubt.
Yonder's a work, now, of that famous youth
The Urbinate who died five years ago.   *105*
('Tis copied, George Vasari sent it me.)
Well, I can fancy how he did it all,
Pouring his soul, with kings and popes to see,
Reaching, that Heaven might so replenish him,
Above and through his art—for it gives way;   *110*
That arm is wrongly put—and there again—
A fault to pardon in the drawing's lines,
Its body, so to speak: its soul is right,
He means right—that, a child may understand.
Still, what an arm! and I could alter it.   *115*
But all the play, the insight and the stretch—
Out of me! out of me! And wherefore out?
Had you enjoined them on me, given me soul,
We might have risen to Rafael, I and you.
Nay, Love, you did give all I asked, I think—   *120*
More than I merit, yes, by many times.
But had you—oh, with the same perfect brow,

93 Morello: mountain in the Apennines.   *104 youth:* the painter Raphael (1483–1520), born at Urbino.   *106 Vasari:* (1511–1574), Italian artist and author.

And perfect eyes, and more than perfect mouth,
And the low voice my soul hears, as a bird
The fowler's pipe, and follows to the snare—   125
Had you, with these the same, but brought a mind!
Some women do so. Had the mouth there urged
"God and the glory! never care for gain.
The Present by the Future, what is that?
Live for fame, side by side with Angelo—   130
Rafael is waiting. Up to God all three!"
I might have done it for you. So it seems—
Perhaps not. All is as God over-rules.
Beside, incentives come from the soul's self;
The rest avail not. Why do I need you?   135
What wife had Rafael, or has Angelo?
In this world, who can do a thing, will not—
And who would do it, cannot, I perceive:
Yet the will's somewhat—somewhat, too, the power—
And thus we half-men struggle. At the end,   140
God, I conclude, compensates, punishes.
'Tis safer for me, if the award be strict,
That I am something underrated here,
Poor this long while, despised, to speak the truth.
I dared not, do you know, leave home all day,   145
For fear of chancing on the Paris lords.
The best is when they pass and look aside;
But they speak sometimes; I must bear it all.
Well may they speak! That Francis, that first time,
And that long festal year at Fontainebleau!   150
I surely then could sometimes leave the ground,
Put on the glory, Rafael's daily wear,
In that humane great monarch's golden look,—
One finger in his beard or twisted curl
Over his mouth's good mark that made the smile,   155
One arm about my shoulder, round my neck,
The jingle of his gold chain in my ear,
I painting proudly with his breath on me,
All his court round him, seeing with his eyes,
Such frank French eyes, and such a fire of souls   160
Profuse, my hand kept plying by those hearts,—
And, best of all, this, this, this face beyond,
This in the background, waiting on my work,
To crown the issue with a last reward!

---

130 *Angelo:* Michaelangelo (1475–1564).   149 *Francis:* King Francis I of France
invited Andrea to Fontainebleau; Andrea is said to have misused funds given him
by Francis (see lines 247–249).

A good time, was it not, my kingly days?   165
And had you not grown restless—but I know—
'Tis done and past; 'twas right, my instinct said;
Too live the life grew, golden and not grey,
And I'm the weak-eyed bat no sun should tempt
Out of the grange whose four walls make his world.   170
How could it end in any other way?
You called me, and I came home to your heart.
The triumph was, to have ended there; then if
I reached it ere the triumph, what is lost?
Let my hands frame your face in your hair's gold,   175
You beautiful Lucrezia that are mine!
"Rafael did this, Andrea painted that—
The Roman's is the better when you pray,
But still the other's Virgin was his wife—"
Men will excuse me. I am glad to judge   180
Both pictures in your presence; clearer grows
My better fortune, I resolve to think.
For, do you know, Lucrezia, as God lives,
Said one day Angelo, his very self,
To Rafael . . . I have known it all these years . . .   185
(When the young man was flaming out his thoughts
Upon a palace-wall for Rome to see,
Too lifted up in heart because of it)
"Friend, there's a certain sorry little scrub
Goes up and down our Florence, none cares how,   190
Who, were he set to plan and execute
As you are, pricked on by your popes and kings,
Would bring the sweat into that brow of yours!"
To Rafael's!—And indeed the arm is wrong.
I hardly dare—yet, only you to see,   195
Give the chalk here—quick, thus the line should go!
Ay, but the soul! he's Rafael! rub it out!
Still, all I care for, if he spoke the truth,
(What he? why, who but Michael Angelo?
Do you forget already words like those?)   200
If really there was such a chance, so lost,—
Is, whether you're—not grateful—but more pleased.
Well, let me think so. And you smile indeed!
This hour has been an hour! Another smile?
If you would sit thus by me every night   205
I should work better, do you comprehend?
I mean that I should earn more, give you more.
See, it is settled dusk now; there's a star;
Morello's gone, the watch-lights show the wall,
The cue-owls speak the name we call them by.   210

Come from the window, Love,—come in, at last,
Inside the melancholy little house
We built to be so gay with. God is just.
King Francis may forgive me. Oft at nights
When I look up from painting, eyes tired out,   215
The walls become illumined, brick from brick
Distinct, instead of mortar, fierce bright gold,
That gold of his I did cement them with!
Let us but love each other. Must you go?
That Cousin here again? he waits outside?   220
Must see you—you, and not with me? Those loans?
More gaming debts to pay? you smiled for that?
Well, let smiles buy me! have you more to spend?
While hand and eye and something of a heart
Are left me, work's my ware, and what's it worth?   225
I'll pay my fancy. Only let me sit
The grey remainder of the evening out,
Idle, you call it, and muse perfectly
How I could paint, were I but back in France,
One picture, just one more—the Virgin's face,   230
Not your's this time! I want you at my side
To hear them—that is, Michael Angelo—
Judge all I do and tell you of its worth.
Will you? To-morrow, satisfy your friend.
I take the subjects for his corridor,   235
Finish the portrait out of hand—there, there,
And throw him in another thing or two
If he demurs; the whole should prove enough
To pay for this same Cousin's freak. Beside,
What's better and what's all I care about,   240
Get you the thirteen scudi for the ruff.
Love, does that please you? Ah, but what does he,
The Cousin! what does he to please you more?

   I am grown peaceful as old age to-night.
I regret little, I would change still less.   245
Since there my past life lies, why alter it?
The very wrong to Francis!—it is true
I took his coin, was tempted and complied,
And built this house and sinned, and all is said.
My father and my mother died of want.   250
Well, had I riches of my own? you see
How one gets rich! Let each one bear his lot.
They were born poor, lived poor, and poor they died:
And I have laboured somewhat in my time

---

241 *thirteen scudi:* coins not quite worth a dollar.

And not been paid profusely. Some good son   255
Paint my two hundred pictures—let him try!
No doubt, there's something strikes a balance. Yes,
You loved me quite enough, it seems to-night.
This must suffice me here. What would one have?
In Heaven, perhaps, new chances, one more chance—   260
Four great walls in the New Jerusalem
Meted on each side by the angel's reed,
For Leonard, Rafael, Angelo and me
To cover—the three first without a wife,
While I have mine! So—still they overcome   265
Because there's still Lucrezia,—as I choose.

Again the Cousin's whistle! Go, my Love.

263 *Leonard:* Leonardo da Vinci (1452–1519).

WALT WHITMAN
1819–1892

Whitman was thirty-six years old when the first edition of *Leaves of Grass* was published in 1855, and he had already experienced life widely as a farmer, builder, teacher, journalist, printer, and merchant. He believed that the United States had a democratic mission to unite all creation in enlightenment, and his poetry reflects a desire to be in tune with everyone. He advocated complete freedom, personal and sexual.

The range of Whitman's poetry is great, from the formal and symphonic purity of "When Lilacs Last in the Dooryard Bloom'd" through the prose-poem "barbaric yawp" that floods most of his work. Although noticed by poets like Swinburne abroad, Whitman received little attention at home, except when the 1881 edition of *Leaves of Grass* attracted curiosity and profits by being banned in Boston. All of Whitman's work—the diversity in unity so consistent with his ideas—is encompassed within *Leaves of Grass*, which continued to grow right up to the final ninth, or "deathbed," edition of 1892.

Like Wordsworth before him, Whitman truly sought to revolutionize the language of poetry, forcing it back to the rhythms and diction of ordinary speech and using lines of irregular lengths and patterns to effect the staccato of common language.

To a Locomotive in Winter

Thee for my recitative,
Thee in the driving storm even as now, the snow, the
    winter-day declining,
Thee in thy panoply, thy measur'd dual throbbing and thy
    beat convulsive,
Thy black cylindric body, golden brass and silvery steel,
Thy ponderous side-bars, parallel and connecting rods,
    gyrating, shuttling at thy sides,   5
Thy metrical, new swelling pant and roar, now tapering in
    the distance,
Thy great protruding head-light fix'd in front,
Thy long, pale, floating vapor-pennants, tinged with delicate
    purple,
The dense and murky clouds out-belching from thy smokestack,
Thy knitted frame, thy springs and valves, the tremulous
    twinkle of thy wheels,   10
Thy train of cars behind, obedient, merrily following,
Through gale or calm, now swift, now slack, yet steadily
    careering;
Type of the modern—emblem of motion and power—pulse
    of the continent,
For once come serve the Muse and merge in verse, even as
    here I see thee,
With storm and buffeting gusts of wind and falling snow,   15
By day thy warning ringing bell to sound its notes,
By night thy silent signal lamps to swing.
Fierce-throated beauty!
Roll through my chant with all thy lawless music, thy
    swinging lamps at night,
Thy madly-whistled laughter, echoing, rumbling like an
    earthquake, rousing all,   20
Law of thyself complete, thine own track firmly holding,
(No sweetness debonair of tearful harp or glib piano thine,)

Thy trills of shrieks by rocks and hill return'd,
Launch'd o'er the prairies wide, across the lakes,
To the free skies unpent and glad and strong.   25

A Noiseless Patient Spider

A noiseless patient spider,
I mark'd where on a little promontory it stood isolated,
Mark'd how to explore the vacant vast surrounding,
It launch'd forth filament, filament, filament, out of itself,
Ever unreeling them, ever tirelessly speeding them.   5

And you O my soul where you stand,
Surrounded, detached, in measureless oceans of space,
Ceaselessly musing, venturing, throwing, seeking the spheres
     to connect them,
Till the bridge you will need be form'd, till the ductile
     anchor hold,
Till the gossamer thread you fling catch somewhere, O my soul.   10

There Was a Child Went Forth

There was a child went forth every day,
And the first object he look'd upon, that object he became,
And that object became part of him for the day or a certain
     part of the day,
Or for many years or stretching cycles of years.

The early lilacs became part of this child,   5
And grass and white and red morning-glories, and white and
     red clover, and the song of the phoebe-bird,
And the Third-month lambs and the sow's pink-faint litter,
     and the mare's foal and the cow's calf,
And the noisy brood of the barnyard or by the mire of the
     pond-side,
And the fish suspending themselves so curiously below there,
     and the beautiful curious liquid,
And the water-plants with their graceful flat heads, all
     became part of him.   10

The field-sprouts of Fourth-month and Fifth-month became
    part of him,
Winter-grain sprouts and those of the light-yellow corn, and
    the esculent roots of the garden,
And the apple-trees cover'd with blossoms and the fruit
    afterward, and wood-berries, and the commonest weeds
    by the road,
And the old drunkard staggering home from the outhouse of
    the tavern whence he had lately risen,
And the schoolmistress that pass'd on her way to the school,   *15*
And the friendly boys that pass'd, and the quarrelsome boys,
And the tidy and fresh cheek'd girls, and the barefoot Negro
    boy and girl,
And all the changes of city and country wherever he went.

His own parents, he that had father'd him and she that had
    conceiv'd him in her womb and birth'd him,
They gave this child more of themselves than that,   *20*
They gave him afterward every day, they became part of him.

The mother at home quietly placing the dishes on the
    supper-table,
The mother with mild words, clean her cap and gown, a
    wholesome odor falling off her person and clothes as she
    walks by,
The father, strong, self-sufficient, manly mean, anger'd, unjust,
The blow, the quick loud word, the tight bargain, the crafty lure,   *25*
The family usages, the language, the company, the furniture,
    the yearning and swelling heart,
Affection that will not be gainsay'd, the sense of what is real,
    the thought if after all it should prove unreal,
The doubts of day-time and the doubts of night-time, the
    curious whether and how,
Whether that which appears so is so, or is it all flashes
    and specks?
Men and women crowding fast in the streets, if they are not
    flashes and specks what are they?   *30*
The streets themselves and the façades of houses, and goods
    in the windows,
Vehicles, teams, the heavy-plank'd wharves, the huge
    crossing at the ferries,
The village of the highland seen from afar at sunset, the river
    between,
Shadows, aureola and mist, the light falling on roofs and
    gables of white or brown two miles off,

There Was a Child: *34 aureola:* halo or glory.

The schooner near by sleepily dropping down the tide, the
    little boat slack-tow'd astern,   35
The hurrying tumbling waves, quick-broken crests, slapping,
The strata of color'd clouds, the long bar of maroon-tint away
    solitary by itself, the spread of purity it lies motionless in,
The horizon's edge, the flying sea-crow, the fragrance of salt
    marsh and shore mud,
These became part of that child who went forth every day, and
    who now goes, and will always go forth every day.

Out of the Cradle Endlessly Rocking

Out of the cradle endlessly rocking,
Out of the mocking-bird's throat, the musical shuttle,
Out of the Ninth-month midnight,
Over the sterile sands and the fields beyond, where the child
    leaving his bed wandered alone, bareheaded, barefoot,
Down from the showered halo,   5
Up from the mystic play of shadows twining and twisting as if
    they were alive,
Out from the patches of briers and blackberries,
From the memories of the bird that chanted to me,
From your memories, sad brother, from the fitful risings and
    fallings I heard,
From under that yellow half-moon late-risen and swollen as if
    with tears,   10
From those beginning notes of yearning and love there in the
    mist,
From the thousand responses of my heart never to cease,
From the myriad thence-aroused words,
From the word stronger and more delicious than any,
From such as now they start the scene revisiting,   15
As a flock, twittering, rising, or overhead passing,
Borne hither, ere all eludes me, hurriedly,
A man, yet by these tears a little boy again,
Throwing myself on the sand, confronting the waves,
I, chanter of pains and joys, uniter of here and hereafter,   20
Taking all hints to use them, but swiftly leaping beyond them,
A reminiscence sing.

Once Paumanok,
When the lilac-scent was in the air and Fifth-month grass was
    growing,

Out of the Cradle: *23 Paumanok:* Long Island.

Up this seashore in some briers,   25
Two feathered guests from Alabama, two together,
And their nest, and four light-green eggs spotted with brown,
And every day the he-bird to and fro near at hand,
And every day the she-bird crouched on her nest, silent, with
    bright eyes,
And every day I, a curious boy, never too close, never
    disturbing them,   30
Cautiously peering, absorbing, translating.

Shine! shine! shine!
Pour down your warmth, great sun!
While we bask, we two together.
Two together!   35
Winds blow south, or winds blow north,
Day come white, or night come black,
Home, or rivers and mountains from home,
Singing all time, minding no time,
While we two keep together.   40

Till of a sudden,
Maybe killed, unknown to her mate,
One forenoon the she-bird crouched not on the nest,
Nor returned that afternoon, nor the next,
Nor ever appeared again.   45
And thenceforward all summer in the sound of the sea,
And at night under the full of the moon in calmer weather,
Over the hoarse surging of the sea,
Or flitting from brier to brier by day,
I saw, I heard at intervals the remaining one, the he-bird,   50
The solitary guest from Alabama.

Blow! blow! blow!
Blow up sea-winds along Paumanok's shore;
I wait and I wait till you blow my mate to me.

Yes, when the stars glistened,   55
All night long on the prong of a moss-scalloped stake,
Down almost amid the slapping waves,
Sat the lone singer wonderful causing tears.

He called on his mate,
He poured forth the meanings which I of all men know.   60
Yes, my brother, I know,—
The rest might not, but I have treasured every note,
For more than once dimly down to the beach gliding,
Silent, avoiding the moonbeams, blending myself with the
    shadows,

Recalling now the obscure shapes, the echoes, the sounds and
    sights after their sorts, 65
The white arms out in the breakers tirelessly tossing,
I, with bare feet, a child, the wind wafting my hair,
Listened long and long.
Listened to keep, to sing, now translating the notes,
Following you, my brother. 70

Soothe! soothe! soothe!
Close on its wave soothes the wave behind,
And again another behind embracing and lapping, every one
    close,
But my love soothes not me, not me.

Low hangs the moon, it rose late, 75
It is lagging—O I think it is heavy with love, with love.

O madly the sea pushes upon the land,
With love, with love.

O night! do I not see my love fluttering out among the breakers?
What is that little black thing I see there in the white? 80

Loud! loud! loud!
Loud I call to you, my love!

High and clear I shoot my voice over the waves,
Surely you must know who is here, is here,
You must know who I am, my love. 85

Low-hanging moon!
What is that dusky spot in your brown yellow?
O it is the shape, the shape of my mate!
O moon, do not keep her from me any longer.

Land! land! O land! 90
Whichever way I turn, O I think you could give me my
    mate back again if you only would,
For I am almost sure I see her dimly whichever way I look.
O rising stars!
Perhaps the one I want so much will rise, will rise with some
    of you.
O throat! O trembling throat! 95
Sound clearer through the atmosphere!
Pierce the woods, the earth,
Somewhere listening to catch you must be the one I want.

Shake out carols!
Solitary here, the night's carols!   100
Carols of lonesome love! death's carols!
Carols under that lagging, yellow, waning moon!
O under that moon where she droops almost down into the sea!
O reckless despairing carols!

But soft! sink low!   105
Soft! let me just murmur,
And do you wait a moment, you husky-noised sea,
For somewhere I believe I heard my mate responding to me,
So faint, I must be still, be still to listen,
But not altogether still, for then she might not come
      immediately to me.   110

Hither, my love!
Here I am! here!
With this just-sustained note I announce myself to you,
This gentle call is for you my love, for you.

Do not be decoyed elsewhere: 115
That is the whistle of the wind, it is not my voice,
That is the fluttering, the fluttering of the spray,
Those are the shadows of leaves.

O darkness! O in vain!
O I am very sick and sorrowful.   120
O brown halo in the sky near the moon, drooping upon the sea!
O troubled reflection in the sea!
O throat! O throbbing heart!
And I singing uselessly, uselessly all the night.

O past! O happy life! O song of joy!   125
In the air, in the woods, over fields,
Loved! loved! loved! loved! loved!
But my mate no more, no more with me!
We two together no more.

The aria sinking.   130
All else continuing, the stars shining,
The winds blowing, the notes of the bird continuous echoing,
With angry moans the fierce old mother incessantly moaning,
On the sands of Paumanok's shore gray and rustling,
The yellow half-moon enlarged, sagging down, drooping, the
      face of the sea almost touching,   135

The boy ecstatic, with his bare feet the waves, with his hair
    the atmosphere dallying,
The love in the heart long pent, now loose, now at last
    tumultuously bursting,
The aria's meaning, the ears, the soul, swiftly depositing,
The strange tears down the cheeks coursing,
The colloquy there, the trio, each uttering,   140
The undertone, the savage old mother incessantly crying,
To the boy's soul's questions sullenly timing, some drowned
    secret hissing,
To the outsetting bard.

Demon or bird (said the boy's soul)
Is it indeed toward your mate you sing? or is it really to me?   145
For I, that was a child, my tongue's use sleeping, now I have
    heard you,
Now in a moment I know what I am for, I awake,
And already a thousand singers, a thousand songs, clearer,
    louder and more sorrowful than yours,
A thousand warbling echoes have started to life within me,
    never to die.

O you singer solitary, singing by yourself, projecting me,   150
O solitary me listening, never more shall I cease perpetuating
    you,
Never more shall I escape, never more the reverberations,
Never more the cries of unsatisfied love be absent from me.
Never again leave me to be the peaceful child I was before
    what there in the night,
By the sea under the yellow and sagging moon,   155
The messenger there aroused, the fire, the sweet hell within,
The unknown want, the destiny of me.
O give me the clew! (It lurks in the night here somewhere)
O if I am to have so much, let me have more!
A word then, (for I will conquer it)   160
The word final, superior to all,
Subtle, sent up—what is it?—I listen;
Are you whispering it, and have been all the time you
    sea-waves?
Is that it from your liquid rims and wet sands?

Whereto answering, the sea,   165
Delaying not, hurrying not,
Whispered me through the night, and very plainly before
    daybreak,
Lisped to me the low and delicious word death,

158 clew: clue.

And again death, death, death, death,
Hissing melodious, neither like the bird nor like my aroused
    child's heart,   *170*
But edging near as privately for me, rustling at my feet,
Creeping thence steadily up to my ears and laving me softly
    all over,
Death, death, death, death, death.

Which I do not forget,
But fuse the song of my dusky demon and brother,   *175*
That he sang to me in the moonlight on Paumanok's gray beach,
With the thousand responsive songs at random,
My own songs awaked from that hour,
And with them the key, the word up from the waves,
The word of the sweetest song and all songs,   *180*
That strong and delicious word which, creeping to my feet,
(Or like some old crone rocking the cradle, swathed in sweet
    garments, bending aside)
The sea whispered me.

To Think of Time

I

To think of time—of all that retrospection,
To think of to-day, and the ages continued henceforward.
Have you guess'd you yourself would not continue?
Have you dreaded these earth-beetles?
Have you fear'd the future would be nothing to you?   *5*
Is to-day nothing? is the beginningless past nothing?
If the future is nothing they are just as surely nothing.
To think that the sun rose in the east—that men and women
    were flexible, real, alive—that everything was alive,
To think that you and I did not see, feel, think, nor bear our part,
To think that we are now here and bear our part.   *10*

II

Not a day passes, not a minute or second without an
    accouchement,
Not a day passes, not a minute or second without a corpse.
The dull nights go over and the dull days also,
The soreness of lying so much in bed goes over,

To Think of Time: *11 accouchement:* delivery in child-bed.

The physician after long putting off gives the silent and
    terrible look for an answer, 15
The children come hurried and weeping, and the brothers and
    sisters are sent for,
Medicines stand unused on the shelf, (the camphor-smell has
    long pervaded the rooms,)
The faithful hand of the living does not desert the hand of
    the dying,
The twitching lips press lightly on the forehead of the dying,
The breath ceases and the pulse of the heart ceases, 20
The corpse stretches on the bed and the living look upon it,
It is palpable as the living are palpable.
The living look upon the corpse with their eyesight,
But without eyesight lingers a different living and looks
    curiously on the corpse.

III

To think the thought of death merged in the thought of materials, 25
To think of all these wonders of city and country, and others
    taking great interest in them, and we taking no interest
    in them.
To think how eager we are in building our houses,
To think others shall be just as eager, and we quite indifferent.
(I see one building the house that serves him a few years, or
    seventy or eighty years at most,
I see one building the house that serves him longer than that.) 30
Slow-moving and black lines creep over the whole earth—
    they never cease—they are the burial lines,
He that was President was buried, and he that is now
    President shall surely be buried.

IV

A reminiscence of the vulgar fate,
A frequent sample of the life and death of workmen,
Each after his kind. 35
Cold dash of waves at the ferry-wharf, posh and ice in the
    river, half-frozen mud in the streets,
A gray discouraged sky overhead, the short last daylight of
    December,
A hearse and stages, the funeral of an old Broadway
    stage-driver, the cortege mostly drivers.
Steady the trot to the cemetery, duly rattles the death-bell,
The gate is pass'd, the new-dug grave is halted at, the living
    alight, the hearse uncloses, 40
The coffin is pass'd out, lower'd and settled, the whip is laid
    on the coffin, the earth is swiftly shovel'd in,

The mound above is flatted with the spades—silence,
A minute—no one moves or speaks—it is done,
He is decently put away—is there any thing more?
He was a good fellow, free-mouth'd, quick-temper'd, not
    bad-looking,   45
Ready with life or death for a friend, fond of women,
    gambled, ate hearty, drank hearty,
Had known what it was to be flush, grew low-spirited toward
    the last, sicken'd, was help'd by a contribution,
Died, aged forty-one years—and that was his funeral.
Thumb extended, finger uplifted, apron, cape, gloves, strap,
    wet-weather clothes, whip carefully chosen,
Boss, spotter, starter, hostler, somebody loafing on you, you
    loafing on somebody, headway, man before and man
    behind,   50
Good day's work, bad day's work, pet stock, mean stock, first
    out, last out, turning-in at night,
To think that these are so much and so nigh to other drivers,
    and he there takes no interest in them.

When Lilacs Last in the Dooryard Bloom'd

I

When lilacs last in the dooryard bloom'd
And the great star early droop'd in the western sky in the
    night,
I mourn'd, and yet shall mourn with ever-returning spring.

Ever-returning spring, trinity sure to me you bring,
Lilac blooming perennial and drooping star in the west,   5
And thought of him I love.

II

O powerful western fallen star!
O shades of night—O moody, tearful night!
O great star disappear'd—O the black murk that hides the
    star!
O cruel hands that hold me powerless—O helpless soul of me!   10
O harsh surrounding cloud that will not free my soul.

III

In the dooryard fronting an old farm-house near the
    white-washed palings,

Stands the lilac-bush tall-growing with heart-shaped leaves of
    rich green,
With many a pointed blossom rising delicate, with the
    perfume strong I love,
With every leaf a miracle—and from this bush in the
    dooryard,   15
With delicate-color'd blossom and heart-shaped leaves of rich
    green,
A sprig with its flower I break.

IV

In the swamp in secluded recesses,
A shy and hidden bird is warbling a song.
Solitary the thrush,   20
The hermit withdrawn to himself, avoiding the settlements,
Sings by himself a song.
Song of the bleeding throat,
Death's outlet song of life, (for well dear brother I know
If thou wast not granted to sing thou would'st surely die.)   25

V

Over the breast of the spring, the land, amid cities,
Amid lanes and through old woods, where lately the violets
    peep'd from the ground, spotting the gray debris,
Amid the grass in the fields each side of the lanes, passing the
    endless grass,
Passing the yellow-spear'd wheat, every grain from it shroud
    in the dark-brown fields uprisen,
Passing the apple-tree blows of white and pink in the
    orchards,   30
Carrying a corpse to where it shall rest in the grave,
Night and day journeys a coffin.

VI

Coffin that passes through lanes and streets,
Through day and night with the great cloud darkening the
    land,
With the pomp of the inloop'd flags with the cities draped in
    black,   35
With the show of the States themselves as of crape-veil'd
    women standing,
With processions long and winding and the flambeaus of the
    night,
With the countless torches lit, with the silent sea of faces and
    the unbared heads,
With the waiting depot, the arriving coffin, and the sombre
    faces,

With dirges through the night, with the thousand voices
　　rising strong and solemn,
With all the mournful voices of the dirges pour'd around the
　　coffin,
The dim-lit churches and the shuddering organs—where amid
　　these you journey,
With the tolling tolling bells' perpetual clang,
Here, coffin that slowly passes,
I give you my sprig of lilac.　　　　　　　　　　　　　　45

VII

(Nor for you, for one alone,
Blossoms and branches green to coffin all I bring,
For fresh as the morning, thus would I chant a song for you
　　O sane and sacred death.
All over bouquets of roses,
O death, I cover you over with roses and early lilies,　　　50
But mostly and now the lilac that blooms the first,
Copious I break, I break the sprigs from the bushes,
With loaded arms I come, pouring for you,
For you and the coffins all of you O death.)

VIII

O western orb sailing the heaven,　　　　　　　　　　　55
Now I know what you must have meant as a month since I
　　walk'd,
As I walk'd in silence the transparent shadowy night,
As I saw you had something to tell as you bent to me night
　　after night,
As you drooped from the sky low down as if to my side,
　　(while the other stars all look'd on,)
As we wander'd together the solemn night, (for something
　　I know not what kept me from sleep,)　　　　　　　60
As the night advanced, and I saw on the rim of the west how
　　full you were of woe,
As I stood on the rising ground in the breeze in the cool
　　transparent night,
As I watch'd where you pass'd and was lost in the netherward
　　black of the night,
As my soul in its trouble dissatisfied sank, as where you, sad
　　orb,
Concluded, dropt in the night, and was gone.　　　　　65

IX

Sing on there in the swamp,
O singer bashful and tender, I hear your notes, I hear your
　　call,

I hear, I come presently, I understand you,
But a moment I linger, for the lustrous star has detain'd me,
The star my departing comrade holds and detains me.   70

X

O how shall I warble myself for the dead one there I loved?
And how shall I deck my song for the large sweet soul that
    has gone?
And what shall my perfume be for the grave of him I love?

Sea-winds blown from east and west,
Blown from the Eastern sea and blown from the Western sea,
    till there on the prairies meeting,   75
These and with these and the breath of my chant,
I'll perfume the grave of him I love.

XI

O what shall I hang on the chamber walls?
And what shall the pictures be that I hang on the walls,
To adorn the burial-house of him I love?   80

Pictures of growing spring and farms and homes,
With the Fourth-month eve at sundown, and the gray smoke
    lucid and bright,
With floods of the yellow gold of the gorgeous, indolent,
    sinking sun, burning, expanding the air,
With the fresh sweet herbage under foot, and the pale green
    leaves of the trees prolific,
In the distance the flowing glaze, the breast of the river, with
    a wind-dapple here and there,   85
With ranging hills on the banks, with many a line against the
    sky, and shadows,
And the city at hand with dwellings so dense, and stacks of
    chimneys,
And all the scenes of life and the workshops, and the
    workmen homeward returning.

XII

Lo, body and soul—this land,
My own Manhattan with spires, and the sparkling and
    hurrying tides, and the ships,   90
The varied and ample land, the South and the North in the
    light, Ohio's shores and flashing Missouri,
And ever the far-spreading prairies cover'd with grass and
    corn.

Lo, the most excellent sun so calm and haughty,
The violet and purple morn with just-felt breezes,
The gentle soft-born measureless light,   95
The miracle spreading bathing all, the fulfill'd noon,
The coming eve delicious, the welcome night and the stars,
Over my cities shining all, enveloping man and land.

XIII

Sing on, sing on you gray-brown bird,
Sing from the swamps, the recesses, pour your chant from
    the bushes,   100
Limitless out of the dusk, out of the cedars and pines.

Sing on dearest brother, warble your reedy song,
Loud human song, with voice of uttermost woe,
O liquid and free and tender!
O wild and loose to my soul—O wondrous singer!   105
You only I hear—yet the star holds me, (but will soon depart,)
Yet the lilac with mastering odor holds me.

XIV

Now while I sat in the day and look'd forth,
In the close of the day with its light and the fields of spring,
    and the farmers preparing their crops,
In the large unconscious scenery of my land with its lakes
    and forests,   110
In the heavenly aerial beauty, (after the perturb'd winds and
    the storms,)
Under the arching heavens of the afternoon swift passing,
    and the voices of children and women,
The many-moving sea-tides, and I saw the ships how they
    sail'd,
And the summer approaching with richness, and the fields all
    busy with labor,
And the infinite separate houses, how they all went on, each
    with its meals and minutia of daily usages,   115
And the streets how their throbbings throbb'd, and the cities
    pent—lo, then and there,
Falling upon them all and among them all, enveloping me
    with the rest,
Appear'd the cloud, appear'd the long black trail,
And I knew death, its thought, and the sacred knowledge of
    death.

Then with the knowledge of death as walking one side of me,   120
And the thought of death close-walking the other side of me,

And I in the middle as with companions, and as holding the
    hands of companions,
I fled forth to the hiding receiving night that talks not,
Down to the shores of the water, the path by the swamp in
    the dimness,
To the solemn shadowy cedars and ghostly pines so still.   *125*
And the singer so shy to the rest receiv'd me,
The gray-brown bird I know receiv'd us comrades three,
And he sang the carol of death, and a verse for him I love.
From deep secluded recesses,
From the fragrant cedars and the ghostly pines so still,   *130*
Came the carol of the bird.
And the charm of the carol rapt me,
As I held as if by their hands my comrades in the night,
And the voice of my spirit tallied the song of the bird.

Come lovely and soothing death,   *135*
Undulate round the world, serenely arriving, arriving,
In the day, in the night, to all, to each,
Sooner or later delicate death.
Prais'd be the fathomless universe,
For life and joy, and for objects and knowledge curious,   *140*
And for love, sweet love—but praise! praise! praise!
For the sure-enwinding arms of cool-enfolding death.
Dark mother always gliding near with soft feet,
Have none chanted for thee a chant of fullest welcome?
Then I chant it for thee, I glorify thee above all,   *145*
I bring thee a song that when thou must indeed come, come
    unfalteringly.
Approach strong deliveress,
When it is so, when thou has taken them I joyously sing the
    dead,
Lost in the loving floating ocean of thee,
Laved in the flood by thy bliss O death.   *150*
From me to thee glad serenades,
Dances for thee I propose saluting thee, adornments and
    feastings for thee,
And the sights of the open landscape and the high-spread
    sky are fitting,
And life and the fields, and the huge and thoughtful night.
The night in silence under many a star,   *155*
The ocean shore and the husky whispering wave whose voice
    I know,
And the soul turning to thee O vast and well-veil'd death,
And the body gratefully nestling close to thee.
Over the tree-tops I float thee a song,

Over the rising and sinking waves, over the myriad fields and
    the prairies wide,   160
Over the dense-pack'd cities all and the teeming wharves and
    ways,
I float this carol with joy, with joy to thee O death.

XV

To the tally of my soul,
Loud and strong kept up the gray-brown bird,
With pure deliberate notes spreading filling the night.   165
Loud in the pines and cedars dim,
Clear in the freshness moist and the swamp-perfume,
And I with my comrades there in the night.
While my sight that was bound in my eyes unclosed,
As to long panoramas of visions.   170
And I saw askant the armies,
I saw as in noiseless dreams hundreds of battle-flags,
Borne through the smoke of the battles and pierc'd with
    missiles I saw them,
And carried hither and yon through the smoke, and torn and
    bloody,
And at last but a few shreds left on the staffs, (and all in
    silence,)   175
And the staffs all splinter'd and broken.
I saw battle-corpses, myriads of them,
And the white skeletons of young men, I saw them,
I saw the debris and debris of all the slain soldiers of the war,
But I saw they were not as was thought,   180
They themselves were fully at rest, they suffered not,
The living remain'd and suffer'd, the mother suffer'd,
And the wife and the child and the musing comrade suffer'd,
And the armies that remain'd suffer'd.

XVI

Passing the visions, passing the night,   185
Passing, unloosing the hold of my comrades' hands,
Passing the song of the hermit bird and the tallying song of
    my soul,
Victorious song, death's outlet song, yet varying
    ever-altering song,
As low and wailing, yet clear the notes, rising and falling,
    flooding the night,

Sadly sinking and fainting, as warning and warning, and yet
    again bursting with joy,   190
Covering the earth and filling the spread of the heaven,

As that powerful psalm in the night I heard from recesses,
Passing, I leave thee lilac with heart-shaped leaves,
I leave thee there in the door-yard, blooming, returning with
    spring.
I cease from my song for thee,   195
From my gaze on thee in the west, fronting the west,
    communing with thee,
O comrade lustrous with silver face in the night.

Yet each to keep and all, retrievements out of the night,
The song, the wondrous chant of the gray-brown bird,
And the tallying chant, the echo arous'd in my soul,   200
With the lustrous and drooping star with the countenance
    full of woe,
With the holders holding my hand nearing the call of the bird,
Comrades mine and I in the midst, and their memory ever to
    keep, for the dead I loved so well,
For the sweetest, wisest soul of all my days and lands—and
    this for his dear sake,
Lilac and star and bird twined with the chant of my soul,   205
There in the fragrant pines and the cedars dusk and dim.

MATTHEW ARNOLD
1822–1888

As a critic of culture and literature in the 1860s, Matthew Arnold spoke of "high seriousness," a quality he and a generation of Rugby students absorbed during the 1830s from his headmaster father, Dr. Thomas Arnold. Rebelling briefly as a student at Oxford, Matthew affected being a giddy fop and barely graduated. The sense of humor survived in the satirical chiding of his prose style, but his poetry, written mainly during the 1850s, tends to be far darker. His years as poet span from the publication of *The Strayed Reveler* in 1849 to his election to Professor of Poetry at Oxford in 1857, a position attained despite a pressing fulltime career as inspector of schools.

Arnold's theme is one of dissatisfaction with the moral and cultural achievements of his time. Despite the confidence in material progress so swelling to his middle-class contemporaries, Arnold thought himself "wandering between two worlds, one dead, the other powerless to be born." The two worlds he speaks of had to do with nobility and high cultural achievement, not conquest or gross national product. All periods in history are "transitional," but Arnold saw the rawness of his times—in which city life and masses of ill-educated middle classes took precedence—as especially ripe for cultural disaster; undoubtedly he would have felt the twentieth century had realized his worst apprehensions.

Dover Beach

The sea is calm to-night.
The tide is full, the moon lies fair
Upon the straits;—on the French coast the light
Gleams and is gone; the cliffs of England stand
Glimmering and vast, out in the tranquil bay.   5

Come to the window, sweet is the night-air!
Only, from the long line of spray
Where the sea meets the moon-blanch'd land,
Listen! you hear the grating roar
Of pebbles which the waves draw back, and fling,   10
At their return, up the high strand,
Begin and cease, and then again begin,
With tremulous cadence slow, and bring
The eternal note of sadness in.

Sophocles long ago   15
Heard it on the Aegean, and it brought
Into his mind the turbid ebb and flow,
Of human misery; we
Find also in the sound a thought,
Hearing it by this distant northern sea.   20

The Sea of Faith
Was once, too, at the full, and round earth's shore
Lay like the folds of a bright girdle furl'd.
But now I only hear
Its melancholy, long, withdrawing roar,   25
Retreating, to the breath
Of the night-wind, down the vast edges drear
And naked shingles of the world.

Ah, love, let us be true
To one another! for the world, which seems   30
to lie before us like a land of dreams,
So various, so beautiful, so new,
Hath really neither joy, nor love, nor light,
Nor certitude, nor peace, nor help for pain;
And we are here as on a darkling plain   35
Swept with confused alarms of struggle and flight,
Where ignorant armies clash by night.

The Forsaken Merman

Come, dear children, let us away;
Down and away below!
Now my brothers call from the bay,
Now the great winds shoreward blow,
Now the salt tides seaward flow;   5
Now the wild white horses play,
Champ and chafe and toss in the spray.
Children dear, let us away!
This way, this way!

Call her once before you go—   10
Call once yet!
In a voice that she will know:
'Margaret! Margaret!'
Children's voices should be dear
(Call once more) to a mother's ear;   15
Children's voices, wild with pain—
Surely she will come again!
Call her once and come away;
This way, this way!
'Mother dear, we cannot stay!   20
The wild white horses foam and fret.'
Margaret! Margaret!

Come, dear children, come away down;
Call no more!
One last look at the white-wall'd town,   25
And the little grey church on the windy shore;
Then come down!
She will not come though you call all day;
Come away, come away!

Children dear, was it yesterday   30
We heard the sweet bells over the bay?
In the caverns where we lay,
Through the surf and through the swell,
The far-off sound of a silver bell?
Sand-strewn caverns, cool and deep,   35
Where the winds are all asleep;
Where the spent lights quiver and gleam
Where the salt weed sways in the stream,
Where the sea-beast, ranged all round,
Feed in the ooze of their pasture-ground;   40
Where the sea-snakes coil and twine,
Dry their mail and bask in the brine;
Where great whales come sailing by,
Sail and sail, with unshut eye,
Round the world for ever and aye?   45
When did music come this way?
Children dear, was it yesterday?

Children dear, was it yesterday
(Call yet once) that she went away?
Once she sate with you and me,   50
On a red gold throne in the heart of the sea,
And the youngest sate on her knee.
She comb'd its bright hair, and she tended it well,
When down swung the sound of a far-off bell.
She sigh'd, she look'd up through the clear green sea;   55
She said: 'I must go, for my kinsfolk pray
In the little grey church on the shore to-day
'Twill be Easter-time in the world—ah me!
And I lose my poor soul, Merman! here with thee.'
I said: 'Go up, dear heart, through the waves;   60
Say thy prayer, and come back to the kind sea-caves!'
She smiled, she went up through the surf in the bay
Children dear, was it yesterday?

Children dear, were we long alone?
'The sea grows stormy, the little ones moan: 65
Long prayers,' I said, 'in the world they say;
Come!' I said; and we rose through the surf in the bay
We went up the beach, by the sandy down
Where the sea-stocks bloom, to the white-wall'd town;
Through the narrow paved streets, where all was still,   70
To the little grey church on the windy hill.
From the church came a murmur of folk at their prayers,
But we stood without in the cold blowing airs.

We climb'd on the graves, on the stones worn with rains,
And we gazed up the aisle through the small leaded panes.   *75*
She sate by the pillar; we saw her clear:
'Margaret, hist! come quick, we are here!
Dear heart,' I said, 'we are long alone;
The sea grows stormy, the little ones moan.'
But, ah, she gave me never a look,   *80*
For her eyes were seal'd to the holy book!
Loud prays the priest; shut stands the door.
Come away, children, call no more!
Come away, come down, call no more!

Down, down, down!   *85*
Down to the depths of the sea!
She sits at her wheel in the humming town,
Singing most joyfully.
Hark what she sings: 'O joy, O joy,
For the humming street, and the child with its toy!   *90*
For the priest, and the bell, and the holy well;
For the wheel where I spun,
And the blessed light of the sun!'
And so she sings her fill,
Singing most joyfully,   *95*
Till the spindle drops from her hand,
And the whizzing wheel stands still.
She steals to the window, and looks at the sand,
And over the sand at the sea;
And her eyes are set in a stare;   *100*
And anon there breaks a sigh,
And anon there drops a tear,
From a sorrow-clouded eye,
And a heart sorrow-laden,
A long, long sigh;   *105*
For the cold strange eyes of a little Mermaiden
And the gleam of her golden hair.

Come away, away children;
Come children, come down!
The hoarse wind blows coldly;   *110*
Lights shine in the town.
She will start from her slumber
When gusts shake the door;
She will hear the winds howling,
Will hear the waves roar.   *115*
We shall see, while above us
The waves roar and whirl,

A ceiling of amber,
A pavement of pearl.
Singing: 'Here came a mortal,   120
But faithless was she!
And alone dwell for ever
The kings of the sea.'

But, children, at midnight,
When soft the winds blow,   125
When clear falls the moonlight,
When spring-tides are low;
When sweet airs come seaward
From heaths starr'd with broom,
And high rocks throw mildly   130
On the blanch'd sands a gloom;
Up the still, glistening beaches,
Up the creeks we will hie,
Over banks of bright seaweed
The ebb-tide leaves dry.   135
We will gaze, from the sand-hills,
At the white, sleeping town;
At the church on the hill-side—
And then come back down.
Singing: 'There dwells a loved one,   140
But cruel is she!
She left lonely for ever
The kings of the sea.'

To Marguerite ———

From SWITZERLAND *

Yes! in the sea of life enisled,
With echoing straits between us thrown,
Dotting the shoreless watery wild,
We mortal millions live alone.
The islands feel the enclasping flow,   5
And then their endless bounds they know.

But when the moon their hollows lights,
And they are swept by balms of spring,
And in their glens, on starry nights,

* "Switzerland" is a suite of love lyrics, of which this is the fifth. It is uncertain
whether Marguerite was a real or imagined person.

The nightingales divinely sing;   10
And lovely notes, from shore to shore,
Across the sounds and channels pour—

Oh! then a longing like despair
Is to their farthest caverns sent;
For surely once, they feel, we were   15
Parts of a single continent!
Now round us spreads the watery plain—
Oh might our marges meet again!

Who order'd that their longing's fire
Should be, as soon as kindled, cool'd?   20
Who renders vain their deep desire?—
A God, a God their severance ruled!
And bade betwixt their shores to be
The unplumb'd, salt, estranging sea.

The Scholar-Gypsy

Go, for they call you, shepherd, from the hill;
  Go, shepherd, and untie the wattled cotes!
    No longer leave thy wistful flock unfed,
  Nor let thy bawling fellows rack their throats,
    Nor the cropped herbage shoot another head.   5
      But when the fields are still,
  And the tired men and dogs all gone to rest,
    And only the white sheep are sometimes seen
    Cross and recross the strips of moon-blanched green,
  Come, shepherd, and again begin the quest!   10

Here, where the reaper was at work of late—
  In this high field's dark corner, where he leaves
    His coat, his basket, and his earthen cruse,
    And in the sun all morning binds the sheaves,
      Then here, at noon, comes back his stores to use—   15
      Here will I sit and wait,
  While to my ear from uplands far away
    The bleating of the folded flocks is borne,
    With distant cries of reapers in the corn—
  All the live murmur of a summer's day.   20
Screened is this nook o'er the high, half-reaped field,
  And here till sun-down, shepherd! will I be.

The Scholar-Gypsy: 2 *wattled cotes*: sheepfolds.

Through the thick corn the scarlet poppies peep,
And round green roots and yellowing stalks I see
  Pale pink convolvulus in tendrils creep;   25
    And air-swept lindens yield
Their scent, and rustle down their perfumed showers
  Of bloom on the bent grass where I am laid,
  And bower me from the August sun with shade;
And the eye travels down to Oxford's towers.   30

And near me on the grass lies Glanvil's book—
  Come, let me read the oft-read tale again!
    The story of the Oxford scholar poor,
  Of pregnant parts and quick inventive brain,
    Who, tired of knocking at preferment's door,   35
      One summer-morn forsook
His friends, and went to learn the gypsy-lore,
  And roamed the world with that wild brotherhood,
  And came, as most men deemed, to little good,
But came to Oxford and his friends no more.   40

But once, years after, in the country-lanes,
  Two scholars, whom at college erst he knew,
    Met him, and of his way of life inquired;
  Whereat he answered that the gypsy-crew,
    His mates, had arts to rule as they desired   45
      The workings of men's brains,
And they can bind them to what thoughts they will.
  "And I," he said, "the secret of their art,
  When fully learned, will to the world impart;
But it needs heaven-sent moments for this skill."   50

This said, he left them, and returned no more.—
  But rumors hung about the country-side,
    That the lost Scholar long was seen to stray,
  Seen by rare glimpses, pensive and tongue-tied,
    In hat of antique shape, and cloak of gray,   55
      The same the gypsies wore,
Shepherds had met him on the Hurst in spring;
  At some lone alehouse in the Berkshire moors,
  On the warm ingle-bench, the smock-frocked boors
Had found him seated at their entering.   60
But, 'mid their drink and clatter, he would fly.
  And I myself seem half to know thy looks,
  And put the shepherds, wanderer! on thy trace;

31 *Glanvil's book:* The poem is based upon a story in Joseph Glanvil's *Vanity of
Dogmatizing* (1661), retold in stanzas 4 through 7. 59 *boors:* rustics.

And boys who in lone wheatfields scare the rooks
  I ask if thou hast passed their quiet place;   65
    Or in my boat I lie
Moored to the cool bank in the summer-heats,
  'Mid wide grass meadows which the sunshine fills,
  And watch the warm, green-muffled Cumner hills,
And wonder if thou haunt'st their shy retreats.   70

For most, I know, thou lov'st retired ground!
  Thee at the ferry Oxford riders blithe,
    Returning home on summer-nights, have met
Crossing the stripling Thames at Bab-lock-hithe,
    Trailing in the cool stream thy fingers wet,   75
    As the punt's rope chops round;
  And leaning backward in a pensive dream,
    And fostering in thy lap a heap of flowers
    Plucked in shy fields and distant Wychwood bowers,
And thine eyes resting on the moonlit stream.   80

And then they land, and thou art seen no more!—
  Maidens, who from the distant hamlets come
    To dance around the Fyfield elm in May,
Oft through the darkening fields have seen thee roam,
    Or cross a stile into the public way.   85
    Oft thou hast given them store
Of flowers—the frail-leafed, white anemone,
    Dark bluebells drenched with dews of summer eves,
    And purple orchises with spotted leaves—
But none hath words she can report of thee.   90

And, above Godstow Bridge, when hay-time's here
  In June, and many a scythe in sunshine flames,
    Men who through those wide fields of breezy grass
Where black-winged swallows haunt the glittering Thames,
    To bathe in the abandoned lasher pass,   95
    Have often passed thee near
Sitting upon the river bank o'ergrown;
    Marked thine outlandish garb, thy figure spare,
    Thy dark vague eyes, and soft abstracted air—
But, when they came from bathing, thou wast gone!   100

At some lone homestead in the Cumner hills,
  Where at her open door the housewife darns,
    Thou hast been seen, or hanging on a gate

95 *Lasher:* a pool below a dam.

To watch the threshers in the mossy barns.
    Children, who early range these slopes and late 105
      For cresses from the rills,
  Have known thee eying, all an April-day,
    The springing pastures and the feeding kine;
    And marked thee, when the stars come out and shine,
Through the long dewy grass move slow away. 110

In autumn, on the skirts of Bagley Wood—
  Where most the gypsies by the turf-edged way
    Pitch their smoked tents, and every bush you see
  With scarlet patches tagged and shreds of gray,
    Above the forest-ground called Thessaly— 115
      The blackbird, picking food,
  Sees thee, nor stops his meal, nor fears at all;
    So often has he known thee past him stray,
    Rapt, twirling in thy hand a withered spray,
And waiting for the spark from heaven to fall. 120

And once, in winter, on the causeway chill
  Where home through flooded fields foot-travelers go,
    Have I not passed thee on the wooden bridge,
  Wrapped in thy cloak and battling with the snow,
    Thy face tow'rd Hinksey and its wintry ridge? 125
      And thou hast climbed the hill,
  And gained the white brow of the Cumner range;
    Turned once to watch, while thick the snowflakes fall,
    The line of festal light in Christ-Church hall—
Then sought thy straw in some sequestered grange. 130

But what—I dream! Two hundred years are flown
  Since first thy story ran through Oxford halls,
    And the grave Glanvil did the tale inscribe
  That thou wert wandered from the studious walls
    To learn strange arts, and join a gypsy tribe; 135
      And thou from earth art gone
  Long since, and in some quiet churchyard laid—
    Some country-nook, where o'er thy unknown grave
    Tall grasses and white flowering nettles wave,
Under a dark, red-fruited yew-tree's shade. 140

—No, no, thou hast not felt the lapse of hours!
  For what wears out the life of mortal men?
    'Tis that from change to change their being rolls;

---

108 kine: archaic for *cows* or *cattle.* *129 Christ-Church hall:* the great dining hall of Christ Church College at Oxford.

'Tis that repeated shocks, again, again,
    Exhaust the energy of strongest souls 145
        And numb the elastic powers,
  Till having used our nerves with bliss and teen,
    And tired upon a thousand schemes our wit,
    To the just-pausing Genius we remit
Our worn-out life, and are—what we have been. 150

Thou hast not lived, why should'st thou perish, so?
  Thou hadst *one* aim, *one* business, *one* desire;
    Else wert thou long since numbered with the dead!
  Else hadst thou spent, like other men, thy fire!
    The generations of thy peers are fled, 155
        And we ourselves shall go;
  But thou possessest an immortal lot,
    And we imagine thee exempt from age
    And living as thou liv'st on Glanvil's page,
Because thou hadst—what we, alas! have not. 160

For early didst thou leave the world, with powers
  Fresh, undiverted to the world without,
    Firm to their mark, not spent on other things;
  Free from the sick fatigue, the languid doubt,
    Which much to have tried, in much been baffled, brings. 165
        O life unlike to ours!
Who fluctuate idly without term or scope,
    Of whom each strives, nor knows for what he strives,
    And each half lives a hundred different lives;
Who wait like thee, but not, like thee, in hope. 170

Thou waitest for the spark from heaven! and we,
  Light half-believers of our casual creeds,
    Who never deeply felt, nor clearly willed,
  Whose insight never has borne fruit in deeds,
    Whose vague resolves never have been fulfilled; 175
        For whom each year we see
  Breeds new beginnings, disappointments new;
    Who hesitate and falter life away,
    And lose tomorrow the ground won today—
Ah! do not we, wanderer! await it too? 180

Yes, we await it!—but it still delays,
  And then we suffer! and amongst us one,
    Who most hast suffered, takes dejectedly
  His seat upon the intellectual throne;
    And all his store of sad experience he 185
        Lays bare of wretched days;

Tells us his misery's birth and growth and signs,
   And how the dying spark of hope was fed,
   And how the breast was soothed, and how the head,
And all his hourly varied anodynes.   190

This for our wisest! and we others pine,
   And wish the long unhappy dream would end,
   And waive all claim to bliss, and try to bear;
With close-lipped patience for our only friend,
   Sad patience, too near neighbor to despair—   195
     But none has hope like thine!
Thou through the fields and through the woods dost stray,
   Roaming the country-side, a truant boy,
   Nursing thy project in unclouded joy,
And every doubt long blown by time away.   200

O born in days when wits were fresh and clear,
   And life ran gayly as the sparkling Thames;
   Before this strange disease of modern life,
With its sick hurry, its divided aims,
   Its head o'ertaxed, its palsied hearts, was rife—   205
     Fly hence, our contact fear!
Still fly, plunge deeper in the bowering wood!
   Averse, as Dido did with gesture stern
   From her false friend's approach in Hades turn,
Wave us away, and keep thy solitude!   210

Still nursing the unconquerable hope,
   Still clutching the inviolable shade,
   With a free, onward impulse brushing through,
By night, the silvered branches of the glade—
   Far on the forest-skirts, where none pursue,   215
     On some mild pastoral slope
Emerge, and resting on the moonlit pales
   Freshen thy flowers as in former years
   With dew, or listed with enchanted ears,
From the dark dingles, to the nightingales!   220

But fly our paths, our feverish contact fly!
   For strong the infection of our mental strife,
   Which, though it gives no bliss, yet spoils for rest;
And we should win thee from thy own fair life,
   Like us distracted, and like us unblest.   225

208–209: Deserted by Aeneas, Dido committed suicide. In his journey into the underworld Aeneas encountered her in Hades; he pleaded with her, but she refused to speak and turned away from him (see *Aeneid* 6. 450–471).

Soon, soon thy cheer would die,
Thy hopes grow timorous, and unfixed thy powers,
And thy clear aims be cross and shifting made;
And then thy glad perennial youth would fade,
Fade, and grow old at last, and die like ours.   230

Then fly our greetings, fly our speech and smiles!
—As some grave Tyrian trader, from the sea,
Descried at sunrise an emerging prow
Lifting the cool-haired creepers stealthily,
The fringes of a southward-facing brow   235
Among the Aegaean isles;
And saw the merry Grecian coaster come,
Freighted with amber grapes, and Chian wine,
Green, bursting figs, and tunnies steeped in brine—
And knew the intruders on his ancient home,   240

The young light-hearted masters of the waves—
And snatched his rudder, and shook out more sail;
And day and night held on indignantly
O'er the blue Midland waters with the gale,
Betwixt the Syrtes and soft Sicily,   245
To where the Atlantic raves
Outside the western straits; and unbent sails
There, where down cloudy cliffs, through sheets of foam,
Shy traffickers, the dark Iberians come;
And on the beach undid his corded bales.   250

Rugby Chapel

NOVEMBER 1857

Coldly, sadly descends
The autumn-evening. The field
Strewn with its dank yellow drifts
Of wither'd leaves, and the elms,
Fade into dimness apace,   5
Silent;—hardly a shout
From a few boys late at their play!

232 *Tyrian:* from Tyre, in Phoenicia.   238 *Chian:* from Chios, a Greek island in the Aegean.   244 *Midland waters:* the Mediterrean.   245 *Syrtes:* quicksands on the northern coast of Africa.   249 *Iberians:* ancient inhabitants of the Iberian (Spanish) Peninsula.

The lights come out in the street,
In the school-room windows;—but cold,
Solemn, unlighted, austere,   10
Through the gathering darkness, arise
The chapel-walls, in whose bound
Thou, my father! art laid.

There thou dost lie, in the gloom
Of the autumn evening. But ah!   15
That word, gloom, to my mind
Brings thee back, in the light
Of thy radiant vigour, again;
In the gloom of November we pass'd
Days not dark at thy side;   20
Seasons impair'd not the ray
Of thy buoyant cheerfulness clear.
Such thou wast! and I stand
In the autumn evening, and think
Of bygone autumns with thee.   25

Fifteen years have gone round
Since thou arosest to tread,
In the summer-morning, the road
Of death, at a call unforeseen,
Sudden. For fifteen years,   30
We who till then in thy shade
Rested as under the boughs
Of a mighty oak, have endured
Sunshine and rain as we might,
Bare, unshaded, alone,   35
Lacking the shelter of thee.

O strong soul, by what shore
Tarriest thou now? For that force,
Surely, has not been left vain!
Some where, surely, afar,   40
In the sounding labour-house vast
Of being, is practised that strength,
Zealous, beneficent, firm!

Yes, in some far-shining sphere,
Conscious or not of the past,   45
Still thou performest the word
Of the Spirit in whom thou dost live—
Prompt, unwearied, as here!
Still thou upraisest with zeal

The humble good from the found,   50
Sternly repressest the bad!
Still, like a trumpet, dost rouse
Those who with half-open eyes
Tread the border-land dim
'Twixt vice and virtue; reviv'st   55
Succourest!—this was thy work,
This way thy life upon earth.

What is the course of the life
Of mortal men on the earth?—
Most men eddy about   60
Here and there—eat and drink,
Chatter and love and hate,
Gather and squander, are raised
Aloft, are hurl'd in the dust,
Striving blindly, achieving   65
Nothing; and then they die—
Perish;—and no one asks
Who or what they have been,
More than he asks what waves,
In the moonlit solitudes mild   70
Of the midmost Ocean, have swell'd,
Foam'd for a moment, and gone.

And there are some, whom a thirst
Ardent, unquenchable, fires,
Not with the crowd to be spent,   75
Not without aim to go round
In an eddy of purposeless dust,
Effort unmeaning and vain.
Ah yes! some of us strive
Not without action to die   80
Fruitless, but something to snatch
From dull oblivion, nor all
Glut the devouring grave!
We, we have chosen our path—
Path to a clear-purposed goal,   85
Path of advance!—but it leads
A long, steep journey, through sunk
Gorges, o'er mountains in snow.
Cheerful, with friends, we set forth—
Then, on the height, comes the storm.   90
Thunder crashes from rock
To rock, the cataracts reply,
Lightnings dazzle our eyes.

Roaring torrents have breach'd
The track, the stream-bed descends   95
In the place where the wayfarer once
Planted his footstep—the spray
Boils o'er its borders! aloft
The unseen snow-beds dislodge
Their hanging ruin; alas,   100
Havoc is made in our train!
Friends, who set forth at our side,
Falter, are lost in the storm.
We, we only are left!
With frowning foreheads, with lips   105
Sternly compress'd, we strain on,
On—and at nightfall at last
Come to the end of our way,
To the lonely inn 'mid the rocks;
Where the gaunt and taciturn host   110
Stands on the threshold, the wind
Shaking his thin white hairs—
Holds his lantern to scan
Our storm-beat figures, and asks:
Whom in our party we bring?   115
Whom we have left in the snow?

Sadly we answer: We bring
Only ourselves! we lost
Sight of the rest in the storm.
Hardly ourselves we fought through,   120
Stripp'd, without friends, as we are.
Friends, companions, and train;
The avalanche swept from our side.

But thou would'st not alone
Be saved, my father! alone   125
Conquer and come to thy goal,
Leaving the rest in the wild.
We were weary, and we
Fearful, and we in our march
Fain to drop down and to die.   130
Still thou turnedst, and still
Beckonedst the trembler, and still
Gavest the weary thy hand.

If, in the paths of the world,
Stones might have wounded thy feet,   135
Toil or dejection have tried

Thy spirit, of that we saw
Nothing—to us thou wast still
Cheerful, and helpful, and firm!
Therefore to thee it was given   140
Many to save with thyself;
And, at the end of thy day,
O faithful shepherd! to come,
Bringing thy sheep in thy hand.

And through thee I believe   145
In the noble and great who are gone;
Pure souls honour'd and blest
By former ages who else—
Such, so soulless, so poor,
Is the race of men whom I see—   150
Seem'd but a dream of the heart,
Seem'd but a cry of desire.
Yes! I believe that there lived
Others like thee in the past,
Not like the men of the crowd   155
Who all round me to-day
Bluster or cringe, and make life
Hideous, and arid, and vile;
But souls temper'd with fire,
Fervent, heroic, and good,   160
Helpers and friends of mankind.

Servants of God!—or sons
Shall I not call you? because
Not as servants ye knew
Your Father's innermost mind,   165
His, who unwillingly sees
One of his little ones lost—
Yours is the praise, if mankind
Hath not as yet in its march
Fainted, and fallen, and died!   170

See! In the rocks of the world
Marches the host of mankind,
A feeble, wavering line.
Where are they tending—A God
Marshall'd them, gave them their goal   175
Ah, but the way is so long!
Years they have been in the wild!
Sore thirst plagues them, the rocks
Rising all round, overawe;

Factions divide them, their host   180
Threatens to break, to dissolve.
—Ah, keep, keep them combined!
Else, of the myriads who fill
That army; not one shall arrive;
Sole they shall stray; in the rocks   185
Stagger for ever in vain,
Die one by one in the waste.

Then, in such hour of need
Of your fainting, dispirited race,
Ye, like angels, appear,   19(
Radiant with ardour divine!
Beacons of hope, ye appear!
Langour is not in your heart,
Weakness is not in your word,
Weariness not on your brow.   195
Ye alight in our van! at your voice,
Panic, despair, flee away.
Ye move through the ranks, recall
The stragglers, refresh the outworn
Praise, re-inspire the brave!   200
Order, courage, return.
Eyes rekindling, and prayers,
Follow your steps as ye go.
Ye fill up the gaps in our files,
Strengthen the wavering line,   205
Stablish, continue our march,
On, to the bound of the waste,
On, to the City of God.

Stanzas from the Grande Chartreuse

Through Alpine meadows soft-suffused
With rain, where thick the crocus blows,
Past the dark forges long disused,
The mule-track from Saint Laurent goes.
The bridge is crossed, and slow we ride,   5
Through forest, up the mountain side.

Stanzas from the Grande Chartreuse: *Title:* The Grande Chartreuse, once the
principal monastery of the Carthusian monks, is in the French Alps near Gre-
noble. 4 *Saint Laurent:* like *Dead Guier* (line 10) and *Courrerie* (line 18), near
the monastery.

The autumnal evening darkens round,
The wind is up, and drives the rain;
While, hark! far down, with strangled sound
Doth the Dead Guier's stream complain,   10
Where that wet smoke, among the woods,
Over his boiling caldron broods.

Swift rush the spectral vapors white
Past limestone scars with ragged pines,
Showing—then blotting from our sight!—   15
Halt—through the cloud-drift something shines!
High in the valley, wet and drear,
The huts of Courrerie appear.

Strike leftward! cries our guide; and higher
Mounts up the stony forest-way.   20
At last the encircling trees retire;
Look! through the showery twilight gray,
What pointed roofs are these advance?
A palace of the kings of France?

Approach, for what we seek is here!   25
Alight, and sparely sup, and wait
For rest in this outbuilding near;
Then cross the sward, and reach that gate;
Knock; pass the wicket. Thou art come
To the Carthusians' world-famed home.   30

The silent courts, where night and day
Into their stone-carved basins cold
The splashing icy fountains play,
The humid corridors behold,
Where, ghost-like in the deepening night,   35
Cowled forms brush by in gleaming white!

The chapel, where no organ's peal
Invests the stern and naked prayer!
With penitential cries they kneel
And wrestle; rising then, with bare   40
And white uplifted faces stand,
Passing the Host from hand to hand;

Each takes, and then his visage wan
Is buried in his cowl once more.
The cells!—the suffering Son of man   45
Upon the wall; the knee-worn floor;

And where they sleep, that wooden bed,
Which shall their coffin be when dead!

The library, where tract and tome
Not to feed priestly pride are there,   50
To hymn the conquering march of Rome,
Nor yet to amuse, as ours are:
They paint of souls the inner strife,
Their drops of blood, their death in life.

The garden, overgrown—yet mild,   55
See, fragrant herbs are flowering there;
Strong children of the Alpine wild
Whose culture is the brethren's care;
Of human tasks their only one,
And cheerful works beneath the sun.   60

Those halls, too, destined to contain
Each its own pilgrim-host of old,
From England, Germany, or Spain,—
All are before me! I behold
The house, the brotherhood austere.   65
And what am I, that I am here?

For rigorous teachers seized my youth,
And purged its faith, and trimmed its fire,
Showed me the high, white star of Truth,
There bade me gaze, and there aspire.   70
Even now their whispers pierce the gloom:
What dost thou in this living tomb?

Forgive me, masters of the mind!
At whose behest I long ago
So much unlearned, so much resigned: 75
I come not here to be your foe!
I seek these anchorites, not in ruth,
To curse and to deny your truth;

Not as their friend, or child, I speak!
But as, on some far northern strand,   80
Thinking of his own Gods, a Greek
In pity and mournful awe might stand
Before some fallen Runic stone;
For both were faiths, and both are gone.

Wandering between two worlds, one dead,   85
The other powerless to be born,

With nowhere yet to rest my head,
Like these, on earth I wait forlorn.
Their faith, my tears, the world deride:
I come to shed them at their side. 90

Oh, hide me in your gloom profound,
Ye solemn seats of holy pain!
Take me, cowled forms, and fence me round,
Till I possess my soul again;
Till free my thoughts before me roll, 95
Not chafed by hourly false control!

For the world cries, your faith is now
But a dead time's exploded dream;
My melancholy, sciolists say,
Is a passed mode, an outworn theme.— 100
As if the world had ever had
A faith, or sciolists been sad!

Ah! if it *be* passed, take away,
At least, the restlessness, the pain!
Be man henceforth no more a prey 105
To these out-dated stings again!
The nobleness of grief is gone:
Ah, leave us not the fret alone!

But,—if you cannot give us ease,—
Last of the race of them who grieve, 110
Here leave us to die out with these
Last of the people who believe!
Silent, while years engrave the brow;
Silent—the best are silent now.

Achilles ponders in his tent, 115
The kings of modern thought are dumb;
Silent they are, though not content,
And wait to see the future come.
They have the grief men had of yore,
But they contend and cry no more. 120

Our fathers watered with their tears
This sea of time whereon we sail;
Their voices were in all men's ears
Who passed within their puissant hail.

99 sciolists: pretenders to learning whose knowledge is superficial.

Still the same ocean round us raves,   125
But we stand mute, and watch the waves.

For what availed it, all the noise
And outcry of the former men?
Say, have their sons achieved more joys?
Say, is life lighter now than then?   130
The sufferers died, they left their pain;
The pangs which tortured them remain.

What helps it now, that Byron bore,
With haughty scorn which mocked the smart,
Through Europe to the Etolian shore   135
The pageant of his bleeding heart?
That thousands counted every groan,
And Europe made his woe her own?

What boots it, Shelley! that the breeze
Carried thy lovely wail away,   140
Musical through Italian trees
Which fringe thy soft blue Spezzian bay?
Inheritors of thy distress,
Have restless hearts one throb the less?

Or are we easier, to have read,   145
O Obermann! the sad, stern page,
Which tells us how thou hidd'st thy head
From the fierce tempest of thine age
In the lone brakes of Fontainebleau,
Or chalets near the Alpine snow?   150

Ye slumber in your silent grave!—
The world, which for an idle day
Grace to your mood of sadness gave,
Long since hath flung her weeds away.
The eternal trifler breaks your spell;   155
But we—we learnt your lore too well!

Years hence, perhaps, may dawn an age,
More fortunate, alas! than we,
Which without hardness will be sage,
And gay without frivolity.   160
Sons of the world, oh! speed those years;
But, while we wait, allow our tears!

146 *Obermann:* Étienne Pivert de Sénancour (1770–1846), author of the autobio-
graphical novel *Obermann.* 149 *Fontainebleau:* city near Paris with a famous
forest.

Allow them! We admire with awe
The exulting thunder of your race;
You give the universe your law,   165
You triumph over time and space:
Your pride of life, your tireless powers,
We praise them, but they are not ours.

We are like children reared in shade
Beneath some old-world abbey wall,   170
Forgotten in a forest-glade,
And secret from the eyes of all.
Deep, deep the greenwood round them waves,
Their abbey, and its close of graves!

But, where the road runs near the stream,   175
Oft through the trees they catch a glance
Of passing troops in the sun's beam,—
Pennon, and plume, and flashing lance;
Forth to the world those soldiers fare,
To life, to cities, and to war.   180

And through the woods, another way,
Faint bugle-notes from far are borne,
Where hunters gather, staghounds bay,
Round some old forest-lodge at morn.
Gay dames are there, in sylvan green;   185
Laughter and cries—those notes between!

The banners flashing through the trees
Make their blood dance, and chain their eyes;
That bugle-music on the breeze
Arrests them with a charmed surprise.   190
Banner by turns and bugle woo:
Ye shy recluses, follow too!

O children, what do ye reply?
"Action and pleasure, will ye roam
Through these secluded dells to cry   195
And call us? but too late ye come!
Too late for us your call ye blow,
Whose bent was taken long ago.

"Long since we pace this shadowed nave;
We watch those yellow tapers shine,   200
Emblems of hope over the grave,
In the high altar's depth divine.

The organ carries to our ear
Its accents of another sphere

"Fenced early in this cloistral round   205
Of revery, of shade, of prayer,
How should we grow in other ground?
How can we flower in foreign air?
—Pass, banners, pass, and bugles, cease;
And leave our desert to its peace!"   210

EMILY DICKINSON
1830–1886

There are few public dates in the life of this woman from Amherst whose privacy has been interpreted by biographers to shroud every trait from rationality to madness. Emily Dickinson went to Mount Holyoke for one year in 1847, but then turned her journeys inward to a few small rooms at home; she conquered the world with the stern and simple expedient of rejecting it. Her relation to her father, a Calvinist lawyer, may have been one of driving attraction-repulsion and may be reflected in her poetic quarrels with Christ, nature, sin, and love itself. Whether inspired naturally or through intellectual calculation, she is made a great poet by the tension and release of her feelings. She seems, sometimes, to mysticize her poems in order to animate and examine objects of nature and emotion, then to discard the vibration completely, leaving a reader with sharp realizations of the difficult contradictions in being alive. During her life she published only seven poems, anonymously; she wrote 1,775.

A narrow fellow in the grass

A narrow fellow in the grass
Occasionally rides;
You may have met him,—did you not?
His notice sudden is.

The grass divides as with a comb,   5
A spotted shaft is seen;
And then it closes at your feet
And opens further on.

He likes a boggy acre,
A floor too cool for corn.   10
Yet when a child, and barefoot,
I more than once, at morn,

Have passed, I thought, a whip-lash
Unbraiding in the sun,—
When, stooping to secure it,   15
It wrinkled, and was gone.

Several of nature's people
I know, and they know me;
I feel for them a transport
Of cordiality;   20

But never met this fellow,
Attended or alone,
Without a tighter breathing,
And zero at the bone.

Success is counted sweetest

Success is counted sweetest
By those who ne'er succeed.

To comprehend a nectar
Requires sorest need.

Not one of all the purple host   5
Who took the flag to-day
Can tell the definition,
So clear, of victory,

As he, defeated, dying,
On whose forbidden ear   10
The distant strains of triumph
Break, agonized and clear.

A wounded deer leaps highest

A wounded deer leaps highest,
I've heard the hunter tell;
'Tis but the ecstasy of death,
And then the brake is still.

The smitten rock that gushes,   5
The trampled steel that springs:
A cheek is always redder
Just where the hectic stings!

Mirth is the mail of anguish,
In which it caution arm,   10
Lest anybody spy the blood
And "You're hurt" exclaim!

My life closed twice before its close

My life closed twice before its close;
     It yet remains to see
If Immortality unveil
     A third event to me,

A wounded deer: *4 brake:* thicket. *8 hectic:* fever.

So huge, so hopeless to conceive,
    As these that twice befell.
Parting is all we know of heaven,
    And all we need of hell.

I taste a liquor never brewed

I taste a liquor never brewed,
From tankards scooped in pearl;
Not all the vats upon the Rhine
Yield such an alcohol!

Inebriate of air am I,   *5*
And debauchee of dew,
Reeling, through endless summer days,
From inns of molten blue.

When landlords turn the drunken bee
Out of the foxglove's door,   *10*
When butterflies renounce their drams,
I shall but drink the more!

Till seraphs swing their snowy hats,
And saints to windows run,
To see the little tippler   *15*
Leaning against the sun!

I like to see it lap the miles

I like to see it lap the miles,
And lick the valleys up,
And stop to feed itself at tanks;
And then, prodigious, step

Around a pile of mountains,   *5*
And, supercilious, peer
In shanties by the sides of roads;
And then a quarry pare

I taste a liquor: *3 Rhine:* Rhine wine (Rhenish) is famous.

To fit its sides, and crawl between,
Complaining all the while   10
In horrid, hooting stanza;
Then chase itself down hill

And neigh like Boanerges;
Then, punctual as a star,
Stop—docile and omnipotent—   15
At its own stable door.

A bird came down the walk

A bird came down the walk:
He did not know I saw;
He bit an angle-worm in halves
And ate the fellow, raw.

And then he drank a dew   5
From a convenient grass,
And then hopped sidewise to the wall
To let a beetle pass.

He glanced with rapid eyes
That hurried all abroad,—   10
They looked like frightened beads, I thought
He stirred his velvet head

Like one in danger; cautious,
I offered him a crumb,
And he unrolled his feathers   15
And rowed him softer home

Than oars divide the ocean,
Too silver for a seam,
Or butterflies, off banks of noon,
Leap, plashless, as they swim.   20

I like to see it: 13 *Boanerges:* probably derived from a word meaning "sons of thunder"; hence, a loud-voiced speaker, etc.

Because I could not stop for death

Because I could not stop for Death,
He kindly stopped for me;
The carriage held but just ourselves
And Immortality.

We slowly drove, he knew no haste,   5
And I had put away
My labor, and my leisure too,
For his civility.

We passed the school where children played
At wrestling in a ring;   10
We passed the fields of gazing grain,
We passed the setting sun.

We paused before a house that seemed
A swelling of the ground;
The roof was scarcely visible,   15
The cornice but a mound.

Since then 'tis centuries; but each
Feels shorter than the day
I first surmised the horses' heads
Were toward eternity.   20

I felt a funeral in my brain

I felt a funeral in my brain,
    And mourners, to and fro,
Kept treading, treading, till it seemed
    That sense was breaking through.

And when they all were seated,   5
    A service like a drum
Kept beating, beating, till I thought
    My mind was going numb.

And then I heard them lift a box,
    And creak across my soul   10

With those same boots of lead, again.
    Then space began to toll

As all the heavens were a bell,
    And Being but an ear,
And I and silence some strange race,   *15*
    Wrecked, solitary, here.

I heard a fly buzz when I died

I heard a fly buzz when I died;
    The stillness round my form
Was like the stillness in the air
    Between the heaves of storm.

The eyes beside had wrung them dry,   *5*
    And breaths were gathering sure
For that last onset, when the king
    Be witnessed in his power.

I willed my keepsakes, signed away
    What portion of me I   *10*
Could make assignable,—and then
    There interposed a fly,

With blue, uncertain, stumbling buzz,
    Between the light and me;
And then the windows failed, and then   *15*
    I could not see to see.

After great pain a formal feeling comes

After great pain a formal feeling comes—
The nerves sit ceremonious like tombs;
The stiff Heart questions—was it He that bore?
And yesterday—or centuries before?

The feet mechanical   *5*
Go round a wooden way

Of ground or air or Ought, regardless grown,
A quartz contentment like a stone.

This is the hour of lead
Remembered if outlived,   10
As freezing persons recollect the snow—
First chill, then stupor, then the letting go.

The last night that she lived

The last night that she lived,
It was a common night,
Except the dying; this to us
Made nature different.

We noticed smallest things,—   5
Things overlooked before,
By this great light upon our minds
Italicized, as 'twere.

That others could exist
While she must finish quite,   10
A jealousy for her arose
So nearly infinite.

We waited while she passed;
It was a narrow time,
Too jostled were our souls to speak,   15
At length the notice came.

She mentioned, and forgot;
Then lightly as a reed
Bent to the water, shivered scarce,
Consented, and was dead.   20

And we, we placed the hair
And drew the head erect;
And then an awful leisure was,
Our faith to regulate.

Pain has an element of blank

Pain has an element of blank;
It cannot recollect
When it began, or if there were
A day when it was not.

It has no future but itself,
Its infinite realms contain
Its past, enlightened to perceive
New periods of pain.

They say that "time assuages"

They say that "time assuages,"—
Time never did assuage;
An actual suffering strengthens,
As sinews do, with age.

Time is a test of trouble,
But not a remedy.
If such it prove, it prove too
There was no malady.

The brain is wider than the sky

The brain is wider than the sky,
For, put them side by side,
The one the other will include
With ease, and you beside.

The brain is deeper than the sea,   5
For, hold them, blue to blue,
The one the other will absorb,
As sponges, buckets do.

The brain is just the weight of God,
For, lift them, pound for pound,   10

And they will differ, if they do,
 As syllable from sound.

I died for beauty, but was scarce

I died for beauty, but was scarce
Adjusted in the tomb,
When one who died for truth was lain
In an adjoining room.

He questioned softly why I failed?   5
"For beauty," I replied.
"And I for truth,—the two are one;
We brethren are," he said.

And so, as kinsmen met a night,
We talked between the rooms,   10
Until the moss had reached our lips,
And covered up our names.

Bring me the sunset in a cup

Bring me the sunset in a cup,
Reckon the morning's flagons up,
 And say how many dew;
Tell me how far the morning leaps,
Tell me what time the weaver sleeps   5
 Who spun the breadths of blue!

Write me how many notes there be
In the new robin's ecstasy
 Among astonished boughs;
How many trips the tortoise makes,   10
How many cups the bee partakes,—
 The debauchee of dews!

Also, who laid the rainbow's piers,
Also, who leads the docile spheres
 By withes of supple blue?   15

Whose fingers string the stalactite,
Who counts the wampum of the night,
    To see that none is due?

Who built this little Alban house
And shut the windows down so close   20
    My spirit cannot see?
Who'll let me out some gala day,
With implements to fly away,
    Passing pomposity?

Forever is composed of Nows

Forever is composed of Nows—
'Tis not a different time,
Except for infiniteness
And latitude of home.

From this, experienced here,   5
Remove the dates to these,
Let months dissolve in further months,
And years exhale in years.

Without certificate or pause
Or celebrated days,   10
As infinite our years would be
As Anno Domini's.

The bustle in a house

The bustle in a house
The morning after death
Is solemnest of industries
Enacted upon earth,—

The sweeping up of heart,
And putting love away
We shall not want to use again
Until eternity.

It sifts from leaden sieves

It sifts from leaden sieves,
It powders all the wood,
It fills with alabaster wool
The wrinkles of the road.

It makes an even face   5
Of mountain and of plain,—
Unbroken forehead from the east
Unto the east again.

It reaches to the fence,
It wraps it, rail by rail,   10
Till it is lost in fleeces;
It flings a crystal veil

On stump and stack and stem,—
The summer's empty room,
Acres of seams where harvests were,   15
Recordless, but for them.

It ruffles wrists of posts
As ankles of a queen,—
Then stills its artisans like ghosts,
Denying they have been.   20

To hear an Oriole sing

To hear an Oriole sing
May be a common thing,
Or only a divine.

It is not of the bird
Who sings the same, unheard,   5
As unto crowd.

The fashion of the ear
Attireth that it hear
In dun or fair.

So whether it be rune,   *10*
Or whether it be none,
Is of within;

The "tune is in the tree,"
The sceptic showeth me;
"No, sir! In thee!"   *15*

GERARD MANLEY
HOPKINS
1844–1889

Hopkins, like Emily Dickinson, was published posthumously, and his reputation and influence is virtually that of a modern poet. Though he abandoned all to become a Jesuit and was perfectly disciplined and obedient in orders, Hopkins as a poet is supremely sensuous and conscious of beauty. One of a gifted family, he was encouraged in the arts, but —caught in the revival of ritualism and dogma called "The Oxford Movement" while at Balliol—he gave up his intention of becoming an Anglican divine and entered the Catholic Church under the tutelage of John Henry Newman in 1866. For seven years he abandoned poetry completely, but two years before his ordination as a Jesuit in 1877 he wrote a major poem, *The Wreck of the Deutschland*; like all the poems to come, it was never published in his lifetime. As a priest, he experienced enough of life amid the poverty of Liverpool to disturb and broaden him. His complex love of language and the private theories of "inscape" and "sprung rhythem" make him appear an aesthete in black robes, but he was moved by other people's lives (see "Felix Randal"), and the substance of his poetry is metaphysical in impact. Hopkins's poems are especially apt examples of the intellectual creativity and varieties of pleasure possible in fine poetry.

The Wreck of the Deutschland

To the happy memory of five Franciscan Nuns exiled by the Falk Laws drowned between midnight and morning of Dec. 7th, 1875

PART THE FIRST

I

    Thou mastering me
  God! giver of breath and bread;
World's strand, sway of the sea;
  Lord of living and dead;
Thou hast bound bones and veins in me, fastened me flesh,   5
And after it almost unmade, what with dread,
  Thy doing: and dost thou touch me afresh?
Over again I feel thy finger and find thee.

II

    I did say yes
  O at lightning and lashed rod;   10
Thou heardst me truer than tongue confess
  Thy terror, O Christ, O God;
Thou knowest the walls, altar and hour and night:
The swoon of a heart that the sweep and the hurl of thee trod
  Hard down with a horror of height: 15
And the midriff astrain with leaning of, laced with fire of stress.

III

    The frown of his face
  Before me, the hurtle of hell
Behind, where, where was a, where was a place?
  I whirled out wings that spell   20
And fled with a fling of the heart to the heart of the Host.

The Wreck of the *Deutschland: Epigraph:* Catholicism and German imperialism collided under Bismarck, and the German government took severe measures against the Catholic Church. In 1872 the Jesuits were expelled; a year later, Dr. Adalbert Falk drafted the May Laws (or Falk Laws), even more stringent.

My heart, but you were dovewinged, I can tell,
    Carrier-witted, I am bold to boast,
To flash from the flame to the flame then, tower from the grace
        to the grace.

IV

    I am soft sift   25
      In an hourglass—at the wall
    Fast, but mined with a motion, a drift,
      And it crowds and it combs to the fall;
I steady as a water in a well, to a poise, to a pane,
    But roped with, always, all the way down from the tall   30
      Fells or flanks of the voel, a vein
Of the gospel proffer, a pressure, a principle, Christ's gift.

V

    I kiss my hand
      To the stars, lovely-asunder
    Starlight, wafting him out of it; and   35
      Glow, glory in thunder;
Kiss my hand to the dappled-with-damson west:
Since, tho' he is under the world's splendour and wonder,
    His mystery must be instressed, stressed;
For a I greet him the days I meet him, and bless when I under-
        stand.   40

VI

    Not out of his bliss
      Springs the stress felt
    Nor first from heaven (and few know this)
      Swings the stroke dealt—
Stroke and a stress that stars and storms deliver,   45
    That guilt is hushed by, hearts are flushed by and melt—
      But it rides time like riding a river
(And here the faithful waver, the faithless fable and miss).

VII

    It dates from day
      Of his going in Galilee;   50
    Warm-laid grave of a womb-like grey;
      Manger, maiden's knee;
The dense and the driven Passion, and frightful sweat;

---

28 *combs:* rolls over, as the crest of a wave rolls over as it falls. *29 poise:* balance, the water being level as balanced scales. *pane:* a sheet of glass, the water being steady and level. *32 Fells or flanks of the voel:* pastures and flanks of a bare hill or mountain; Hopkins has in mind a mountain in North Wales, where he wrote this poem. *37 damson:* damson plum. *39 instressed:* felt in the very depths of one's being, through God's grace.

Thence the discharge of it, there its swelling to be,
    Though felt before, though in high flood yet—   *55*
What none would have known of it, only the heart, being hard
        at bay,

VIII

    Is out with it! Oh,
      We lash with the best or worst
    Word last! How a lush-kept plush-capped sloe
      Will, mouthed to flesh-burst,   *60*
Gush!—flush the man, the being with it, sour or sweet,
    Brim, in a flash, full!—Hither then, last or first,
      To hero of Calvary, Christ's feet—
Never ask if meaning it, wanting it, warned of it—men go.

IX

    Be adored among men,   *65*
      God, three-numberèd form;
    Wring thy rebel, dogged in den,
      Man's malice, with wrecking and storm.
Beyond saying sweet, past telling of tongue,
    Thou art lightning and love, I found it, a winter and warm;   *70*
      Father and fondler of heart thou hast wrung:
Hast thy dark descending and most art merciful then.

X

    With an anvil-ding
      And with fire in him forge thy will
    Or rather, rather then, stealing as Spring   *75*
      Through him, melt him but master him still:
Whether at once, as once at a crash Paul,
Or as Austin, a lingering-out sweet skill,
      Make mercy in all of us, out of us all
Mastery, but be adored, but be adored King.   *80*

PART THE SECOND
XI

    "Some find me a sword; some
      The flange and the rail; flame,
    Fang, or flood" goes Death on drum,
      And storms bugle his fame.
But wé dream we are rooted in earth—Dust!   *85*
Flesh falls within sight of us, we, through our flower the
        same,

77 *Paul:* St. Paul, martyred in A.D. 67(?).   78 *Austin:* St. Augustine (354–430),
Bishop of Hippo.

Wave with the meadow, forget that there must
The sour scythe cringe, and the blear share come.

XII

On Saturday sailed from Bremen,
American-outward-bound,   90
Take settler and seamen, tell men with women,
Two hundred souls in the round—
O Father, not under thy feathers nor ever as guessing
The goal was a shoal, of a fourth the doom to be drowned;
Yet did the dark side of the bay of thy blessing   95
Not vault them, the millions of rounds of thy mercy not reeve
even them in?

XIII

Into the snows she sweeps,
Hurling the haven behind,
The Deutschland, on Sunday; and so the sky keeps,
For the infinite air is unkind,   100
And the sea flint-flake, black-backed in the regular blow,
Sitting Eastnortheast, in cursed quarter, the wind;
Wiry and white-fiery and whirlwind-swivellèd snow
Spins to the widow-making unchilding unfathering deeps.

XIV

She drove in the dark to leeward,   105
She struck—not a reef or a rock
But the combs of a smother of sand: night drew her
Dead to the Kentish Knock;
And she beat the bank down with her bows and the ride of
her keel:
The breakers rolled on her beam with ruinous shock;   110
And canvas and compass, the whorl and the wheel
Idle for ever to waft her or wind her with, these she endured.

XV

Hope had grown grey hairs,
Hope had mourning on,
Trenched with tears, carved with cares,   115
Hope was twelve hours gone;
And frightful a nightfall folded rueful a day
Nor rescue, only rocket and lightship, shone,
And lives at last were washing away:

89 *Bremen:* German city on the North Sea. 91 *tell:* count or reckon. 96 *reeve:*
fasten, as with ropes. 108 *Kentish Knock:* a sandbank in the Thames estuary.

To the shrouds they took,—they shook in the hurling and
      horrible airs. 120

XVI

One stirred from the rigging to save
  The wild woman-kind below,
With a rope's end round the man, handy and brave—
  He was pitched to his death at a blow,
For all his dreadnought breast and braids of thew: 125
They could tell him for hours, dandled the to and fro
  Through the cobbled form-fleece, what could he do
With the burl of the fountains of air, buck and the flood of the
      wave?

XVII

They fought with God's cold—
  And they could not and fell to the deck 130
(Crushed them) or water (and drowned them) or rolled
  With the sea-romp over the wreck.
Night roared, with the heart-break hearing a heart-broke
      rabble,
The woman's wailing, the crying of child without check—
  Till a lioness arose breasting the babble, 135
A prophetess towered in the tumult, a virginal tongue told.

XVIII

Ah, touched in your bower of bone
  Are you! turned for an exquisite smart,
Have you! make words break from me here all alone,
  Do you!—mother of being in me, heart. 140
O unteachably after evil, but uttering truth,
  Why, tears! is it? tears, such a melting, a madrigal start!
  Never-eldering revel and river of youth,
What can it be, this glee? the good you have there of your own?

XIX

Sister, a sister calling 145
  A master, her master and mine!—
And the inboard seas run swirling and hawling;
  The rash smart sloggering brine
Blinds her; but she that weather sees one thing, one;
Has one fetch in her: she rears herself to divine 150
  Ears, and the call of the tall nun
To the men in the tops and the tackle rode over the storm's
      brawling.

147 *hawling:* hauling.

XX

    She was first of a five and came
  Of a coifèd sisterhood.
    (O Deutschland, double a desperate name!   *155*
    O world wide of its good!
  But Gertrude, lily, and Luther, are two of a town,
  Christ's lily and beast of the waste wood:
    From life's dawn it is drawn down,
Abel is Cain's brother and breasts they have sucked the same.)   *160*

XXI

    Loathed for a love men knew in them,
  Banned by the land of their birth,
    Rhine refused them. Thames would ruin them;
    Surf, snow, river and earth
  Gnashed: but thou art above, thou Orion of light;   *165*
  Thy unchancelling poising palms were weighing the worth,
    Thou martyr-master: in thy sight
Storm flakes were scroll-leaved flowers, lily showers—sweet
      heaven was astrew in them.

XXII

    Five! the finding and sake
  And cipher of suffering Christ.   *170*
    Mark, the mark is of man's make
  And the word of it Sacrificed.
  But he scores it in scarlet himself on his own bespoken,
  Before-time-taken, dearest prizèd and priced—
    Stigma, signal, cinquefoil token   *175*
For lettering of the lamb's fleece, ruddying of the rose flake.

XXIII

    Joy fall to thee, father Francis,
  Drawn to the Life that died;
    With the gnarls of the nails in thee, niche of the lance, his
    Lovescape crucified   *180*

155: Deutschland is the name of both the ship which carries them to their doom and of the country which banished them; it is therefore "double a desperate name." *157 Gertrude:* St. Gertrude of Eisleben, Germany, the birthplace of Luther. *Luther:* Martin Luther (1483–1546), whose rebellion against the Church Hopkins, a Catholic, would naturally view as evil. *165 Orion:* the most brilliant constellation. *169–170: finding:* that which is emblematic of something, or by which something is discovered. *sake:* "the being something has, as a voice by its echo, a face by its reflection, a body by its shadow, a man by his name, face, or memory, *and also* that in the thing by virtue of which it has this being abroad" (Hopkins). *175 cinquefoil:* five-leaved. *177 Francis:* St. Francis of Assisi (1182–1226), on whose body the stigmata were said to have appeared. *180 Lovescape:* word coined by Hopkins: the pattern of Christ's wounds.

And seal of his seraph-arrival and these thy daughters
And five-livèd and leavèd favour and pride,
    Are sisterly sealed in wild waters,
To bathe in his fall-gold mercies, to breathe in his all-fire
        glances.

XXIV

    Away in the loveable west,   *185*
    On a pastoral forehead of Wales,
  I was under a roof here, I was at rest,
    And they the prey of the gales;
She to the black-about air, to the breaker, the thickly
Falling flakes, to the throng that catches and quails   *190*
  Was calling "O Christ, Christ, come quickly":
The cross to her she calls Christ to her, christens her wild-worst
        Best.

XXV

    The majesty! what did she mean?
    Breathe, arch and original Breath.
  Is it love in her of the being as her lover had been?   *195*
    Breathe, body of lovely Death.
They were else-minded then, altogether, the men
Woke thee with a *we are perishing* in the weather of Genne-
        sareth.
  Or is it that she cried for the crown then,
The keener to come at the comfort for feeling the combating
        keen?   *200*

XXVI

    For how to the heart's cheering
    The down-dugged ground-hugged grey
  Hovers off, the jay-blue heavens appearing
    Of pied and peeled May!
Blue-beating and hoary-glow height; or night, still higher,   *205*
With belled fire and the moth-soft Milky Way,
  What by your measure is the heaven of desire,
The treasure never eyesight got, nor was ever guessed what
        for the hearing?

XXVII

    No, but it was not these.
    The jading and jar of the cart,   *210*

---

198 Gennesareth: Sea of Galilee, where Christ miraculously calmed the storm
(Matt. 14:204).

Time's tasking, it is fathers that asking for ease
    Of the sodden-with-its-sorrowing heart,
  Not danger, electrical horror; then further it finds
    The appealing of the Passion is tenderer in prayer apart:
      Other, I gather, in measure her mind's   215
Burden, in wind's burly and beat of endragonèd seas.

XXVIII

    But how shall I . . . make me room there:
      Reach me a . . . Fancy, come faster—
  Strike you the sight of it? look at it loom there,
    Thing that she . . . there then! the Master,   220
      Ipse, the only one, Christ, King, Head:
  He was to cure the extremity where he had cast her;
    Do, deal, lord it with living and dead;
Let him ride, her pride, in his triumph, despatch and have
      done with his doom there.

XXIX

    Ah! there was a heart right!   225
      There was single eye!
  Read the unshapeable shock night
    And knew the who and the why;
  Wording it how but by him that present and past,
    Heaven and earth are word of, worded by?—   230
      The Simon Peter of a soul! to the blast
Tarpeian-fast, but a blown beacon of light.

XXX

    Jesu, heart's light,
      Jesu, maid's son,
  What was the feast followed the night   235
    Thou hadst glory of this nun?—
  Feast of the one woman without stain.
  For so conceivèd, so to conceive thee is done;
    But here was heart-throe, birth of a brain,
Word, that heard and kept thee and uttered thee outright.   240

XXXI

    Well, she has thee for the pain, for the
      Patience; but pity of the rest of them!
  Heart, go and bleed at a bitterer vein for the
    Comfortless unconfessed of them—

221 *Ipse:* Latin for "He himself." 226 *single eye:* "The light of the body is the eye; if therefore thine eye be single, thy whole body shall be full of light" (Matt. 6:22). 232 *Tarpeian-fast:* as steadfast as the Tarpeian Rock, on the Roman Capitoline. 235 *feast:* December 8, the feast of the Immaculate Conception.

No not uncomforted: lovely-felicitous Providence 245
Finger of a tender of, O of a feathery delicacy, the breast of
    the
Maiden could obey so, be a bell to, ring of it, and
Startle the poor sheep back! is the shipwreck then a harvest,
        does tempest carry the grain for thee?

XXXII

I admire thee, master of the tides,
    Of the Yore-flood, of the year's fall; 250
The recurb and the recovery of the gulf's sides,
    The girth of it and the wharf of it and the wall;
Stanching, quenching ocean of a motionable mind;
Ground of being, and granite of it: past all
    Grasp God, throned behind 255
Death with a sovereignty that heeds but hides, bodes but abides;

XXXIII

With a mercy that outrides
    The all of water, an ark
For the listener; for the lingerer with a love glides
    Lower than death and the dark; 260
A vein for the visiting of the past-prayer, pent in prison,
The-last-breath penitent spirits—the uttermost mark
    Our passion-plungèd giant risen,
The Christ of the Father compassionate, fetched in the storm
        of his strides.

XXXIV

Now burn, new born to the world, 265
    Double-naturèd name,
The heaven-flung, heart-fleshed, maiden-furled
    Miracle-in-Mary-of-flame,
Mid-numbered He in three of the thunder-throne!
Not a dooms-day dazzle in his coming nor dark as he came; 270
    Kind, but royally reclaiming his own;
A released shower, let flash to the shire, not a lilghtning of fire
        hard-hurled.

XXXV

Dame, at our door
    Drowned, and among our shoals,
Remember us in the roads, the heaven-haven of the
    Reward: 275
    Our King back, oh; upon English souls!

250 *Yore-flood:* either the Deluge or the primal waters described in Gen. 1:2.

Let him easter in us, be a dayspring to the dimness of us,
       be a crimson-cresseted east,
   More brightening her, rare-dear Britain, as his reign rolls,
       Pride, rose, prince, hero of us, high-priest,
   Our hearts' charity's hearth's fires, our thoughts' chivalry's
       throng's Lord.   *280*

The Habit of Perfection

Elected Silence, sing to me
And beat upon my whorlèd ear,
Pipe me to pastures still and be
The music that I care to hear.

Shape nothing, lips; be lovely-dumb: *5*
It is the shut, the curfew sent
From there where all surrenders come
Which only makes you eloquent.

Be shellèd, eyes, with double dark
And find the uncreated light: *10*
This ruck and reel which you remark
Coils, keeps, teases simple sight.

Palate, the hutch of tasty lust,
Desire not to be rinsed with wine:
The can must be so sweet, the crust   *15*
So fresh that come in fasts devine!

Nostrils, your careless breath that spend
Upon the stir and keep of pride,
What relish shall the censers send
Along the sanctuary side!   *20*

O feel-of-primrose hands, O feet
That want the yield of plushy sward,
But you shall walk the golden street
And you unhouse and house the Lord.

And, Poverty, be thou the bride   *25*
And now the marriage feast begun,

277 *easter:* Easter is the feast of the Resurrection; Hopkins turns the noun into
a verb, meaning "be resurrected."

298   *Gerard Manley Hopkins*

And lily-coloured clothes provide
Your spouse not laboured-at nor spun.

God's Grandeur

The world is charged with the grandeur of God.
   It will flame out, like a shining from shook foil;
   It gathers to a greatness, like the ooze of oil
Crushed. Why do men then now not reck his rod?
Generations have trod, have trod, have trod;   5
   And all is seared with trade; bleared, smeared with toil;
   And wears man's smudge and shares man's smell: the soil
Is bare now, nor can foot feel, being shod.

And for all this, nature is never spent;
   There lives the dearest freshness deep down things;   10
And though the last lights off the black West went
   Oh, morning, at the brown brink eastward, springs—
Because the Holy Ghost over the bent
   World broods with warm breast and with ah! bright winds.

The Starlight Night

Look at the stars! look, look up at the skies!
   O look at all the fire-folk sitting in the air!
   The bright boroughs, the circle-citadels there!
Down in dim woods the diamond delves! the elves'-eyes!
The gray lawns cold where gold, where quickgold lies!   5
   Wind-beat whitebeam! airy abeles set on a flare!
   Flake-doves sent floating forth at a farmyard scare!
Ah, well! it is all a purchase, all is a prize.

Buy then! bid then!—What?—Prayer, patience, alms, vows.
   Look, look: a May-mess, like on orchard boughs!   10
Look! March-bloom, like on mealed-with-yellow sallows!
   These are indeed the barn; withindoors house
The shocks. This piece-bright paling shuts the spouse
   Christ home, Christ and his mother and all his hallows.

The Starlight Night: *6 abeles:* poplars.   *11 sallows:* willows.   *13 paling:* fencing.

Spring

Nothing is so beautiful as spring—
    When weeds, in wheels, shoot long and lovely and lush;
    Thrush's eggs look little low heavens, and thrush
Through the echoing timber does so rinse and wring
The ear, it strikes like lightnings to hear him sing;   5
    The glassy peartree leaves and blooms, they brush
    The descending blue; that blue is all in a rush
With richness; the racing lambs too have fair their fling.

What is all this juice and all this joy?
    A strain of the earth's sweet being in the beginning   10
In Eden garden.—Have, get, before it cloy,
    Before it cloud, Christ, lord, and sour with sinning,
Innocent mind and Mayday in girl and boy,
    Most, O maid's child, thy choice and worthy the winning.

The Windhover

TO CHRIST OUR LORD

I caught this morning morning's minion, kingdom of
    daylight's dauphin, dapple-dawn-drawn Falcon, in his riding
    Of the rolling level underneath him steady air, and striding
High there, how he rung upon the rein of a wimpling wing
In his ecstasy! then off, off forth on swing,   5
    As a skate's heel sweeps smooth on a bow-bend: the hurl
        and gliding
    Rebuffed the big wind. My heart in hiding
Stirred for a bird,—the achieve of, the mastery of the thing!

Brute beauty and valor and act, oh, air, pride, plume here
    Buckle! AND the fire that breaks from thee then, a billion   10
Times told lovelier, more dangerous, O my chevalier!

    No wonder of it: shéer plód makes plough down sillion
Shine, and blue-bleak embers, ah my dear,
    Fall, gall themselves, and gash gold-vermilion.

The Windhover: *4 rung:* in horsemanship, a horse rings upon the rein when he runs in a circle at the end of a long rein held by a trainer; falcons "ring" when they rise in spirals. *12 sillion:* the side of a furrow.

Pied Beauty

Glory be to God for dappled things—
    For skies of couple-colour as a brindled cow;
      For rose-moles all in stipple upon trout that swim;
Fresh-firecoal chestnut-falls; finches wings;
    Landscape plotted and pieced—fold, fallow, and plough;   5
      And áll trádes, their gear and tackle and trim.

All things, counter, original, spare, strange;
    Whatever is fickle, freckled (who knows how?)
      With swift, slow; sweet, sour; adazzle, dim;
He father's-forth whose beauty is past change: Praise him.   10

Felix Randal

Felix Randal the farrier, O he is dead then? my duty all ended,
Who have watched his mould of man, big-boned and
    hardy-handsome
Pining, pining, till time when reason rambled in it and some
Fatal four disorders, fleshed there, all contended?

Sickness broke him. Impatient he cursed at first, but mended   5
Being anointed and all; though a heavenlier heart began some
Months earlier, since I had our sweet reprieve and ransom
Tendered to him. Ah well, God rest him all road ever he
    offended!

This seeing the sick endears them to us, us too it endears.
My tongue had taught thee comfort, touch had quenched
    thy tears,   10
Thy tears that touched my heart, child, Felix, poor Felix
    Randal;

How far from then forethought of, all thy more boisterous
    years,
When thou at the random grim forge, powerful amidst peers,
Didst fettle for the great grey drayhorse his bright and
    battering sandal!

Felix Randal: *1 farrier:* a blacksmith who shoes horses. *13 random:* built of irregular stones (W. H. Gardner). *14 fettle:* prepare, make ready.

Spring and Fall
TO A YOUNG CHILD

Márgarét, are you gríeving
Over Goldengrove unleaving?
Leáves, líke the things of man, you
With your fresh thoughts care for, can you?
Ah! ás the heart grows older   5
It will come to such sights colder
By and by, nor spare a sigh
Though worlds of wanwood leafmeal lie;
And yet you wíll weep and know why.
Now no matter, child, the name: 10
Sórrow's spríngs áre the same.
Nor mouth had, no nor mind, expressed
What heart heard of, ghost guessed:
It ís the blight man was born for,
It is Margaret you mourn for.   15

Inversnaid

This darksome burn, horseback brown,
His rollrock highroad roaring down,
In coop and in comb the fleece of his foam
Flutes and low to the lake falls home.

A windpuff-bonnet of fáwn-fróth   5
Turns and twindles over the broth
Of a pool so pitchblack, féll-frówning,
It rounds and rounds Despair to drowning.

Degged with dew, dappled with dew
Are the groins of the braes that the brook treads through,   10
Wiry heathpacks, flitches of fern,
And the beadbonny ash that sits over the burn.

Spring and Fall: 8 *wanwood leafmeal*: Both words were coined by Hopkins; the first comes from *wan* (pale) and *wood*, and the second is formed by analogy with *piecemeal.*

Inversnaid: 2 *rollrock*: a coined word. The force of the water rolls the rocks. 3 *coop . . . comb*: The water is pent in by rocks or it combs over them. 9 *degged*: sprinkled. 10 *braes*: banks of a stream, slopes. 11 *flitches*: strips, tufts.

What would the world be, once bereft
Of wet and of wildness? Let them be left,
O let them be left, wildness and wet;   15
Long live the weeds and the wilderness yet.

No Worst, There Is None

No worst, there is none. Pitched past pitch of grief,
More pangs will, schooled at forepangs, wilder wring.
Comforter, where, where is your comforting?
Mary, mother of us, where is your relief?
My cries heave, herds-long; huddle in a man, a chief   5
Woe, wórld-sorrow; on an áge-old anvil wince and sing—
Then lull, then leave off. Fury had shrieked "No ling-
ering! Let me be fell: force I must be brief."

  O the mind, mind has mountains; cliffs of fall
Frightful, sheer, no-man-fathomed. Hold them cheap   10
May who ne'er hung there. Nor does long our small
Durance deal with that steep or deep. Here! creep,
Wretch, under a comfort serves in a whirlwind: all
Life death does end and each day dies with sleep.

I Wake and Feel the Fell of Dark

I wake and feel the fell of dark, not day.
What hours, O what black hoürs we have spent
This night! what sights you, heart, saw; ways you went!
And more must, in yet longer light's delay.
With witness I speak this. But where I say   5
Hours I mean years, mean life. And my lament
Is cries countless, cries like dead letters sent
To dearest him that lives alas! away.

I am gall, I am heartburn. God's most deep decree
Bitter would have me taste: my taste was me;   10
Bones built in me, flesh filled, blood brimmed the curse.
Selfyeast of spirit a dull dough sours. I see
The lost are like this, and their scourge to be
As I am mine, their sweating selves; but worse.

Patience, Hard Thing!

Patience, hard thing! the hard thing but to pray,
But bid for, Patience is! Patience who asks
Wants war, wants wounds; weary his times, his tasks;
To do without, take tosses, and obey.
    Rare patience roots in these, and, these away,   5
Nowhere. Natural heart's ivy, Patience masks
Our ruins of wrecked past purpose. There she basks
Purple eyes and seas of liquid leaves all day.

We hear our hearts grate on themselves: it kills
To bruise them dearer. Yet the rebellious wills   10
Of us we do bid God bend to him even so.
    And where is he who more and more distils
Delicious kindness?—He is patient. Patience fills
His crisp combs, and that comes those ways we know.

Thou Art Indeed Just, Lord

Justus quidem tu es, Domine, si disputem tecum: verumtamen justa loquar
ad te: Quare via impiorum prosperatur? etc.

Thou art indeed just, Lord, if I contend
With thee; but, sir, so what I plead is just.
Why do sinners' ways prosper? and why must
Disappointment all I endeavour end?
Wert thou my enemy, O thou my friend,   5
How wouldst thou worse, I wonder, than thou dost
Defeat, thwart me? Oh, the sots and thralls of lust
Do in spare hours more thrive than I that spend,
Sir, life upon thy cause. See, banks and brakes
Now, leavèd how thick! lacèd they are again   10
With fretty chervil, look, and fresh wind shakes
Them; birds build—but not I build; no, but strain,
Time's eunuch, and not breed one work that works.
Mine, O thou lord of life, send my roots rain.

Patience, Hard Thing: *14 combs:* honeycombs.

Thou Art Indeed Just, Lord: *Epigraph:* The Latin quotation is from Jer. 13:1;
the first three lines of the sonnet translate it.   *11 chervil:* cow parsley.

WILLIAM BUTLER YEATS
1865–1939

Son of an Irish painter whose religion was art, Yeats partly fol-
lowed suit in his youth, writing sensual abstractions after Rosetti
and Shelley and finding himself a founder of the *fin de siecle* Rhymers' Club
in 1891. Equally interested in Blake and mysticism, Yeats participated in
occult secret societies, mainly The Order of the Golden Dawn. Participating
in Irish revolutionary and cultural ambitions, his Dublin friends reinforced
his interest in native folklore and directed him to the heroic myths of early
Gaelic history. All this was woven into his poetry and drama by 1910, lend-
ing weight to his imagery and symbolism. A lifelong search for the core of
things, both emotionally and spiritually, was underway.

Yeats was madly in love for many years with a beautiful actress,
Maud Gonne, but she would never marry him. (Years later, he proposed

to her daughter, but no one concerned would hear of it.) Yeats's friends, who composed an elite of literary and landed gentry, were pleased when he finally accepted an eligible young candidate for his affections and settled down in marriage at the age of fifty-two. His new wife demonstrated an ability at automatic writing which enabled him to pull his imaginative and mystical themes into a system of symbols for a multileveled universe. These writings, as developed in *A Vision* (1925, 1937), dominate his later poems which, even after winning the Nobel Prize in 1923, entered still another stage of achievement. From 1922 to 1928 he was an active senator of the Irish Free State, where he continued to promote national culture, particularly the theater. Yeats's last poetry is, if anything, even more youthful and lusty. The tightness of his lyrics and perfection of his symbolism continued to advance.

A Dialogue of Self and Soul

I

My Soul   I summon to the winding ancient stair;
    Set all your mind upon the steep ascent,
    Upon the broken, crumbling battlement,
    Upon the breathless starlit air,
    Upon the star that marks the hidden pole;   *5*
    Fix every wandering thought upon
    That quarter where all thought is done:
    Who can distinguish darkness from the soul?

My Self   The consecrated blade upon my knees
    Is Sato's ancient blade, still as it was,   *10*
    Still razor-keen, still like a looking-glass
    Unspotted by the centuries;
    That flowering, silken, old embroidery, torn
    From some court lady's dress and round
The wooden scabbard bound and wound,   *15*
    Can, tattered, still protect, faded adorn.

My Soul   Why should the imagination of a man
Long past his prime remember things that are
    Emblematical of love and war?
    Think of ancestral night that can,   *20*
    If but imagination scorn the earth
    And intellect its wandering

10 Sato's ancient blade: Sato, a friend of Yeats, gave him an ancient sword.

To this and that and t' other thing,
Deliver from the crime of death and birth.

My Self   Montashigi, third of his family, fashioned it   *25*
Five hundred years ago, about it lie
Flowers from I know not what embroidery—
Heart's purple—and all these I set
For emblems of the day against the tower
Emblematical of the night,   *30*
And claim as by a soldier's right
A charter to commit the crime once more.

My Soul   Such fullness in that quarter overflows
And falls into the basin of the mind
That man is stricken deaf and dumb and blind,   *35*
For intellect no longer knows
Is from the *Ought,* or *Knower* from the *Known*—
That is to say, ascends to Heaven;
Only the dead can be forgiven;
But when I think of that my tongue's a stone.   *40*

II

My Self   A living man is blind and drinks his drop.
What matter if the ditches are impure?
What matter if I live it all once more?
Endure that toil of growing up;
The ignominy of boyhood; the distress   *45*
Of boyhood changing into man;
The unfinished man and his pain
Brought face to face with his own clumsiness;

The finished man among his enemies?—
How in the name of Heaven can he escape   *50*
That defiling and disfigured shape
The mirror of malicious eyes
Casts upon his eyes until at last
He thinks that shape must be his shape?
And what's the good of an escape   *55*
If honour find him in the wintry blast?

I am content to live it all again
And yet again, if it be life to pitch
Into the frog-spawn of a blind man's ditch,
A blind man battering blind men;   *60*
Or into that most fecund ditch of all,
The folly that man does

Or must suffer, if he woos
A proud woman not kindred of his soul.

I am content to follow to its source,   65
Every event in action or in thought;
Measure the lot; forgive myself the lot!
When such as I cast out remorse
So great a sweetness flows into the breast
We must laugh and we must sing,   70
We are blest by everything,
Everything we look upon is blest.

The Lake Isle of Innisfree

I will arise and go now, and go to Innisfree,
And a small cabin build there, of clay and wattles made:
Nine bean-rows will I have there, a hive for the honeybee,
And live alone in the bee-loud glade.

And I shall have some peace there, for peace comes dropping
    slow,   5
Dropping from the veils of the morning to where the cricket
    sings;
There midnight's all a glimmer, and noon a purple glow,
And evening full of the linnet's wings.

I will arise and go now, for always night and day
I hear lake water lapping with low sounds by the shore;   10
While I stand on the roadway, or on the pavements grey,
I hear it in the deep heart's core.

To a Friend Whose Work
Has Come to Nothing

Now all the truth is out,
Be secret and take defeat
From any brazen throat,

The Lake Isle: *1 Innisfree:* an island in Lough Gill in western Ireland, near
where Yeats spent much of his boyhood.

For how can you compete,
Being honour bred, with one   5
Who, were it proved he lies,
Were neither shamed in his own
Nor in his neighbours' eyes?
Bred to a harder thing
Than Triumph, turn away   10
And like a laughing string
Whereon mad fingers play
Amid a place of stone,
Be secret and exult,
Because of all things known   15
That is most difficult.

The Second Coming

Turning and turning in the widening gyre
The falcon cannot hear the falconer;
Things fall apart; the centre cannot hold;
Mere anarchy is loosed upon the world,
The blood-dimmed tide is loosed, and everywhere   5
The ceremony of innocence is drowned;
The best lack all conviction, while the worst
Are full of passionate intensity.

Surely some revelation is at hand;
Surely the Second Coming is at hand.   10
The Second Coming! Hardly are those words out
When a vast image out of *Spiritus Mundi*
Troubles my sight: somewhere in sands of the desert
A shape with lion body and the head of a man,
A gaze blank and pitiless as the sun,   15
Is moving its slow thighs, while all about it
Reel shadows of the indignant desert birds.

The Second Coming: *Title:* Yeats combined the idea of a Second Coming of
Christ with the ancient idea of the Magnus Annus ("Great Year") of 2,200 years,
when a new era would begin. *1 gyre:* a spiral. Yeats pronounced it with a
hard g. In his book *A Vision* (1925), Yeats described the process of human his-
tory in terms of eras brought about by two interpenetrating cones; thus the
Babylonian era was succeeded by the Greek, the Greek by the Christian, and
now, as Yeats sees it, the Christian era is in decay and about to be succeeded
by another. *12 Spiritus Mundi:* "The Spirit of the World," Yeats's name for a
collective human memory which transcends the individual.

The darkness drops again; but now I know
That twenty centuries of stony sleep
Were vexed to nightmare by a rocking cradle,   20
And what rough beast, its hour come round at last,
Slouches towards Bethlehem to be born?

Sailing to Byzantium

I

That is no country for old men. The young
In one another's arms, birds in the trees
—Those dying generations—at their song,
The salmon-falls, the mackerel-crowded seas,
Fish, flesh, or fowl, commend all summer long   5
Whatever is begotten, born, and dies.
Caught in that sensual music all neglect
Monuments of unageing intellect.

II

An aged man is but a paltry thing,
A tattered coat upon a stick, unless   10
Soul clap its hands and sing, and louder sing
For every tatter in its mortal dress,
Nor is there singing school but studying
Monuments of its own magnificence;
And therefore I have sailed the seas and come   15
To the holy city of Byzantium.

III

O sages standing in God's holy fire
As in the gold mosaic of a wall,
Come from the holy fire, perne in a gyre,
And be the singing-masters of my soul.   20
Consume my heart away; sick with desire
And fastened to a dying animal
It knows not what its is; and gather me
Into the artifice of eternity.

Sailing to Byzantium: *Title:* Now the city of Istanbul in Turkey, Byzantium was
once the capital of the Eastern Roman Empire. Yeats thought that the Byzantine
life achieved a perfect unity of art, religion, and practical activity.   *19 perne in
a gyre:* a perne is a spindle, a gyre a spiral; hence, the ages are to come in a
spiral motion, for circular motions are those of eternity (a circle never ends).

IV

Once out of nature I shall never take   *25*
My bodily form from any natural thing,
But such a form as Grecian goldsmiths make
Of hammered gold and gold enamelling
To keep a drowsy Emperor awake;
Or set upon a golden bough to sing   *30*
To lords and ladies of Byzantium
Of what is past, or passing, or to come.

Youth and Age

Much did I rage when young,
Being by the world oppressed,
But now with flattering tongue
It speeds the parting guest.

The Tower

I

What shall I do with this absurdity—
O heart, O troubled heart—this caricature,
Decrepit age that has been tied to me
As to a dog's tail?
                              Never had I more
Excited, passionate, fantastical   *5*
Imagination, nor an ear and eye
That more expected the impossible—
No, not in boyhood when with rod and fly,
Or the humbler worm, I climbed Ben Bulben's back
And had the livelong summer day to spend.   *10*
It seems that I must bid the Muse go pack,
Choose Plato and Plotinus for a friend
Until imagination, ear and eye,
Can be content with argument and deal
In abstract things; or be derided by   *15*
A sort of battered kettle at the heel.

The Tower: *Title:* refers to the Norman tower of Thoor Ballylee, which Yeats
owned and in which he had his study. *12 Plato and Plotinus:* Both philosophers
spurned the world of sense and dealt "in abstract things."

II

I pace upon the battlements and stare
On the foundations of a house, or where
Tree, like a sooty finger, starts from the earth;
And send imagination forth   20
Under the day's declining beam, and call
Images and memories
From ruin or from ancient trees,
For I would ask a question of them all.

Beyond that ridge lived Mrs. French, and once   25
When every silver candlestick or sconce
Lit up the dark mahogany and the wine,
A serving man, that could divine
That most respected lady's every wish,
Ran and with the garden shears   30
Clipped an insolent farmer's ears
And brought them in a little covered dish.

Some few remembered still when I was young
A peasant girl commended by a song,
Who'd lived somewhere upon that rocky place,   35
And praised the colour of her face,
And had the greater joy in praising her,
Remembering that, if walked she there,
Farmers jostled at the fair
So great a glory did the song confer.   40

And certain men, being maddened by those rhymes,
Or else by toasting her a score of times,
Rose from the table and declared it right
To test their fancy by their sight;
But they mistook the brightness of the moon   45
For the prosaic light of day—
Music had driven their wits astray—
And one was drowned in the great bog of Cloone.

Strange, but the man who made the song was blind;
Yet, now I have considered it, I find   50
That nothing strange; the tragedy began
With Homer that was a blind man,
And Helen has all living hearts betrayed.
O may the moon and sunlight seem

48 *Cloone:* in the vicinity of the tower.   57 *Hanrahan:* the hero of Yeats *Stories of Red Hanrahan.*

One inextricable beam,   55
For if I triumph I must make men mad.

And I myself created Hanrahan
And drove him drunk or sober through the dawn
From somewhere in the neighbouring cottages.
Caught by an old man's juggleries   60
He stumbled, tumbled, fumbled to and fro
And had but broken knees for hire
And horrible splendour of desire;
I thought it all out twenty years ago:

Good fellows shuffled cards in an old bawn;   65
And when that ancient ruffian's turn was on
He so bewitched the cards under his thumb
That all but the one card became
A pack of hounds and not a pack of cards,
And that he changed into a hare.   70
Hanrahan rose in frenzy there
And followed up those baying creatures towards—

O towards I have forgotten what—enough!
I must recall a man that neither love
Nor music nor an enemy's clipped ear   75
Could, he was so harried, cheer;
A figure that has grown so fabulous
There's not a neighbour left to say
When he finished his dog's day:
An ancient bankrupt master of this house.   80

Before that ruin came, for centuries,
Rough men-at-arms, cross-gartered to the knees
Or shod in iron, climbed the narrow stairs,
And certain men-at-arms there were
Whose images, in the Great Memory stored,   85
Come with loud cry and panting breast
To break upon a sleeper's rest
While their great wooden dice beat on the board.

As I would question all, come all who can;
Come old, necessitous, half-mounted man;   90
And bring beauty's blind rambling celebrant;
The red man the juggler sent
Through God-forsaken meadows; Mrs. French,
Gifted with so fine an ear;
The man drowned in a bog's mire,   95
When mocking muses chose the country wench.

Did all old men and women, rich and poor,
Who trod upon these rocks or passed this door,
Whether in public or in secret rage
As I do now against old age?   *100*
But I have found an answer in those eyes
That are impatient to be gone;
Go therefore; but leave Hanrahan,
For I need all his mighty memories.

Old lecher with a love on every wind,   *105*
Bring up out of that deep considering mind
All that you have discovered in the grave,
For it is certain that you have
Reckoned up every unforeknown, unseeing
Plunge, lured by a softening eye,   *110*
Or by a touch or a sigh,
Into the labyrinth of another's being;

Does the imagination dwell the most
Upon a woman won or woman lost?
If on the lost, admit you turned aside   *115*
From a great labyrinth out of pride,
Cowardice, some silly over-subtle thought
Or anything called conscience once;
And that if memory recur, the sun's
Under eclipse and the day blotted out.   *120*

III

It is time that I wrote my will;
I choose upstanding men
That climb the streams until
The fountain leap, and at dawn
Drop their cast at the side   *125*
Of dripping stone; I declare
They shall inherit my pride,
The pride of people that were
Bound neither to Cause nor to State,
Neither to slaves that were spat on,   *130*
Nor to the tyrants that spat,
The people of Burke and Grattan
That gave, though free to refuse—
Pride, like that of the morn,
When the headlong light is loose,   *135*

---

132 Burke: Edmund Burke (1729–1797), the great statesman, orator, and political
writer. He was born in Dublin. *Grattan:* Henry Grattan (1746–1820), the Irish
statesman and orator.

Or that of the fabulous horn,
Or that of the sudden shower
When all streams are dry,
Or that of the hour
When the swan must fix his eye   140
Upon a fading gleam,
Float out upon a long
Last reach of glittering stream
And there sing his last song.
And I declare my faith: 145
I mock Plotinus' thought
And cry in Plato's teeth,
Death and life were not
Till man made up the whole,
Made lock, stock and barrel   150
Out of his bitter soul,
Aye, sun and moon and star, all,
And further add to that
That, being dead, we rise,
Dream and so create   155
Translunar Paradise.
I have prepared my peace
With learned Italian things
And the proud stones of Greece,
Poet's imaginings   160
And memories of love,
Memories of the words of women,
All those things whereof
Man makes a superhuman
Mirror-resembling dream.   165

As at the loophole there
The daws chatter and scream,
And drop twigs layer upon layer.
When they have mounted up,
The mother bird will rest   170
On their hollow top,
And so warm her wild nest.

I leave both faith and pride
To young upstanding men
Climbing the mountain side,   175
That under the bursting dawn
They may drop a fly;
Being of that metal made
Till it was broken by
This sedentary trade.   180

Now shall I make my soul,
Compelling it to study
In a learned school
Till the wreck of body,
Slow decay of blood,   185
Testy delirium
Or dull decrepitude,
Or what worse evil come—
The death of friends, or death
Of every brilliant eye   190
That made a catch in the breath—
Seem but the clouds of the sky
When the horizon fades;
Or a bird's sleepy cry
Among the deepening shades.   195

Leda and the Swan

A sudden blow: the great wings beating still
Above the staggering girl, her thighs caressed
By the dark webs, her nape caught in his bill,
He holds her helpless breast upon his breast.

How can those terrified vague fingers push   5
The feathered glory from her loosening thighs?
And how can body, laid in that white rush,
But feel the strange heart beating where it lies?

A shudder in the loins engenders there
The broken wall, the burning roof and tower   10
And Agamemnon dead.
                            Being so caught up,
So mastered by the brute blood of the air,
Did she put on his knowledge with his power
Before the indifferent beak could let her drop?

Leda and the Swan: *Title:* In the form of a swan, Zeus made love to Leda, the
wife of the king of Sparta. In consequence Leda bore Castor, Pollux, Helen, and
Clytemnestra. After Helen married Menelaus, Paris abducted her, an act which
resulted in the Trojan War and the destruction of Troy (line 10). Clytemnestra
married Agamemnon, King of Argos; she murdered him on his return from
Troy (line 11).

Two Songs from a Play

I

I saw a staring virgin stand
Where holy Dionysus died,
And tear the heart out of his side,
And lay the heart upon her hand
And bear that beating heart away;   5
And then did all the Muses sing
Of Magnus Annus at the spring,
As though God's death were but a play.

Another Troy must rise and set,
Another lineage feed the crow,   10
Another Argo's painted prow
Drive to a flashier bauble yet.
The Roman Empire stood appalled:
It dropped the reigns of peace and war
When that fierce virgin and her Star   15
Out of the fabulous darkness called.

II

In pity for man's darkening thought
He walked that room and issued thence
In Galilean turbulence;
The Babylonian starlight brought   20
A fabulous, formless darkness in;
Odour of blood when Christ was slain
Made all Platonic tolerance vain
And vain all Doric discipline.

Everything that man esteems   25
Endures a moment or a day.
Love's pleasure drives his love away,
The painter's brush consumes his dreams;

Two Songs from a Play: *Title:* The play is *The Resurrection* (1931), for which the first song is the prologue and the second is the epilogue. In the first, the Greek age has come to an end; its symbol, the god Dionysus, lies dead, having been destroyed by the Virgin Mary. A Magnus Annus has ended and a new one begins (see "The Second Coming," page 309). The new cycle will bring another Troy and more deaths as in the Trojan War, and a new Argo will sail in search of something "flashier" than the Golden Fleece. The lines echo Virgil's fourth ecologue, "The Pollio," which was thought by many Christians to prophesy the Christian era. The "Star" (line 15) is the Star of Bethlehem. In the second song, the decline of the Babylonian age introduces the Greek, its fall, and the rise of the Christian era: man's desire consumes itself in its very accomplishment.

The herald's cry, the soldier's tread
Exhaust his glory and his might: 30
Whatever flames upon the night
Man's own resinous heart has fed.

*A*mong School Children

I walk through the long schoolroom questioning,
A kind old nun in a white hood replies;
The children learn to cipher and to sing,
To study reading-books and history,
To cut and sew, be neat in everything   5
In the best modern way—the children's eyes
In momentary wonder stare upon
A sixty year old smiling public man.

I dream of a Ledaean body, bent
Above a sinking fire, a tale that she   10
Told of a harsh reproof, or trivial event
That changed some childish day to tragedy—
Told, and it seemed that our two natures blent
Into a sphere from youthful sympathy,
Or else, to alter Plato's parable,   15
Into the yolk and white of the one shell.

And thinking of that fit of grief or rage
I look upon one child or t'other there
And wonder if she stood so at that age—
For even daughters of the swan can share   20
Something of every paddler's heritage—
And had that color upon cheek or hair;
And thereupon my heart is driven wild:
She stands before me as a living child.

Her present image floats into the mind—   25
Did quattrocento finger fashion it
Hollow of cheek as though it drank the wind
And took a mess of shadows for its meat?

Among School Children: *9 Ledaean body:* a body like Leda's (see page 316).
15 Plato's parable: In Plato's *Symposium,* Aristophanes proffers a myth in which
man was spherical, having four legs and four arms; but the gods found such
men too powerful, and Zeus divided the spheres into halves. The halves in search
of each other explain the nature of love. *26 quattrocento:* the fifteenth century.

And I though never of Ledaean kind
Had pretty plumage once—enough of that,   30
Better to smile on all that smile, and show
There is a comfortable kind of old scarecrow.

What youthful mother, a shape upon her lap
Honey of generation had betrayed,
And that must sleep, shriek, struggle to escape   35
As recollection or the drug decide,
Would think her son, did she but see that shape
With sixty or more winters on its head,
A compensation for the pang of his birth,
Or the uncertainty of his setting forth?   40

Plato thought nature but a spume that plays
Upon a ghostly paradigm of things;
Soldier Aristotle played the taws
Upon the bottom of a king of kings;
World-famous golden-thighed Pythagoras   45
Fingered upon a fiddle stick or strings
What a star sang and careless Muses heard:
Old clothes upon old sticks to scare a bird.

Both nuns and mothers worship images,
But those the candles light are not as those   50
That animate a mother's reveries,
But keep a marble or a bronze repose.
And yet they too break hearts—O Presences
That passion, piety or affection knows,
And that all heavenly glory symbolize—   55
O self-born mockers of man's enterprise;

Labor is blossoming or dancing where
The body is not bruised to pleasure soul,
Nor beauty born out of its own despair,
Nor blear-eyed wisdom out of midnight oil.   60

34 *Honey of generation:* a phrase from Porphyry (233–306?), a Neoplatonic
philosopher, in *The Cave of the Nymphs;* a soul is attracted by the honey, and
so conception occurs. Yeats fuses this with the Platonic notion that the soul for-
gets its previous knowledge. *41–48:* Plato thought all experiences of the senses
were imitations of Ideas, which alone were real. Aristotle dealt with concrete,
not abstract, ideas; Alexander the Great was his pupil, and perhaps Aristotle
whipped him (*played the taws:* played a whip). Pythagoras is said to have had
a golden thigh; his mathematical philosophy found an analogy between musical
proportions and the motions of the heavenly bodies (the music of the spheres).
Great as these men were, old age reduced all to mere scarecrows, effigies. *49:*
Note that we have had three kinds of love: the lover for the beloved, the nun
for God, the mother for her child—"passion, piety or affection."

O chestnut tree, great rooted blossomer,
Are you the leaf, the blossom or the bole?
O body swayed to music, O brightening glance,
How can we know the dancer from the dance?

Crazy Jane and the Bishop

Bring me to the blasted oak
That I, midnight upon the stroke,
(*All find safety in the tomb.*)
May call down curses on his head
Because of my dear Jack that's dead.   5
Coxcomb was the least he said:
The solid man and the coxcomb.

Nor was he Bishop when his ban
Banished Jack the Journeyman,
(*All find safety in the tomb.*)   10
Nor so much as parish priest,
Yet he, an old book in his fist,
Cried that we lived like beast and beast:
The solid man and the coxcomb.

The Bishop has a skin, God knows,   15
Wrinkled like the foot of a goose,
(*All find safety in the tomb.*)
Nor can he hide in holy black
The heron's bunch upon his back,
But a birch-tree stood my Jack: 20
The solid man and the coxcomb.

Jack had my virginity,
And bids me to the oak, for he
(*All find safety in the tomb.*)
Wanders out into the night   25
And there is shelter under it,
But should that other come, I spit:
The solid man and the coxcomb.

Crazy Jane Talks with the Bishop

I met the Bishop on the road
And much said he and I.
'Those breasts are flat and fallen now,
Those veins must soon be dry;
Live in a heavenly mansion,   5
Not in some foul sty.'

'Fair and foul are near of kin,
And fair needs foul,' I cried.
'My friends are gone, but that's a truth
Nor grave or bed denied,   10
Learned in bodily lowliness
And in the heart's pride.

'A woman can be proud and stiff
When on love intent;
But Love has pitched his mansion in   15
The place of excrement;
For nothing can be sole or whole
That has not been rent.'

Lapis Lazuli

I have heard that hysterical women say
They are sick of the palette and fiddle-bow,
Of poets that are always gay,
For everybody knows or else should know
That if nothing drastic is done   5
Aeroplane and Zeppelin will come out,
Pitch like King Billy bomb-balls in
Until the town lie beaten flat.

All perform their tragic play,
There struts Hamlet, there is Lear,   10
That's Ophelia, that Cordelia;
Yet they, should the last scene be there,
The great stage curtain about to drop,
If worthy their prominent part in the play,

Lapis Lazuli: 7 *King Billy*: Kaiser Wilhelm II, Emperor of Germany 1888–1918.

Do not break up their lines to weep.   15
They know that Hamlet and Lear are gay;
Gaiety transfiguring all that dread.
All men have aimed at, found and lost;
Black out; Heaven blazing into the head:
Tragedy wrought to its uttermost.   20
Though Hamlet rambles and Lear rages,
And all the drop-scenes drop at once
Upon a hundred thousand stages,
It cannot grow by an inch or an ounce.

On their own feet they came, or on shipboard,   25
Camel-back, horse-back, ass-back, mule-back,
Old civilisations put to the sword.
Then they and their wisdom went to rack:
No handiwork of Callimachus,
Who handled marble as if it were bronze,   30
Made draperies that seemed to rise
When sea-wind swept the corner, stands;
His long lamp-chimney shaped like the stem
Of a slender palm, stood but a day;
All things fall and are built again,   35
And those that build them again are gay.

Two Chinamen, behind them a third,
Are carved in lapis lazuli,
Over them flies a long-legged bird,
A symbol of longevity;   40
The third, doubtless a serving-man,
Carries a musical instrument.

Every discoloration of the stone,
Every accidental crack or dent,
Seems a water-course or an avalanche,   45
Or lofty slope where it still snows
Though doubtless plum or cherry-branch
Sweetens the little half-way house
Those Chinamen climb towards, and I
Delight to imagine them seated there;   50
There, on the mountain and the sky,
On all the tragic scene they stare.
One asks for mournful melodies;

29 *Callimachus:* name of a sculptor, painter, and gold engraver of the second
half of the fifth century B.C. He was famous for the finish of his marbles and is
the reputed inventor of the running drill, which permits extremely fluid treat-
ment of the folds in marble drapery.

Accomplished fingers begin to play.
Their eyes mid many wrinkles, their eyes,
Their ancient, glittering eyes, are gay.

The Circus Animals' Desertion

I

I sought a theme and sought for it in vain,
I sought it daily for six weeks or so.
Maybe at last, being but a broken man,
I must be satisfied with my heart, although
Winter and summer till old age began   5
My circus animals were all on show,
Those stilted boys, that burnished chariot,
Lion and woman and the Lord knows what.

II

What can I but enumerate old themes?
First that sea-rider Oisin led by the nose   10
Through three enchanted islands, allegorical dreams,
Vain gaiety, vain battle, vain repose,
Themes of the embittered heart, or so it seems,
That might adorn old songs or courtly shows;
But what cared I that set him on to ride,   15
I, starved for the bosom of his faery bride?

And then a counter-truth filled out its play,
The Countess Cathleen was the name I gave it;
She, pity-crazed, had given her soul away,
But masterful Heaven had intervened to save it.   20
I thought my dear must her own soul destroy
So did fanaticism and hate enslave it,
And this brought forth a dream and soon enough
This dream itself had all my thought and love.

And when the Fool and Blind Man stole the bread   25
Cuchulain fought the ungovernable sea;
Heart-mysteries there, and yet when all is said

The Circus Animals' Desertion: Yeats here refers to his works as "circus animals"; the covers of his books had such figures stamped on them, and they became symbols of great meaning for Yeats. Now that the animals have deserted him, he can no longer write. In the second section he mentions legendary figures that he used as themes in his poems and plays.

It was the dream itself enchanted me:
Character isolated by a deed
To engross the present and dominate memory.   *30*
Players and painted stage took all my love,
And not those things that they were emblems of.

III

Those masterful images because complete
Grew in pure mind, but out of what began?
A mound of refuse or the sweepings of a street,   *35*
Old kettles, old bottles, and a broken can,
Old iron, old bones, old rags, that raving slut
Who keeps the till. Now that my ladder's gone,
I must lie down where all the ladders start,
In the foul rag-and-bone shop of the heart.   *40*

ROBERT FROST
1874–1963

Frost married his fellow valedictorian from Lawrence (Mass.) High School in 1895. He tried Harvard from 1897 to 1899 but then rejected the professionalism of formal education. His poetry being uniformly ignored since 1890 and his life as teacher, farmer, and family man not nearly satisfying enough, he finally sold his farm in 1912 and moved to England to join the Georgian literary world. The stratagem worked. *A Boy's Will* (1913) and *North of Boston* (1914) were both acclaimed in England, then in America, and so Frost's distinguished career as a poet was finally launched. At the age of forty, he moved back to act out the New England sage of his poems and become poet-in-residence to the entire United States.

Frost created, through his poems, the most likable *persona* in American letters, and it was no wonder, since he encouraged it, that readers assumed he was the warm, humorous stoic of his poetry. Since his death, the inevitable shaking down of reputation which occurs in both literary and historical studies has taken place. In Frost's case, this reevaluation has focused mainly on his personality, which diverged considerably in real life from what it appears to be in his poetry. (Indeed, the poetry itself is probably even greater in technique than it was judged during his life!)

Frost shows a classic mastery of structure and metrics which ranks him equal to any poet in this volume. His sonnets, for instance, are not embarrassed in the presence of Shakespeare's, Milton's, and Wordsworth's, the greatest sonneteers. And, more than any poet in this volume, Frost brought the real language of his time to the highest forms of classical poetic expression.

Directive

Back out of all this now too much for us,
Back in a time made simple by the loss
Of detail, burned, dissolved, and broken off
Like graveyard marble sculpture in the weather,
There is a house that is no more a house   5
Upon a farm that is no more a farm
And in a town that is no more a town.
The road there, if you'll let a guide direct you
Who only has at heart your getting lost,
May seem as if it should have been a quarry—   10
Great monolithic knees the former town
Long since gave up pretense of keeping covered.
And there's a story in a book about it:
Besides the wear of iron wagon wheels
The ledges show lines ruled southeast-northwest,   15
The chisel work of an enormous Glacier
That braced his feet against the Arctic Pole.
You must not mind a certain coolness from him
Still said to haunt this side of Panther Mountain.
Nor need you mind the serial ordeal   20
Of being watched from forty cellar holes
As if by eye pairs out of forty firkins.
As for the woods' excitement over you
That sends light rustle rushes to their leaves,
Charge that to upstart inexperience.   25
Where were they all not twenty years ago?
They think too much of having shaded out
A few old pecker-fretted apple trees.

Make yourself up a cheering song of how
Someone's road home from work this once was,   *30*
Who may be just ahead of you on foot
Or creaking with a buggy load of grain.
The height of the adventure is the height
Of country where two village cultures faded
Into each other. Both of them are lost.   *35*
And if you're lost enough to find yourself
By now, pull in your ladder road behind you
And put a sign up CLOSED to all but me.
Then make yourself at home. The only field
Now left's no bigger than a harness gall.   *40*
First there's the children's house of make-believe,
Some shattered dishes underneath a pine,
The playthings in the playhouse of the children.
Weep for what little things could make them glad.
Then for the house that is no more a house,   *45*
But only a belilaced cellar hole,
Now slowly closing like a dent in dough.
This was no playhouse but a house in earnest.
Your destination and your destiny's
A brook that was the water of the house,   *50*
Cold as a spring as yet so near its source,
Too lofty and original to rage.
(We know the valley streams that when aroused
Will leave their tatters hung on barb and thorn.)
I have kept hidden in the instep arch   *55*
Of an old cedar at the waterside
A broken drinking goblet like the Grail
Under a spell so the wrong ones can't find it,
So can't get saved, as Saint Mark says they mustn't.
(I stole the goblet from the children's playhouse.)   *60*
Here are your waters and your watering place.
Drink and be whole again beyond confusion.

*P*rovide, *P*rovide

The witch that came (the withered hag)
To wash the steps with pail and rag
Was once the beauty Abishag,

The picture pride of Hollywood.
Too many fall from great and good   *5*
For you to doubt the likelihood.

Die early and avoid the fate.
Or if predestined to die late,
Make up your mind to die in state.

Make the whole stock exchange your own!   10
If need be occupy a throne,
Where nobody can call *you* crone.

Some have relied on what they knew,
Others on being simply true.
What worked for them might work for you.   15

No memory of having starred
Atones for later disregard,
Or keeps the end from being hard.

Better to go down dignified
With boughten friendship at your side   20
Than none at all. Provide, provide!

Mending Wall

Something there is that doesn't love a wall,
That sends the frozen-ground-swell under it
And spills the upper boulders in the sun,
And makes gaps even two can pass abreast.
The work of hunters is another thing: 5
I have come after them and made repair
Where they have left not one stone on a stone,
But they would have the rabbit out of hiding,
To please the yelping dogs. The gaps I mean,
No one has seen them made or heard them made,   10
But at spring mending-time we find them there.
I let my neighbour know beyond the hill;
And on a day we meet to walk the line
And set the wall between us once again.
We keep the wall between us as we go.   15
To each the boulders that have fallen to each.
And some are loaves and some so nearly balls
We have to use a spell to make them balance:
"Stay where you are until our backs are turned!"
We wear our fingers rough with handling them.   20
Oh, just another kind of out-door game,

One on a side. It comes to little more:
There where it is we do not need the wall:
He is all pine and I am apple orchard.
My apple trees will never get across   25
And eat the cones under his pines, I tell him.
He only says, "Good fences make good neighbours."
Spring is the mischief in me, and I wonder
If I could put a notion in his head:
"*Why* do they make good neighbours? Isn't it   30
Where there are cows? But here there are no cows.
Before I built a wall I'd ask to know
What I was walling in or walling out,
And to whom I was like to give offense.
Something there is that doesn't love a wall,   35
That wants it down." I could say "Elves" to him,
But it's not elves exactly, and I'd rather
He said it for himself. I see him there,
Bringing a stone grasped firmly by the top
In each hand, like an old-stone savage armed.   40
He moves in darkness as it seems to me,
Not of woods only and the shade of trees.
He will not go behind his father's saying,
And he likes having thought of it so well
He says again, "Good fences make good neighbours."   45

*A*fter Apple-Picking

My long two-pointed ladder's sticking through a tree
Toward heaven still,
And there's a barrel that I didn't fill
Beside it, and there may be two or three
Apples I didn't pick upon some bough.   5
But I am done with apple-picking now.
Essence of winter sleep is on the night,
The scent of apples: I am drowsing off.
I cannot rub the strangeness from my sight
I got from looking through a pane of glass   10
I skimmed this morning from the drinking trough
And held against the world of hoary grass.
It melted, and I let it fall and break.
But I was well
Upon my way to sleep before it fell,   15
And I could tell

What form my dreaming was about to take.
Magnified apples appear and disappear
Stem end and blossom end,
And every fleck of russet showing clear.   20
My instep arch not only keeps the ache,
It keeps the pressure of a ladder-round.
I feel the ladder sway as the boughs bend.
And I keep hearing from the cellar bin
The rumbling sound   25
Of load on load of apples coming in.
For I have had too much
Of apple-picking: I am overtired
Of the great harvest I myself desired.
There were ten thousand thousand fruit to touch,   30
Cherish in hand, lift down, and not let fall.
For all
That struck the earth,
No matter if not bruised or spiked with stubble,
Went surely to the cider-apple heap   35
As of no worth.
One can see what will trouble
This sleep of mine, whatever sleep it is.
Were he not gone,
The woodchuck could say whether it's like his   40
Long sleep, as I describe its coming on,
Or just some human sleep.

The Road Not Taken

Two roads diverged in a yellow wood,
And sorry I could not travel both
And be one traveler, long I stood
And looked down one as far as I could
To where it bent in the undergrowth;   5

Then took the other, as just as fair,
And having perhaps the better claim,
Because it was grassy and wanted wear;
Though as for that, the passing there
Had worn them really about the same,   10

And both that morning equally lay
In leaves no step had trodden black.

Oh, I kept the first for another day!
Yet knowing how way leads on to way,
I doubted if I should ever come back.   15

I shall be telling this with a sigh
Somewhere ages and ages hence:
Two roads diverged in a wood, and I—
I took the one less traveled by,
And that has made all the difference.   20

The Oven Bird

There is a singer everyone has heard,
Loud, a mid-summer and a mid-wood bird,
Who makes the solid tree trunks sound again.
He says that leaves are old and that for flowers
Mid-summer is to spring as one to ten.   5
He says the early petal-fall is past,
When pear and cherry bloom went down in showers
On sunny days a moment overcast;
And comes that other fall we name the fall.
He says the highway dust is over all.   10
The bird would cease and be as other birds
But that he knows in singing not to sing.
The question that he frames in all but words
Is what to make of a diminished thing.

Birches

When I see birches bend to left and right
Across the lines of straighter darker trees,
I like to think some boy's been swinging them.
But swinging doesn't bend them down to stay
As ice storms do. Often you must have seen them   5
Loaded with ice a sunny winter morning
After a rain. They click upon themselves
As the breeze rises, and turn many-colored
As the stir cracks and crazes their enamel.
Soon the sun's warmth makes them shed crystal shells   10

Shattering and avalanching on the snowcrust—
Such heaps of broken glass to sweep away
You'd think the inner dome of heaven had fallen.
They are dragged to the withered bracken by the load,
And they seeem not to break; though once they are bowed   15
So low for long, they never right themselves:
You may see their trunks arching in the woods
Years afterwards, trailing their leaves on the ground
Like girls on hands and knees that throw their hair
Before them over their heads to dry in the sun.   20
But I was going to say when Truth broke in
With all her matter of fact about the ice storm,
I should prefer to have some boy bend them
As he went out and in to fetch the cows—
Some boy too far from town to learn baseball.   25
Whose only play was what he found himself,
Summer or winter, and could play alone.
One by one he subdued his father's trees
By riding them down over and over again
Until he took the stiffness out of them,   30
And not one but hung limp, not one was left
For him to conquer. He learned all there was
To learn about not launching out too soon
And so not carrying the tree away
Clear to the ground. He always kept his poise   35
To the top branches, climbing carefully
With the same pains you use to fill a cup
Up to the brim, and even above the brim.
Then he flung outward, feet first, with a swish,
Kicking his way down through the air to the ground.   40
So was I once myself a swinger of birches.
And so I dream of going back to be.
It's when I'm weary of considerations,
And life is too much like a pathless wood
Where your face burns and tickles with the cobwebs   45
Broken across it, and one eye is weeping
From a twig's having lashed across it open.
I'd like to get away from earth a while
And then come back to it and begin over.
May no fate willfully misunderstand me   50
And half grant what I wish and snatch me away
Not to return. Earth's the right place for love.
I don't know where it's likely to go better.
I'd like to go by climbing a birch tree,
And climb black branches up a snow-white trunk   55
Toward heaven, till the tree could bear no more,

But dipped its top and set me down again.
That would be good both going and coming back
One could do worse than be a swinger of birches.

The Cow in Apple Time

Something inspires the only cow of late
To make no more of a wall than an open gate,
And think no more of wall-builders than fools.
Her face is flecked with pomace and she drools
A cider syrup. Having tasted fruit,   5
She scorns a pasture withering to the root.
She runs from tree to tree where lie and sweeten
The windfalls spiked with stubble and worm-eaten.
She leaves them bitten when she has to fly.
She bellows on a knoll against the sky.   10
Her udder shrivels and the milk goes dry.

The Runaway

Once when the snow of the year was beginning to fall,
We stopped by a mountain pasture to say "Whose colt?"
A little Morgan had one forefoot on the wall,
The other curled at his breast. He dipped his head
And snorted at us. And then he had to bolt.   5
We heard the miniature thunder where he fled,
And we saw him, or thought we saw him, dim and gray,
Like a shadow against the curtain of falling flakes.
"I think the little fellow's afraid of the snow.
He isn't winter-broken. It isn't play   10
With the little fellow at all. He's running away.
I doubt if even his mother could tell him, 'Sakes,
It's only weather.' He'd think she didn't know!
Where is his mother? He can't be out alone."
And now he comes again with clatter of stone,   15
And mounts the wall again with whited eyes
And all his tail that isn't hair up straight.

The Runaway: 3 *Morgan:* an American breed of light horse that originated in
Vermont.

He shudders his coat as if to throw off flies.
"Whoever it is that leaves him out so late,
When other creatures have gone to stall and bin,   20
Ought to be told to come and take him in."

Stopping by Woods on a Snowy Evening

Whose woods these are I think I know.
His house is in the village, though;
He will not see me stopping here
To watch his woods fill up with snow.

My little horse must think it queer   5
To stop without a farmhouse near
Between the woods and frozen lake
The darkest evening of the year.

He gives his harness bells a shake
To ask if there is some mistake.   10
The only other sound's the sweep
Of easy wind and downy flake.

The woods are lovely, dark, and deep.
But I have promises to keep,
And miles to go before I sleep,   15
And miles to go before I sleep.

The Onset

Always the same, when on a fated night
At last the gathered snow lets down as white
As may be in dark woods, and with a song
It shall not make again all winter long
Of hissing on the yet uncovered ground,   5
I almost stumble looking up and round,
As one who overtaken by the end
Gives up his errand, and lets death descend
Upon him where he is, with nothing done
To evil, no important triumph won,   10
More than if life had never begun.

Yet all the precedent is on my side:
I know that winter death has never tried
The earth but it has failed: the snow may heap
In long storms an undrifted four feet deep   15
As measured against maple, birch, and oak,
It cannot check the peeper's silver croak;
And I shall see the snow all go down hill
In water of a slender April rill
That flashes tail through last year's withered brake   20
And dead weeds, like a disappearing snake.
Nothing will be left white but here a birch,
And there a clump of houses with a church.

To Earthward

Love at the lips was touch
As sweet as I could bear;
And once that seemed too much;
I lived on air

That crossed me from sweet things,   5
The flow of—was it musk
From hidden grapevine springs
Downhill at dusk?

I had the swirl and ache
From sprays of honeysuckle   10
That when they're gathered shake
Dew on the knuckle.

I craved strong sweets, but those
Seemed strong when I was young;
The petal of the rose   15
It was that stung.

Now no joy but lacks salt,
That is not dashed with pain
And weariness and fault;
I crave the stain   20

Of tears, the aftermark
Of almost too much love,
The sweet of bitter bark
And burning clove.

When stiff and sore and scarred   25
I take away my hand
From leaning on it hard
In grass and sand,

The hurt is not enough:
I long for weight and strength   30
To feel the earth as rough
To all my length.

Once by the Pacific

The shattered water made a misty din.
Great waves looked over others coming in,
And thought of doing something to the shore
That water never did to land before.
The clouds were low and hairy in the skies,   5
Like locks blown forward in the gleam of eyes.
You could not tell, and yet it looked as if
The shore was lucky in being backed by cliff,
The cliff in being backed by continent;
It looked as if a night of dark intent   10
Was coming, and not only a night, an age.
Someone had better be prepared for rage.
There would be more than ocean-water broken
Before God's last *Put out the Light* was spoken.

Bereft

Where had I heard this wind before
Change like this to a deeper roar?
What would it take my standing there for,
Holding open a restive door,
Looking downhill to a frothy shore?   5
Summer was past and day was past.
Somber clouds in the west were massed.
Out in the porch's sagging floor,
Leaves got up in a coil and hissed,

Bereft: *9 coil:* Frost's intention is to suggest a striking snake.

Blindly struck at my knee and missed.   *10*
Something sinister in the tone
Told me my secret must be known:
Word I was in the house alone
Somehow must have gotten abroad,
Word I was in my life alone,   *15*
Word I had no one left but God.

*T*wo Tramps in Mud Time

Out of the mud two strangers came
And caught me splitting wood in the yard.
And one of them put me off my aim
By hailing cheerily "Hit them hard!"
I knew pretty well why he dropped behind   *5*
And let the other go on a way.
I knew pretty well what he had in mind:
He wanted to take my job for pay.

Good blocks of beech it was I split,
As large around as the chopping block;   *10*
And every piece I squarely hit
Fell splinterless as a cloven rock.
The blows that a life of self-control
Spares to strike for the common good,
That day, giving a loose to my soul,   *15*
I spent on the unimportant wood.

The sun was warm but the wind was chill.
You know how it is with an April day
When the sun is out and the wind is still,
You're one month on in the middle of May.   *20*
But if you so much as dare to speak,
A cloud comes over the sunlit arch,
A wind comes off a frozen peak,
And you're two months back in the middle of March.

A bluebird comes tenderly up to alight   *25*
And turns to the wind to unruffle a plume
His song so pitched as not to excite
A single flower as yet to bloom.
It is snowing a flake: and he half knew
Winter was only playing possum.   *30*

Except in color he isn't blue,
But he wouldn't advise a thing to blossom.

The water for which we may have to look
In summertime with a witching wand,
In every wheelrut's now a brook,   35
In every print of a hoof a pond.
Be glad of water, but don't forget
The lurking frost in the earth beneath
That will steal forth after the sun is set
And show on the water its crystal teeth.   40

The time when most I loved my task
These two must make me love it more
By coming with what they came to ask.
You'd think I never had felt before
The weight of an ax-head poised aloft,   45
The grip on earth of outspread feet,
The life of muscles rocking soft
And smooth and moist in vernal heat.

Out of the woods two hulking tramps
(From sleeping God knows where last night,   50
But not long since in the lumber camps).
They thought all chopping was theirs of right.
Men of the woods and lumberjacks,
They judged me by their appropriate tool.
Except as a fellow handled an ax   55
They had no way of knowing a fool.

Nothing on either side was said.
They knew they had but to stay their stay
And all their logic would fill my head:
As that I had no right to play   60
With what was another man's work for gain.
My right might be love but theirs was need.
And where the two exist in twain
Theirs was the better right—agreed.

But yield who will to their separation,   65
My object in living is to unite
My avocation and my vocation
As my two eyes make one in sight.
Only where love and need are one,
And the work is play for mortal stakes,   70
Is the deed ever really done
For Heaven and the future's sakes.

Design

I found a dimpled spider, fat and white,
On a white heal-all, holding up a moth
Like a white piece of rigid satin cloth—
Assorted characters of death and blight
Mixed ready to begin the morning right,   5
Like the ingredients of a witches' broth—
A snow-drop spider, a flower like froth,
And dead wings carried like a paper kite.
What had that flower to do with being white,
The wayside blue and innocent heal-all?   10
What brought the kindred spider to that height,
Then steered the white moth thither in the night?
What but design of darkness to appall?—
If design govern in a thing so small.

The Gift Outright

The land was ours before we were the land's.
She was our land more than a hundred years
Before we were her people. She was ours
In Massachusetts, in Virginia,
But we were England's, still colonials,   5
Possessing what we still were unpossessed by,
Possessed by what we now no more possessed.
Something we were withholding made us weak
Until we found out that it was ourselves
We were withholding from our land of living,   10
And forthwith found salvation in surrender.
Such as we were we gave ourselves outright
(The deed of gift was many deeds of war)
To the land vaguely realizing westward,
But still unstoried, artless, unenhanced,   15
Such as she was, such as she would become.

Design: 2 heal-all: the weedy perennial *Prunella vulgaris*, also called self-heal.
A member of the mint family, it was once used as a remedy for sore throats and
other ailments.

Questioning Faces

The winter owl banked just in time to pass
And save herself from breaking window glass.
And her wings straining, suddenly aspread
Caught color from the last of evening red
In a display of underdown and quill
To glassed-in children at the window sill.

WALLACE STEVENS
1879–1955

To his neighbors and associates in suburban Connecticut, the portly, respectable Mr. Stevens was an insurance executive who had made it: from 1934 he was a vice-president of the Hartford Accident and Indemnity Company. His life as a poet, if known, would have served no advantage.

Stevens believed in order, in "hard" reality and adjusting to it, in paying Caesar. Matthew Arnold's career was at least as exacting, but a career and a life in the arts were not inconsistent to the Victorian English mind. Wallace Stevens's vocation as "big businessman" in twentieth-century America was jealous and demanding, but he believed in it just as firmly as Hopkins believed in his.

Stevens left Harvard without his degree and, up to 1916, tasted the

Bohemian life in New York City while working as reporter, law student, and lawyer. He had literary contacts and attempted some highly experimental verse plays. But it was not until 1923, when he was forty-four, that Stevens spoke and presented himself as a mature poet in *Harmonium*. Later volumes, such as *Ideas of Order* (1935) and *The Man with the Blue Guitar* (1937), achieved a sophisticated audience that appreciated his fantastic verbal music. His poetry chills with its reminders of death and limitation, then warms with a luxuriance of sensual imagery. His single, endlessly permutable theme is that we can face our finite and temporary human condition through the infinite and eternal uses of the imagination to conceive beauty.

Sunday Morning

Complacencies of the peignoir, and late
Coffee and oranges in a sunny chair,
And the green freedom of a cockatoo
Upon a rug mingle to dissipate
The holy hush of ancient sacrifice.   5
She dreams a little, and she feels the dark
Encroachment of that old catastrophe,
As a calm darkens among water-lights.
The pungent oranges and bright, green wings
Seem things in some procession of the dead,   10
Winding across wide water, without sound.
The day is like wide water, without sound,
Stilled for the passing of her dreaming feet
Over the seas, to silent Palestine,
Dominion of the blood and sepulchre.   15

Why should she give her bounty to the dead?
What is divinity if it can come
Only in silent shadows and in dreams?
Shall she not find in comforts of the sun,
In pungent fruit and bright, green wings, or else   20
In any balm or beauty of the earth,
Things to be cherished like the thought of heaven?
Divinity must live within herself:
Passions of rain, or moods in falling snow;
Grievings in loneliness, or unsubdued   25
Elations when the forest blooms; gusty
Emotions on wet roads on autumn nights;
All pleasures and all pains, remembering
The bough of summer and the winter branch.
These are the measures destined for her soul.   30

Jove in the clouds had his inhuman birth.
No mother suckled him, no sweet land gave
Large-mannered motions to his mythy mind.
He moved among us, as a muttering king,
Magnificent, would move among his hinds.   35
Until our blood, commingling, virginal,
With heaven, brought such requital to desire
The very hinds discerned it, in a star.
Shall our blood fail? Or shall it come to be
The blood of paradise? And shall the earth   40
Seem all of paradise that we shall know?
The sky will be much friendlier then than now,
A part of labor and a part of pain,
And next in glory to enduring love,
Not this dividing and indifferent blue.   45

She says, "I am content when wakened birds,
Before they fly, test the reality
Of misty fields, by their sweet questionings;
But when the birds are gone, and their warm fields
Return no more, where, then, is paradise?"   50
There is not any haunt of prophecy,
Nor any old chimera of the grave,
Neither the golden underground, nor isle
Melodious, where spirits gat them home,
Nor visionary south, nor cloudy palm   55
Remote on heaven's hill, that has endured
As April's green endures; or will endure
Like her remembrance of awakened birds,
Or her desire for June and evening, tipped
By the consummation of the swallow's wings.   60

She says, "But in contentment I still feel
The need of some imperishable bliss."
Death is the mother of beauty; hence from her,
Alone, shall come fulfilment to our dreams
And our desires. Although she strews the leaves   65
Of sure obliteration on our paths,
The path sick sorrow took, the many paths
Where triumph rang its brassy phrase, or love
Whispered a little out of tenderness,
She makes the willow shiver in the sun   70
For maidens who were wont to sit and gaze
Upon the grass, relinquished to their feet.
She causes boys to pile new plums and pears
On disregarded plate. The maidens taste
And stray impassioned in the littering leaves.   75

Is there no change of death in paradise?
Does ripe fruit never fall? Or do the boughs
Hang always heavy in that perfect sky,
Unchanging, yet so like our perishing earth,
With rivers like our own that seek for seas   80
They never find, the same receding shores
That never touch with inarticulate pang?
Why set the pear upon those river-banks
Or spice the shores with odors of the plum?
Alas, that they should wear our colors there,   85
The silken weavings of our afternoons,
And pick the strings of our insipid lutes!
Death is the mother of beauty, mystical,
Within whose burning bosom we devise
Our earthly mothers waiting, sleeplessly.   90

Supple and turbulent, a ring of men
Shall chant in orgy on a summer morn
Their boisterous devotion to the sun,
Not as a god, but as a god might be,
Naked among them, like a savage source.   95
Their chant shall be a chant of paradise,
Out of their blood, returning to the sky;
And in their chant shall enter, voice by voice,
The windy lake wherein their lord delights,
The trees, like serafim, and echoing hills,   100
That choir among themselves long afterward.
They shall know well the heavenly fellowship
Of men that perish and of summer morn.
And whence they came and whither they shall go
The dew upon their feet shall manifest.   105

She hears, upon that water without sound,
A voice that cries, "The tomb in Palestine
Is not the porch of spirits lingering.
It is the grave of Jesus, where He lay."
We live in an old chaos of the sun,   110
Or old dependency of day and night,
Or island solitude, unsponsored, free,
Of that wide water, inescapable.
Deer walk upon our mountains, and the quail
Whistle about us their spontaneous cries;   115
Sweet berries ripen in the wilderness;
And, in the isolation of the sky,
At evening, casual flocks of pigeons make
Ambiguous undulations as they sink,
Downward to darkness, on extended wings.   120

Ploughing on Sunday

The white cock's tail
Tosses in the wind.
The turkey-cock's tail
Glitters in the sun.

Water in the fields.   5
The wind pours down.
The feathers flare
And bluster in the wind.

Remus, blow your horn!
I'm ploughing on Sunday,   10
Ploughing North America.
Blow your horn!

Tum-ti-tum,
Ti-tum-tum-tum!
The turkey-cock's tail   15
Spreads to the sun.

The white cock's tail
Streams to the moon.
Water in the fields.
The wind pours down.   20

The Emperor of Ice-cream

Call the roller of big cigars,
The muscular one, and bid him whip
In kitchen cups concupiscent curds.
Let the wenches dawdle in such dress
As they are used to wear, and let the boys   5
Bring flowers in last month's newspapers.
Let be be finale of seem.
The only emperor is the emperor of ice-cream.

Take from the dresser of deal,
Lacking the three glass knobs, that sheet   10

The Emperor of Ice-cream: *7*: "Let reality put an end to appearance." *9 deal*:
an inexpensive wood.

On which she embroidered fantails once
And spread it so as to cover her face.
If her horny feet protrude, they come
To show how cold she is, and dumb.
Let the lamp affix its beam.   15
The only emperor is the emperor of ice-cream.

Peter Quince at the Clavier

I

Just as my fingers on these keys
Make music, so the self-same sounds
On my spirit make a music too.

Music is feeling, then, not sound;
And thus it is that what I feel,   5
Here in this room, desiring you,

Thinking of your blue-shadowed silk,
Is music. It is like the strain
Waked in the elders by Susanna:

Of a green evening, clear and warm,   10
She bathed in her still garden, while
The red-eyed elders, watching, felt

The basses of their being throb
In witching chords, and their thin blood
Pulse pizzicati of Hosanna.   15

II

In the green water, clear and warm,
Susanna lay.
She searched
The touch of springs,
And found   20
Concealed imaginings.
She sighed
For so much melody.

Peter Quince at the Clavier: *Title:* Peter Quince is a character in Shakespeare's
Midsummer Night's Dream, but Stevens seems to have used the name without
specific reference to this.   *9 Susanna:* Her story is told in Dan. 13, a chapter sub-
sequently removed to the Apocrypha; Stevens retells it here.

Upon the bank she stood
In the cool   25
Of spent emotions.
She felt, among the leaves,
The dew
Of old devotions.

She walked upon the grass,   30
Still quavering.
The winds were like her maids,
On timid feet,
Fetching her woven scarves,
Yet wavering.   35

A breath upon her hand
Muted the night.
She turned—
A cymbal clashed,
And roaring horns.   40

III

Soon, with a noise like tambourines,
Came her attendant Byzantines.

They wondered why Susanna cried
Against the elders by her side:

And as they whispered, the refrain   45
Was like a willow swept by rain.

Anon their lamps' uplifted flame
Revealed Susanna and her shame.

And then the simpering Byzantines
Fled, with a noise like tambourines.   50

IV

Beauty is momentary in the mind—
The fitful tracing of a portal;
But in the flesh it is immortal.

The body dies; the body's beauty lives.
So evenings die, in their green going,   55
A wave, interminably flowing

So gardens die, their meek breath scenting
The cowl of Winter, done repenting.

So maidens die to the auroral
Celebration of a maiden's choral.   60

Susanna's music touched the bawdy strings
Of those white elders; but, escaping,
Left only Death's ironic scraping.
Now in its immortality, it plays
On the clear viol of her memory,   65
And makes a constant sacrament of praise.

Thirteen Ways of Looking at a Blackbird

I

Among twenty snowy mountains,
The only moving thing
Was the eye of the blackbird.

II

I was of three minds,
Like a tree   5
In which there are three blackbirds.

III

The blackbird whirled in the autumn winds.
It was a small part of the pantomime.

IV

A man and a woman
Are one.   10
A man and a woman and a blackbird
Are one.

V

I do not know which to prefer,
The beauty of inflections
Or the beauty of innuendoes,   15
The blackbird whistling
Or just after.

VI

Icicles filled the long window
With barbaric glass.
The shadow of the blackbird   20

Crossed it, to and fro.
The mood
Traced in the shadow
An indecipherable cause.

VII

O thin men of Haddam,   25
Why do you imagine golden birds?
Do you not see how the blackbird
Walks around the feet
Of the women about you?

VIII

I know noble accents   30
And lucid, inescapable rhythms;
But I know, too,
That the blackbird is involved
In what I know.

IX

When the blackbird flew out of sight,   35
It marked the edge
Of one of many circles.

X

At the sight of blackbirds
Flying in a green light,
Even the bawds of euphony   40
Would cry out sharply.

XI

He rode over Connecticut
In a glass coach
Once, a fear pierced him,
In that he mistook   45
The shadow of his equipage
For blackbirds.

XII

The river is moving
The blackbird must be flying.

XIII

It was evening all afternoon   50
It was snowing

---

25 *Haddam:* a town in Connecticut. Stevens uses the name without real reference
to the town.   46 *equipage:* the "glass coach," which is, of course, his car.

And it was going to snow.
The blackbird sat
In the cedar-limbs.

The Idea of Order in Key West

She sang beyond the genius of the sea.
The water never formed to mind or voice,
Like a body wholly body, fluttering
Its empty sleeves; and yet its mimic motion
Made constant cry, caused constantly a cry,   *5*
That was not ours although we understood,
Inhuman, of the veritable ocean.

The sea was not a mask. No more was she.
The song and water were not medleyed sound,
Even if what she sang was what she heard,   *10*
Since what she sang she uttered word by word.
It may be that in all her phrases stirred
The grinding water and the gasping wind;
But it was she and not the sea we heard.

For she was the maker of the song she sang.   *15*
The ever-hooded, tragic-gestured sea
Was merely a place by which she walked to sing.
Whose spirit is this? we said, because we knew
It was the spirit that we sought and knew
That we should ask this often as she sang.   *20*

If it was only the dark voice of the sea
That rose, or even colored by many waves;
If it was only the outer voice of sky
And cloud, of the sunken coral water-walled,
However clear, it would have been deep air,   *25*
The heaving speech of air, a summer sound
Repeated in a summer without end
And sound alone. But it was more than that,
More even than her voice, and ours, among
The meaningless plungings of water and the wind,   *30*
Theatrical distances, bronze shadows heaped
On high horizons, mountainous atmospheres
Of sky and sea.

It was her voice that made
The sky acutest at its vanishing.
She measured to the hour its solitude.   35
She was the single artificer of the world
In which she sang. And when she sang, the sea,
Whatever self it had, became the self
That was her song, for she was maker. Then we,
As we beheld her striding there alone,   40
Knew that there never was a world for her
Except the one she sang and, singing, made.

Ramon Fernandez, tell me, if you know,
Why, when the singing ended and we turned
Toward the town, tell why the glassy lights,   45
The lights in the fishing boats at anchor there,
As the night descended, tilting in the air,
Mastered the night and portioned out the sea,
Fixing emblazoned zones and fiery poles,
Arranging, deepening, enchanting night.   50

Oh! Blessed rage for order, pale Ramon,
The maker's rage to order words of the sea,
Words of the fragrant portals, dimly-starred,
And of ourselves and of our origins,
In ghostlier demarcations, keener sounds.   55

The Glass of Water

That the glass would melt in heat,
That the water would freeze in cold,
Shows that this object is merely a state,
One of many, between two poles. So,
In the metaphysical, there are these poles.   5

Here in the centre stands the glass. Light
Is the lion that comes down to drink. There
And in that state, the glass is a pool.
Ruddy are his eyes and ruddy are his claws
When light comes down to wet his frothy jaws.   10

The Idea of Order: *43 Ramon Fernandez:* Stevens tells us that he made this
name up, using two common Spanish names; he found later that it was the pen
name of a French critic.

And in the water winding weeds move round.
And there and in another state—the refractions,
The *metaphysica*, the plastic parts of poems
Crash in the mind—But, fat Jocundus, worrying
About what stands here in the centre, not the glass,   15

But in the centre of our lives, this time, this day,
It is a state, this spring among the politicians
Playing cards. In a village of the indigenes,
One would have still to discover. Among the dogs and dung,
One would continue to contend with one's ideas.   20

The Glass of Water: *14 Jocundus:* a name for a cheerful person, possibly meant
to refer to Stevens himself. *18 indigenes:* natives.

T. S. ELIOT
1888–1965

Thomas Stearns Eliot succeeded in becoming the leader of modern criticism and poetry during his lifetime even as, paradoxically, he rejected modernity, individualism, and all but the most conservative values in his personal life. This pruning culminated in *For Lancelot Andrewes* (1928), when he declared himself "an Anglo-Catholic in religion, a classicist in literature, and a royalist in politics." His boyhood in St. Louis presents itself as a bitter exile, later tempered by a brilliant career at Harvard, where the echoes of his nineteenth-century ancestors fueled his search for an older world. He studied at the Sorbonne (fulfilling an avid interest in Laforgue mainly), then at Oxford. Hard times as teacher, banker, and husband followed. Helped extensively by Ezra Pound, Eliot earned his reputation in 1922 with the publication of *The Wasteland*. "Ash Wednesday" followed in 1930, although his impressive critical writing had greater impact than any poem or even than his influential role as editor of *The Criterion. After Strange Gods: A Primer of Modern Heresy* (1934) further charts his pursuit of orthodoxy and is a sharp example of his position toward the individualism of such other contemporaries as Joyce, Lawrence, and Yeats. His religious focus finds its most ambitious poetic expression in *The Four Quartets*, written from 1935 to 1943. In 1948 he won the Nobel Prize.

The Love Song of J. Alfred Prufrock

S'io credesse che mia risposta fosse
A persona che mai tornasse al mondo,
Questa fiamma staria senza piu scosse.
Ma perciocche giammai di questo fondo
Non torno vivo alcun, s'i'odo il vero,
Senza tema d'infamia ti rispondo.

Let us go then, you and I,
When the evening is spread out against the sky
Like a patient etherised upon a table;
Let us go, through certain half-deserted streets,
The muttering retreats   5
Of restless nights in one-night cheap hotels
And sawdust restaurants with oyster-shells:
Streets that follow like a tedious argument
Of insidious intent
To lead you to an overwhelming question. . . .   10
Oh, do not ask, "What is it?"
Let us go and make our visit.

In the room the women come and go
Talking of Michelangelo.

The yellow fog that rubs its back upon the window-panes,   15
The yellow smoke that rubs its muzzle on the window-panes,
Licked its tongue into the corners of the evening,
Lingered upon the pools that stand in drains,
Let fall upon its back the soot that falls from chimneys,
Slipped by the terrace, made a sudden leap,   20

The Love Song of J. Alfred Prufrock: *Epigraph:* "If I thought my response were to someone who could ever return to the world, this flame would shake no longer. But since no one ever returned alive from this pit, if what I hear is true, I answer thee without fear of infamy." Guido da Montefeltro is speaking to Dante (*Inferno* 27. 61–66). Prufrock, like Guido, is making a confession he would not make if it would be known to others.

And seeing that it was a soft October night,
Curled once about the house, and fell asleep.

And indeed there will be time
For the yellow smoke that slides along the street,
Rubbing its back upon the window-panes;   25
There will be time, there will be time
To prepare a face to meet the faces that you meet;
There will be time to murder and create,
And time for all the works and days of hands
That lift and drop a question on your plate;   30
Time for you and time for me,
And time yet for a hundred indecisions,
And for a hundred visions and revisions,
Before the taking of a toast and tea.

In the room the women come and go   35
Talking of Michelangelo.

And indeed there will be time
To wonder, "Do I dare?" and, "Do I dare?"
Time to turn back and descend the stair,
With a bald spot in the middle of my hair—   40
(They will say: "How his hair is growing thin!")
My morning coat, my collar mounting firmly to the chin,
My necktie rich and modest, but asserted by a simple pin—
(They will say: "But how his arms and legs are thin!")
Do I dare   45
Disturb the universe?
In a minute there is time
For decisions and revisions which a minute will reverse.

For I have known them all already, known them all:
Have known the evenings, mornings, afternoons,   50
I have measured out my life with coffee spoons;
I know the voices dying with a dying fall
Beneath the music from a farther room.
   So how should I presume?

And I have known the eyes already, known them all—   55
The eyes that fix you in a formulated phrase,
And when I am formulated, sprawling on a pin,
When I am pinned and wriggling on the wall,
Then how should I begin
To spit out all the butt-ends of my days and ways?   60
   And how should I presume?

And I have known the arms already, known them all—
Arms that are braceleted and white and bare
(But in the lamplight, downed with light brown hair!)
Is it perfume from a dress   65
That makes me so digress?
Arms that lie along a table, or wrap about a shawl,
   And should I then presume?
   And how should I begin?

         . . . .

Shall I say, I have gone at dusk through narrow streets   70
And watched the smoke that rises from the pipes
Of lonely men in shirt-sleeves, leaning out of windows? . . .

I should have been a pair of ragged claws
Scuttling across the floors of silent seas.

         . . . .

And the afternoon, the evening, sleeps so peacefully!   75
Smoothed by long fingers,
Asleep . . . tired . . . or it malingers,
Stretched on the floor, here beside you and me.
Should I, after tea and cakes and ices,
Have the strength to force the moment to its crisis?   80
But though I have wept and fasted, wept and prayed,
Though I have seen my head (grown slightly bald) brought in
     upon a platter,
I am no prophet—and here's no great matter;
I have seen the moment of my greatness flicker,
And I have seen the eternal Footman hold my coat, and snicker, 85
And in short, I was afraid.

And would it have been worth it, after all,
After the cups, the marmalade, the tea,
Among the porcelain, among some talk of you and me,
Would it have been worth while,   90
To have bitten off the matter with a smile,
To have squeezed the universe into a ball
To roll it toward some overwhelming question,
To say: "I am Lazarus, come from the dead,
Come back to tell you all, I shall tell you all"—   95
If one, settling a pillow by her head,
   Should say: "That is not what I meant at all.
   That is not it, at all."

83 *prophet:* the prophet John the Baptist was beheaded, and his head was brought
on a platter to Salome.   94 *Lazarus:* resurrected by Jesus.

And would it have been worth it, after all,
Would it have been worth while,   *100*
After the sunsets and the dooryards and the sprinkled streets,
After the novels, after the teacups, after the skirts that trail
        along the floor—
And this, and so much more?—
It is impossible to say just what I mean!
But as if a magic lantern threw the nerves in patterns on a
        screen: *105*
Would it have been worth while
If one, settling a pillow or throwing off a shawl,
And turning toward the window, should say:
        "That is not it at all,
        That is not what I meant, at all."   *110*

                        .   .   .   .   .

No! I am not Prince Hamlet, nor was meant to be;
Am an attendant lord, one that will do
To swell a progress, start a scene or two,
Advise the prince; no doubt, an easy tool,
Deferential, glad to be of use,   *115*
Politic, cautious, and meticulous;
Full of high sentence, but a bit obtuse;
At times, indeed, almost ridiculous—
Almost, at times, the Fool.

I grow old . . . I grow old . . .   *120*
I shall wear the bottoms of my trousers rolled.

Shall I part my hair behind? Do I dare to eat a peach?
I shall wear white flannel trousers, and walk upon the beach.
I have heard the mermaids singing, each to each.

I do not think that they will sing to me.   *125*

I have seen them riding seaward on the waves
Combing the white hair of the waves blown back
When the wind blows the water white and black.

We have lingered in the chambers of the sea
By sea-girls wreathed with seaweed red and brown   *130*
Till human voices wake us, and we drown.

112 an attendant lord: a courtier, someone who attends on royalty. *121 rolled:*
with cuffs. Cuffed trousers had just come into fashion when this poem was com-
posed. Prufrock is thinking of dressing fashionably to hide his age and of part-
ing his hair differently to hide his bald spot.

Preludes

I

The winter evening settles down
With smell of steaks in passageways.
Six o'clock.
The burnt-out ends of smoky days.
And now a gusty shower wraps   5
The grimy scraps
Of withered leaves about your feet
And newspapers from vacant lots;
The showers beat
On broken blinds and chimney-pots,   10
At the corner of the street
A lonely cab-horse steams and stamps.
And then the lighting of the lamps.

II

The morning comes to consciousness
Of faint stale smells of beer   15
From the sawdust-trampled street
With all its muddy feet that press
To early coffee-stands.
With the other masquerades
That time resumes,   20
One thinks of all the hands
That are raising dingy shades
In a thousand furnished rooms.

III

You tossed a blanket from the bed,
You lay upon your back, and waited;   25
You dozed, and watched the night revealing
The thousand sordid images
Of which your soul was constituted;
They flickered against the ceiling.
And when all the world came back   30
And the light crept up between the shutters
And you heard the sparrows in the gutters,
You had such a vision of the street
As the street hardly understands;
Sitting along the bed's edge, where   35
You curled the papers from your hair,
Or clasped the yellow soles of feet
In the palms of both soiled hands.

IV

His soul stretched tight across the skies
That fade behind a city block,   *40*
Or trampled by insistent feet
At four and five and six o'clock;
And short square fingers stuffing pipes,
And evening newspapers, and eyes
Assured of certain certainties,   *45*
The conscience of a blackened street
Impatient to assume the world.

I am moved by fancies that are curled
Around these images, and cling:
The notion of some infinitely gentle   *50*
Infinitely suffering thing.

Wipe your hand across your mouth, and laugh;
The worlds revolve like ancient women
Gathering fuel in vacant lots.

Morning at the Window

They are rattling breakfast plates in basement kitchens,
And along the trampled edges of the street
I am aware of the damp souls of housemaids
Sprouting despondently at area gates.

The brown waves of fog toss up to me
Twisted faces from the bottom of the street,
And tear from a passer-by with muddy skirts
An aimless smile that hovers in the air
And vanishes along the level of the roofs.

Gerontion

Thou hast nor youth nor age
But as it were an after dinner sleep
Dreaming of both.

Here I am, an old man in a dry month,
Being read to by a boy, waiting for rain.
I was neither at the hot gates
Nor fought in the warm rain
Nor knee deep in the salt marsh, heaving a cutlass,   5
Bitten by flies, fought.
My house is a decayed house,
And the jew squats on the window sill, the owner,
Spawned in some estaminet of Antwerp,
Blistered in Brussels, patched and peeled in London.   10
The goat coughs at night in the field overhead;
Rocks, moss, stonecrop, iron, merds.
The woman keeps the kitchen, makes tea,
Sneezes at evening, poking the peevish gutter.
        I an old man,   15
A dull head among windy spaces.

Signs are taken for wonders. "We would see a sign!"
The word within a word, unable to speak a word,
Swaddled with darkness. In the juvescence of the year
Came Christ the tiger   20
In depraved May, dogwood and chestnut, flowering judas,
To be eaten, to be divided, to be drunk
Among whispers; by Mr. Silvero
With caressing hands, at Limoges
Who walked all night in the next room;   25

By Hakagawa, bowing among the Titians;
By Madame de Tornquist, in the dark room
Shifting the candles; Fräulein von Kulp
Who turned in the hall, one hand on the door.
        Vacant shuttles   30
Weave the wind. I have no ghosts,
An old man in a draughty house
Under a windy knob.

Gerontion: *Title:* diminutive of the Greek word for "old man," therefore, "little old man." It is not the name of the speaker, but a name for his condition; at one stage of its development, the soul becomes like a little old man. *Epigraph:* from Shakespeare's *Measure for Measure* 3. 1. *9 estaminet:* a cheap cafe. *12 merds:* droppings. *19 juvescence:* rejuvenation.

After such knowledge, what forgiveness? Think now
History has many cunning passages, contrived corridors   35
And issues, deceives with whispering ambitions,
Guides us by vanities. Think now
She gives when our attention is distracted
And what she gives, gives with such supple confusions
That the giving famishes the craving. Gives too late   40
What's not believed in, or if still believed,
In memory only, reconsidered passion. Gives too soon
Into weak hands, what's thought can be dispensed with
Till the refusal propagates a fear. Think
Neither fear nor courage saves us. Unnatural vices   45
Are fathered by our heroism. Virtues
Are forced upon us by our impudent crimes.
These tears are shaken from the wrath-bearing tree.

The tiger springs in the new year. Us he devours.
    Think at last   50
We have not reached conclusion, when I
Stiffen in a rented house. Think at last
I have not made this show purposelessly
And it is not by any concitation
Of the backward devils   55
I would meet you upon this honestly.
I that was near your heart was removed therefrom
To lose beauty in terror, terror in inquisition.
I have lost my passion: why should I need to keep it
Since what is kept must be adulterated?   60
I have lost my sight, smell, hearing, taste and touch:
How should I use them for your closer contact?

These with a thousand small deliberations
Protract the profit of their chilled delirium,
Excite the membrane, when the sense has cooled,   65
With pungent sauces, multiply variety
In a wilderness of mirrors. What will the spider do,
Suspend its operations, will the weevil
Delay? De Bailhache, Fresca, Mrs. Cammel, whirled
Beyond the circuit of the shuddering Bear   70
In fractured atoms. Gull against the wind, in the windy straits

71–72 *straits of Belle Isle:* The northern entrance to the Gulf of St. Lawrence; a
small rock island there was the first land sighted by ships from Europe.

Of Belle Isle, or running on the Horn,
White feathers in the snow, the Gulf claims,
And an old man driven by the Trades
To a sleepy corner.

                    Tenants of the house,   75
Thoughts of a dry brain in a dry season.

Sweeney Among the Nightingales

ὦμοι, πέπληγμαι χαιρίαν πληγὴν ἔσω.

Apeneck Sweeney spreads his knees
Letting his arms hang down to laugh,
The zebra stripes along his jaw
Swelling to maculate giraffe.

The circles of the stormy moon   5
Slide westward to the River Plate,
Death and the Raven drift above
And Sweeney guards the hornèd gate.

Gloomy Orion and the Dog
Are veiled; and hushed the shrunken seas;   10
The person in the Spanish cape
Tries to sit on Sweeney's knees

Slips and pulls the table cloth
Overturns a coffee cup,
Reorganized upon the floor   15
She yawns and draws a stocking up;

The silent man in mocha brown
Sprawls at the window-sill and gapes;

Sweeney Among the Nightingales: *Title:* Sweeney appears in several of Eliot's poems, always as a vulgar person, more animal than human. *Epigraph:* The death cry of Agamemnon in Aeschylus's tragedy of that name. While being killed by his wife Clytemnestra and her paramour Aegisthus, he cries, "Ah, me! I have been struck deep with a mortal blow!" *6 River Plate:* The Rio de la Plata, an estuary formed by the Parana and Uruguay rivers, separating Uruguay and Argentina. *7 Raven:* the constellation Corvus. *8 hornèd gate:* probably a reference to the horns of the crescent moon, associated with Diana and her worship in the grove at Nemi.

The waiter brings in oranges,
Bananas, figs and hot-house grapes;   20

The silent vertebrate exhales,
Contracts and concentrates, withdraws;
Rachel *née* Rabinovitch
Tears at the grapes with murderous paws;

She and the lady in the cape   25
Are suspect, thought to be in league;
Therefore the man with heavy eyes
Declines the gambit, shows fatigue,

Leaves the room and reappears
Outside the window, leaning in,   30
Branches of wistaria
Circumscribe a golden grin;

The host with someone indistinct
Converses at the door apart,
The nightingales are singing near   35
The Convent of the Sacred Heart,

And sang within the bloody wood
When Agamemnon cried aloud,
And let their liquid siftings fall
To stain the stiff dishonoured shroud.   40

The Hollow Men

Mistah Kurtz—he dead.

A penny for the Old Guy

I

We are the hollow men
We are the stuffed men
Leaning together
Headpiece filled with straw. Alas!
Our dried voices, when   5

The Hollow Men: *Epigraphs:* (1) from Joseph Conrad's *Heart of Darkness* (1902); (2) from the chant of British children collecting money for fireworks and bonfires on Guy Fawkes day. They carry straw effigies to burn later and cry, "Remember, remember, the Fifth of November / A penny for the Old Guy." In 1605 Fawkes was caught preparing to blow up the Houses of Parliament.

We whisper together
Are quiet and meaningless
As wind in dry grass
Or rats' feet over broken glass
In our dry cellar   10

Shape without form, shade without colour,
Paralysed force, gesture without motion;

Those who have crossed
With direct eyes, to death's other Kingdom
Remember us—if at all—not as lost   15
Violent souls, but only
As the hollow men
The stuffed men.

II

Eyes I dare not meet in dreams
In death's dream kingdom   20
These do not appear:
There, the eyes are
Sunlight on a broken column
There, is a tree swinging
And voices are   25
In the wind's singing
More distant and more solemn
Than a fading star.

Let me be no nearer
In death's dream kingdom   30
Let me also wear
Such deliberate disguises
Rat's coat, crowskin, crossed staves
In a field
Behaving as the wind behaves   35
No nearer—

Not that final meeting
In the twilight kingdom

III

This is the dead land
This is cactus land   40
Here the stone images
Are raised, here they receive
The supplication of a dead man's hand
Under the twinkle of a fading star.

Is it like this   45
In death's other kingdom
Waking alone
At the hour when we are
Trembling with tenderness
Lips that would not kiss   50
Form prayers to broken stone.

IV
The eyes are not here
There are no eyes here
In this valley of dying stars
In this hollow valley   55
This broken jaw of our lost kingdoms

In this last of meeting places
We grope together
And avoid speech
Gathered on this beach of the tumid river   60

Sightless, unless
The eyes reappear
As the perpetual star
Multifoliate rose
Of death's twilight kingdom   65
The hope only
Of empty men

V
Here we go round the prickly pear
Prickly pear prickly pear
Here we go round the prickly pear   70
At five o'clock in the morning.

Between the idea
And the reality
Between the motion
And the act   75
Falls the shadow
        For Thine is the Kingdom.

        Between the conception
And the creation
Between the emotion   80
And the response

Falls the Shadow
    Life is very long.

    Between the desire
And the spasm   *85*
Between the potency
And the existence
Between the essence
And the descent
Falls the Shadow   *90*
    For Thine is the Kingdom.

    For Thine is
Life is
For Thine is the

    This is the way the world ends   *95*
This is the way the world ends
This is the way the world ends
Not with a bang but with a whimper.

Journey of the Magi

    "A cold coming we had of it,
Just the worst time of the year
For a journey, and such a long journey:
The ways deep and the weather sharp,
The very dead of winter."   *5*
And the camels galled, sore-footed, refractory,
Lying down in the melting snow.
There were times we regretted
The summer palaces on slopes, the terraces,
And the silken girls bringing sherbet.   *10*
Then the camel men cursing and grumbling
And running away, and wanting their liquor and women,
And the night-fires going out, and the lack of shelters,
And the cities hostile and the towns unfriendly
And the villages dirty and charging high prices: *15*
A hard time we had of it.
At the end we preferred to travel at night,

Journey of the Magi: *1–5:* Eliot's adaptation of a passage in Lancelot Andrewes's
Nativity sermon.

Sleeping in snatches,
With the voices singing in our ears, saying
That this was all folly.   20

Then at dawn we came down to a temperate valley,
Wet, below the snow line, smelling of vegetation;
With a running stream and a water-mill beating the darkness,
And three trees on the low sky,
And an old white horse galloped away in the meadow.   25
Then we came to a tavern with vine-leaves over the lintel,
Six hands at an open door dicing for pieces of silver,
And feet kicking the empty wine-skins.
But there was no information, and so we continued
And arrived at evening, not a moment too soon   30
Finding the place; it was (you may say) satisfactory.

All this was a long time ago, I remember,
And I would do it again, but set down
This set down
This: were we led all that way for   35
Birth or Death? There was a Birth, certainly,
We had evidence and no doubt. I had seen birth and death,
But had thought they were different; this Birth was
Hard and bitter for us, like Death, our death.
We returned to our places, these Kingdoms,   40
But no longer at ease here, in the old dispensation,
With an alien people clutching their gods.
I should be glad of another death.

24 *three trees:* a symbol, since three "trees" or crosses were involved in the
Crucifixion. 25 *white horse:* the rider of the white horse is Christ (Rev. 19).
26: *vine-leaves:* indicating that new wine was ready. 27: a reference both to
the soldiers dicing at the foot of the Cross and to the thirty pieces of silver that
Judas got for betraying Christ. Thus the Tree Magi, Three Wise Men, or Three
Kings, as they are sometimes called, encounter several omens in their journey
toward the stable where Jesus is to be born.

ADDITIONAL POEMS

Lord Randal

"O where hae ye been, Lord Randal, my son?
O where hae ye been, my handsome young man?"
"I hae been to the wild wood; mother, make my bed soon,
For I'm weary wi hunting, and fain wald lie down."

"Where gat ye your dinner, Lord Randal, my son?   5
Where gat ye your dinner, my handsome young man?"
"I din'd wi my true-love; mother, make my bed soon,
For I'm weary wi hunting, and fain wald lie down."

"What gat ye to your dinner, Lord Randal, my son?
What gat ye to your dinner, my handsome young man?"   10
"I gat eels boiled in broo; mother, make my bed soon,
For I'm weary wi hunting, and fain wald lie down."

"What became of your bloodhounds, Lord Randal, my son?
What became of your bloodhounds, my handsome young
      man?"
"O they swelld and they died; mother, make my bed soon,   15
For I'm weary wi hunting, and fain wald lie down."

"O I fear ye are poisond, Lord Randal, my son!
O I fear ye are poisond, my handsome young man!"
"O yes! I am poisond; mother, make my bed soon,
For I'm sick at the heart, and I fain wald lie down."   20

Sir Patrick Spens

The king sits in Dumferling toune,
    Drinking the blude-reid wine:
"O whar will I get guid sailor,
    To sail this schip of mine?"

Up and spak an eldern knicht,   5
    Sat at the kings richt kne:
"Sir Patrick Spens is the best sailor
    That sails upon the se "

The king has written a braid letter,
    And signed it wi his hand,   10
And sent it to Sir Patrick Spens,
    Was walking on the sand.

The first line that Sir Patrick red,
    A loud lauch lauchèd he;
The next line that Sir Patrick red,   15
    The teir blinded his ee.

"O wha is this has don this deid,
    This ill deid don to me,
To send me out this time o' the yeir,
    To sail upon the se!   20

"Mak hast, mak hast, my mirry men all,
    Our guid schip sails the morne:"
"O say na sae, my master deir,
    For I feir a deadlie storme.

"Late, late yestreen I saw the new moone,   25
    Wi the auld moone in hir arme,
And I feir, I feir, my deir master,
    That we will cum to harme."

O our Scots nobles wer richt laith
    To weet their cork-heild schoone;   30
Bot lang owre a' the play wer playd,
    Thair hats they swam aboone.

O lang, lang may their ladies sit,
    Wi thair fans into their hand,
Or eir they se Sir Patrick Spens   35
    Cum sailing to the land.

O lang, lang may the ladies stand,
    Wi thair gold kems in their hair,
Waiting for thair ain deir lords,
    For they'll se thame na mair.   40

Haf owre, haf owre to Aberdour,
    It's fiftie fadom deip,
And thair lies guid Sir Patrick Spens,
    Wi the Scots lords at his feit.

SIR THOMAS WYATT (1503?–1542)

They Flee from Me

They flee from me, that sometime did me seek,
    With naked foot stalking within my chamber:
Once have I seen them gentle, tame and meek,
    That now are wild, and do not once remember,
    That sometime they have put themselves in danger   5
To take bread at my hand; and now they range
Busily seeking in continual change.

Thankéd be Fortune, it hath been otherwise
    Twenty times better; but once especial,

In thin array, after a pleasant guise,   10
    When her loose gown did from her shoulders fall,
    And she me caught in her arms long and small,
And therewithal so sweetly did me kiss,
And softly said, "Dear heart, how like you this?"

It was no dream; for I lay broad awaking: 15
    But all is turn'd now, through my gentleness,
Into a bitter fashion of forsaking;
    And I have leave to go of her goodness;
    And she also to use new fangleness.
But since that I unkindly so am served: 20
How like you this, what hath she now deserved?

EDMUND SPENSER (1552?–1599)

Sonnet 70

From AMORETTI

Fresh spring, the herald of Love's mighty king,
In whose coat-armour richly are displayed
All sorts of flowers, the which on earth do spring,
In goodly colours gloriously arrayed;
Go to my love, where she is careless laid,   5
Yet in her winter's bower will not awake;
Tell her the joyous time will not be stayed
Unless she do him by the forelock take;
Bid her therefore herself soon ready make
To wait on Love among his lovely crew;   10
Where every one that misseth then her make
Shall be by him amerced with penance due.
Make haste, therefore, sweet love, whilst it is prime,
For none can call again the passéd time.

Sonnet 75

From AMORETTI

One day I wrote her name upon the strand;
But came the waves and washéd it away;
Again I wrote it with a second hand;

But came the tide, and made my pains his prey.
"Vain man," said she, "that dost in vain essay   5
A mortal thing so to immortalise,
For I myself shall like to this decay,
And eke my name be wipéd out likewise."
"Not so," quoth I, "let baser things devise
To die in dust, but you shall live by fame;   10
My verse your virtues rare shall eternise,
And in the heavens write your glorious name.
Where, whenas death shall all the world subdue,
Our love shall live, and later life renew."

SIR PHILIP SIDNEY (1554–1586)

Sonnet 39

From ASTROPHEL AND STELLA

Come, Sleep; O Sleep! the certain knot of peace,
The baiting-place of wit, the balm of woe,
The poor man's wealth, the prisoner's release,
Th'indifferent judge between the high and low;
With shield of proof shield me from out the prease   5
Of those fierce darts Despair at me doth throw:
O make in me those civil wars to cease;
I will good tribute pay, if thou do so.
Take thou of me smooth pillows, sweetest bed,
A chamber deaf to noise and blind to light,   10
A rosy garland and a weary head;
And if these things, as being thine by right,
Move not thy heavy grace, thou shalt in me,
Livelier than elsewhere, Stella's image see.

Leave Me, O Love

Leave me, O love which reachest but to dust;
And thou, my mind, aspire to higher things;
Grow rich in that which never taketh rust,
Whatever fades but fading pleasure brings.
Draw in thy beams, and humble all thy might   5

To that sweet yoke where lasting freedoms be;
Which breaks the clouds and opens forth the light,
That doth both shine and give us sight to see.
O take fast hold; let that light be thy guide
In this small course which birth draws out to death,   10
And think how evil becometh him to slide,
Who seeketh heav'n and comes of heav'nly breath.
Then farewell, world; thy uttermost I see;
Eternal Love, maintain thy life in me.

CHRISTOPHER MARLOWE (1564–1593)

The Passionate Shepherd to His Love

Come live with me and be my love,
And we will all the pleasures prove,
That valleys, groves, hills and fields,
Woods or steepy mountains yields.

And we will sit upon the rocks,   5
Seeing the shepherds feed their flocks
By shallow rivers, to whose falls
Melodious birds sing madrigals.

And I will make thee beds of roses,
And a thousand fragrant posies,   10
A cap of flowers and a kirtle
Embroidered all with leaves of myrtle;

A gown made of the finest wool,
Which from our pretty lambs we pull;
Fair-linéd slippers for the cold,   15
With buckles of the purest gold;

A belt of straw and ivy buds,
With coral clasps and amber studs;
And if these pleasures may thee move,
Come live with me and be my love.   20

The shepherd swains shall dance and sing
For thy delight each May morning;
If these delights thy mind may move,
Then live with me and be my love.

THOMAS CAMPION (1567–1620)

There Is a Garden in Her Face

There is a garden in her face
Where roses and white lilies grow;
A heavenly paradise is that place
Wherein all pleasant fruits do flow.
    There cherries grow which none may buy,   *5*
    Till "Cherry ripe" themselves do cry.

Those cherries fairly do enclose
Of orient pearl a double row,
Which when her lovely laughter shows,
They look like rose-buds filled with snow;   *10*
    Yet them nor peer nor prince can buy,
    Till "Cherry ripe" themselves do cry.

Her eyes like angels watch them still,
Her brows like bended bows do stand,
Threatening with piercing frowns to kill   *15*
All that attempt, with eye or hand,
    Those sacred cherries to come nigh
    Till "Cherry ripe" themselves do cry.

BEN JONSON 1573?–1637

On My First Son

Farewell, thou child of my right hand, and joy;
My sin was too much hope of thee, loved boy.
Seven years thou wert lent to me, and I thee pay,
Exacted by thy fate, on the just day.
O, could I lose all father now! for why   *5*
Will man lament the state he should envy—
To have so soon 'scaped world's and flesh's rage,
And, if no other misery, yet age?
Rest in soft peace; and, asked, say, "Here doth lie
Ben Johnson his best piece of poetry;   *10*
For whose sake henceforth all his vows be such
As what he loves may never like too much."

Song: To Celia

Drink to me only with thine eyes,
    And I will pledge with mine;
Or leave a kiss but in the cup,
    And I'll not look for wine.
The thirst, that from the soul doth rise,   *5*
    Doth ask a drink divine.
But might I of Jove's nectar sup,
    I would not change for thine.

I sent thee, late, a rosy wreath,
    Not so much honoring thee,   *10*
As giving it a hope, that there
    It could not whither'd be.
But thou theron did'st only breathe,
    And sent'st it back to me.
Since when, it grows, and smells, I swear,   *15*
    Not of itself, but thee.

ROBERT HERRICK (1591–1674)

To the Virgins, to Make Much of Time

Gather ye rose-buds while ye may,
    Old Time is still a-flying:
And this same flower that smiles to-day,
    To-morrow will be dying.

The glorious lamp of Heaven, the sun,   *5*
    The higher he's a-getting;
The sooner will his race be run,
    And nearer he's to setting.

That age is best, which is the first,
    When youth and blood are warmer;   *10*
But being spent, the worse, and worst
    Times, still succeed the former.

Then be not coy, but use your time;
    And while ye may, go marry:
For having lost but once your prime,   *15*
    You may forever tarry.

Upon Julia's Clothes

Whenas in silks my Julia goes,
Then, then, methinks, how sweetly flows
The liquefaction of her clothes!

Next, when I cast mine eyes and see
That brave vibration each way free,
—O how that glittering taketh me!

GEORGE HERBERT (1593–1633)

The Collar

I struck the board and cried, No more!
 I will abroad.
What? Shall I ever sigh and pine?
My lines and life are free, free as the road,
 Loose as the wind, as large as store.   5
  Shall I be still in suit?
Have I no harvest but a thorn
To let my blood, and not restore
What I have lost with cordial fruit?
  Sure there was wine   10
Before my sighs did dry it; there was corn
 Before my tears did drown it.
Is the year only lost to me?
 Have I no bays to crown it?
No flowers, no garlands gay? All blasted?   15
 All wasted?
Not so, my heart! But there is fruit,
 And thou hast hands.
Recover all thy sigh-blown age
On double pleasures. Leave thy cold dispute   20
Of what is fit and not. Forsake thy cage,
 Thy rope of sands,
Which petty thoughts have made, and made to thee
 Good cable, to enforce and draw,
  And be thy law,   25
While thou didst wink and wouldst not see.
  Away! Take heed!
  I will abroad.

Call in thy death's head there. Tie up thy fears.
                He that forbears   30
          To suit and serve his need
                Deserves his load.
But as I raved and grew more fierce and wild
          At every word,
Methought I heard one calling, *Child*!   35
          And I replied, *My Lord.*

SIR JOHN SUCKLING (1609–1642)

Song

Why so pale and wan, fond lover?
     Prithee, why so pale?
Will, when looking well can't win her,
     Looking ill prevail?
     Prithee, why so pale?   5

Why so dull and mute, young sinner?
     Prithee, why so mute?
Will, when speaking well can't win her,
     Saying nothing do't?
     Prithee, why so mute?   10

Quit, quit for shame, this will not move;
     This cannot take her.
If of herself she will not love,
     Nothing can make her;
     The devil take her!   15

HENRY VAUGHAN (1622–1695)

The World

I saw eternity the other night
Like a great ring of pure and endless light,
     All calm as it was bright;
And round beneath it, time in hours, days, years,
          Driv'n by the spheres,   5

Like a vast shadow moved in, in which the world
    And all her train were hurled:
The doting lover in his quaintest strain
    Did there complain;
Near him his lute, his fancy, and his flights,   *10*
    Wit's sour delights,
With gloves and knots, the silly snares of pleasure,
    Yet his dear treasure,
All scattered lay, while he his eyes did pore
    Upon a flower.   *15*

The darksome statesman, hung with weights and woe,
Like a thick midnight fog moved there so slow
    He did not stay, nor go;
Condemning thoughts, like sad eclipses, scowl
    Upon his soul,   *20*
And clouds of crying witnesses without
    Pursued him with one shout;
Yet digged the mole, and lest his ways be found
    Worked underground,
Where he did clutch his prey, but One did see   *25*
    That policy;
Churches and altars fed him; perjuries
    Were gnats and flies;
It rained about him blood and tears, but he
    Drank them as free.   *30*

The fearful miser on a heap of rust
Sat pining all his life there, did scarce trust
    His own hands with the dust,
Yet would not place one piece above, but lives
    In fear of thieves.   *35*
Thousands there were as frantic as himself,
    And hugged each one his pelf:
The downright epicure placed heav'n in sense,
    And scorned pretense;
While others, slipped into a wide excess,   *40*
    Said little less;
The weaker sort slight trivial wares enslave,
    Who think them brave;
And poor despisèd truth sat counting by
    Their victory.   *45*

Yet some, who all this while did weep and sing,
And sing and weep, soared up into the ring;
    But most would use no wing.

O fools, said I, thus to prefer dark night
      Before true light,   50
To live in grots and caves, and hate the day
     Because it shows the way,
The way which from this dead and dark abode
     Leads up to God,
A way where you might tread the sun, and be   55
     More bright than he.
But as I did their madness so discuss,
     One whispered thus:
This ring the bridegroom did for none provide
     But for his bride.   60

JOHN DRYDEN (1631–1700)

I *Feed a Flame Within*

From SECRET LOVE

I feed a flame within, which so torments me,
That it both pains my heart, and yet contents me:
'Tis such a pleasing smart, and I so love it,
That I had rather die than once remove it.

Yet he for whom I grieve shall never know it;   5
My tongue does not betray, nor my eyes show it:
Not a sigh, nor a tear, my pain discloses,
But they fall silently, like dew on roses.

Thus to prevent my love from being cruel,
My heart's the sacrifice, as 't is the fuel: 10
And while I suffer this, to give him quiet,
My faith rewards my love, tho' he deny it.

On his eyes will I gaze, and there delight me;
Where I conceal my love, no frown can fright me;
To be more happy, I dare not aspire;   15
Nor can I fall more low, mounting no higher.

Fair Iris I Love

From AMPHITRYON

Fair Iris I love, and hourly I die,
But not for a lip, nor a languishing eye:
She's fickle and false, and there we agree,
For I am as false and as fickle as she.
We neither believe what either can say;   5
And, neither believing, we neither betray.
'Tis civil to swear, and say things of course;
We mean not the taking for better or worse.
When present, we love; when absent, agree:
I think not of Iris, nor Iris of me.   10
The legend of love no couple can find,
So easy to part, or so equally join'd.

JONATHAN SWIFT (1667–1745)

A Description of the Morning

Now hardly here and there a hackney coach
Appearing, showed the ruddy morn's approach.
Now Betty from her master's bed had flown,
And softly stole to discompose her own;
The slip-shod 'prentice from his master's door   5
Had pared the dirt and sprinkled round the floor.
Now Moll had whirled her mop with dext'rous airs,
Prepared to scrub the entry and the stairs.
The youth with broomy stumps began to trace
The kennel's edge, where wheels had worn the place.   10
The small-coal man was heard with cadence deep,
Till drowned in shriller notes of chimney-sweep:
Duns at his lordship's gate began to meet;
And brickdust Moll had screamed through half the street.
The turnkey now his flock returning sees,   15
Duly let out a-nights to steal for fees:
The watchful bailiffs take their silent stands,
And schoolboys lag with satchels in their hands.

WILLIAM COLLINS (1721–1759)

*O*de to Evening

If aught of oaten stop, or pastoral song,
May hope, chaste Eve, to soothe thy modest ear,
　　Like thy own brawling springs,
　　Thy springs, and dying gales;

O Nymph reserved, while now the bright-haired sun　　5
Sits in yon western tent, whose cloudy skirts,
　　With brede ethereal wove,
　　O'erhang his wavy bed:

Now air is hushed, save where the weak-eyed bat
With short shrill shriek flits by on leathern wing;　　10
　　Or where the beetle winds
　　His small but sullen horn,

As oft he rises midst the twilight path,
Against the pilgrim borne in heedless hum:
　　Now teach me, maid composed,　　15
　　To breathe some softened strain,

Whose numbers, stealing through thy darkening vale,
May not unseemly with its stillness suit;
　　As, musing slow, I hail
　　Thy genial loved return.　　20

For when thy folding-star arising shows
His paly circlet, at his warning lamp
　　The fragrant Hours, and Elves
　　Who slept in buds the day,

And many a Nymph who wreathes her brow with sedge,　　25
And sheds the freshening dew, and lovelier still,
　　The pensive Pleasures sweet,
　　Prepare thy shadowy car;

Then let me rove some wild and heathy scene;
Or find some ruin, midst its dreary dells,　　30
　　Whose walls more awful nod
　　By thy religious gleams.

Or, if chill blustering winds, or driving rain,
Prevent my willing feet, be mine the hut,

That, from the mountain's side,
Views wilds, and swelling floods,

And hamlets brown, and dim-discovered spires;
And hears their simple bell, and marks o'er all
Thy dewy fingers draw
The gradual dusky veil. 40

While Spring shall pour his showers, as oft he wont,
And bathe thy breathing tresses, meekest Eve!
While Summer loves to sport
Beneath thy lingering light;

While sallow Autumn fills thy lap with leaves; 45
Or Winter, yelling through the troublous air,
Affrints thy shrinking train,
And rudely rends thy robes;

So long, regardful of thy quiet rule,
Shall Fancy, Friendship, Science, smiling Peace, 50
Thy gentlest influence own,
And love thy favourite name!

ROBERT BURNS (1759–1796)

A Red, Red Rose

O my luve is like a red, red rose,
That's newly sprung in June;
O my luve is like the melodie
That's sweetly played in tune.

As fair thou art, my bonie lass, 5
So deep in luve am I;
And I will luve thee still, my dear,
Till a' the seas gang dry.

Till a' the seas gang dry, my dear,
And the rocks melt wi' the sun; 10
And I will luve thee still, my dear,
While the sands o' life shall run.

And fare thee weel, my only luve,
   And fare thee weel a while;
And I will come again, my luve,   *15*
   Tho' it were ten thousand mile!

GEORGE GORDON, LORD BYRON (1788–1824)

She Walks in Beauty

She walks in beauty, like the night
   Of cloudless climes and starry skies;
And all that's best of dark and bright
   Meet in her aspect and her eyes:
Thus mellowed to that tender light   *5*
   Which heaven to gaudy day denies.

One shade the more, one ray the less,
   Had half impaired the nameless grace
Which waves in every raven tress,
   Or softly lightens o'er her face;   *10*
Where thoughts serenely sweet express
   How pure, how dear their dwelling-place.

And on that cheek, and o'er that brow,
   So soft, so calm, yet eloquent,
The smiles that win, the tints that glow,   *15*
   But tell of days in goodness spent,
A mind at peace with all below,
   A heart whose love is innocent!

WILLIAM CULLEN BRYANT (1794–1878)

To a Waterfowl

   Whither, 'midst falling dew,
While glow the heavens with the last steps of day,
Far, through their rosy depths, dost thou pursue
   Thy solitary way?

Vainly the fowler's eye   5
Might mark thy distant flight, to do thee wrong,
    As, darkly seen against the crimson sky,
      Thy figure floats along.

    Seek'st thou the plashy brink
Of weedy lake, or marge of river wide,   10
Or where the rocking billows rise and sink
      On the chafed ocean side?

    There is a Power, whose care
Teaches thy way along that pathless coast,—
The desert and illimitable air,   15
      Lone wandering, but not lost.

All day thy wings have fann'd,
At that far height, the cold thin atmosphere;
Yet stoop not, weary, to the welcome land,
      Though the dark night is near.   20

    And soon that toil shall end,
Soon shalt thou find a summer home, and rest,
And scream among thy fellows; reeds shall bend,
      Soon, o'er thy sheltered nest.

    Thou'rt gone, the abyss of heaven   25
Hath swallowed up thy form, yet, on my heart
Deeply hath sunk the lesson thou has given,
      And shall not soon depart.

    He, who, from zone to zone,
Guides through the boundless sky thy certain flight,   30
In the long way that I must trace alone,
      Will lead my steps aright.

EDGAR ALLAN POE (1809–1849)

To Helen

    Helen, thy beauty is to me
      Like those Nicaean barks of yore,
    That gently o'er a perfumed sea,
      The weary, wayworn wanderer bore
      To his own native shore.   5

On desperate seas long wont to roam,
   Thy hyacinth hair, thy classic face,
Thy Naiad airs have brought me home
    To the glory that was Greece
    And the grandeur that was Rome.   *10*

Lo! in yon brilliant window-niche
   How statue-like I see thee stand,
The agate lamp within thy hand!
    Ah, Psyche, from the regions which
    Are Holy Land!   *15*

HERMAN MELVILLE (1819–1891)

The Maldive Shark

About the Shark, phlegmatical one,
Pale sot of the Maldive sea,
The sleek little pilot-fish, azure and slim,
How alert in attendance be.
From his saw-pit of mouth, from his charnel of maw   *5*
They have nothing of harm to dread,
But liquidly glide on his ghastly flank
Or before his Gorgonian head;
Or lurk in the port of serrated teeth
In white triple tiers of glittering gates,   *10*
And there find a haven when peril's abroad,
An asylum in jaws of the Fates!
They are friends; and friendly they guide him to prey,
Yet never partake of the treat—
Eyes and brains to the dotard lethargic and dull,   *15*
Pale ravener of horrible meat.

THOMAS HARDY (1840–1928)

The Ruined Maid

"O 'Melia, my dear, this does everything crown!
Who could have supposed I should meet you in Town?
And whence such fair garments, such prosperi—ty?"—
"O didn't you know I'd been ruined?" said she.

—"You left us in tatters, without shoes or socks,   5
Tired of digging potatoes, and spudding up docks;
And now you've gay bracelets and bright feathers three!"—
"Yes: that's how we dress when we're ruined," said she.

—"At home in the barton you said 'thee' and 'thou',
And 'thik oon', and 'theäs oon', and 't 'other'; but now   10
Your talking quite fits 'ee for high compa—ny!"—
"Some polish is gained with one's ruin," said she.

—"Your hands were like paws then, your face blue and bleak
But now I'm bewitched by your delicate cheek,
And your little gloves fit as on any la—dy!"—   15
"We never do work when we're ruined," says she.

—"You used to call home-life a hag-ridden dream,
And you'd sigh, and you'd sock; but at present you seem
To know not of megrims or melancho—ly!"—
"True. One's pretty lively when ruined," said she.   20

—"I wish I had feathers, a fine sweeping gown,
And a delicate face, and could strut about Town!"—
"My dear—a raw country girl, such as you be,
Cannot quite expect that. You ain't ruined," said she.

Neutral Tones

We stood by a pond that winter day,
And the sun was white, as though chidden of God,
And a few leaves lay on the starving sod;
    —They had fallen from an ash, and were gray.

Your eyes on me were as eyes that rove   5
Over tedious riddles of years ago;
And some words played between us to and fro
    On which lost the more by our love.

The smile on your mouth was the deadest thing
Alive enough to have strength to die;   10
And a grin of bitterness swept thereby
    Like an ominous bird a-wing. . . .

Since then, keen lessons that love deceives,
And wrings with wrong, have shaped to me
Your face, and the God-curst sun, and a tree,   15
    And a pond edged with grayish leaves.

A. E. HOUSMAN (1859–1936)

To an Athlete Dying Young

The time you won your town the race
We chaired you through the market-place;
Man and boy stood cheering by,
And home we brought you shoulder-high.

To-day, the road all runners come,   5
Shoulder-high we bring you home,
And set you at your threshold down,
Townsman of a stiller town.

Smart lad, to slip betimes away
From fields where glory does not stay   10
And early though the laurel grows
It withers quicker than the rose.

Eyes the shady night has shut
Cannot see the record cut,
And silence sounds no worse than cheers   15
After earth has stopped the ears:

Now you will not swell the rout
Of lads that wore their honours out,
Runners whom renown outran
And the name died before the man.   20

So set, before its echoes fade,
The fleet foot on the sill of shade,
And hold to the low lintel up
The still-defended challenge-cup.

And round that early-laurelled head   25
Will flock to gaze the strengthless dead,
And find unwithered on its curls
The garland briefer than a girl's.

Eros Turannos

She fears him, and will always ask
   What fated her to choose him;
She meets in his engaging mask
   All reasons to refuse him;
But what she meets and what she fears   5
Are less than are the downward years,
Drawn slowly to the foamless weirs
   Of age, were she to lose him.

Between a blurred sagacity
   That once had power to sound him,   10
And Love, that will not let him be
   The Judas that she found him,
Her pride assuages her almost,
As if it were alone the cost.—
He sees that he will not be lost,   15
   And waits and looks around him.

A sense of ocean and old trees
   Envelops and allures him;
Tradition, touching all he sees,
   Beguiles and reassures him;   20
And all her doubts of what he says
Are dimmed with what she knows of days—
Till even prejudice delays
   And fades, and she secures him.

The falling leaf inaugurates   25
   The reign of her confusion;
The pounding wave reverberates
   The dirge of her illusion;
And home, where passion lived and died,
Becomes a place where she can hide,   30
While all the town and harbor side
   Vibrate with her seclusion.

We tell you, tapping on our brows,
   The story as it should be,—
As if the story of a house   35
   Were told, or ever could be;
We'll have no kindly veil between

Her visions and those we have seen,—
As if we guessed what hers have been,
    Or what they are or would be.   40

Meanwhile we do no harm; for they
    That with a god have striven,
Not hearing much of what we say,
    Take what the god has given;
Though like waves breaking it may be,   45
Or like a changed familiar tree,
Or like a stairway to the sea
    Where down the blind are driven.

Richard Cory

Whenever Richard Cory went down town,
We people on the pavement looked at him:
He was a gentleman from sole to crown,
Clean favored, and imperially slim.

And he was always quietly arrayed,   5
And he was always human when he talked;
But still he fluttered pulses when he said,
"Good-morning," and he glittered when he walked.

And he was rich—yes, richer than a king—
And admirably schooled in every grace: 10
In fine, we thought that he was everything
To make us wish that we were in his place.

So on we worked, and waited for the light,
And went without the meat, and cursed the bread;
And Richard Cory, one calm summer night,   15
Went home and put a bullet through his head.

The Red Wheelbarrow

so much depends
upon

a red wheel
barrow

glazed with rain
water

beside the white
chickens

To Waken an Old Lady

Old age is
a flight of small
cheeping birds
skimming
bare trees   5
above a snow glaze.
Gaining and failing
they are buffetted
by a dark wind—
But what?   10
On harsh weedstalks
the flock has rested,
the snow
is covered with broken
seedhusks   15
and the wind tempered
by a shrill
piping of plenty.

The Garden

Like a skein of loose silk blown against a wall
She walks by the railing of a path in Kensington Gardens,
And she is dying piece-meal of a sort of emotional anemia.

And round about her there is a rabble
Of the filthy, sturdy, unkillable infants of the very poor.   5
They shall inherit the earth.

In her is the end of breeding.
Her boredom is exquisite and excessive.
She would like someone to speak to her,
And is almost afraid that I will commit that indiscretion.   10

The Age Demanded an Image

From HUGH SELWYN MAUBERLEY

The age demanded an image
Of its accelerated grimace,
Something for the modern stage,
Not, at any rate, an Attic grace;

Not, not certainly, the obscure reveries   5
Of the inward gaze;
Better mendacities
Than the classics in paraphrase!

The "age demanded" chiefly a mould in plaster,
Made with no loss of time,   10
A prose kinema, not, not assuredly, alabaster
Or the "sculpture" of rhyme.

MARIANNE MOORE (1887–1972)

Poetry

I, too, dislike it: there are things that are important beyond
        all this fiddle.
    Reading it, however, with a perfect contempt for it,
        one discovers in
  it after all, a place for the genuine.
        Hands that can grasp, eyes
        that can dilate, hair that can rise   5
           if it must, these things are important not
           because a

high-sounding interpretation can be put upon them but
        because they are
  useful. When they become so derivative as to become
        unintelligible,
  the same thing may be said for all of us, that we
        do not admire what   10
        we cannot understand: the bat
           holding on upside down or in quest of
           something to

eat, elephants pushing, a wild horse taking a roll, a tireless
        wolf under
  a tree, the immovable critic twitching his skin like a
        horse that feels a flea, the base-
  ball fan, the statistician—   15
        nor is it valid
           to discriminate against 'business documents and

school books'; all these phenomena are important. One must
        make a distinction
  however: when dragged into prominence by half poets,
        the result is not poetry,
  nor till the poets among us can be   20
        'literalists of
        the imagination'—above
           insolence and triviality and can present

for inspection, imaginary gardens with real toads in them,
        shall we have
  it. In the meantime, if you demand on the one hand,   25
  the raw material of poetry in

all its rawness and
that which is on the other hand
genuine, then you are interested in poetry.

ARCHIBALD MacLEISH (1892–   )

Ars Poetica

A poem should be palpable and mute
As a globed fruit

Dumb
As old medallions to the thumb

Silent as the sleeve-worn stone   5
Of casement where the moss has grown—

A poem should be wordless
As the flight of birds

          .   .   .   .   .

A poem should be motionless in time
As the moon climbs   10

Leaving, as the moon releases
Twig by twig the night-entangled trees,

Leaving, as the moon behind the winter leaves,
Memory by memory the mind—

A poem should be motionless in time   15
As the moon climbs

          .   .   .   .   .

A poem should be equal to:
Not true

For all the history of grief
An empty doorway and a maple leaf   20

For love
The leaning grasses and two lights above the sea—

A poem should not mean
But be.

Buffalo Bill's

Buffalo Bill's
defunct
        who used to
        ride a watersmooth-silver
                        stallion   5
and break onetwothreefourfive pigeonsjustlikethat
                                 Jesus

he was a handsome man
                   and what i want to know is
how do you like yourblueeyed boy   10
Mister Death

My sweet old etcetera

my sweet old etcetera
aunt lucy during the recent

war could and what
is more did tell you just
what everybody was fighting   5

for,
my sister
isabel created hundreds
(and
hundreds)of socks not to   10
mention shirts fleaproof earwarmers

etcetera wristers etcetera, my
mother hoped that

i would die etcetera
bravely of course my father used   15
to become hoarse talking about how it was
a privilege and if only he
could meanwhile my

self etcetera lay quietly
in the deep mud et   20

cetera
(dreaming,
et
   cetera, of
Your smile   25
eyes knees and of your Etcetera)

HART CRANE (1899–1932)

To Brooklyn Bridge

From THE BRIDGE

How many dawns, chill from his rippling rest
The seagull's wings shall dip and pivot him,
Shedding white rings of tumult, building high
Over the chained bay waters Liberty—

Then, with inviolate curve, forsake our eyes   5
As apparitional as sails that cross
Some page of figures to be filed away;
—Till elevators drop us from our day . . .

I think of cinemas, panoramic sleights
With multitudes bent toward some flashing scene   10
Never disclosed, but hastened to again,
Foretold to other eyes on the same screen;

And Thee, across the harbor, silver-paced
As though the sun took step of thee, yet left
Some motion ever unspent in thy stride,—   15
Implicitly thy freedom staying thee!

Out of some subway scuttle, cell or loft
A bedlamite speeds to thy parapets,
Tilting there momently, shrill shirt ballooning,
A jest falls from the speechless caravan.   20

Down Wall, from girder into street noon leaks,
A rip-tooth of the sky's acetylene;

All afternoon the cloud-flown derricks turn . . .
Thy cables breathe the North Atlantic still.

And obscure as that heaven of the Jews,   25
Thy guerdon . . . Accolade thou dost bestow
Of anonymity time cannot raise:
Vibrant reprieve and pardon thou dost show.

O harp and altar, of the fury fused,
(How could mere toil align thy choiring strings!)   30
Terrific threshold of the prophet's pledge,
Prayer of pariah, and the lover's cry,—

Again the traffic lights that skim thy swift
Unfractioned idiom, immaculate sigh of stars,
Beading thy path—condense eternity: 35
And we have seen night lifted in thine arms.

Under thy shadows by the piers I waited;
Only in darkness is thy shadow clear.
The City's fiery parcels all undone,
Already snow submerges an iron year . . .   40

O Sleepless as the river under thee,
Vaulting the sea, the prairies' dreaming sod,
Unto us lowliest sometime sweep, descend
And of the curveship lend a myth to God.

W. H. AUDEN (1907–   )

Musée des Beaux Arts

About suffering they were never wrong,
The Old Masters: how well they understood
Its human position; how it takes place
While someone else is eating or opening a window or just
        walking dully along;
How, when the aged are reverently, passionately waiting   5
For the miraculous birth, there always must be
Children who did not specially want it to happen, skating
On a pond at the edge of the wood:
They never forgot
That even the dreadful martyrdom must run its course   10

Anyhow in a corner, some untidy spot
Where the dogs go on with their doggy life and the
    torturer's horse
Scratches its innocent behind on a tree.

In Brueghel's *Icarus*, for instance: how everything turns away
Quite leisurely from the disaster; the ploughman may   *15*
Have heard the splash, the forsaken cry,
But for him it was not an important failure; the sun shone
As it had to on the white legs disappearing into the green
Water; and the expensive delicate ship that must have seen
Something amazing, a boy falling out of the sky,   *20*
Had somewhere to get to and sailed calmly on.

The Unknown Citizen

(To JS/07/M/378
This Marble Monument
Is Erected by the State)

He was found by the Bureau of Statistics to be
One against whom there was no official complaint,
And all the reports on his conduct agree
That, in the modern sense of an old-fashioned word, he was a
    saint,
For in everything he did he served the Greater Community.   *5*
Except for the War till the day he retired
He worked in a factory and never got fired,
But satisfied his employers, Fudge Motors Inc.
Yet he wasn't a scab or odd in his views,
For his Union reports that he paid his dues,   *10*
(Our report on his Union shows it was sound)
And our Social Psychology workers found
That he was popular with his mates and liked a drink.
The Press are convinced that he bought a paper every day
And that his reactions to advertisements were normal in every
    way.   *15*
Policies taken out in his name prove that he was fully insured,
And his Health-card shows he was once in hospital but left it
    cured.
Both Producers Research and High-Grade Living declare
He was fully sensible to the advantages of the Instalment Plan
And had everything necessary to the Modern Man,   *20*

A phonograph, a radio, a car and a frigidaire.
Our researchers into Public Opinion are content
That he held the proper opinions for the time of year;
When there was peace, he was for peace; when there was war,
    he went.
He was married and added five children to the population,   25
Which our Eugenist says was the right number for a parent
    of his generation,
And our teachers report that he never interfered with their
    education.
Was he free? Was he happy? The question is absurd:
Had anything been wrong, we should certainly have heard.

THEODORE ROETHKE (1908–1963)

I Knew a Woman

I knew a woman, lovely in her bones,
When small birds sighed, she would sigh back at them;
Ah, when she moved, she moved more ways than one:
The shapes a bright container can contain!
Of her choice virtues only gods should speak,   5
Or English poets who grew up on Greek
(I'd have them sing in chorus, cheek to cheek).

How well her wishes went! She stroked my chin,
She taught me Turn, and Counter-turn, and Stand;
She taught me Touch, that undulant white skin;   10
I nibbled meekly from her proffered hand;
She was the sickle; I, poor I, the rake,
Coming behind her for her pretty sake
(But what prodigious mowing we did make).

Love likes a gander, and adores a goose: 15
Her full lips pursed, the errant note to seize;
She played it quick, she played it light and loose;
My eyes, they dazzled at her flowing knees;
Her several parts could keep a pure repose,
Or one hip quiver with a mobile nose   20
(She moved in circles, and those circles moved).

Let seed be grass, and grass turn into hay:
I'm martyr to a motion not my own;

What's freedom for? To know eternity.
I swear she cast a shadow white as stone.   25
But who would count eternity in days?
These old bones live to learn her wanton ways:
(I measure time by how a body sways).

Dolor

I have known the inexorable sadness of pencils,
Neat in their boxes, dolor of pad and paper-weight,
All the misery of manilla folders and mucilage,
Desolation in immaculate public places,
Lonely reception room, lavatory, switchboard,   5
The unalterable pathos of basin and pitcher.
Ritual of multigraph, paper-clip, comma,
Endless duplication of lives and objects.
And I have seen dust from the walls of institutions,
Finer than flour, alive, more dangerous than silica,   10
Sift, almost invisible, through long afternoons of tedium,
Dropping a fine film on nails and delicate eyebrows,
Glazing the pale hair, the duplicate gray standard faces.

DYLAN THOMAS (1914–1953)

Do Not Go Gentle into That Good Night

Do not go gentle into that good night,
Old age should burn and rave at close of day;
Rage, rage against the dying of the light.

Though wise men at their end know dark is right,
Because their words had forked no lightning they   5
Do not go gentle into that good night.

Good men, the last wave by, crying how bright
Their frail deeds might have danced in a green bay,
Rage, rage against the dying of the light.

Wild men who caught and sang the sun in flight,   10
And learn, too late, they grieved it on its way,
Do not go gentle into that good night.

Grave men, near death, who see with blinding sight
Blind eyes could blaze like meteors and be gay,
Rage, rage against the dying of the light.   *15*

And you, my father, there on the sad height,
Curse, bless, me now with your fierce tears, I pray.
Do not go gentle into that good night.
Rage, rage against the dying of the light.

JOHN BERRYMAN (1914–1972)

They may suppose, because I would not cloy your ear

SONNET 23

They may suppose, because I would not cloy your ear—
If ever these songs by other ears are heard—
With 'love' and 'love', I loved you not, but blurred
Lust with strange images, warm, not quite sincere,
To switch a bedroom black. O mutineer   *5*
With me against these empty captains! gird
Your scorn again above all at *this* word
Pompous and vague on the stump of his career.

Also I fox 'heart', striking a modern breast
Hollow as a drum, and 'beauty' I taboo;   *10*
I want a verse fresh as a bubble breaks,
As little false. . . Blood of my sweet unrest
Runs all the same—I am in love with you—
Trapped in my rib-cage something throes and aches!

Dinch me, dark God, having smoked me out

DREAM SONG 266

Dinch me, dark God, having smoked me out.
Let Henry's ails fail, pennies on his eyes
never to open more,
the shires are voting him out of time & place,
they'll drop his bundle, drunkard & Boy Scout,   *5*
where he was once before:

nowhere, nowhere. Was then the thing all planned?
I mention what I do not understand.
I mention for instance Love:
God loves his creatures when he treats them so?   *10*
Surely one grand *exception* here below
his presidency of

the widespread galaxies might once be made
for perishing Henry, whom let not then die.
He can advance no claim,   *15*
save that he studied thy Word & grew afraid,
work & fear be the basis for his terrible cry
not to forget his name.

ROBERT LOWELL (1917–   )

The Holy Innocents

Listen, the hay-bells tinkle as the cart
Wavers on rubber tires along the tar
And cindered ice below the burlap mill
And ale-wife run. The oxen drool and start
In wonder at the fenders of a car,   *5*
And blunder hugely up St. Peter's hill.
These are the undefiled by woman—their
Sorrow is not the sorrow of this world:
King Herod shrieking vengeance at the curled
Up knees of Jesus choking in the air,   *10*
A king of speechless clods and infants. Still
The world out-Herods Herod; and the year,
The nineteen-hundred forty-fifth of grace,
Lumbers with losses up the clinkered hill
Of our purgation; and the oxen near   *15*
The worn foundations of their resting-place,
The holy manger where their bed is corn
And holly torn for Christmas. If they die,
As Jesus, in the harness, who will mourn?
Lamb of the shepherds, Child, how still you lie.   *20*

INDEX OF AUTHORS
AND TITLES

INDEX OF FIRST LINES